Agency in the Margins

Agency in the Margins

Stories of Outsider Rhetoric

Edited by
Anne Meade Stockdell-Giesler

Madison • Teaneck
Fairleigh Dickinson University Press

© 2010 by Rosemont Publishing & Printing Corp.

All rights reserved. Authorization to photocopy items for internal or personal use, or the internal or personal use of specific clients, is granted by the copyright owner, provided that a base fee of $10.00, plus eight cents per page, per copy is paid directly to the Copyright Clearance Center, 222 Rosewood Drive, Danvers, Massachusetts 01923. [978-0-8366-4214-6/10 $10.00 + 8¢ pp, pc.]

Associated University Presses
2010 Eastpark Boulevard
Cranbury, NJ 08512

The paper used in this publication meets the requirements of the American National Standard for permanence of Paper for Printed Library Materials Z39.48-1984

Library of Congress Cataloging-in-Publication Data

Agency in the margins : stories of outsider rhetoric / edited by Anne Meade Stockdell-Giesler.
   p. cm.
  Includes bibliographical references and index.
  ISBN 978-0-8386-4214-6 (alk. paper)
  1. Rhetoric—Political aspects—United States. 2. Rhetoric—Social aspects—United States. 3. Rhetoric—United States—History. 4. Marginality, Social—United States. I. Stockdell-Giesler, Anne Meade, 1967–
  P301.5.P67A44 2010
  818.5'108694—dc22

2009008223

PRINTED IN THE UNITED STATES OF AMERICA

Contents

Introduction Anne Meade Stockdell-Giesler	9
Freedom of Speech and the Politics of Silence: The Case of Ward Churchill Michael Donnelly	23
Recovering the Voices of the Florida Turpentine Slaves: A Lost Rhetoric of Resistance Linda Bannister and James E. Hurd, Jr.	39
A Hole Story: The Space of Historical Memory in the Abolitionist Imagination Zoe Trodd	68
"Mirrors of hard, distorting glass": *Invisible Man* as Outsider Rhetoric Ian Edwards	91
Historical Moments, Historical Words: The Continuing Legacy of Malcolm X's Black Nationalist Rhetoric and Huey P. Newton in Common's Rap Music Coretta Pittman	119
Outsider Rhetoric in Italian American Immigrant Autobiographies Ilaria Serra	143
"To Live Outside the Law, You Must Be Honest": Words, Walls, and the Rhetorical Practices of *The Angolite* Scott Whiddon	165
"Protect yourself at all times": *Million Dollar Baby*, Boxing, and Feminine Agency Ian Edwards	197

(Still) Calling Out from the Closet?: The Rhetoric of
Visibility in Queer TV and Film 225
   Rebecca Ingalls

Modernity Baptized in the Spirit: Early Pentecostal Rhetoric
in America 241
   Joseph W. Williams

Techno-Mob Movements: Public Performances and the
Collective Voices of Outsiders 261
   Jessica Ketcham Weber

Strategic Essentialism and the Representation of the Natural:
The Case of Ecofeminist/Scientist Wangari Maathai 287
   Raymond Oenbring

Conclusion 307
   Anne Meade Stockdell-Giesler and Rebecca Ingalls

Notes on Contributors 313

Index 316

Agency in the Margins

Introduction
Anne Meade Stockdell-Giesler

The western rhetorical tradition, as we know it, extends back at least 2,500 years to its roots in the philosophies of Socrates, Plato, and Aristotle. That tradition has long honored individual orations delivered by men in privileged male-dominated forums such as the political office, the pulpit, and the marketplace. In recent years scholars have begun to look at individual oratorical performances by marginalized figures. Heated debates over who "owns" rhetoric and what consists of legitimate rhetorical performance have taken place. Scholars have put forth theories of rhetoric encompassing diverse situations and exigencies.

What we have not offered, I would contend, is an interpretation and theorization of the rhetoric of outsider groups *as a type or class of rhetoric*. This collection of essays studies the rhetoric of Otherness and explores how outsiders to mainstream sites for rhetorical participation find ways to make themselves heard while retaining marginal identities. The question that this collection attempts to answer is: how do people who are defined as outsiders create agency—how do they become agents of change, of social, political, spiritual, and cultural power—outside of those spaces that we traditionally understand as belonging to the powerful?

The subjects in this collection vary: authors discuss contemporary hip-hop music; early twentieth-century literature; prison publications; post-Civil War treatment of "free" African Americans; queer culture; and more. The common thread in each essay is the study of how the groups have managed to successfully use rhetoric to exert social power and establish agency in a world that denies them privileged status. Each of these groups' work helps to establish a constitutive rhetoric of otherness, a contribution to a genre of "Outsider Rhetoric" in which the rhetor(s) create a narrative in which they as subjects have legitimacy as rhetors, and in which the audience then is reconstituted to perceive this legitimacy. As Maurice Charland points out, "much of what we as rhetorical critics consider to be a product or consequence of discourse, including social identity, religious faith, sexuality, and ideology is beyond the realm of rational or even free choice, beyond the realm of persuasion";[1] our rhetorical constructions in terms of who we are as rhetors and as audience members is prerhetorical, and must be reconstituted by outsiders to our own known group identities should an outsider want to reach us. What the essays in this book attempt to illuminate are examples of outsiders creating agency through constitutive rhetorics which attempt to create a narrative in which the outsider has a legitimate right to speak; "narratives offer a world in which human agency is possible and acts can be meaningful."[2] Additionally, Charland argues, "one must already be an interpellated subject and exist as a discursive position in order to be a part of the audience of a rhetorical situation in which persuasion could occur."[3] Constitutive rhetoric serves to create communities of audiences—to define new boundaries and group-identities for rhetorical situations. This action is, of course, always tied up in concepts of power—and outsiders, by definition, are not empowered.

How the agents in each of the examples presented by these essays garners power varies; as Foucault explains in regard to discourse and power relations:

> We must conceive discourse as a series of discontinuous segments whose tactical function is neither uniform nor stable . . . we must not imagine a world of discourse divided between accepted discourse and excluded discourse, or between dominant discourse and the dominated one; but as a multiplicity of discursive elements that can come into play in various strategies. Discourses are not once and for all subservient to power or raised up against it, any more than silences are. . . . Discourse transmits and produces power; it reinforces it, but also undermines and exposes it, renders it fragile and makes it possible to thwart it.[4]

In the spirit of Foucault's ideas about discourse, this book attempts to highlight the discourse of marginalized groups who have been considered silenced, disenfranchised, or rhetorically unempowered, and how they found place and access to create and disperse that discourse through constitutive rhetorics. The essays will perhaps undo the black-and-white notions of "mainstream" and "marginalized" rhetorical ethos and will instead focus on the very art of outsider rhetoric in its complexity; after all, "a rhetoric to Athenians in praise of Athens would be relatively insignificant compared to a rhetoric that constitutes Athenians as such."[5]

Theories of social-movement rhetoric may at first seem relevant here, and the spirit and intentions of individual rhetors discussed in this book may often be linked to those of social movement rhetorics.

However, social movement rhetoric is somewhat limited in its scope in relation to many outsiders who lack the institutionalization, order, leadership, and/or citizenship authority that formal organization in a social movement grants; in her essay, Coretta Pittman notes how hip-hop performer Common Sense, while a member of the rap music community, struggles in his own way to communicate his social and political messages from the margins of a genre whose superstars have garnered criticism for lyrics full of violence and sexism. In a once-marginalized genre that has gone mainstream, Common remains an outsider with his socially conscious themes. As Charland notes about the Athenians, social movement rhetorics are created by groups who have formally identified and organized themselves—and speak from an established ethos (they are, in other words, Athenians praising Athens). In this book, outsiders remain on the fringes of such formalization, which is defined by Stewart, Smith, and Denton as composed of recognizable leaders with identifiable memberships and formal organization; they write, however, that "social movements are always *out-groups* that society views as illegitimate."[6] Stewart, Smith, and Denton limit the scope of persuasion in society at large, though—the scope of their work is restricted to the organized formality and group identity of social movements; many of the subjects discussed in this new collection simply cannot access formal social movements, or choose to express themselves otherwise. The key in this text is to look at those who are not affiliated with an organized social movement or who have tended to remain on the margins of such a movement—who have no real access to such a movement as a tool to persuasion. Harriet Jacobs, for example, as a slave in the American South, could not join the abolitionist movement; she could not safely articulate an argument against her condition as a member of a social movement in her own community. Her persistence in her desire to be heard led her to an alternative site for communication.

Outsider rhetoric can lack the sort of formalized structure and strictures of institutional academic rhetoric and that of social movements, but does not lack deliberation, artfulness, or purpose. Foucault's concept of heterotopia is relevant here. He proposes that "the problem of the human site or living space is . . . that of knowing what relations of propinquity, what type of storage, circulation, marking, and classification of human elements should be adopted in a given situation to achieve a given end."[7] The heterotopia, then, is a space which works to help define, within a social or cultural context, the rhetorical tools available for use to achieve a given end. The heterotopia, which Foucault defines as "counter-sites, a kind of effectively enacted utopia in which the real sites, all the other sites that can be found within the culture, are simultaneously represented, contested, and inverted,"[8] are mirrors in which outsiders find themselves reflected in a society which does not really recognize them. For the outsider, the heterotopia creates a space which allows the outsider to both identify him or herself, as well as to "see myself there where I am absent."[9] This collection brings to light the many different ways that politically or socially marginalized people use discourse to garner, access, undermine, or overturn power—to make themselves seen and heard. Though the examples here may not be found in history or literature texts as models of dominant culture, they do represent powerful voices working within a society that has defined them as outsiders. Charland's understanding of constitutive rhetoric is also relevant here:

> Constitutive rhetorics of new subject positions can be understood, therefore, as working upon previous discourses, upon previous constitutive rhetorics. They capture alienated subjects by rearticulating existing subject positions so as to contain or resolve experienced dialectical contradictions between the world and its discourses. The process by which an audience member enters into a new subject position is therefore not one of persuasion. It is akin more to one of conversion that ultimately results in an act of recognition of the "rightness" of a discourse and of one's identity with its reconfigured subject position.[10]

Thusly, as Scott Whiddon argues in his chapter, a prison inmate may reconfigure his audience of "outsiders" into "insiders" who have more in common with him than they might otherwise believe. An inmate's very humanity is constituted to his noninmate audience through his literacy and journalistic integrity. A group of almost-slaves in the post-Civil War South can create their own community and humanity (Bannister and Hurd); and so on. These essays cannot encompass all contributions to outsider rhetoric, nor do they attempt to codify outsider rhetoric, but they do provide scholars with a diverse resource to begin their own theorizing and explorations of rhetoric from the margins.

To be sure, there have been many books and essays focusing on marginal individuals and how they participated in the rhetorical tradition—from Diotima in the ancient world (via Plato) to Sojourner Truth in the Civil War American South, we have numerous examples of individuals who have entered into the mainstream to practice the rhetoric of the dominant culture—in Western rhetoric, that means they have, more or less, stood solitary behind a podium and delivered Aristotelian orations in the style and language of the dominant, mainstream, empowered culture. They have accessed, and inhabited, the utopia. While each of these scholarly contributions (Lunsford's *Re-*

claiming Rhetorica, Jackson's *Understanding African American Rhetoric*, Ritchie and Ronald's *Available Means* are all examples) has its own value, this collection of essays looks at rhetoric from another viewpoint. It explores how those who could not or did not enter the mainstream (the utopia) and speak from the traditional school of rhetoric have in fact produced rhetoric and engaged in discourse intended to wield, undermine, or question power. These rhetors often speak in groups, in nontraditional ways: through song, through images, through literature, worship, and elsewhere. The driving question for this book is: what happens when people have something powerful to say, but they have no access to mainstream political and social forums for saying it? Do they remain silent? Or do they find alternative sites, means, and methods of making themselves heard? For years, women in ancient Greece were assumed to be silent, passive residents of the interior domestic spaces of their world. Scholars dismissed their cultural presence and power. We now know this to be only a partial view of women's lives in the ancient world. I would like to demonstrate a similar uncovering of people's power from marginal spaces.

The premise that distinguishes this book from others that explore marginalized figures in rhetorical history is that each of the essays focuses on outsiders who remained in the margins, who spoke *from* the margins, not from positions of authority and not from the traditional sites for rhetorical practice. Rather than group the essays by race, ethnicity, or class, I group them simply by their marginality. While it is relevant to explore the communication of groups defined by, say, economic status or race or membership to social movements, it is equally valuable to recognize and evaluate the very diversity of otherness in a single text. It is quite telling, I believe, that in a work such as this we find represented groups from across racial, gender, religious, and class lines. The fact remains that until very recently in Western history, the academies, legislature, and religious leaderships have been peopled nearly exclusively by privileged (usually white) men—a group who happens to be a minority in any culture (and yet who, still, dominates the political and social structure of American society). Any "outsider" who managed to work his or her way into the mainstream remained an anomaly, a spot of ink on an otherwise white page. What I strive to represent here is how people have remained in the margins and have managed to speak powerfully and persuasively about their lives and places in the world, ultimately managing to wield significant social power from their positions of Otherness.

In Michael Donnelly's chapter, we see what happens when an outsider's use of traditional rhetoric to wield power comes to the attention of the dominant political forces in a culture: it is quickly and unequivocally quashed. Donnelly explains how the Western notion of "free speech" is anything but free; he argues that "Free Speech has often functioned, and continues to function, as a weapon, wielded by those in power, to silence those in opposition." Donnelly's essay calls into question the very notion that all members of a culture have equal rights to speak publicly or, for that matter, equal access to forums for that sort of speech. His essay helps to define the borders of outsider rhetoric and makes the case that those living in the margins face terrible consequences when they attempt to wield power in a way that is counterproductive to the dominant power structure, and in a forum and style such as is used by those in power. Therefore, outsiders must frequently remain in the margins in order to be heard and, Donnelly argues, if they garner any power whatsoever, they will be drawn into the center in order to be silenced by those in power.

Donnelly uses the example of Professor Ward Churchill, whose academic standing and activism were brought to question and into the center by those in power (in this case, Bill O'Reilly). The very complexity of outsider effectiveness and positioning is made clear in this essay, where Donnelly proposes that "some 'outsider rhetorics'—a certain sub-set, let's say—must push at the extremes. By so doing, such rhetorics force open spaces for discussion—in other words, they dismantle silences—and for less 'radical' but no less 'outsider' rhetorics to be more effective." Donnelly's essay uncovers the myth of free speech for outsiders who want to wield cultural power, and establishes the exigence for a rhetoric that comes from, and remains in, the margins. As long as Churchill remained in academic life and didn't threaten the power structure, his Native American activist "otherness" was tolerated, even appreciated within his academic community (as demonstrated by his considerable status at his place of employment). Donnelly argues that "outsiders have to negotiate some very tricky terrain—the rhetoric that can and will be heard in/from the margins must constantly test the boundaries of 'acceptable speech,' which means breaching those boundaries on occasion, and therefore being silenced." Churchill's negotiation of this terrain was frequently successful, but when his rhetoric of overt social protest and commentary came to the attention of a more powerful ethos—Bill O'Reilly—Churchill's was quickly stripped of credibility.

The next group of essays deals, generally, with issues of race, ethnicity, and rhetorical identity. Linda Bannister and James Hurd's essay tells one story of outsider rhetoric with their discussion of the social experience and rhetorical art of the Florida turpentine industry as viewed through the lenses of the African American indentured workers whose labor brought great wealth to white businessmen in the early-to-middle twentieth century. Bannister and Hurd's essay explores the virtual slavery of the turpentine industry in the post-Civil War era, where a system of debt bondage kept workers imprisoned. These workers, hardly any more free than their enslaved ancestors, faced similar retribution to escaped slaves: "Beatings, bloodhounds, manhunts, and lynchings were commonly used to deter those fleeing the camps." Facing these conditions, and the resultant feelings of powerlessness that surely plagued them, the turpentine workers "developed a system of communicating . . . that featured ironic, stubborn literalness and ingenious lying, as well as subversive foot-dragging on the job, helping them to assert some control over a crushingly oppressive work environment." This system of communication is a particularly artful form of outsider rhetoric, which even includes Aesop-like fables that instruct the workers and their families in social codes and subtleties of subversion.

It is important to remember Aesop, I think, in relation to this chapter of the book, for Aesop was, of course, a slave. Aesop's fables have become nursery stories told to children as moral wisdom that endure today. Rhetorically, they were an artful means for a slave to instruct the more powerful without doing so directly and thereby threatening the powerful. Aesop could not use peer-to-peer rhetorical tactics, as he was not, of course, a peer. Like Aesop, the turpentine workers had to carefully monitor their communication and behavior, always mindful of the very real threat their supervisors represented. The workers also had a long tradition of subversive and veiled language of their own, having descended from slaves who had their very lives at stake if they spoke out of turn or on an equal level to their masters. Bannister and Hurd note that "turpentine workers used two kinds of rhetoric available to those on the margins: subversive conversation (marked by subtleties unavailable to the whites they engaged) and folktales." These rhetorical tactics create the mirror in a heterotopia which reflects the workers into a power structure in which they appear to be absent (to the whites). They are not there—to the whites—but for them, they are present and hold the upper hand, at least in particular situations.

Zoe Trodd's essay, "A Hole Story: Outsider Rhetoric in the African American Literary Tradition," explores the metaphor of architectural space in the African American literary tradition. African American writers, she proposes, "imagined characters . . . in the margins and loopholes of America's founding documents. They performed something similar to the Winnebago Tribe of Nebraska's cultural dialogue between *worak* stories (things as they are) and *waika* stories (things as they might have been)." In addition, she theorizes, these literary figures used their art to set forth how things *ought to be*. Trodd cites Frederick Douglass's interpretation of artists: "Poets, prophets, and reformers are all picture-makers . . . they see what ought to be by the reflection of what is, and endeavor to remove the contradiction." For Trodd, literature by figures such as Ralph Ellison, Harriet Jacobs, Richard Wright, and others represents a body of outsider rhetoric which uses the literary art form to reflect, correct, and spotlight the glaring absence of black representation in American culture. Literature is a means of accessing power, agency, and voice in a culture that erases the African American visage from the public view. For these writers, literature becomes a means of achieving visibility, of filling in the gaps or holes in the otherwise very white and very partial perspective.

Ian Edwards's chapter also concerns African American literature. His focus is on Ellison's *Invisible Man* and how Ellison's uses of style "imply an open-ended, dialogical statement of the expressive possibilities open to the outsider in fiction in general, and a 'working-through' of the productive tensions implicit in the African-American's position." He explores how *Invisible Man* constitutes a model of outsider rhetoric "as a response, on two different if intimately related levels, to the various *discursive* and *subjective* problematics implicit in the marginalized agent's relations to hegemony." Edwards, an outsider himself in some ways as an Englishman writing about African American literary forms, argues that *Invisible Man* "interrogates fundamental precepts of the traditional rhetoric of U.S. society, such as 'freedom' and 'democracy.'" This interrogation appears through the guise of literature, a safer, more subtle, and perhaps far more powerful means of rhetorical influence than direct political attempts at articulating the problems of race relations in twentieth-century American culture. As an African American man, Ellison had to negotiate a particularly hazardous set of rhetorical constraints, and thus his literature becomes a Foucauldian opportunity to use discourse—to carry on a conversation with the reading audience—to undermine and question the status quo, to expose the hypocrisies in American notions of freedom and liberty.

Coretta Pittman's essay is an analysis of the rhetoric of rap artist "Common," Huey P. Newton, and Malcolm X. Much as fiction served as a space for African American writers to voice their resistance to social norms of their day, rap music has become a means for rhetorical action by marginalized members of a culture such as Common. Her example ties rap musician "Common" to leading social/political activists such as Newton and Malcolm X, categorizing them together as socially conscious resistors to the status quo. All three of these figures are not only outsiders to the dominant community—the white middle class—they are also outsiders within their own communities, to a degree. Common's socially conscious rap stays away from the sex-and-violence themes that seem to pervade contemporary rap. Malcolm X and Huey Newton are often compared negatively to Martin Luther King and his accommodationist, passive-resistance policies of leadership.

Pittman observes that "because enslavement taught Black Americans that language was so important, they recognized its potential for harm and liberation." Malcolm X, then, gave Black Americans courage and a voice to make themselves heard despite monumental opposition which included Jim Crow laws and, all too often, violence. Newton, cofounder of the Black Panthers, felt dissatisfied with King's leadership and adopted a revolutionary rhetoric influenced by Mao Tse-tung and Che Guevara, among others. His was, Pittman argues, a rhetoric of self-empowerment which was "shaped by the desires and needs of the community." For Pittman, these three figures represent a tradition of Black American rhetoric from the margins aimed at changing the "utopia" and to reflect themselves onto a largely white picture—even when it means sidestepping and speaking against those other Black Americans who have made inroads into white culture.

Ilaria Serra explores an outsider group within the American culture, the Italian immigrant who arrived over the course of the twentieth century. While the stories of the earliest immigrants to the United States are relatively well-known, Serra argues that the Italian immigrants' stories remain lost, mute, and forgotten. The texts that she has uncovered which tell immigration stories "must be considered rhetoric on the margins." Certainly immigration has had a powerful impact on the American identity, yet most of us do not know the immigrants' stories. The autobiographies of the ordinary twentieth-century immigrants, unlike those of the "founding fathers" of American mythology (which tends to represent itself as the story of white intellectual-class Englishmen), are stories of the working class that built the country as it moved from an agrarian to an industrial society. Serra classifies these uncovered stories as a type of generative rhetoric, one which brings forth "a reversal of an existing social condition and a crossing of cultural boundaries." These immigrants reflect themselves onto their culture and attempt to expose their invisibility, to quite literally write themselves into identity, and into the middle class.

Scott Whiddon discusses a group of outsiders who live quite literally outside of mainstream society—prisoners at the Louisiana State Penitentiary at Angola. Unlike the other outsiders discussed in this collection who live among the mainstream society and negotiate within it as outsiders, this population is physically displaced and outside of the regular, everyday culture. His essay focuses on the *Angolite*, an award-winning news magazine written and produced by the inmates of Angola. Unquestionably outsiders, the *Angolite* staff has won numerous awards and its former editor, Wilbert Rideau, was the first black staff member and lived at Angola on death row. Whiddon proposes that

> *The Angolite*—as a body of writing by inmates, a group of marginalized rhetors, a physical space within a historically troubled institution—is an impressive rhetorical act both in its longevity as a publication and the power of its prose. Despite its physical and ideological marginalization, *The Angolite* works as a site of resistance by maintaining an ethos of responsible journalism and by using genres and methods that are valued by both the inmates at LSP and mainstream, "free" audiences.

Whiddon's essay explores how the inmate staff of the *Angolite* work to represent themselves to the free society and to make themselves known and heard by an audience who usually not merely ignores them but doesn't even consciously recognize that they exist. The physical space of the prison is way outside the fringes of desirable places to live and function, and thus the prisoners are out of sight, out of mind. Writing for the *Angolite* grants the prisoners voices and visibility, and even in a way empowers them despite their incarceration. The *Angolite* staff, according to Whiddon, "recognizes the complex nature of power that marks their hours as writers and inmates, yet it continues to enact contemplation and social change from the unlikeliest of locations." Whiddon has himself brought to light a population so ignored that they might as well not exist for most members of free society, and he has exposed and theorized into legitimacy their discursive attempts at negotiating life and power from behind prison bars.

Next in the collection are a series of essays that discuss issues of gender and faith identity and public perception. In his essay concerning gender and agency, Ian Edwards explores the complexities of women engaged in the über-masculine world of boxing. In fact, he questions the identity of the sport's gendered nature, asking: "is the gendered status of boxing itself merely provisional, its putatively masculine status merely a contingent fact based on the gender of the vast majority of its participants to this point?" Women are, at least on the surface, clearly outsiders in the world of boxing, if only for the sport's inherently violent nature—women are, after all, presumed to be the nonviolent gender, inclined more to collaboration and negotiation than to hand-to-hand combat. But, as Edwards argues, the very masculine stereotype of boxing permits women an agency when they do choose to participate: "If boxing seems an incongruous arena in which to demonstrate feminine agency, one of the masculine preserves least likely to cede to the equality of women, it is surely also an opportunity for women to reverse gender norms most spectacularly and unexpectedly (and therefore with more subversive force)." In fact, their outsider status within the sport is necessary for their success. Were women to become mainstream as boxers, they would, perhaps, lose the spectacular rhetorical effect of their presence there.

Rebecca Ingalls considers the concept of outsider through queer theory and popular culture. She explores the metaphor of the closet as a space for queer rhetoric within the broader American culture, arguing that "the gay community and its audience still seems to be holding on to the closet as a rhetorical shelter in the margin." Despite the fact that the presence of queer culture has expanded exponentially in recent years in popular culture, Ingalls argues that it has in no way become normalized or mainstreamed. In fact, as her title suggests, the closet is alive and well and providing both confinement and refuge. Ingalls explores the complexities of human sexuality and rhetorical access to mainstream pop culture venues, asserting that "when we think about what it means to assert rhetorical power from the margin, we have to ask what being 'here' means." The rhetorical choices made by openly queer actors, writers, and other figures have a powerful effect on access to and perceptions of general audiences; these rhetorical players must negotiate the rhetorical spaces they find themselves in (and perhaps want to remove themselves from) especially artfully.

Joseph Williams's essay discusses another outsider group in American culture: the religious group known as Pentecostals. Known for speaking in tongues and experiencing the Holy Spirit quite literally through physical, supernatural experiences, Pentecostals have been the subject of much skepticism, ostracism, and prejudice in American Protestantism. Williams discusses how Pentecostals incorporated industrial and technological terminology to relate their religious experiences: "despite their outsider status in early twentieth-century America, Pentecostals imbibed the intoxicating spirit of the times, transposing themes in the broader American culture into their own plainfolk nomenclature." Williams states that "Pentecostals tapped an evidentiary rhetorical tradition within American evangelicalism that sought empirical proof to support belief in the supernatural."

For Williams, this group of outsiders uses the mainstream popular culture to exist within and even undermine it. While remaining an outsider to other Christian protestant religious groups in mainstream American culture, Pentecostals harnessed much of the language and terminology of the secular culture to root itself in the community.

Williams argues that in setting themselves outside of mainstream churches while simultaneously incorporating terminology of the rapidly industrializing culture, the Pentecostals' rhetoric "reveals how 'outsiders' can adopt key components of a dominant culture's rhetorical tools even as they work to subvert that very culture." Williams's essay is a unique look into the Pentecostal culture and history, as well as an exploration of how an outsider group can deliberately and artfully challenge mainstream culture through discourse, even through superimposing themselves onto the center through the use of language. Much like Serra's immigration stories, which represent marginal, everyday workers' attempts to inscribe themselves into American mainstream culture and society by appropriating an art form usually known to the educated classes, the Pentecostal linguistic choices that Williams discusses show how religious outsiders can circumvent mainstream church choices and connect the supernatural to the technological/industrial to make themselves heard and understood.

The last two essays in this collection explore very modern issues that have been brought about in part by globalization and technology. Jessica Ketcham's essay is an exploration of how pop culture—specifically modern technology—can be used for rhetorical means. In "Techno-Mob Movements: Public Performances and the Collective Voices of Outsiders," Ketcham explains how contemporary technology has enabled people across the world to mobilize themselves in social activism. Ketcham defines the term "Techno-Mob" as "the creative use of **techno**logy to **mob**ilize citizens." These "mobs" are "dynamic, fluid collectives of citizens whose voices are being heard despite their lack of traditional political power." She describes how large groups of people are able to garner social and/or political power that the individual usually lacks in society. Technological advances permit the organization of the groups; "everyday citizens have begun to embrace their outsider position by creating alternative news and media sources, and through technology they are building upon the fact that collective social action is the only way for resistance to turn into political change." Ketcham shows how technologies such as Weblogs, text messaging, and the internet have enabled people to take up social action in ways unimaginable just a generation ago. She proposes that the actions taken up by techno-mobs are "a politically aware rhetorical method, which citizens are participating in across the world to gain agency, transform the meaning of outsider, and to unsettle normalizing practices of society."

The final essay in the collection also explores the international rhetorical agent—Wangari Maathai, African Nobel Prize winner—and her deliberate positioning of herself as an outsider to Western values.

By doing so, Oenbring argues, Maathai "engages in what Spivak calls 'strategic essentialism.'" Maathai, despite receiving adequate acclaim to earn her the prestigious Nobel Prize, sets herself apart from Western values and customs through her expression of controversial views. By doing so she deliberately set her *ethos* as that of the Outsider. She chooses to remain on the outside rather than stepping inside through the access that the Nobel and her fame have allowed her. Maathai was educated in part in the United States and is arguably an "insider" by virtue of her status, education, and recognition by the West. Her rhetorical move to maintain on the outside and garner power and voice there, rather than from the mainstream, is a strategic device chosen for its effectiveness to her particular cause. Oenbring argues that "Maathai's (hidden) instrumentalism, . . . in conjunction with her strategic representation of aspects of the natural world in order to increase attention for her project among the postmodern Western left, makes rhetorical redescription of her activist texts a particularly valuable task." Oenbring's exploration of Maathai's rhetorical choices uncover a very artful, deliberate, and effective use of insider/outsider status and ethos.

Although each of these articles explores separate aspects of Western culture and ethos, they all have in common the analysis of how speakers who perceive themselves as Outsiders use that status and identity to rhetorical effect. Each of the subjects of these chapters is identified as unempowered; and, where traditional academic studies of rhetoric may ignore them, they are in fact effective in their goals to reach an audience from the margins. Each of the subjects in these essays have created a heterotopia where they are able to be reflected upon the mainstream society. They create spaces for themselves where their participation doesn't minimize their value through being discounted as exceptions to a rule. Exceptions don't make inroads into the power structure—they enter, become footnotes, and depart. The Outsider ethos allows for identity creation and power from the margins.

It is important to remember that politics is only one means of wielding social influence, and it is an increasingly distrusted one in American culture. And although many have charged into the mainstream (Martin Luther King, Jr.; Susan B. Anthony; Anita Hill) and tried to make changes there, these figures generally remained outsiders by virtue of their very uncommonness. And increasingly, those outsiders who do enter into mainstream politics and social movements earn a sense of mistrust from their peers, who question their ability to remain loyal to their cause, and to maintain their true identity. As such, Outsiders who position themselves on the outside and call attention to their marginality may have more power, more effect, and more followers. They use an artful, thoughtful, rhetoric which is especially complex due to the multiple audiences they must consider, and the care with which they must choose their words. Though the subjects of each of the essays in this collection may initially seem to bear little resemblance to the classical notion of "A good man speaking well," they *do* have a clear understanding of Aristotle's definition of rhetoric as the art of finding the available means of persuasion. And perhaps these examples are even more compelling, as they are Outsiders to formal rhetorical training as well as access to traditional rhetoric, yet they have a very astute understanding of the notion of "available means."

Notes

1. Maurice Charland, "Constitutive Rhetoric and the Case of the 'People Quebecois,'" *Quarterly Journal of Speech* 73 (2) 1987: 215.
2. Ibid., 221.
3. Ibid., 220.
4. Michel Foucault, *The History of Sexuality*, vol. 1, trans. Robert Hurley (New York: Pantheon, 1978), 100–101.
5. Charland, "Constitutive Rhetoric," 214.
6. Charles J. Stewart, Craig Allen Smith, and Robert E. Denton, Jr., *Persuasion and Social Movements*, 4th ed. (Prospect Heights, IL: Waveland Press, 2001), 6.
7. Michel Foucault, "Of Other Spaces," *Diacritics* 16, no. 1 (Spring 1986): 22–27.
8. Ibid.
9. Ibid.
10. Charland, "Constitutive Rhetoric," 226.

Bibliography

Charland, Maurice. "Constitutive Rhetoric and the Case of the 'People Quebecois'" *Quarterly Journal of Speech* 73, no. 2 (1987): 133–50.

Foucault, Michel. *The History of Sexuality*. Vol. 1. Translated by Robert Hurley. New York: Pantheon, 1978.

Foucault, Michel. "Of Other Spaces," *Diacritics* 16, no. 1 (Spring 1986): 22–27.

Stewart, Charles J., Craig Allen Smith, and Robert E. Denton, Jr. *Persuasion and Social Movements*. 4th ed. Prospect Heights, IL: Waveland Press, 2001.

Freedom of Speech and the Politics of Silence: The Case of Ward Churchill

Michael Donnelly

"Freedom of speech" is a major element of the cultural context in which we live, think, work, and write. Indeed, it is generally considered, in U.S. cultural and political parlance, the major structuring principle of a "free" society, the principle *qua* principle of democracy. It is frequently understood as the "foundation" upon which (all) democracy must rest. Without it, the argument goes, all else is for naught. Furthermore, on a broad cultural basis, the First Amendment is often perceived as somehow "most important." This follows quasi-logically in a culture steeped in a hierarchical paradigm of thought and organization—"First" signifies something; it designates an order, a kind of priority. There are of course, with some regularity, debates over whether a certain expression of "speech" is (or should be) protected under the First Amendment, but virtually all of these debates assume the same definition (or assume they are using the same definition) of "Freedom of Speech." There is rarely any public discussion of what Freedom of Speech means, or, at least, there is general agreement that Freedom of Speech is a universally recognizable and identifiable thing.

Most histories and discussion of the First Amendment tend to focus on the "Law"—i.e., court decisions, especially emanating from the Supreme Court. My position is somewhat different: that Freedom of Speech is a *cultural* concept, not merely, or even primarily, a legal one. It should be understood in terms of how it functions in the culture at large, and not merely on the basis of those, relatively few, cases that make it into a court of law, much less the even fewer that reach the Supreme Court. Certainly, the cultural concept of Free Speech includes and is sometimes impacted by Court rulings; but even Supreme Court justices are not outside the realm of culture, and an examination of Court decisions can demonstrate the ways in which those decisions have reflected and/or been shaped by dominant cultural attitudes. The invocation of "freedom of speech" is always and already political—it is invoked by someone (or some group) in a particular sociopolitical position, with a greater or lesser degree of power, at a specific historical moment, for specific ends. It is not merely a neutral term requiring clarification by the Court, or application to a particular case. To begin to understand how the concept functions *culturally*—rather than, as most studies do, merely *legally*—we must consider the contextual elements of the uses of freedom of speech. In doing so, we find that Free Speech has often functioned, and continues to function, as a weapon, wielded by those in power, to silence those in opposition.

In particular, "outsider rhetorics" are theoretically protected by the First Amendment; in fact, one might reasonably argue that the purpose of the First Amendment was primarily to protect "outsider rhetorics." One can point to numerous examples of how this has worked—the simple fact that I can drive over to the nearest bookstore and purchase a copy of *Malcolm X Speaks* indicates that this is true to some extent, but not to *what* extent. As it functions culturally, the notion of Free Speech has, in fact, served more often to protect and insulate the insider-center (i.e., those in positions of power and privilege) than the outsider, and, in fact, is frequently used to silence the "outsider." Because of this, some "outsider rhetorics"—a certain subset, let's say—must push at the extremes. By so doing, such rhetorics force open spaces for discussion—in other words, they dismantle silences—and for less "radical" but no less "outsider" rhetorics to be more effective. There is, of course, no way to gauge this in terms of winners or losers. Despite its best attempts, the conservative-Center cannot silence, once and for all, Outsiders; and yet its efforts are not without effect. Perhaps no case illustrates this in so interesting a way as the case of Ward Churchill.

Theoretical Context

In his 1994 book *There's No Such Thing as Free Speech (and it's a good thing, too!)*, Stanley Fish argues that there is no stable, transcendent "thing" to which "free speech" refers, that, like concepts of "fair" and "just," its definition(s) "flow from local contexts rather than from the identification of transcendent or general standards."[1] A principle like Freedom of Speech does not transcend politics, as its proponents would contend—it is not merely a neutral principle that can function for good or ill, because it always functions in a context, a context delimited (partly, not entirely) by who is invoking it, what power(s) they possess (tangible and intangible), and to what end they hope to use it. The invocation of freedom of speech is always and already political—

which is to say, it always represents a particular, political interest: "Short of an absolutely absolutist position . . . , a line must be drawn between protected speech and speech that might in some circumstances be regulated, and *that line will always reflect a political decision to indemnify some kinds of verbal behavior and devalue others.*"[2]

According to Fish, the intellectual and political left's "mistake"—in debates like the one over hate speech—has been to appeal to a "higher standard," or a more "fair" or more "just" principle; which is to say, in confronting racism and sexism, the left has appealed to their own concepts of "justice" or "fairness," maintaining a foundational paradigm of argumentation. This is, in Fish's words, a "trap": one must either argue (or appear to argue) against "fairness," "justice," "free speech"; or, "if you respond . . . by declaring that you too are committed to the disinterested search for truth and eschew politics, you will be playing the game on the other fellow's field, . . . giving yourself the herculean task . . . of explaining why feminist, African American and gay concerns are universal."[3] A better response, says Fish, "would be to acknowledge the political implications of a revised curriculum but point out that any alternative curriculum—say, a diet of exclusively Western or European texts—would be no less politically invested, only differently so."[4] Fish admits "that the absence of independent standards" inherent in this move

> becomes disabling, . . . that there is nowhere to go, no locus of judgment to which disputants can appeal for an authoritative announcement. But this doesn't mean that they must throw up their hands or toss the dice; it means that they must argue, thrash it out, present bodies of evidence to one another and to relevant audiences, try to change one another's mind. . . . authority does not preside over the debate from a position outside it but is the prize for which the debaters vie.[5]

Suggesting that we "must argue, thrash it out, present bodies of evidence, . . . and try to change one another's mind," Fish claims that these arguments should be based not on abstracted principles, but on the actual material consequences of varying ideas and policies. At the same time, however, "The structure that is supposed to permit ideological/political agendas to fight it out fairly . . . is itself always ideologically and politically constructed."[6] In effect, the "debating table" is always politically slanted, so that while, as Fish says, "authority does not preside over the debate from a position outside it but is the prize for which the debaters vie,"[7] it is also true that different participators in the debate will bring different degrees of authority with them to the table; some will wield tremendous power, some little or none at all. In fact, some possess enough power, enough influence over the structure of debate as to exclude certain others from the debate entirely, or (and this may be more important) to allow those others to participate, only to effectively silence them again within the forum of debate.

Fish is therefore able to acknowledge that in "actual" debate, in the "real world" arena, the playing field is not level; yet at the same time he can describe an idealized form of debate that could only function if in fact the playing field was level: "argue, thrash it out, present bodies of evidence . . ." Thus the important question, I think, is what does Fish's argument "mean" in that "real world arena," what does it mean for actual people in actual situations? Fish's answer is "not very much":

> Strange as it may seem, those who are persuaded by the arguments of this chapter can do nothing with them—can derive from them no program or set of marching orders—without being unfaithful to them. The most you can do is employ them as I have here, as a means of denying to those on the other side the high ground of purity so essential to their polemic; but once that has been done (and I urge that it be done unceasingly), you cannot claim a new purity that has somehow arisen, like a phoenix, from the ashes of absolutist discourse.[8]

One is left to wonder what effect denying the "other side" their "high ground," even unceasingly, can possibly have, when in fact those on the "other side" wield very real power—power that includes the leisure to ignore (the denial), as well as the power to silence; when the concept of free speech is appropriated by those who "have the power to do so."[9] The potential effectiveness of this denial, it seems to me, presumes precisely the kind of "level playing field" Fish elsewhere acknowledges does not exist; it presumes, in fact, the "free-marketplace of ideas" created, culturally and conceptually, by the notion of Freedom of Speech. We can deny until we are blue in the face—but to what effect? What might it mean to "thrash it out" on the basis of real, material consequences, when some of those gathered at the debating table already wield very real cultural, political, and economic power over their opponents?

In the specific cultural context of the United States, this means the concept of Free Speech functions only in (terms of) its relationship to Silence(ing) Others. Silence is enforced not entirely or even primarily by militaristic force (as in a totalitarian state), but by rhetorical force brought to bear through various forms of institutional, sociopolitical, and economic power. It is in many cases a reality only for those who wield cultural, economic, and (therefore) political power, who define what constitutes "Free Speech," and the limits thereon. The "Free Speech" of the Outsider is too often illusory and transient, and depends in large part on not crossing an invisible line defined and drawn by those in power.

This is not to say that Outsiders are powerless, or never able to speak at all. Indeed, Outsider rhetorics, with and without the protection of the First Amendment, have been and continue to be forces for change. My argument is simply that, first, Freedom of Speech functions *differently* for different groups according to their positions in the social matrix (insider/outsider, top/bottom), and that therefore Outsider rhetorics must constantly test, challenge, and stretch the "acceptable speech" boundaries defined by those in power.

Controversy in Context

Churchill's is clearly an outsider rhetoric—the rhetoric of indigenous rights, anti-capitalist-imperialism, and especially of political dissent. At the center of the Churchill controversy, it seemed, was an essay originally published (on the internet) in 2001, shortly after 9/11. In "Some People Push Back: On the Justice of Roosting Chickens," Churchill, in his usual uncompromising polemic, argued that the "terrorists" were merely responding to an undeclared war waged by the United States and others on Iraq, and that the victims of 9/11 (at least many or most of those in the WTC) were not "innocent" but willing participants in the economic exploitation and oppression of peoples around the globe, and perhaps at best willingly ignorant of the military force being used on their behalf; his point, as he later summarized it, was simply that "we cannot allow the U.S. government, acting in our name, to engage in massive violations of international law and fundamental human rights and not expect to reap the consequences."[10]

Yet, the publication of "Some People Push Back" did not itself generate controversy. As Scott Smallwood reported in the *Chronicle of Higher Education*, "other than a brief mention in *The Burlington Free-Press* during a December 2001 visit to the University of Vermont, the essay never made the news."[11] The 2003 publication of the follow-up book, *On the Justice of Roosting Chickens*, which Churchill describes as "a detailed chronology of U.S. military interventions since 1776 and U.S. violations of international law since World War II,"[12] likewise created not a stir (and, in fact, was all but ignored in later controversy). What, then, was the context within which the controversy emerged? Reports uniformly identify a Churchill speaking engagement at Hamilton College, scheduled for February 3, 2005, which is true as far as it goes. The "debate" over whether or not Churchill's speech should be cancelled, instigated by a single Hamilton professor, should be situated in the broader climate of conservative dissatisfaction with what they see as overly liberal (and often radical) higher education.

In addition, and often overlooked, is Churchill's participation, as part of the Colorado Chapter of the American Indian Movement (A. I. M.), in the annual blocking and halting of the Columbus Day parade in Denver. His 1991 essay "Bringing the Law Home" details the brief, based largely on the United Nations' 1948 Convention on Punishment and Prevention of the Crime of Genocide, filed by the defendants in court following their subsequent arrest, which led to their acquittal. In 2004, A.I.M. once again blocked the Columbus Day parade, and once again the protestors were both arrested and acquitted. This appears to have raised the ire of conservative disc jockeys in Denver. What even this limited chronology[13] suggests is that the rhetoric itself is of less consequence than a particular historical moment—though one is forced to wonder what would have happened (or not happened) had Churchill merely omitted "little Eichmanns" from the essay.

Tellingly, the controversy that followed did not focus on the "accuracy" or "inaccuracy," or "validity" (or lack of) of "Some People Push Back"—indeed, if and how the essay might be "accurate," or even from what perspective, are not questions on the table; the notion that it is simply, utterly, and completely wrong is taken as a matter of course. There was no broad discussion of the argument made in "Some People Push Back," and still less of the book that followed. Instead, those with power define the terrain, the boundaries of public discussion, and therefore preempt any actual dialogue. Antagonists used a few selected and rhetorically effective snippets—primarily a single phrase ("little Eichmanns"), and, rather than attack Churchill's ideas (in the spirit of fighting speech with more speech), they chose to attack his character—questioning his legitimacy as a Native American and his credentials for professorship.

Put another way, if the appropriate response to "offensive speech" is "more speech," then we should consider the effects of "more speech"—if indeed it has any. In this case, one might identify Churchill's essay as the "offensive speech," to which Bill O'Reilly, Colorado Governor Bill Owens, David Horowitz, Ann Coulter, and other conservatives responded. The effect of this "more speech" was, first, to silence Churchill—his scheduled appearance at Hamilton College was eventually cancelled, as were other already scheduled appearances. Second, they provoked a full-scale investigation of Churchill that resulted, eventually, in his firing, as well as, more broadly, reviews of tenure and promotion processes. The message to liberal (never mind radical) academics and intellectuals everywhere becomes clear. In the favorite words of Bill O'Reilly: "Just shut up." Yet Churchill's dismissal, and the discussion of tenure and promotion, had nothing to do with the original case of "offensive speech." Churchill was not fired because his writing was "offensive," nor because his "speech" was not protected by the First Amendment. The essay and later book were not found to be untrue, inaccurate, or obscene (though many used that word to describe it). Indeed, the University of Colorado administration *affirmed* the First Amendment protection of Churchill's work. Even David Horowitz and governor Bill Owens were forced to concede as much.[14]

If, instead, we consider Churchill's work not as the originally offensive speech, but as "more speech" in response *to* "offensive speech," things look somewhat different. The offensive speech in this case might be said to include (but not be limited to) Madeleine Albright's assertion that the deaths of half a million Iraqi children were "worth the cost," the senior George Bush's pronouncement that "the world must learn that what we say, goes," repeated media references to "collateral damage," and so on.[15] But more speech, in this case, is no longer the appropriate response to "offensive speech"—Churchill should not be permitted to speak at colleges and universities, still less should he be allowed to teach. Further, those making this argument were able to bring about these ends through the marshaling of cultural and political power, and not through the validity of their arguments, which, after all, had nothing to do with the text in question.

THE CONSERVATIVE BACKLASH

Speaking on The O'Reilly Factor that aired on February 15, 2005, David Horowitz explained,

> you can't fire some professor or anybody working in a state institution for opinions they put on the internet, because they have citizenship rights. But, I said Ward Churchill—this is a man who teaches his—all his books really are about America being a genocidal nation, worse than Hitler. That's why everybody in the World Trade Center's a "little Eichmann." But, if you look at the real world, if it were true that America was conducting genocide against brown people and black people, why do all those Mexicans want to come here? You know, why are there Haitians tryin' to get into the United States? It shows utter contempt for them. This guy is not controversial. He's certifiable. This is a lunatic. That's when I said he's a kook and a loon, and the situation at the University is out of control.[16]

After acknowledging that Churchill has "citizenship rights" (by which I assume he means the right to Free Speech), he quickly changes the subject to "all his books," implying that you *can* fire someone for writing books that "are about America being a genocidal nation." (Later in the interview, he says simply, "I think he should be fired for impersonating an Indian."[17]) Horowitz further relies upon that fact that "worse than Hitler," appealing to the sentiments of patriotic Americans, will clinch the censure of Churchill's work without the need for any close examination or further discussion. Then, adopting a favorite conservative strategy, he begs the question (and an irrelevant question at that), "if it were true . . . why do all those Mexicans want to come here?" Finally, he lapses into name-calling, and generalizes from his opinion of Churchill to "the situation at the University," later telling O'Reilly "they should put the whole Ethnic Studies Department on probation . . . they need to get an outside audit of that University and look at their hiring, promotion, tenure practices."[18] O'Reilly, agreeing, says, "Oh, absolutely. It's a radical campus, is it not?" To which Horowitz marshals the testimony of twelve College Republicans (at a university of nearly twenty-five thousand undergraduates), every one of whom has "had a professor rant against the war in Iraq and George Bush in a class" and "seen OUTFOXED." "They're radical!" concludes Horowitz,[19] who, a year later, published a book on the *101 Most Dangerous Academics in America*. Just two weeks later, O'Reilly asserts "Ward Churchill is a traitor," and "continues to speak around the country, getting paid for telling people that the civilians in the World Trade Center on 9/11 were legitimate military targets."[20] O'Reilly then runs a video clip in which Churchill explains: "The Central Intelligence Agency had located facilities in the World Trade Center. The Defense Department had located facilities in the World Trade Center. There were other entities that could be considered part of command and control infrastructure that had been deliberately situated by the government of the United States in the towers. By U.S. rules, which I absolutely object to, by U.S. rules, that made them legitimate targets."[21] O'Reilly, of course, very conveniently ignores Churchill's reference to "U.S. rules," never mind that he "absolutely objects to" those rules. Instead, because he can't actually address the issues of CIA facilities, the Defense Department, "other entities . . . deliberately situated by the government," or "U.S. rules," O'Reilly responds only with "Now Churchill's view is just hateful. . . . Clear-thinking Americans have already rejected Churchill's hatred. And, no person should confront the man in any way."[22] What this means is that no one (including, obviously, O'Reilly) should engage in any debate with Churchill. Later, like Horowitz, he reveals what this is really about:

"This story is not about Churchill anymore. It's about the people who enable him. What say you, University of Colorado?"[23]

Likewise, Ann Coulter writes "Not Crazy Horse, Just Crazy," and "Why Does Ward Churchill Still Teach at Colorado?" (Both published in *Human Events* in February of 2005, roughly six weeks after the story broke.) In the former, she begins with a few carefully selected quotes, which she cannot actually examine, only assume the reader will find as outrageous as she does, and then writes, "To grasp the current state of higher education in America, consider that if Churchill is at any risk at all of being fired, it is only because he smokes." "Tenure," she says, "was supposed to create an atmosphere of open debate and inquiry [except, one assumes, with radical left professors], but instead has created havens for talentless cowards who want to be insulated from life."[24] In the latter article, published a week earlier, Coulter makes no pretense that this is about anything but Churchill's legitimacy as a Native American, despite her repeated references to "Some People Push Back."[25]

Of course, these three are "right-wing," and not necessarily representative of the mainstream. Except that one finds both their sentiments and their strategies echoed in more prominent places. Colorado governor Bill Owens wrote to the University's Board of Regents, calling on Churchill to resign from the University altogether. Yet his letter is not addressed to Churchill, but "Dear Friends": "All decent people," he writes, "whether Republican or Democrat, liberal or conservative, should denounce the views of Ward Churchill. Not only are his writings outrageous and insupportable, they are at odds with the facts of history."[26] Yet the only facts of history he can muster are that those who died on 9/11 were "innocent" and "murdered by evil cowards." Owens concedes that "no one wants to infringe on Mr. Churchill's right to express himself"—though surely this is precisely what he wants—"But we are not compelled to accept his pro-terrorist views at state taxpayer subsidy nor under the banner of the University of Colorado."[27] Here, Churchill's "right to express himself" is transformed into "we are not compelled to accept," Churchill himself becomes "pro-terrorist," and an essay published on the internet (not classroom teaching, mind—Churchill was not fired for classroom diatribes) falls "under the banner of the University." On the same day, the Colorado House passed a resolution condemning Churchill's essay as "deplorable" and expressing its "heartfelt sympathy for the victims" of 9/11. The resolution concludes: "Be It Further Resolved, That copies of the Joint Resolution be sent to University of Colorado President Elizabeth Hoffman, the University of Colorado at Boulder Chancellor's office, the University of Colorado Board of Regents, and University of Colorado at Boulder Department of Ethics Chairman [though Churchill had already resigned this post] Ward L. Churchill."[28]

The University of Colorado, for its part, must certainly have heard Owens and the conservative backlash behind him. By April 1, interim chancellor Philip P. DiStefano, echoing both Horowitz and Owens (to differing degrees), affirmed that "Churchill's political expression is constitutionally protected."[29] Even so, DiStefano first took the opportunity to explain that he, too, "found the essay to be profoundly repugnant and hurtful to everyone touched by the tragedy of September 11, 2001."[30] *Then* he said that charges of plagiarism and fabrication, as well as Churchill's ancestry, would be referred to the Standing Committee on Research Misconduct.

The Rhetoric of Ward Churchill

Ward Churchill's polemics are, in a word, uncompromising. They are certainly inflammatory, even vitriolic—and have always been so, no doubt intentionally. "Some People Push Back" is not even remotely out of character in this regard—he's been writing such attacks on U.S. ideology and imperialism since the 1980s. What's shocking is not that "Some People" provoked such a response (even one that took three years), but that his previous writings never did. Comparisons to Nazi Germany and the Holocaust are a regular feature of Churchill's attacks on genocidal U.S. policies, historical and contemporary. Looked at in the broader context of his writings, which are (perhaps unfortunately) riddled with biting sarcasm and a tendency toward hyperbole, Churchill's rhetoric should nonetheless be understood as based on a single premise: "So's your old man"[31] is simply an insufficient and ineffectual response to the continued soft-peddling and broad acceptance of aggression, military and nonmilitary, at home and abroad. He has long lost any patience with even liberal and antiwar sentiment: those "who expressed opposition to what was/is being done to the children of Iraq. . . . by-and-large contented themselves with signing petitions and conducting candle-lit prayer vigils, bearing 'moral witness.'"[32]

He relies heavily on accumulated history—"detailed chronology" of the sort provided by the book *On the Justice of Roosting Chickens*—exposing singular events as not merely isolated incidents, but as fundamentally related to a series of ongoing events. These histories are, plagiarism and fabrication charges not withstanding,[33] painstakingly documented (endnotes sometimes run on for pages, even for a single essay). Churchill also relies heavily on definition—the entirety of the

"Some People Push Back" essay hinges on definitions of a series of words: innocent, ignorance, cowards, fanatics, desperate, insane, "evil," terrorist. He takes words and phrases which are commonly bandied about with assumed definitions and says, basically, "let's look at what this word really means" as a way of inverting the groups to which the terms apply. Iraqi children are "innocent," the U.S. President is a "terrorist." These definitions are often shaded with the above sarcasm: "Evil . . . was perfectly incarnated in that malignant toad known as Madeleine Albright, squatting in her studio chair like Jaba the Hutt."[34] No one (apparently) blinked, save perhaps Albright herself, at this characterization.

The reference to "little Eichmanns," of course, is an inversion of definition of monumental proportions. Though it is not different in kind from others of Churchill's Nazi analogies, it does differ in terms of the specific group of people to which it was applied. Never mind that many "Americans" have only the vaguest notion, if any at all, of who Adolf Eichmann actually was, or had any opportunity to understand it in the context in which it was used.[35] This is not to say that the phrase was simply "taken out of context," and that once re-placed (in the context of its usage) it then loses its offensive dimension. It is to point out, once again, that there was no substantive discussion of the point or the essay. Churchill did write later, in response to the controversy, "It should be emphasized that I applied the 'little Eichmanns' characterization only to those described as 'technicians.' Thus, it was obviously not directed to the children, janitors, food service workers, firemen and random passers-by killed in the 9-1-1 attack";[36] and,

> Finally, I have never characterized all the September 11 victims as "Nazis." What I said was that the "technocrats of empire" working in the World Trade Center were the equivalent of "little Eichmanns." Adolf Eichmann was not charged with direct killing but with ensuring the smooth running of the infrastructure that enabled the Nazi genocide. Similarly, German industrialists were legitimately targeted by the Allies.[37]

From a rhetorical standpoint, Churchill's explanation, of course, did nothing to calm things—he won't back off, though he will try to "explain." Even so, the worst one can accuse him of in this case, aside from a serious lack of tact, is a false analogy. Even so, if that is the case, such should be debated and discussed, rather than merely dismissed.

Conclusion

Earlier I asserted that Freedom of Speech functions *differently* for different groups according to their positions in the social matrix (insider/outsider, top/bottom), and that therefore Outsider rhetorics must constantly test, challenge, and stretch the "acceptable speech" boundaries defined by those in power. Some "outsider rhetorics," at least, must push at the extremes in order to dismantle silences and force open spaces for discussion. These "extreme" rhetorics are often silenced via the cultural and political power of those in the "Center." Certainly Churchill's rhetoric pushes at the boundaries. It may be too much to say that he has been silenced, but he has been fired (appeal pending). The larger point, however, is that despite conservative efforts to silence—and I would argue that conservative rhetoric has been largely successful in those efforts on a broad, cultural (i.e., mainstream) level—the Churchill controversy has engendered much debate in other, less widely viewed arenas. It has served, in many ways, and fortunately or unfortunately, to galvanize ideological forces on both the left and the right. This polarization should be viewed, in my estimation, as both a benefit and a cost. To the degree that such polarization closes down real discussion and debate, it is costly. But to the degree that it has forced academics to "push back," in defense of both academic freedom and freedom of speech, to respond to the conservative attack on higher education, it has had its benefits. It has likewise provoked others—perhaps not so radical—to see and to think and to talk about the issues raised;[38] what is most unfortunate is that those discussions get no broad media attention. Still, the boundaries have been stretched, and new spaces are open.

Notes

1. Stanley Fish, *There's No Such Thing as Free Speech (and it's a good thing, too!)* (New York: Oxford University Press, 1994), 10.
2. Ibid., 15.
3. Ibid., 9.
4. Ibid.
5. Ibid., 10–11.
6. Ibid., 116.
7. Ibid., 11.
8. Ibid., 20.
9. Ibid., 102.
10. Ward Churchill, "Press Release," *Colorado Communities for Justice and Peace*, January 31, 2005, http://www.coloradopeace.org/2005/WardChurchill/PressRelease-2005jan31.html.
11. Scott Smallwood, "Inside a Free-Speech Firestorm," *Chronicle of Higher Education* 51, no. 24 (February 18, 2005).
12. Churchill, "Press Release."
13. For a detailed chronology, see Smallwood, "Inside a Free-Speech Firestorm."

14. David Horowitz, interview with Bill O'Reilly, *The O'Reilly Factor*, February 15, 2005; Owens, letter to the University of Colorado, February 2, 2005.
15. Ward Churchill, "Some People Push Back: On the Justice of Roosting Chickens," *Pockets of Resistance* 11 (September 2001), http://www.darknightpress.org/index.php?i=print&article=9.
16. Marie Therese, "David Horowitz Takes Pot Shots at Ward Churchill, U of Colorado, and OUTFOXED," *News Hounds*, February 17, 2005, http://www.newshounds.us/2005/02/17/david_horowitz_takes_pot_shots_at_ward_churchill_u_of_colorado_and_outfoxed.php.
17. Ibid.
18. Ibid.
19. Ibid.
20. Bill O'Reilly, "Professor Ward Churchill is a Traitor," *The O'Reilly Factor*, March 3, 2005, http://www.foxnews.com/story/0,2933,149295,00.html.
21. Ibid.
22. Ibid.
23. Ibid.
24. Ann Coulter, "Not Crazy Horse, Just Crazy," *Human Events* 61, no. 7 (February 21, 2005): 5.
25. Ann Coulter, "Why Does Ward Churchill Still Teach at Colorado?," *Human Events* 61, no. 6 (February 14, 2005): 6.
26. Bill Owens, letter, February 1, 2005, http://www.colorado.gov/governor/press/february05/churchill.pdf.
27. Ibid.
28. Resolution of Colorado House of Representatives, February 2, 2005, http://www.kersplebedeb.com/mystuff/s11/churchill_hor.html.
29. Scott Smallwood, "U. of Colorado Will Investigate Allegations of Misconduct Against Controversial Professor," *Chronicle of Higher Education* 51, no. 30 (April 1, 2005): A36.
30. Ibid.
31. "[A]s if the effects of speech could be canceled out by additional speech, . . . [as] if the pain and humiliation caused by racial or religious epithets could be ameliorated by saying something like 'So's your old man.'" Stanley Fish, *There's No Such Thing as Free Speech (and it's a good thing, too!)* (New York: Oxford University Press, 1994), 109.
32. Churchill, "Some People Push Back," 3.
33. Tom Mayer, professor of sociology at the University of Colorado, has recently (June 2007) written: "Although the report by the committee on research misconduct clearly entailed prodigious labor, it is a flawed document requiring careful analysis. The central flaw in the report is grotesque exaggeration about the magnitude and gravity of the improprieties committed by Ward Churchill. . . .

"The text of the report suggests that the committee's judgments about the seriousness of Churchill's misconduct were contaminated by political considerations. This becomes evident on page 97 where the committee acknowledges that 'damage done to the reputation of . . . the University of Colorado as an academic institution is a consideration in our assessment of the seriousness of Professor Churchill's conduct.' Whatever damage the University may have sustained by employing Ward Churchill derives from his controversial political statements and certainly not from the obscure footnoting practices nor disputed authorship issues investigated by the committee. Indeed, the two plagiarism charges refer to publications that are now fourteen years old. Although these charges had been made years earlier, they were not considered worthy of investigation until Ward Churchill became a political cause celebre. Using institutional reputation to measure misconduct severity amounts to importing politics through the back door." http://wardchurchill.net/files/mayer.doc.

34. Churchill, "Some People Push Back," 5.

35. The passage in its entirety: "As to those in the World Trade Center . . .

"Well, really. Let's get a grip here, shall we? True enough, they were civilians of a sort. But innocent? Gimme a break. They formed a technocratic corps at the very heart of America's global financial empire—the 'mighty engine of profit' to which the military dimension of U.S. policy has always been enslaved—and they did so both willingly and knowingly. Recourse to 'ignorance'—a derivative, after all, of the word 'ignore'—counts as less than an excuse among this relatively well-educated elite. To the extent that any of them were unaware of the costs and consequences to others of what they were involved in—and in many cases excelling at—it was because of their absolute refusal to see. More likely, it was because they were too busy braying, incessantly and self-importantly, into their cell phones, arranging power lunches and stock transactions, each of which translated, conveniently out of sight, mind and smelling distance, into the starved and rotting flesh of infants. If there was a better, more effective, or in fact any other way of visiting some penalty befitting their participation upon the little Eichmanns inhabiting the sterile sanctuary of the twin towers, I'd really be interested in hearing about it."

36. Churchill, "Press Release."

37. Ibid.

38. See "Feedback from the Internet" on the Web site *Kersplebedeb*, which posted Churchill's original essay and an assortment of related material. http://www.kersplebedeb.com/mystuff/s11/churchill_feedback.html.

Bibliography

Allen, David S., and Robert Jensen. *Freeing the First Amendment: Critical Perspectives on Freedom of Expression*. New York: New York University Press, 1995.

Churchill, Ward. "Bringing the Law Home." *Indians Are Us? Culture and Genocide in Native North America*. Monroe, ME: Common Courage, 1994.

———. "Press Release." *Colorado Communities for Justice and Peace*. January 31, 2005. http://www.coloradopeace.org/2005/WardChurchill/PressRelease-2005jan31.html.

———. "Some People Push Back: On the Justice of Roosting Chickens." *Pockets of Resistance* 11 (September 2001). http://www.darknightpress.org/index.php?i=print&article=9.

Cockburn, Alexander. "Ward Churchill and the Mad Dogs of the Right." *Nation* 280, no. 7 (February 21, 2005): 9.

Colorado House of Representatives. Resolution. February 2, 2005. http://www.kersplebedeb.com/ mystuff/s11/churchill_hor.html.

Coulter, Ann. "Not Crazy Horse, Just Crazy." *Human Events* 61, no. 7 (February 21, 2005): 5.

———. "Why Does Ward Churchill Still Teach at Colorado?" *Human Events* 61, no. 6 (February 14, 2005): 6.

"Feedback from the Internet." *Kersplebedeb*. http://www.kersplebedeb.com/mystuff/s11/churchill_feedback.html.

Fish, Stanley. "Chickens: the Ward Churchill and Larry Summers Story." *Chronicle of Higher Education* 51, no. 36 (May 13, 2005): B9–B11.

———. *There's No Such Thing as Free Speech (and it's a good thing too!)*. New York: Oxford University Press, 1994.

Fiss, Owen M. *Liberalism Divided: Freedom of Speech and the Many Uses of State Power*. Boulder, CO: Westview, 1996.

Fraleigh, Douglas. *Freedom of Speech in the Marketplace of Ideas*. New York: St. Martin's, 1997.

Gabbard, David. "Academic Bills of Rights Assault Education." *Free Inquiry* 25, no. 5 (August/September 2005): 21–22.

Garvey, John H., and Frederick Schauer, eds. *The First Amendment: A Reader*. St. Paul, MN: West, 1996.

Harrison, Maureen, and Steve Gilbert, eds. *Freedom of Speech Decisions of the United States Supreme Court*. San Diego: Excellent Books, 1996.

Hentoff, Nat. *The First Freedom: A Tumultuous History of Free Speech in America*. New York: Delacorte Press, 1980.

Jaimes, M. Annette. "The Trial of the 'Columbus Day Four.'" *Lies of Our Times*, 3, n. 9 (September 1992): 8–9.

Kalven, Harry, Jr. *A Worthy Tradition: Freedom of Speech in America*. New York: Harper & Row, 1988.

Leahy, James E. *The First Amendment, 1791–1991: Two Hundred Years of Freedom*. Jefferson, NC: McFarland, 1991.

Lipka, Sara. "Panel Calls for Probe of Ward Churchill." *Chronicle of Higher Education* 52, no. 5 (September 23, 2005): A24.

Matsuda, Mari J., Charles R. Lawrence III, Richard Delgado, and Kimberle Williams Crenshaw. *Words that Wound: Critical Race Theory, Assaultive Speech, and the First Amendment*. Boulder, CO: Westview, 1993.

Mayer, Tom. "The Report on Ward Churchill." (June 2007). http://wardchurchill.net/files/mayer.doc.

O'Reilly, Bill. "Professor Ward Churchill is a Traitor." *The O'Reilly Factor* (March 3, 2005). http://www.foxnews.com/story/0,2933,149295,00.html.

Owens, Bill. Letter February 1, 2005. http://www.colorado.gov/governor/press/february05/churchill.pdf.

Roof, Judith and Robyn Wiegman. *Who Can Speak? Authority and Critical Identity*. Urbana: Uniersityre of Illinois Press, 1995.

Schauer, Frederick. "The First Amendment as Ideology." *William and Mary Law Review* 33, no. 3 (1992): 856.

Shapiro, Bruce. "Free-Speech Fights." *Nation* 280, no. 9 (March 7, 2005): 10. Smallwood, Scott. "Inside a Free-Speech Firestorm." *Chronicle of Higher Education* 51, no. 24 (February 18, 2005).

———. "U. of Colorado Will Investigate Allegations of Misconduct Against Controversial Professor." *Chronicle of Higher Education* 51, no. 30 (April 1, 2005): A36.

Smolla, Rodney A. *Free Speech in an Open Society*. New York: Knopf, 1992. Stewart, James Brewer. *The Constitution, the Law, and Freedom of Expression, 1787–1987*. Carbondale: Southern Illinois University Press, 1987.

Sunstein, Cass R. *Democracy and the Problem of Free Speech*. New York: Free Press, 1993.

Therese, Marie. "David Horowitz Takes Pot Shots at Ward Churchill, U of Colorado, and OUTFOXED." *News Hounds* (February 17, 2005). http://www.newshounds.us/2005/02/17/david_horowitz_takes_pot_shots_at_ward_churchill_u_of_colorado_and_outfoxed.php.

Recovering the Voices of the Florida Turpentine Slaves: A Lost Rhetoric of Resistance

LINDA BANNISTER AND JAMES E. HURD, JR.

INTRODUCTION

THE RISE OF THE POST-CIVIL WAR "NEW SOUTH" WAS MARKED BY INdustrial development and the establishment of an ostensible "free labor" society. However, debt bondage or peonage was common practice in the lucrative Florida turpentine industry. A vestige of antebellum slavery, peonage was a labor system that exploited the poor, homeless, immigrants, and petty criminals who became indebted to the turpentine manufacturing companies by virtue of their employment. Always earning less than the cost of their food and housing, which was provided by the company, turpentine workers were held in debt servitude.[1]

Turpentine profits were staggering; the industry grossed over twenty million dollars in 1902 according to a U.S. Census Report.[2] Florida was one of the largest producers, with an outlay of 2.3 million barrels of turpentine that year. Profits were high because wages were extremely low. Boys were paid ten cents a day, men fifteen or twenty cents. Workers amassed numerous advances from the company stores and were threatened with violence if they tried to escape the camps and their debt. Beatings, bloodhounds, manhunts, and lynching were commonly used to deter those fleeing the camps. Men on horseback, woodsriders, would run fleeing workers down and drag them, bruised and bloodied, back to camp. Debt peonage flourished in the deep South until the 1940s (though turpentine production and peonage did continue at a reduced rate until the 1970s) when the turpentine industry waned because synthetic products began replacing pine resin, and the paper mills became king in the South.

Black turpentine laborers were particularly adept at surviving life in the camps, developing a system of communicating between them and the quarter bosses and woodsriders that featured ironic, stubborn literalness and ingenious lying, as well as subversive foot-dragging on the job, helping them to assert some control over a crushingly oppressive work environment.[3] A number of turpentine workers also became gifted storytellers, inventing and passing on folktales that became a rich oral history replete with encoded lessons about resisting masters and about the critical relationship between the turpentiners and the natural or supernatural. Both the natural world around them and the supernatural world became sources of strength in their condition of servitude. Though technically "free," these indebted workers were no less slaves than their brothers and sisters in the cotton fields and plantations of the nineteenth century, and the turpentine camp owners no less masters than the southern plantation owners.

In brief, turpentine workers used two kinds of rhetoric available to those on the margins: subversive conversation (marked by subtleties unavailable to the whites they engaged) and folktales (marked by a glorification of the physical and mental prowess of the worker heroes featured and noting their strong connection to the natural world, and dependence on the supernatural world it represented). These workers were outsiders, unempowered, lacking traditional institutional identities and political clout, yet their rhetoric had power. They participated through clever manipulation of those who would exclude them, and through an inner strength, a spirituality nurtured by the world around them.

The turpentine industry and debt peonage, which enabled the industry's profitability and oppressed thousands of poor blacks for nearly three-quarters of a century beyond the Emancipation Proclamation, has always been a muted element of popular American history. Though not entirely silenced (the Georgia Agrirama Museum and the Tallahassee Junior Museum in Florida feature re-creations of turpentine stills, a commissary, and other turpentine quarters' buildings, and display various turpentining tools), turpentining has been infrequently the subject of critical and creative work, very probably because it is now defunct in America, as well as a black mark on the economic and political power structures that benefited by it. The less said about a period of oppression the better, particularly when the existing naval stores industry has been mechanized and relocated to China and South America, and is now a dramatically more cost-effective industry.[4] But nonagenarian American turpentine workers and their progeny still live in the small towns of southern Georgia, "Wiregrass Country," and in the Florida Panhandle from Escambia County to Port St. Joe to Appalachicola, where the pines flourished. Jake Hurd, who was a turpentine worker in the forests around Wewahitcka, Florida, from roughly 1910 until 1940, leaves behind his grandson, James E. Hurd, Jr. (the coauthor of this work). Originally, our sole intention and the inspiration for this research was to write a dramatic play about Jake Hurd's life and times, a story well-known in the Hurd family, and the community of "Wewa," but little known elsewhere. In order to learn as much about "Turpentine Jake" as we could, we decided to go down to Florida and Georgia and talk to as many surviving turpentine workers and their families as we could find, beginning with people who knew or had heard of Jake. It was ethnographic research, primarily the collecting of retrospective personal narrative, in the service of dramatic art. Not unlike the travels of Zora Neale Hurston and Stetson Kennedy, who began the Florida folklife project, funded by the Works Progress Administration, we hoped to collect stories, songs, and folktales to uncover the (still) hidden history of the pine workers and the lower-class blacks of the rural south. But what we found in Florida and Georgia was not merely a collection of memories and details of life in the camps, though those were fascinating. We also found evidence of a powerful rhetoric of resistance, a well-established tradition of storytelling, folktales, and fables that both educated rural blacks and gave them the strength and tools to resist the bosses and the turpentine culture that "enslaved" them under debt peonage.

Methodology

The ethnographic research we collected took the form of a series of formal and informal interviews of residents of Appalachicola, Port St. Joe, Wewahitchka, Tallahassee, Panama City (Florida), and Tifton (Georgia). Interviewees were both black and white, and had personally participated in the turpentine industry, either as a worker, camp follower, woodsrider or camp boss, pine forest lessor or lessee, or lived in one of the neighboring towns or ports where turpentine was distilled, barreled, and/or shipped. Descendents and family members of many of the above were also interviewed. Some interviews took place over lunch or coffee, and were "recorded" only with the handwritten notes. Some were digitally recorded on a front porch, with natural light provided by the hot Florida Indian summer sun, others in the back of a church after services, or on the steps of a reconstructed turpentine commissary, in the conference room of the Wewahitchka Public Library, with pictures of turpentiners at work on the walls, or in a museum tea shop with a view of a turpentine still. We collected stories, memories, descriptions of life in and out of the camps. Collecting these retrospective accounts seemed an ideal marriage of methodology and the discourse we were examining, turpentine rhetoric, because the discourse became what it was through telling and retelling, through using and re-using. It was an oral tradition practiced and observed by users new and experienced, honed and altered as time passed and the rhetorical context of the piney woods under debt peonage evolved.

Our primary research is both enthnographic, drawing on taped interviews of surviving turpentine workers and their relatives, and autobiographical, drawing on coauthor James E. Hurd, Jr.'s personal memories of his grandfather Jake and the stories he told James as he grew up on Jake's farm in Wewahitchka, Florida, in the 1960s and 70s. We did the interviews in the fall of 2004 during a two-week road trip from Atlanta throughout the Florida Panhandle, and in the spring of 2005 during a three-week crossing of central and northern Florida (including Eatonville, Hurston's hometown), and back again east through the Panhandle to Pensacola. We also draw on the Florida Folk Life Project, which recorded the stories and songs of blacks during the Depression. Part of the Works Progress Administration created during Franklin Roosevelt's New Deal, the Folklife Project[5] was headed by Stetson Kennedy and Zora Neale Hurston, who traveled throughout Florida from 1937 to 1942 collecting stories and local folklore from the sawmills, turpentine camps, citrus groves, and fishing boats.

As Tiffany Ruby Patterson observes in her compelling book, *Zora Neale Huston and A History of Southern Life*, Hurston's brand of research results in an expanded personal history, a history of private life and folk knowledge with all its "beauty and tragedy, its tensions, its contradictions, and its ethos of resistance."[6] In Hurston's folk art collecting, "location was a historical agent and producer of culture. In the south black culture emanated from the workers—debt peons, sharecroppers, and small-town dwellers. Hurston resituated the folk in the south, recognizing that their language, songs, folklore, etc., gave these people specific regional characteristics. At the same time she illuminated the heterogeneity of black people. In works like *Mules and Men*, Hurston depicted southern folk life as a cultural reference point for the construction of black interior life."[7] We too found a certain heterogeneity among black people in the South, a common respect for the power of language and an unmistakable attraction for stories, stories that illustrated that black people "knew things that gave them power," as Hurston herself believed (unpublished short story "Black Death").[8] In her book, Patterson speaks of "past presents," and argues for combining the traditional historical methodology with Hurston's ethnography and imaginative work to study black culture.

This is a fitting description of our secondary research methodology as well. Our ethnography resulted in an imaginative work, *Turpentine Jake*, and we drew on both the historical record and Hurston's own "auto-ethnography" (or collection of autobiographical <u>and</u> ethnographical writings) to help construct the world of the play. Auto-ethnography, a term coined by Francoise Lionnet in *Autobiographical Voice: Race, Gender, Self-Portraiture* and refined in an essay about Michelle Cliff's *Abeng*,[9] is a fitting description of Hurston's "I" interwoven with the culture of the "we" of the rural southern black in her fictional and non-fictional texts and recordings. Mark Marino, in an unpublished manuscript, "Multimedia Hurston," suggests that Hurston's "multimedia self-portraits" are also truly anthropological. He says Hurston defines herself with regard to a community, and also defines the community, revising cultural stereotypes and revealing the "autobiographical mythologies of empowerment" that revise recorded history, which all but ignores the power of the rural southern black, a power vested in him primarily linguistically.

Patterson goes on to explain why the sometimes written and usually oral record that constructs the "past present" is legitimate history. By past present, Patterson means the "spoken and written documents that embodied for their producers a real present, but that necessarily belongs to our own real past . . . our past is the present of Hurston's subjects,"[10] and Bannister and Hurd's, we argue. "It is the world that they can take for granted in a way we cannot. The producers of these documents and stories lived in a past in which certain events had not yet occurred. We return to our past from a present in which those events have occurred and we take our knowledge of those events with us and seek a past that makes sense of our present."[11] Patterson cautions that we neither romanticize our past nor exaggerate its horrors. We cannot take the past for granted: it is both foreign and deeply familiar. Certainly we experienced this foreignness and deep familiarity in the interviews we conducted. It was particularly apparent because one of the researchers, James Hurd, was also a Floridian, well taught in the tradition of storytelling, and very familiar with the rhetorical strategies so ably used by his ancestors who were turpentiners. Many linguists and language philosophers have argued that proficiency in language use is inextricably bound up with the emerging self.[12] We think it is also reasonable to assume that language use is also bound up with the emerging portrait of a culture, however distant its "past present."

Ordinary language philosopher and American Book Award winner Keith Gilyard says an "autobiographical account, despite its subjectivity, provides an important record of events the author has responded to—in short, what has shaped him or her as a social being. In a quest for such significance, the chronological facts of an individual's existence are not nearly as important as the psychological facts of forging a life."[13] When we collected our data, these autobiographical retrospective accounts, these personal narratives looking back on the past, we had no particular interest in validating its legitimacy for a scholarly audience, but only in writing a historically accurate play; we are relieved that so many respected researchers have validated our approach. We certainly did not collect a perfectly accurate chronological record of events from the people we interviewed; they were often elderly and had no written documents (diaries, letters, etc.) to support their memories of what occurred. Still, they were quite certain of the psychological facts of the lives they had forged.

The Turpentine Camp and Its Inhabitants

Before we further describe the rhetoric of the turpentiners, it is important to get a sense of time and place, to walk a bit in the pine forests and turpentine quarters of the twenties, thirties, and forties. Turpentine camps varied in size depending on the number of crops of timber worked, but each camp consisted of a turpentine still that was used to process the rosin, a copper shed where barrels were made, and a barn and lot for the work animals. The center of the camp was the commissary where workers purchased food, clothing, tools, and expendables.

The living quarters for the camps were divided into two sections, with shanties for the workers and houses for the bosses. Shanties ranged from one to three rooms depending on family size. The exterior walls of the shanties were made of slab waste materials left over from sawmills. The roofs were made of corrugated tin, and the interior had no ceilings. Windows were covered by solid wood slats with hinges, no glass. Newspapers were pasted on the interior walls with flour paste to fill cracks and cover holes. Fireplaces and chimneys were used for both heating and cooking before the wood stove became common. Almost all shanties had open porches. Shanties were positioned in rows, usually on either side of the road that ran through the camp. A pitcher pump was placed nearby so several families could have access to water. Eight or nine shanties were typical in a small camp; twenty-four in a large camp. Separated from these turpentine shanties were better constructed houses where the boss and his supervisory personnel, the woodsrider, the commissary boss, and the stiller, lived. These dwellings were larger, made of pinewood, and supported by lightwood log blocks. The structures were better sealed and had glass windows. Sometimes they were better constructed with two chimneys, one for cooking food and one for heating. Some turpentine camps had a shanty that was used as a school and church. When available, ministers and teachers traveled from camp to camp performing their duties. Each camp had two cemeteries, one for blacks, one for whites. If a camp boss leased convicts, a barracks with a stockade was used to house them. The convicts were chained at night and armed guards were placed around the perimeter of this area.

The process of harvesting gum or rosin from the longleaf pine was difficult and dangerous work. The workers were exposed to the blistering heat and humidity of the summer and the cold, even icy, conditions of winter. Heatstroke and frostbite were common ailments. Workers were always on the lookout for poisonous snakes, spiders, scorpions, and hornets. Other indigenous animals included bears, panthers, wild hogs, and alligators, who were happy to include the occasional lone worker in their diet. Snakes, spiders, scorpions, and small rodents regularly invaded turpentiner shanties.

A turpentine worker's day would begin at four a.m. in order to be in the woods by sunup. Workers would first assemble at the commissary to buy tobacco, snuff, and lunch items. Mules and oxen were fed and hitched up to wagons and carts for the trip into the woods, which lengthened as more pines were harvested. Three to eight miles' walk was typical. Workers would walk to and from their work locations; a lucky few would ride in the wagon. The wagons often moved more slowly than the workers on foot, making the ride an opportunity to shorten the day's work. One-gallon syrup buckets were used to carry lunch, usually a "streak" of white-side, cornbread, cane syrup, beans or peas, rice, and syrup-sweetened water, "sweet water." Lunch buckets were hung in the trees in the "hang-in ground" to prevent them from being scavenged by bears.

The turpentine harvesting process was laborious, backbreaking work. Cup and tin hangers would use mauls and box axes to cut one-half-inch-deep incisions into the tree trunk so tins could be inserted. Using a tool called a hogal, the rough bark was removed from the tree and the first "streak" was formed. The tins would later funnel the flow of rosin into a clay cup, which was attached to the tree beneath the tins. Depending on the size of the crew, ranging from three to six men, 2,000 to 5,000 cups were expected to be hung in a day. In a week, a crew was expected to prepare and harvest two or more crops of trees; a crop was 10,500 pines.[14] Chippers would cut a streak on each tree, enabling the tree's rosin to flow down the face into the cup. A good chipper could work a crop (10,500 pines) in a week. He was paid $1.00 to $1.25 per day. The dip squad performed the next step in the turpentining process, removing the rosin that was collected in the tin or clay cups with dip paddles, then placing the rosin into a dip bucket, which was filled and then taken to a wagon and emptied into a fifty-gallon barrel. It would take about 275 to 300 cups filled with rosin to fill one barrel. A good dipper would fill five barrels a day and earn $0.40 to $0.60 a barrel.[15] After the barrels were filled with rosin, the wagoner would take them to the still to be distilled. The stiller who performed this work was often white because it was believed blacks couldn't handle the task since decisions about timing and appropriate mixtures had to be made. The turpentine distilled from the rosin earned a profit of approximately $50–60 per barrel for the turpentine boss. He would pay the workers who produced that barrel roughly $2.00.[16]

In order to insure the work was done, pines harvested, barrels produced, woodsriders patrolled the forest on horseback, packing rifles and whips. The penalty for shirking was beating. If a worker tried to escape, he was run down and dragged back to camp. Repeat offenders were usually hung or shot. Turpentine workers were prisoners of their debt. Arguably, they could come and go freely between the camp and the forest, as long as they produced the required number of barrels of turpentine, a crushing burden. Workers rarely earned enough to pay off their obligation to the company store and the turpentine boss. Thousands began and ended their lives in debt bondage.

Not an entirely cheerless existence, the turpentining life also included jook joints and skin games, music and dancing, card games and stories, and shanty lyrics that are the forerunners of the spoken word street poetry of 2007. It is a testament to the heartiness and indefatigable spirit of the turpentiners that many of them survived life in the camps, some turpentining twenty or more years, some ultimately able to buy and work their own land and build homes.

It is also important to reiterate that turpentine camp owners were invested in keeping their workers together, moving them along with their few possessions from location to location, isolating them from other communities in the area. Turpentine camp workers formed their own communities owning the clothes on their backs, but little else, and relying primarily on each other for social interaction. There were some camp workers who lived in nearby towns and walked to the crop of pines they were harvesting, but the most common configuration was a movable camp of workers, who "owed their soul(s) to the company store." Turpentine camps were an ideal way to maintain control over scarce labor.[17]

Hurston's Auto-ethnography and Ours

Hurston talks about collecting folktales in *Of Mules and Men*,[18] saying of the folk, "They are most reluctant at times to reveal that which the soul lives by . . . [they] smile and tell him or her something that satisfies the white person because, knowing so little about us, he doesn't know what he is missing. The Negro offers a feather bed resistance. That is, we let the probe enter, but it never comes out. It gets smothered under laughter and pleasantries." She goes on, "The white man is always trying to know into somebody else's business. All right, I'll set something outside the door of my mind for him to play with and handle. He can read my writing, but he sho' can't read my mind. I'll put this play toy in his hand, and he will seize it and go away. Then I'll say my say and sing my song."[19] As Hurston implies, the song the white man never gets to hear is a hidden transcript of everyday resistance, the song sung on the job, in the quarters, and in the jook, the places where ordinary people felt free to articulate their opposition, the resistance embedded in the stories and "idle" talk of the workers. When we went down to Wewahitchka, Port St. Joe, Panama City, and Tallahassee to collect their stories, in a very real sense we went facing the same "hindrance among strangers" that Hurston, essentially an outsider, faced. Even though Hurston (and Hurd) grew up in Florida, they were educated, seeking possibly controversial information, and accompanied by white researchers. Hurston's work was neither exclusively ethnography, nor was it merely autobiographical. It was richly and fortunately both.

In a terrific article published in *African American Review*, David Nicholls suggests that Hurston's *Mules and Men* and its departure from traditional folkloric form should be reframed as a discourse of dissent, even though its subversion is submerged, subtextual, and marginal.[20] He calls the role of Hurston's "narrative frame" in *Of Mules and Men*, a folklore of resistance, particularly the Polk County section, which chronicles the daily lives of the workers in a logging camp. Hurston ultimately wrote a play called *Polk County*,[21] adding a "fictional" work to the "non-fiction" canon she was accumulating. Of course, fictional elements abound in her non-fiction and vice versa. Our research path provides an interesting parallel, since the stories we collected to help us write *Turpentine Jake* were both autobiography (Jake Hurd's as he told it to James Hurd) and ethnography (the recollections of the almost hundred-year-old workers we interviewed). *Turpentine Jake* features the lives and stories (both real and imagined) of turpentine workers who worked in and around Wewahitchka in 1937, and must also be classified as a work of fiction and nonfiction.

To get the real stories that would become *Turpentine Jake*, we interviewed Mr. Buck Clayton, a ninety-six-year-old retired turpentine worker, who remembered wearing rubber tires for boots, and who had to bust ice in the swamp to get the buckets of resin out. Mr. Buck lived in Port St. Joe, with his daughter, Marie Clayton Jackson, who grew up in a turpentine camp and remembered a woodsrider, James Ashberry, who beat a friend, Reverend Langston, until his mouth was permanently twisted (Mr. Buck died in early 2007). Marie also remembers her own mother breast-feeding the white camp owner's child. We interviewed Mrs. Cora Keith, a ninety-three-year-old Wewahitchkan, married at thirteen to a turpentiner. Mrs. Cora remembered carrying a wagon spoke as thick as her wrist to keep the white children from plaguing her as she walked from her home in town to camp, carrying her husband's and her father's lunch. And she spoke of the time her brother was almost lynched because a distracted white woman walked into the side of his parked car and said he tried to run her down (Mrs. Cora died in the spring 2006). We interviewed ninety-two--year old Lorraine Norton, a widow woman whose father owned a series of camps in Florida and South Carolina and who remembers their best "Cooper" or barrel maker, Oscar, who could make a two-hundred-pound barrel in twenty minutes, and played a tune on the hoops with his hammer as he drove them down around the barrel slats. Lorraine remembers her father's wagons carrying the great barrels to Crawkinds Landing, where their "coloreds" loaded the paddlewheelers bound for Pensacola.

We interviewed Charles Arthur Gaskin, who remembers Thanksgiving as a seven-year-old in the camps, with a long table of pine planks where fifty people ate. Charles Arthur remembers his stern, arrogant grandfather Charles who ran a turpentine settlement of twenty families, and owned the last turpentine still in Florida. Charles Gaskin was "rough on the labor, who had a tendency to walk off and leave." He was one of a handful of camp owners indicted and fined in 1942 for "unlawfully arresting James Johnson, a Negro, for the purpose of holding him in involuntary servitude to work off an alleged debt of 22 dollars."

We interviewed Mr. Taylor Jenkins, who told us about his brother-in-law, who was shot in the heart during a skin game, the raucous Saturday night card game that claimed many a turpentiner's meager wages, once the company store had been paid. We interviewed Ms. Vera Shamplain, retired schoolteacher and National Association for the Advancement of Colored People organizer in Panama City, whose father Cy was Jake Hurd's best friend. She told us Jake and Cy were real men, tall, over six feet tall, with straight backs, and everybody respected them, black and white.

We interviewed James "Pappy Joe" Smith, who was a runaway raised by Jake Hurd. Pappy Joe told us about working a ten-hour day and then walking home in a cloud of mosquitoes. He got the fever one time and they put him in a hammock so the breeze would cool him. Pappy Joe said he saw snakes crawling under his hammock to get the coolness under the shanty, escaping the heat of the sun. At night, wild hogs could be heard rooting under the house, eating snakes, snapping their teeth and popping their jaws. As soon as his fever broke, Pappy Joe went back to work.

All of these people we interviewed had vivid memories of the life in turpentine camps, but James's grandfather Jake Hurd and his best friend Cy McClindon were particularly charismatic because they had the gift of storytelling, of making a point with a tale, sometimes a tall one, often humorous, but always with a message, if the listener was sharp enough to grasp it. Oftentimes these stories were overheard by whites, or even told to them directly, but the more subversive shades of meaning were not typically available to them. Certainly some whites, particularly those with long experience in the camps or those who had befriended blacks, understood more. (The real Jake Hurd was well-known in white Wewahitchka, for example, and in *Turpentine Jake*, we put the character based on him into a mentoring relationship with a white camp boss's son, Charlie.) Turpentine workers were hungry for tales well told, partly because they were entertaining, but also because they celebrated and revealed the turpentiner's hidden history, a history of subversion, beneath the veil of their consent, a powerful dissident culture whose weaponry was wordplay, a rhetoric of resistance. Jake Hurd told James Hurd many stories during his boyhood on Jake's farm in Wewahitchka, Florida. We adapted several of them for *Turpentine Jake* and reprint two of them here. They are, of course, a representation or refashioning of the stories James remembers, because no text exists except the text of his memory of his Grandfather Jake telling the stories in a gravelly deep voice, talking of possums and wildcats. The excerpted monologue where the following story is told occurs in act 1, scene 2 of *Turpentine Jake*.

Turpentine Jake: Act 1, Scene 2

Jake. There wuz this boy, lived down the lane, 'round the mudhole, south side of Wewahitchka. His mama had just given him a little sistuh, and one morning she was nursing the baby when the boy comes in from his chores and he sees the baby at the teat. Mama, where'd you get the baby from? Why son, the angels brings the babies and hides 'em in a hollow log. And if you is lucky, like we is, you find 'em and bring 'em home and raise 'em up, just like I did you, and your little sistuh here. Oh mama, says the little boy, I want my own baby to raise up. Well then, you better start lookin', right after you finish breakfast! Yes, mama, and soon as he finishes his grits, he hightails it down to Pappy Bell Branch, the swampy part, looking for hollow logs. Sho' 'nough, 'bout the third one he spies has a curled-up, little white bundle in it, just about baby-size. So he crawls in and grabs it up, fast against his chest just like mama did little sis. Well, that bundle was a possum and it wakes up lickety-split, wraps its tail round the boy's arm, sinks its teeths into that boy's bosom and holds on for dear life. With a yelp and a holler, that boy tears off for home. Momma, Momma he calls out, hep me, hep me. Momma flies out on the porch, what's wrong, son? I got me a baby, found him in a hollow log, but Momma, how do's you wean him?

The possum story always got a big laugh, James remembers, especially when Jake got to the line: "how do's you wean him?" On the surface, the story covers familiar territory, the childish desire to have a baby of one's own, and the unlucky choice of a toothsome possum. But the tag for the story offers the life metaphor. We rejoin the scene with Cy McClindon responding to Jake.

> *Cy. (Laughs.)* That's a good one, Jake, but what's that got to do with Mr. Peavy and tepentime?
>
> *Jake.* Sometimes a varmit gets holt of you and won't let go, and won't be weaned. Then you got to be a man and pull that varmint off of you no matter how much it hurts you, or **him.** You got to, or he'll suck you dry.

It wasn't much of a stretch to name the varmit for what it was—turpentining. Stories like these, that counsel using whatever means necessary to "pull that varmit off of you," were the life blood of the workers. Through them they learned resistance was not futile, that hope lived as long as hearts continued to beat, and ears continued to hear. Stories like these helped turpentiners understand what to do if a white man "got holt" of you; ultimately the possum had to be ripped from the boy's breast, though it might be unbearably painful and might scar him physically and mentally. What seemed good and innocent (a paying job as a turpentiner, a baby) might in fact be dangerous (debt peonage, a possum). It was no wonder so many blacks hungry for jobs optimistically responded to turpentine camp ads: "Wanted: 20 Negro Men, who will chip or pull twenty crops of Turpentine Boxes, or Cups, as they are where they are. Families preferred."[22] They had no idea how hard the road ahead would be and how difficult it would be to leave the piney woods.

The turpentine industry flourished on the backs of the turpentine workers; they **were** the industry, yet they were the outsiders, well outside the conventional power structure, at the mercy of the bosses, subject to the whims of the woodsriders who would whip a worker out of boredom as much as some imagined laziness. Together the workers practiced a cooperative, outsider rhetoric, where storytellers practiced their craft as admired entertainers and sages. Always welcome, these rhetoricians of the piney woods strengthened their fellow laborers' will to survive and resist. In another of Jake's monologues he tells the story of **his** grandfather's encounter with a wildcat, establishing one of the models for resistance that was passed from generation to generation. We rejoin the play still in act 1, scene 2, with Jake addressing Charlie, a camp boss's son.

> *Jake.* Lemme tell you a story, Charlie. My Granpaw was a woodsman up in Alabama. Kilt him a wildcat one day, big cat. Shot 'im right between the eyes. When Granpaw swung that cat up on his shoulder to carry him out for dressin', that cat's head hit him in the heels ev'ry step he took. Now Granpaw was well over six foot, so dat cat was eight or nine foot long, whiskers to tail. Now Granpaw's walkin' back to camp, and he hears growlin'. Is dat you, big cat, he says? Now he knows the cat's dead, but he drops that cat quick, and cuts his throat! When you're dealing with somethin' been known to scratch, and scratch deep, you do what you got to do. Follow me, Charlie?
>
> *Charlie.* Yessuh, I believe I do. But some folks don't mean no harm.
>
> *Jake.* One wildcat looks pretty much like another son.

The wildcat story conveys an essential truth. Wildcats (and white men) can't ever be trusted. Though the story appears to advise violence, it was clear to the audience of turpentiners that Jake's message was one of caution. You didn't take your eye off a woodsrider, but you also didn't let him know you were watching. Turpentine lore includes always facing a door in a skin game, and never taking your eye off the commissary boss when you were filling your lunch bucket or collecting your wages. Overcharging and underpaying turpentiners was common practice. Every turpentiner was well aware that the whites "had been known to scratch and scratch deep." Even in death, turpentiners learned to be wary of a wildcat, and when that wildcat's dangerous side was revealed, to end the encounter quickly. Turpentiner stories were a major component of the resistance rhetoric of oppressed blacks after legalized slavery had ended. This was a critically vital rhetoric because it functioned in an environment where there was an appearance of fair labor practice, but in reality was only a small step removed from slavery. Historian Pete Daniel calls debt peonage the "shadow of slavery,"[23] and certainly the turpentine laborers struggled to survive in its dim light. Some camps had brutal reputations where hopelessness was common, and drunkenness and killings were standard Saturday-night behavior. The function of their rhetoric was multifold: to provide turpentine laborers a source of strength in oppressive circumstances; to uplift worker spirit and build their self-esteem; to raise workers' consciousness about turpentine camp unfair labor practices; to critique and quietly protest camp owner/white **beliefs about** and **practice toward** blacks; and to strengthen the workers' connection to the natural and the supernatural, both of which were sources of comfort and spiritual growth. Turpentining, or harvesting pines for resin, was often practiced carelessly by camp owners who were eager for a maximum profit at the expense of the environment. Entire forests were decimated[24] during the boom years of turpentining (roughly 1880–1940); many longleaf pine trees could have been saved or harvested for longer periods of time by implementing more conservative and careful harvesting techniques. Our research revealed that black turpentine workers often had a respect for the trees and nature in general not shared by the profit-driven camp owners. The relationship with nature was reflected in their stories and songs, and was part of their rhetoric of resistance. It was perhaps the ultimate subversion to be a friend of the trees, when the workers' job was to expeditiously suck the life from them. The foot-dragging black laborers were famous for, was motivated, we believe, by more than just self-preservation.

More Turpentiner Rhetoric

Rhetorical tactics effectively used by turpentiners included: ironic or stubborn literalness, ingenious lying, and subversive subterfuge. Sometimes oversimplified (and punished) as mere insolence, these strategies were often utilized when workers were directly discussing or alluding to the meanness or stupidity of the bosses, the inherent unfairness of the debt peonage system, and the body- and soul-depleting nature of the work itself—"tepentiming." As William Wiethoff argues in *The Insolent Slave,* in a relationship of unbalanced power or status, people discursively gain the upper hand over other people by treating them insolently.[25] Insolence is, we believe, a simplified, "White" characterization of a complex black linguistic behavior. To illustrate this complex rhetorical strategy we include another section of act 1, scene 2, from *Turpentine Jake,* based on stories we were told by Mr. Buck Clayton and Pappy Joe:

> *The woods, the next morning.* JAKE, CY, BUCK, *and* JOE *are "chipping out boxes" (scoring pine trees so they'll ooze resin).* JAKE *and* CY *are wielding chippers (a long-handled turpentining tool).* BUCK *is placing a tin pan on a tree, and* JOE *is clearing brush. In an angry flurry, the* WOODSRIDER *enters stage right. He cracks his whip loudly behind the men.*

Woodsrider. (Yelling.) Ha! Feel the black snake bite!
Joe. (Gasps): Woodsrider!
Woodsrider. You lazy Black sons of bitches are costing me. I never seed sucha gator-faced, gut-footed, liver-lipped buncha niggers in my life.
Buck. (Nervously.) Ye-ye-ye Yessuh.
Jake. Nossuh. Nossuh. We is right on schedule. Cy is on his second drift and so is I. These boys is re-setting pans and clearing brush. They learnin' real good. We all gonna finish a full crop by Friday, right on schedule.
Woodsrider. You talkin' a lot big boy. I jes rode the yearling faces behind you and found more'n hundred palmetto leaves. You know that's the sign for chippin' needed. You need to back up and finish those trees ain't been touched this week. The Black snake gonna bite you sure as I'm standin' here (cracks his whip again).
Jake. Suh, is you callin' me big boy? Elephant is bigger than me and they call him elephant. You know my name.
(WOODSRIDER *bristles and makes a move towards* JAKE.)
Woodsrider. You must wanna see your Jesus.
Cy. Woodsrider, don't jump salty, we gonna check it out. Don' know how we missed 'em. Sun gets in your eyes sometimes, or dem love bugs fly up in your face. Now doze is some nasty critters. Why one time . . .
Woodsrider. Shuddup, you no-account gum-beater. I ain't got time for your yarns. There's a runaway nigger loose in these woods. He ran off of Mr. Blunt's camp and Mr. Peavy is helping with the search. Now you keep your eyes open and don't even think about hidin' 'im. Hide a nigger and I'll stripe your back bloody. You'll run red, boy. Fill-up a dip bucket with your nigger juice. Then you'll see the bugs come.
Buck. Ye-ye-yessuh.
(WOODSRIDER *exits, stage left, crackin' his whip one last time.*)
Jake. Umm, umm, umm. They call us puller, chipper, cooper, woods nigger, tepentimer, poet of the swingin' blade. It's a dance you know, dance of arm and axe and tree, chipper lifted overhead, arcing high and strong and plummeting down, biting into living bark stopping just shy of the heart of the tree, not to kill her, but to open her to your blade and bucket, so she'll drip her precious rosin into your empty cup, treasure of the longleaf pine. A dance it is. Stiff at first, she fears to yield, and then as though she sways to meet your arm and blade, and dips her knees to receive the blow, all in beauty. All day, muscled arm and sturdy axe, sweat and bite, chipping to feed the hunger of the quarter bosses, the hunger of White that would swallow Black. Almighty dollar trumps almighty soul. But Black is strong. Strong arm, strong axe, and the trees bend to us . . . to us, tepentimpers, poets of the swingin' blade.
(*All four men on stage swing an imaginary axe and puller as they sing the following lines to each other.*)
(*Jake singing.*) Oh, Alabam . . . (*All four men singing.*) Huh, Skee
(*Jake singing.*) Oh, Mississip . . . (*All four men singing.*) Huh, Skee

(*Jake singing.*) Oh, Wewa . . . (*All four men singing.*) Huh, Skee
(*Jake singing.*) Oh, in Florida . . . (*All four men singing.*) Huh, Skee
(*All singing.*) Let's chip it
(*All singing.*) Let's pull it
(*All singing.*) Let's dip it
(*All singing.*) Let's roll it . . . Huh, Skee.
(*Jake singing.*) Axe and arm
(*All singing.*) Ox and barrel
(*Jake singing.*) Axe and arm
(*All singing.*) Ox and barrel . . . Huh, Skee.
Cy. Tell it, Jake! (*Laughs.*) Black snake bit me one time . . .
Jake. (*Knowingly.*) What'd you do?
Cy. I snatched 'im up.
Jake. Yeah, and then?
Cy. I popped him 'gainst a stump . . .
Jake. (*Popping his fingers.*) Pop!
Cy. Tore his head clean off! (*Pauses.*) "Bruise the head of the serpent" . . . (*Turning to the boys.*)
Jake. (*Turning to the boys.*) "Or he will bruise your heel." That runaway better be makin' tracks. Woodsrider's got a fire in his eyes. Them Bluntstown boys is gone nigger huntin' and they ain't gonna stop.
Ossie. But Mr. Jake, they can't keep somebody who want's to go if'n he's paid his debt . . .
Jake. A nigger's debt's never paid, son. It's gonna be a turkey shoot. Better make sure your hardware is greased and ready, Cy.
Cy. (*Patting his pocket.*) Yep. Sho 'nuff. Ain't no way out of tepentiming. My daddy used to say, "Onliest way out is to die out."
Jake. Carry you out on a coolin' board, whipped to the red. And, 'dis new cracker woodsrider tryin' to come in sideways on old Upshire Fowler's job. Upshire 'bout the only colored woodsrider I ever seed.
Cy. Upshire's standup.
Ossie. White or Black don't matter. Woodsrider's a woodsrider. My cousin tolt me the law came after their woodsrider up in Tifton. He was roughfin' up the niggers in camp ev'ry week. Those boys couldn't get rid of a bruise before that woodsrider'd flog 'em again. And I heard they arrested him for it.
Buck. Thhaaat's Georgia. This here's Ffffflorida.
Joe. That's right, no law down here in Wewa.
Jake. Ain't that right! Let's go boys, we got's to go palmetto pickin'.
Joe. You mean chippin', right, Mr. Jake?
Cy. No, we gonna save you the trouble, son. See, doze trees is already chipped. We just put the palmetto leaves on 'em to flag the woodsrider. Then we get a nice stroll in the woods and a little rest. Can't work a man hour after hour with no rest. You be dead soon dat way.
Jake. This way, we gets to live a little. Like Cy here, and me, we been tepentiming summer and winter nearly 25 years. Ain't many workers ken say dat.

Cy. (sings) Tepentime's a hard line.
Jake. (*Sings.*) We workin' all the time.

Utilizing rhetorical strategies of "insolence" and subterfuge prevent the Woodsrider's "black snake" (whip) from biting, Jake asks the Woodsrider if he's calling him "big boy" immediately after the Woodsrider does it. Reminiscent of Robert Deniro's repeated "Are you talkin' to me?" speech in *Taxi Driver*, minus its threatening tone, Jake's question is insolent but also coolly matter-of-fact. The diversion Cy offers (Florida sun and love bugs) is a finely tuned rhetorical tactic of the turpentiner often referred to as the "big windy," or meandering story full of unnecessary details and lots of tangents. The Woodsrider is disgusted and his potentially violent attention is diverted away from Jake, who's already scored his point.

Jake's monologue ("They call us puller . . .") is an example of the celebratory rhetoric that sustained the world-weary turpentiner. It applauds the skill of the worker, his physical and mental prowess, and also glorifies and personifies the pines and his relationship with them by likening them to a woman he woos. The monologue also implies the intimate, even spiritual relationship that exists between the turpentiner and the trees. The natural and supernatural were accessible to rural blacks in ways material goods and comforts rarely were. It was easy to look up to the sky and the pines. In the white man's world almighty dollar might trump almighty soul; in the pine forest, black was strong.

The scene ends with Cy and Jake engaging in subversive conversation, figuratively destroying the black snake (his whip) and the Woodsrider, popping him against a stump as they would an intruding camp snake. Even though the turpentiner is "bitten," he survives and triumphs. The rhetorical exchange ends with a classic turpentiner's subterfuge. The workers have falsely marked the pines with palmetto leaves, the sign for "chippin' needed." This enables the workers to merely remove the leaves as they pass and take a stroll through the pines. The Woodsrider will believe they've newly chipped the trees, following his orders, when in truth they've engineered a brief respite from their labors.

The turpentiner rhetoric gathered from the interviews and oral accounts, and then fashioned into representative stories and exchanges in *Turpentine Jake*, is both social critique and personal shield, aiding the turpentiner in surviving life in the camps. But turpentiner rhetoric does have some drawbacks. When whites were attentive enough, or smart enough, to decipher the encoded lessons in the discourse, they likely were quite angry at the hidden but intended effrontery, but more importantly they would have objected to the differing world views and values of the black laborers embedded in their stories, songs, and everyday conversation. The black turpentiner relationship with the natural and supernatural was anathema to the white camp owner.

We have no evidence of a black laborer being killed for telling a story, or "lipping off" to a quarter boss, but there is ample recollection of being silenced ("Shut up, you no-account gum-beater. I ain't got time for your yarns," *Turpentine Jake*, act 1, scene 2) and beaten. It was often an uneasy life in the camps; arguably, these workers lived with constant uncertainty. Their subversive rhetoric risked discovery at any time and might generate violence. Certainly, suspicion thrived in the camps; workers were routinely suspected of cheating the system. Of slacking, an interesting paradox given the inherent unfairness and exploitative nature of debt peonage. Interestingly, whites feared long-time black turpentine laborers more than the laborers feared the whites. The black turpentiner rhetoric was an active accommodation. They had learned to live with turpentining and with the whites in ways the whites never would learn to live with them. Perhaps the oppressor's guilt is too powerful and too present to be utterly ignored. And not surprisingly, white and black townspeople who lived closest to the camps looked "in concern and even horror" at what was happening in the pine forest in the wake of the itinerant camp owner and his "gang of blacks."[26] When a turpentine camp moved on, it left behind not only dead and dying trees, but some of the souls of the blacks who labored there.

Analytic Categories of Turpentiner Rhetoric

Patterns observed in all of our above analyses allowed us to develop some analytic categories that assist in the interpretation of turpentiner rhetoric. First, black turpentiners developed a system of communicating between them and the camp owners, quarter bosses, and woodsriders that was marked by subterfuge and subtleties usually unavailable to the whites they engaged. The features of this subversive discourse included:

1. Ironic, stubborn literalness (often called insolence by whites) ("Elephant is bigger than me and they call him elephant. You know my name.")
2. Ingenious lying/subversive foot-dragging ("Nossuh, we is right on schedule . . . we all gonna finish a full crop by Friday, right on schedule," followed by this comment to

a neophyte turpentiner: "Doze trees is already chipped. We just put the palmetto leaves on 'em to flag the woodsrider. Then we get a nice stroll in the woods. . . . Turpentine's a hard line, we workin' all the time."
3. Subversive metaphor (sometimes including biblical reference) ("Black snake bit me one time, so I popped him against a stump . . . bruise the head of the serpent, or he will bruise your heel.")
4. Agreement/mollification ("making nice") ("Yessuh!") As Hurston says, "the probe enters but never comes out . . . it get smothered under pleasantries and laughter."

In utilizing these four discourse features, the sender of the message (the black turpentiner) communicates directly with one receiver (the white camp owner, quarter boss, or woodsrider) and indirectly with another, the neophyte turpentiner observing the discourse. Whites are routinely compared to animals (possums, wildcats, black snakes, etc.) that are dangerous and capable of great injury. The Bible is sometimes invoked as analogy and verification of the danger. Whites are gently, directly confronted ("Suh, is you calling me big boy?") and then deflected or lied to ("Don't know how we missed 'em. Sun gets in your eyes sometimes, or dem love bugs fly up in your face"). Finally, whites are smiled at and agreed with (the horrific "I'll fill up a dip bucket with your nigger juice" is responded to with a simple nod and a "Yessuh"). Whether direct or indirect, the black turpentiner rhetoric present in everyday discourse in the piney woods was extremely effective. It allowed the turpentiners some small control over a crushingly oppressive work environment, and that small control was often lifesaving.

Secondly, black turpentiners were gifted storytellers and lyricists, inventing and passing on folktales with encoded lessons about resisting their "masters," the camp owners, quarter bosses, and woodsriders. These stories and songs were marked by a glorification of the physical and mental prowess of the worker heroes, and also by a nurturing and celebration of the critical relationship between black turpentiners and the natural and supernatural. The discourse features usually present in these stories and songs may be described thusly:

1. Black turpentiners were characterized as powerful woodland heroes
   ("Now he knows that cat's dead, but he drops that cat quick and cuts his throat." "Black is strong, strong arm, strong axe, and the trees bend to us.")
2. Whites were characterized as grasping, dangerous animals ("Sometimes a varmint gets holt of you and won't let go")

3. The trees and woodland environment were characterized as partnered with the black turpentiner, and as beautiful and spiritually enriching
("It's a dance you know, dance of arm and axe and tree . . . biting into living bark, stopping just shy of the heart of the tree, not to kill her, but to open her to your balde and bucket, so she'll drip her precious rosin into you empty cup . . . all in beauty.")

The black turpentiners and the trees were partnered, physically and spiritually, against the whites, the unthinking, unknowing oppressors who were ready to suck the life from both turpentiner and tree in pursuit of the almighty dollar·("Almighty dollar trumps almighty soul").

The scenes from *Turpentine Jake* we have included qualify as auto-ethnography as well as drama, based as they are on "true" stories and anecdotes we collected and fashioned into a fictional/nonfictional work. In order that the reader might sample the interviews that gave birth to *Turpentine Jake* and this analysis of turpentiner rhetoric, we also include transcripts of excerpts from our interviews of Mr. Buck Clayton and Mrs. Cora Keith, now deceased, who were residents of Port St. Joe and Wewahitchka, Florida, respectively (see appendix). Mr. Buck was a turpentine worker during the twenties through the fifties, working trees owned by H. C. Lister, one of the major turpentine bosses of the Florida Panhandle. Mrs. Cora Keith was the widow of a turpentiner, carrying his lunch into the pines many a hot summer day in Calhoun County, Wewahitchka, Florida.

Conclusion

The turpentine workers created a rhetoric that enabled them to survive and to retain their dignity, even though ready access to "the American dream" was denied them. *Turpentine Jake*, an auto-ethnograhic drama based on traditional historical research, the works of Zora Neale Hurston, and turpentiner memories and stories, tells the Florida turpentiners' stories and celebrates their rhetoric. We conducted over a dozen two to three-hour interviews in the fall of 2004 and the spring of 2005 and have, to date, completed exhaustive transcriptions on only two: Mr. Buck Clayton's interview and Mrs. Cora Keith's.

As you can guess, the transcription process is a laborious one because of a combination of the dialect features and the advanced age of the interviewees. Their words must be carefully reconstructed to insure as accurate as possible rendering of their lexicon and rhetorical strategies. The transcriptions reveal a treasure trove of personal memories and details of life in the turpentine camps, as well as some incredibly rich linguistic detail. Although we attempted to capture much of it in *Turpentine Jake*, a true appreciation is only gained by listening to and viewing the interviews. Mr. Buck's explanations of chipping a box and what a crop is ("7000 trees, some say 10,000") verify the traditional historical research we did, but also adds a face and a flavor to the "mere fact" that is unmistakable and invaluable. Mr. Buck was proud of what he was and what he did; he would never think of himself as a slave, though that is how he was often treated. Everything he said to us was delivered in a tone both quietly matter-of-fact and disarmingly strong. He frequently smiled and chuckled, even when a story had a dark element. And he sat talking to us, at ninety-six, in his own home, with his family around him, still able to tell a story, still able to laugh.

Mrs. Cora Keith's "baby-in-the-hollow-log" story (and similar stories Jake Hurd told his grandson James Hurd) was the inception of the "possum-who-wouldn't-be-weaned" tale in *Turpentine Jake*. Mrs. Cora's tale was one of a thirteen-year-old girl, newly married, unwittingly pregnant, injuring herself until bleeding while roughhousing with other camp children—believing what she'd heard time and again, that people got their babies out of hollow logs and there was no reason for her not to play ball. Her story, Mr. Buck's stories, and the many others we collected, intimated the power that tales well told held for the rural blacks and turpentiners in Florida. They told them, listened to them, and retold them. They were sustenance as much as food was, as necessary to life as air to breathe. Their stories, and Jake Hurd's, who was surely a master storyteller, and who passed his craft onto his grandson James, became the foundation of our play, *Turpentine Jake*. It was the process of refashioning them for the drama that led us to the realization that the act of refashioning, the telling and retelling of stories, the use of subversive language and subversive rhetorical strategies was the turpentiners' means of surviving the camps and "tepentiming." Their language use gave them power, linked them to the natural world around them and the supernatural world beyond, enabled them to derive strength from their servitude. While the trees they worked could easily have become a place to hang a noose, or the materials of yet another crucifixion of the black man in white society, instead the turpentiners used the trees and the images they evoked, they used their facility for language to rise, to climb up out of pine forest into the world beyond it. There is an old turpentiner's adage about turpentining: "The onliest way out is to die out." Certainly many turpentiners ended their days in debt servitude, but for most it was a bearable existence, one in which they made happiness despite the cruelty of their surroundings. Many other turpentiners got out, bought land, built homes, moved north or west, or otherwise conquered debt servitude, not merely escaped it. Jake Hurd was the first man in Calhoun County to own a car, and when he drove it down the main street in Wewahitchka, most of the people in town waved, white and black.

Appendix

Interview with Mr. Buck Clayton (Excerpts)
Port St. Joe, Florida
October 2004

Hurd and Bannister: *What year did you move down there (to Wewahitchka)?*
Mr. Buck: I come here in 19 . . . 1926.
H&B: 1926 . . . So what was your job in the turpentine business?
Mr. B: Well, I chipped boxes.
H&B: You chipped boxes?
Mr. B: You know what that is?
H&B: Tell us what chippin' boxes is. How do you chip a box?
Mr. B: Haha, you gotta, you gotta hack, kinder, pull on a stalk. And you gotta weight to it. Just like pullin'—you ever seen a pull? I know you seen a pull. You know, boxes. Boxes up on trees.
H&B: I never saw a puller but I have an idea what pullin is. You pull the bark off the tree right?
Mr. B: Yeah, cut a streak on it.
H&B: OK, cut a streak on it.
Mr. B: Chippin's the same way, but you just had it in a short stalk.
H&B: A short stalk.
Mr. B: Pullin' boxes was a long stalk. You reach way up the tree.
H&B: I see.
Mr. B: You, you, if you notice round you'll see old boxes that done pulled way up there on the tree.
H&B: So you were a chipper?
Mr. B: I, I done all of it.
H&B: You did chippin' and you did pullin'?
Mr. B: Yeh, pullin' and chippin' and dippin' turpentine.
H&B: Was that hard work?
Mr. B: Yeh it was hard work [laughs] . . . But it didn't bother, didn't bother me.

H&B: It didn't bother you? You look pretty healthy. You look pretty strong.

Mr. B: I done lost my heat though, now. I don't eat like I always did. I don't eat like I oughta eat, if I eat like I oughta eat I'd be the same way. I used to could eat, but I can't eat now.

(Skip to new segment.)

H&B: So how many people worked on the Lister Turpentine Still? How many people did he have working for him?

Mr. B: He had a big whole quarters of people, just like at St. Joe here.

H&B: So he had a whole turpentine quarters, so he probably had over fifty to one hundred people workin for him?

Mr. B: Oh, yes. People comin' in and out of there. Turpentine. It wasn't as big as St. Joc. Oh, he had a whole quarters.

H&B: So he was the biggest turpentine owner in Wewa, in Calhoun County. (Now it's called Gulf County.)

(Skip to new segment.)

H&B: So what was it like working in the woods?

Mr. B: [Laughs.] Well, you go out in the morning, got yo' bucket, do whatever you gonna do, chip boxes, dip turpentine, them old turpentine buckets. Yeah you should have seen 'em. We had sometimes seven or eight boys. I don't know if you've ever seen 'em fill a barrel or not. Your granddaddy Jake and all them boys. They know all about it, them boys would. Old man, uh Jake, we always used to call him Jake Hurd. He was the best one.

H&B: Right, that was his name, Jake, Jake Hurd. So in the morning what time would y'all leave to go out in the woods?

Mr. B: Well sometimes it'd be foreday, sometimes I was up in the day, four or five, I remember waitin' for them oxen.

H&B: So would you all ride the ox wagon out into the woods or would you have to walk out into the woods?

Mr. B: We had to walk out into the woods, you ride the ox wagon if you want to be slow. Them oxen are slow, they pull that turpentine.

H&B: So how many miles would you say it would be from the camp to out in the woods, that you had to walk?

Mr. B: It was about five or six miles out in the woods.

H&B: *So you have like a five or six mile walk in the morning just to get to where you were going to work?*

Mr. B: Yes, to get where you work at.

H&B: And then when you were breaking, in the evening, then you had to walk that same distance back?

Mr. B: Yeah, if you ain't no way to ride, had you walk. Mmm, mm. Yes you did.

H&B: So you work a twelve-hour day then?

Mr. B: Ma'am?

H&B: *You were working twelve hours a day it sounds like?*

Mr. B: Sometimes we was working for twelve hours, I don't know, workin' by your selves, you work like you wanna.

H&B: *If you add in the walking.*

Mr. B: Didn't have no noted time.

H&B: *You just had to get those boxes chipped and dipped within a certain amount of time?*

Mr. B: Yeah, a certain time. We supposed to chip 'em that week.

H&B: *Right. Did you have, how many drifts could you do in a week?*

Mr. B: Well, [laughs] I don't know. I have a crop. I was showing, trying to show it to Marie [his daughter]. I had a crop in the curve going up there by Dalkeath, up there where ya'll [the Hurds] live. I show them over in that pond that I had chipped seven thousand, a crop. Right there, you go in to Wewa, I was showing them where I used to chip.

H&B: *So a crop is seven thousand boxes?*

Mr. B: Seven thousand, yeah. Some say ten.

H&B: *How many is in a drift?*

Mr. B: How many is in a drift?

H&B: *Uh-huh.*

Mr. B: Well you could have . . . could be a two thousand drift.

H&B: *Mmm.*

Mr. B: Mostly, mostly when they put them up they had them in drifts in two thousand, three thousand, four thousand, five thousand.

H&B: *And you had to do that. Now if you were assigned you had to do that much in a week's time?*

Mr. B: Yeah, but a thousand, least a thousand they would do in a day.

H&B: *Really?*

Mr. B: Yeah. Me and my daddy-in-law, we did a crop one day and they was bad lightning and thunder and I told them, I says yeah, if there's lightning and thunder then we don't need to be out here [laughing].

H&B: *[Laughing.]*

Mr. B: Then he (my daddy) says, "What's the matter? You scared God gonna kill you?" [Laughs.]

H&B: *[More laughter.]*

Mr. B: He's a deacon, Christian man. He says, "Boy you know what? We chipped that crop that night in all that weather." He didn't mean to give up. I stayed with him on it though. But I was scared, scared of lightning [Laughs]. "Scared God gonna kill you?" [Laughs.]

Interview with Mrs. Cora Keith (Excerpts)
Wewahitchka, Florida
April 2005

Mrs. Cora Keith: You know, in my day, people told their children all kind of lies. You had to believe them because they . . . [laughter] . . . talking about how you getting babies out the hollow log. I . . . was nervy enough to ask you know. I'd ask them. I'd say, "Where y'all get these babies from?" We go out and get get 'um out a hollow log. Get 'um, put 'um in our suitcase and brang on to who want 'um. I said to myself "Lord, have mercy." Bunch of us would be out there looking, in hollow logs, looking for babies. So just one day. I believe it was Mrs. Norton's momma Mrs. Weed. I was about to get married then young. When I married I was thirteen going into fourteen.

Hurd and Bannister: *When you got married?*

Mrs. C: When I got married. Now that's the truth. You know I was crazy. I'd get out there, a bunch of us playing ball, and my husband come home and . . . course my first child I was along my way with her. And . . . Miss Miles, she had done that number (shaking her finger) for me to get from among them, them young boys and one or two more girls, and for me to go sit down.

H&B: *Cause you were pregnant?*

Mrs. C: But she didn't say the word! I stayed on out there and . . . child, that day was a misery.

H&B: *[laughter] What happened?*

Mrs. C: I fell.

H&B: *Uh oh. Oh dear . . .*

Mrs. C: I fell when I rolled over. The blood just keep comin' . . . and none of them there didn't have no sense cause I didn't have none and I was . . . And then Manuel Miles, he went to hollering "Somebody! Somebody!" Oh, they called me 'Miss C.' "Miss C bleedin to death!" And a white woman lived down there at the branch. She come runnin . . . and she come and after a while her husband come. She bends over and she yell "One of y'all, my horse is hitched up down at the corner. Get on it and go get Myrtle (Myrtle Hurd, who was a midwife) and the child's mother." And I think they met Miss Myrtle on the way, and she come down with her fast-talkin self, nervy, "Y'all oughta told this gal something." [Laughs.]

H&B: *[Laughter.]*

Mrs. C: And I say, "Am I gonna die?" And that's what I asked her. She's all "I don't know, honey." Myrtle looked right at me, she said "You gonna die if this blood ain't stop and quick!" Then Myrtle anyhows, they had those little glass bottles, you know, and she got her bottle and poured some of that in there. Come back and give it to me to drink. "Now you lay flat on your back, and don't you get up til I tell you . . . And then my husband said "I told her to quit playing ball" . . . and I said to myself, I can play ball, just as good as anybody else.

H&B: [Laughter.]

Mrs. C: Cause they sit down there and they told me . . .

H&B: What was that?

Mrs. C: What was what, after I got a little better so I could look at them, and I say "My mama told me you'd get the baby out of a hollow log."

H&B: [Laughter.]

Mrs. C: She brang in them folks . . .

H&B: Oh, goodness.

Mrs. C: "We gonna stop it, we gonna stop it now, we gonna tell em, all of em, where them babies get. And how'd they get up with them. That's what we got to do."

H&B: That's what Grandma (Myrtle Hurd) said?

Mrs. C: [Nods.] Oh, she knew there was too much happenin' and causin' too much of trouble, cause I done fell, hurt myself there, and that was costing they money. So they could of caught a baby while they were there messing with me, caught a baby in and got money.

H&B: So there were babies being born all over the place, weren't there?

Mrs. C: Yeah. People just didn't know nothing to keep you from havin' them then, like they do now.

H&B: Wow.

Mrs. C: Yes suh, you get them babies and twins, my sister and me . . . I had twins!

Notes

1. Butler, Nicholls, and Tegeder all discuss debt peonage as a vestige of antebellum slavery.

2. "Increase in Pine Products," *New York Times*, January 12, 1902.

3. Tegeder discusses at length the oppressive work environment, citing many cases of laborers beaten and bullied by woodsriders and camp owners, amply supporting his book's subtitle "Prisoners of the Pines."

4. Butler comments on the movement of the Turpentine industry overseas. Several museum personnel we spoke with also spoke of turpentining in China and South America.

5. Excerpts from the Folklife Project are available from NPR. "Profile: Florida Folklife Project, Which Recorded the Stories and Songs of Blacks During the Depres-

sion," hosts Jacki Lyden and Noah Adams, *All Things Considered*, NPR, February 28, 2002.

6. Tiffany Ruby Patterson, *Zora Neale Hurston and A History of Southern Life* (Philadelphia: Temple University Press, 2005), 10.

7. Zora Neale Hurston, *Hurston: Folklore, Memoirs, and Other Writings* (New York: Literary Classics of the U.S., 1995), 10.

8. Patterson, *Zora Neale Hurston*, 7.

9. Françoise Lionnet, *Autobiographical Voice: Race, Gender, Self-Portraiture* (New York: Cornell University Press, 1989) and "Of Mangoes and Maroons: Language, History, and the Multicultural Subject of Michelle Cliff's *Abeng*," *Postcolonial Representations: Women, Literature, Identity* (Ithaca: Cornell University Press, 1989), 39.

10. Patterson, *Zora Neale Hurston*, 20.

11. Ibid, 187.

12. Labov, Gilyard, Chomsky, and Smitherman all comment on the link between proficiency and language use and the emerging self.

13. Keith Gilyard, *Voices of the Self: A Study of Language Competence* (Detroit: Wayne State University Press, 1991), 12.

14. Caroll B. Butler, *Treasures of the Longleaf Pines* (Shalimar, Fl: Tarkel Publishing, 1998), 34.

15. Ibid.

16. Ibid.

17. Lawrence S. Early, *Looking for Longleaf: The Fall and Rise of an American Forest* (Chapel Hill: University of North Carolina Press, 2004), 137.

18. Hurston, *Hurston: Folklore, Memoirs, and Other Writings*, 10.

19. Ibid.

20. David G. Nicholls, "Migrant Labor, Folklore, and Resistance in Hurston's Polk County: Reframing Mules and Men," *African American Review* (Fall 1999): 2.

21. Patterson, *Zora Neale Hurston*, 133.

22. Butler, *Treasures of the Longleaf Pines*, 35.

23. Pete Daniel, *The Shadow of Slavery: Peonage in the South, 1901–1969* (Urbana: University of Illinois Press, 1972).

24. Early, *Looking for Longleaf*, 141.

25. William E. Wiethoff, *The Insolent Slave* (Columbia: University of South Carolina Press, 2002), 1.

26. Early, *Looking for Longleaf*, 138.

Bibliography

Bacon, Jacqueline. *The Humblest May Stand Forth: Rhetoric, Empowerment, and Abolition*. Columbia: University of South Carolina Press, 2002.

Begos, Kevin. "Still-Crazy After All These Years." *News Herald*, November 20, 1997.

Boxwell, D. A. "'Sis Cat' as Ethnographer: Self-presentation and Self-inscription in Zora Neale Hurston's Mules and Men." *African American Review* 26 (1992): 605–18.

Boyd, Valerie. *Wrapped in Rainbows: The Life of Zora Neale Hurston*. New York: Scribner, 2004.

Burrison, John A. *Storytellers: Folktales & Legends from the South*. Athens: University of Georgia Press, 1991.

Butler, Caroll B. *Treasures of the Longleaf Pines*. Shalimar, FL: Tarkel Publishing, 1998.

Carmer, Carl. "In the Deep South's 'Palmetto County.'" *New York Times*, December 27, 1942.
Chomsky, Noam. *Language and Mind.* Rev. ed. New York: Harcourt, Brace and Jovanovich, 1972.
Daniel, Pete. *The Shadow of Slavery: Peonage in the South, 1901–1969.* Urbana: University of Illinois Press, 1972.
Du Bois, William. "Searing Novel of the South." *New York Times*, March 5, 1944.
Duck, Leigh Anne. "'Go there tuh know there': Zora Neale Hurston and the Chronotype of theFolk." *American Literary History* 13, no. 2 (2001): 265–94.
Early, Lawrence S. *Looking for Longleaf: The Fall and Rise of an American Forest.* Chapel Hill: University of North Carolina Press, 2004.
Feld, Rose. "The Piney Woods." *New York Times*, October 12, 1941.
Gates, Henry Louis. *The Classic Slave Narratives.* New York: Penguin Group, 1987.
———. ed. *Reading Black, Reading Feminist: A Critical Anthology.* New York: Meridian Book, 1990.
Genovese, Eugene D. *Roll, Jordan, Roll: The World the Slaves Made.* New York: First Vintage Books Edition, 1976.
Gilyard, Keith. *Voices of the Self: A Study of Language Competence.* Detroit: Wayne State University Press, 1991.
Hartman, Saidiya V. *Scenes of Subjection: Terror, Slavery, and Self-making in Nineteenth-Century America.* New York: Oxford University Press, 1997.
Holmes, David G. "Cross-Racial Voicing: Carl Van Vechten's Imagination and the Search for an African American Ethos." *College English* 68 (2006): 291–307.
Hurston, Lucy Anne. *Speak, So You Can Speak Again: The Life of Zora Neale Hurston.* New York: Doubleday, 2004.
Hurston, Zora Neale. *Hurston: Folklore, Memoirs, and Other Writings.* New York: Literary Classics of the U.S., 1995.
Kaplan, Carla, ed. *Zora Neale Hurston: A Life in Letters.* New York: Doubleday, 2003.
Labov, William. *The Study of Nonstandard English.* Rev. ed. Urbana, IL: NCTE, 1981.
Lionnet, Franciose. *Autobiographical Voice: Race, Gender, Self-Portraiture.* New York: Cornell University Press, 1989.
———. "Of Mangoes and Maroons: Language, History, and the Multicultural Subject of Michelle Cliff's *Abeng.*" *Postcolonial Representations: Women, Literature, Identity.* Ithaca: Cornell University Press, 1989.
Marino, Mark. "Multimedia Hurston." Photocopy, Department of English, University of California at Riverside, 2004.
———. "Zora Neale Hurston: First Let Me Set You Straight." Photocopy, Department of English, University of California at Riverside, 2004.
New York Times, "Another Peonage Refugee," August 1, 1906.
———. "Arrested Here for Peonage." July 28, 1906.
———. "Colonization of Blacks in Florida." October 3, 1862.
———. "Grand Jury Indicts Agent for Peonage." October 21, 1906.
———. "Increase in Pine Products." January 12, 1902.
———. "Jail for Rich Men, President Declares." January 7, 1911.
———. "Merger in Pine Products." February 5, 1924.
———. "Peonage Witness Tells of Manhunt." February 26, 1949.

———. "Says Convict Camps Worse Than Slavery." September 1, 1907.

———. "Woman Lawyer Hears of Peonage in Florida." July 23, 1906.

Nicholls, David G. "Migrant Labor, Folklore, and Resistance in Hurston's Polk County: Reframing Mules and Men." *African American Review* (Fall 1999): 3–33.

Patterson, Tiffany Ruby. *Zora Neale Hurston and A History of Southern Life.* Philadelphia: Temple University Press, 2005.

Pavlic, Edward. "What the Music Said: Black Popular Music and Black Popular Culture." *African American Review.* 34, no. 2 (2000): 348–52.

Luden, Jacki, and Noah Adams, hosts. "Profile: Florida Folklife Project, Which Recorded the Stories and Songs of Blacks During the Depression." *All Things Considered.* National Public Radio. February 28, 2002.

Rivers, Larry E. *Slavery in Florida: Territorial Days to Emancipation.* Gainesville: University Press of Florida, 2000.

Sisters in Cinema. Dir. Yvonne Welbon. Harriman, NY: Our Film Works, 2003.

Slaughter, Frank G. "Freud in Turpentine." *New York Times,* October 31, 1948.

Smitherman, G. *Talkin and Testifyin: The Language of Black America.* Boston: Houghton Mifflin, 1977.

Tegeder, Michael David. "Prisoners of the Pines: Debt Peonage in the Southern Turpentine Industry, 1900–1930 (African-Americans)." Diss., University of Florida, 1996.

Wall, Cheryl A, ed. "Introduction." *Sweat,* by Zora Neale Hurston. New Brunswick, NJ: Rutgers University Press, 1997.

Wiethoff, William E. *The Insolent Slave.* Columbia: University of South Carolina Press, 2002.

Zora Is My Name! Videocassette. Directed by Neema Barnette. Perf. Ruby Dee. Beverly Hills, CA: PBS Video, 1990.

Zora Neale Hurston: A Heart with Room for Every Joy. Directed by Pablo Garcia. Perf. Russell Hornsby. Princeton: Films for the Humanities and Sciences, c2005.

A Hole Story: The Space of Historical Memory in the Abolitionist Imagination

ZOE TRODD

> We could have told them a different story."
>
> —Harriet Jacobs, 1861

WHEN HARRIET JACOBS SAT DOWN TO WRITE HER NARRATIVE OF 1861, she knew that *Incidents in the Life of a Slave Girl* would expose a hidden history. Slavery's "secrets" had been "concealed like those of the Inquisition," she notes at one point in the narrative. Nowhere is what Jacobs termed in 1852 "the whole truth": "I never would consent to give my past life to any one for I would not do it without giving the whole truth," she explained in a letter. Instead of this whole truth, Americans have received a clergyman's "South-Side View of Slavery," notes Jacobs in *Incidents*. Complaining of the "exaggerations of abolitionists," the author has assured his readers that slavery is "a beautiful 'patriarchal institution;' that the slaves don't want their freedom." But "what does *he* know?" protests Jacobs. "The slaves dared not tell . . . if he had asked them." Then there are those "Northern travelers,"[1] "who see a partial version of the truth. "*We* could have told them a different story," she concludes.[2]

Jacobs's task in *Incidents* is to tell that "different story." In answer to the clergyman's narrative, for example, Jacobs offers a new version: "What does he know of the half-starved wretches toiling from dawn till dark on the plantations? of mothers shrieking for their children, torn from their arms by slave traders?" And in her introduction to Jacobs's narrative, the abolitionist Lydia Maria Child adds that while aspects of slavery have "been kept veiled," because "ears are too delicate to listen," *Incidents* now offers "the veil withdrawn."[3]

Jacobs's "different story" was part of a broader abolitionist effort to reclaim historical memory. In antebellum America, a host of different stories by passionate outsiders challenged the country's exclusionary narrative of freedom and equality. This historical reclamation was in part an attempt to *change* the course of history as America moved forward. Whether rewriting the Constitution, like John Brown in 1858, or narrating the story of Toussaint Louverture as one of inspiration for American slaves, like William Wells Brown in 1855, abolitionists made history and memory into tools for change. If, as Jacobs observes, her own "bill of sale" will be merely "a useful document to antiquaries, who are seeking to measure the progress of the United States," then perhaps her narrative might achieve something more: "I wished it to be a history of my life entirely by itself which would *do more good*," she insisted in a letter. As Frederick Douglass explained in 1852, the task was to find a past "useful to the present and to the future."[4]

As they focused on history's erasures but also its potentialities as a living past, literary abolitionists like Douglass and Jacobs developed a politics of form—rooting the abolitionist culture of dissent in aesthetics as well as ideologies. This politics of form made their different story a *hole* story: whether the "loophole" in Jacobs's *Incidents*, Harriet Wilson's descriptions of Frado's tiny L-shaped room in *Our Nig* (1861), or the "holes and crevices" in the tavern, the "mantraps" of the decaying portico, and Madison Washington's "cave" in Douglass's *The Heroic Slave* (1853), literary abolitionism included a series of holes and confined places. Within the abolitionist aesthetic, this trope literalized the margins of American historical memory and expressed the present-absence of an elusive "different story."[5]

The abolitionist hole story imagined historical space as physical space, challenging the country's "whole" story of historical progress. The closets, garrets, boxes, crevices, and dark holes of abolitionist literature are the forgotten spaces in history's house, in an anticipation of Walter Benjamin's *Geschichtsraum*, "the space of history." And the trope expressed another kind of historical gap as well: the gulf between what *is* and what *might have been*. Thomas Jefferson had originally drafted a denunciation of the slave trade for the Declaration of Independence and its deletion from the final version left a loophole in America's founding document. Observing this textual marginalization, abolitionist writers spatialized it as a dark hole or confined space, as though the slaves who were erased from America's declaration were consigned to a literal limbo.[6]

Then they used the device of spatialization to imagine closing that gap between past ideal and present reality. They focused on what *ought* to be. "Poets, prophets, and reformers are all picture-makers, and this ability is the secret of their power and achievements," wrote Douglass in 1864; "they see what ought to be by the reflection of what is, and endeavor to remove the contradiction." Examining the American Revolution "by the reflection" of their antebellum present, abolitionist writers found not only a "contradiction" but a usable protest past; a moment of origin for their own outsider rhetoric and a precedent for slave rebellion. The no-place of America's margins became an alternate space of protest history. Challenging a historically confined space with the deep space of activist memory, literary abolitionists demanded liberation from the blank space in between 1776 and the 1850s, and an end to the "contradiction."[7]

THE ABOLITIONISTS' SPATIAL AESTHETIC

On a very real level, space was at the heart of America's slave system. The imposition of negative space began with the middle passage, as Houston Baker explains: "traditional Afro-American geographies [are a] placeless place" because "PLACE is an Afro-American portion of the world which begins in a European DISPLACEMENT of bodies." After that, Baker continues, the "displacement of the slave trade that produced a placeless . . . hole was complemented by a southern agriculture that moved, prodded, drove, 'gangs' of men ceaselessly south and west." Examining the destinations of that journey south and west, John Michael Vlach further explains that plantations were designed to mark slaveowners' "dominance over nature and other men," their spaces reinforcing "a strict hierarchical order." The slaves' living and working spaces enabled surveillance and control, and slaves were "denied the time and resources needed to design and build as they might have wanted."[8]

But, Vlach adds, slaves "appropriated, as marginalized people often do, the environments to which they were assigned." One example of this environmental appropriation was what bell hooks terms "the construction of a homeplace, however fragile and tenuous (the slave hut, the wooden shack)." This had a "radical political dimension," writes hooks, for "one's homeplace was the one site where one could freely confront the issue of humanization, where one could resist." Another was flight—not to the North, but to nearby areas. As Vincent Harding notes, runaway slaves entered the "surrounding forests and swamps, creating microcosmic new societies that remembered the ways of Africa." After the Nat Turner rebellion, which took place around the Great Dismal Swamp of Virginia and North Carolina, the idea of an alternate slave space within the boundaries of the South seemed indelible. Still another was through story-telling. As Eric Sundquist notes, "Nat Turner did not travel, but his message did."[9]

Turner's was one of many messages that traveled, and sometimes traveled physically. In 1830, runaway slaves were allegedly discovered with copies of David Walker's *Appeal to the Coloured Citizens of the World* (1829), and former slaves, including Douglass, traveled the North as lecturers for the major antislavery organizations. But the notion of a "message" shattering the fixed spaces of the slave system involved an imaginary alteration of space as well. Abolitionist appropriated confined space as a usable site of resistance. While Baker insists that "all fixed points are problematical," for "fixity is a function of power" and those who "maintain places, who decide what takes place and dictate what has taken place are power brokers of the traditional," literary abolitionists appropriated these "fixed points" for their protest literature. For example, rooting the battle for free space in the realm of the symbolic, visual artists repeatedly portrayed Henry "Box" Brown climbing out of the box in which he escaped, and accompanied such lithographs with metaphors fashioning the infamous box as slavery's psychological and spiritual suffocation. In one image, set in the office of the Pennsylvania Anti-Slavery Society, Brown emerges from a crate as abolitionists—including William Still, conductor of Philadelphia's Underground Railroad—look on (fig. 1).[10]

Other abolitionists transformed confined space into an alternative

Fig. 1. "The resurrection of Henry Box Brown at Philadelphia, who escaped from Richmond, Va. in a bx 2 feet long 2 ½ ft. deep and 2 ft wide" (1850), lithograph published by A. Donnelly, New York. Courtesy of the Library of Congress, Prints and Photographs Division.

site of historical memory. This particular hole story extended across several mediums, including slave narratives. For example, William Pennington's *The Fugitive Blacksmith* (1849) describes the "mental and spiritual darkness" of slavery in Maryland, its "total moral midnight," which Pennington only comprehended while in the safe space of "six months' concealment" during his flight to freedom. But Pennington reverses this symbolism of dark space with a memory of hiding for "hours in a wood, or behind a fence" to escape his master's "eye"—of chosen invisibility in dark woods and chosen confinement behind a fence. Then he transforms the *master's* space into one more horrific because it collapses as history sweeps through. He describes the "dilapidated dwelling" of a man who "has been guilty of great cruelties to his slaves, and who is dead, or moved away": "the once fine smooth gravel walks, overgrown with grass . . . the once finely painted picket fences, rusted and fallen down—a fine garden in splendid ruins—the lofty ceiling of the mansion thickly curtained with cobwebs—the spacious apartments abandoned. . . . the crying cricket and cockroaches." Borders are breached, for the "walks" are overgrown and the ceiling is hidden. Boundaries are insecure, for the "fences" have fallen down. The master's space is shattered, abandoned, and invaded, for the garden is ruined, the "spacious" apartments are empty, and insects have arrived. And Pennington follows this description with an account of the "decline of slaveholding families." The "old master declines" and slavery has so affected the families of slaveholders that the "decline" in his family line is equally "rapid and marked." In "almost every point of view," Pennington explains, "the children of slaveholders are universally inferior to themselves." Juxtaposing his image of a "dilapidated dwelling" to this mention of familial declension, Pennington suggests that masters, rather than slaves, are about to enter the dead space of American historical memory.[11]

Novelists offered a reconstruction of historical space as well. In Harriet Beecher Stowe's antislavery fiction *Uncle Tom's Cabin* (1852), slaves seize control of space when they inhabit a secret place in the master's house and make that hole tell a story. Cassy and Emmeline hide in a "loophole in the garret." This "fatal garret" is "the garret of the house that Legree occupied . . . a weird and ghostly place," and Cassy and Emmeline take full advantage of its atmosphere. They "play ghost" so that Legree hears "people scuffing" up there, and the "people up garret" scare him. Though he has made the women chattel, Legree now fears the "it" in the garret. As well, Cassy has inserted the neck of an old bottle into the "knot-hole of the garret," so that the wind creates a "shriek" of "horror and despair." This revives "in full force the memory of the old ghost legend." Legree remembers and fears the living past.¹²

Abolitionist histories were themselves another source of appropriative spatialization. In *The Black Man: His Antecedents, His Genius, and His Achievements* (1863), William Wells Brown connects public space and historical memory. His chapter on Crispus Attucks and the Boston Massacre explains: "No monument has yet been erected to him . . . Five generations of accumulated prejudice against the negro had excluded from the American mind all inclination to do justice to one of her bravest sons. When negro slavery shall be abolished in our land, then we may hope to see a monument raised to commemorate the heroism of Crispus Attucks." If not the space of a "monument," Brown's *own* memorialization of Attucks in *The Black Man* creates a space in public memory—the "American mind." And, in reminding his readers of the approaching emancipation (*"shall be* abolished"), Brown suggests that Attucks may well live on in the example of abolitionists. Far from emancipation ending historical amnesia, historical memory assists emancipation. As a living history, not a static monument, the example of Attucks might create space for slaves in history's pantheon *and* the future's citizenship.¹³

Brown's discussion of Attucks was one of many abolitionist invocations of Revolutionary-era protest. Seizing the historical space of 1776, Nat Turner planned his slave revolt on July 4, 1831, while John Brown timed his raid for July 4, 1858, then July 4, 1859 (though had to postpone both times). William Wells Brown's rebel slave George, in *Clotel* (1853), explains his rebellion with reference to 1776 ("You say your fathers fought for freedom—so did we . . . Had we succeeded, we would have been patriots too"), and Stowe's George in *Uncle Tom's Cabin* declares that if "it was right for [your fathers], it is right for me!" But while taking inspiration from the Revolution, abolitionists also pointed to the gap between the Declaration's ideals of equality and the ongoing fact of slavery. Free blacks in New York traditionally celebrated Independence a day late, to protest the long delay in realizing the Declaration's ideals, and *Clotel* evokes the horror of July 4 for slaves. "You make merry on the 4th of July," says George. "Yet while these cannons are roaring . . . one-sixth of the people of this land are in chains." In his autobiography of 1847, Brown had also explained that "the people of the United States boast of their freedom" but "at the same time keep three millions of their own citizens in chains." He added: "while I am seated here in sight of Bunker Hill Monument, writing this narrative, I am a slave, and no law, not even in Massachusetts, can protect me from the slave-holder." Brown saw the risk of summoning 1776 while citizens were in "chains." Returning to America's birth as a protest nation without ending slavery made 1776 a stillbirth.[14]

In spatial terms, this act of remembering a revolution without completing its process had merely created an "aberration within the national narrative by the trope of parenthesis," as Russ Castronovo puts it. "The structure of parenthesis," Castronovo explains, sums up "the political culture of the antebellum era ... 1776 became the pure, originary past, allowing America to remain in continuous temporal and ideological harmony with its own genesis." Like other literary abolitionists, Brown wanted to lift slavery from a structure of parenthesis and summon the "originary past" in order to change, rather than validate, the present. His narrative, written "in sight of Bunker Hill," might remove that contradiction of "freedom" and "chains. With Douglass, Jacobs, Pennington, and numerous others, Brown offered his own words as drops of water to revive the dead landscape of America's historical memory.[15]

Frederick Douglass's Spaces Left

Of all the literary abolitionists, Douglass was the most focused on reconstituting the Revolution's ideals. In his speech "What to the Slave is the Fourth of July?" (1852), Douglass invoked the spirit of '76 to call for another revolution. Choosing to give the speech on July 5, he further reminded his white audience that slavery was an anachronism—a rupture in America's narrative of endless progress. The following year, he again reinterpreted the meaning of July 4. In *The Heroic Slave*, Madison Washington justifies his violence and claims his freedom with the words: "We have done that which you applaud your fathers for doing, and if we are murderers, so were they." Douglass also explained, in an article for *Frederick Douglass's Paper* on September 29, 1854, that fugitive slaves "acted out the declaration of independence" in escaping.[16]

In remembering the Revolution, Douglass was engaged in a form of intellectual *bricolage*—ideas, images, and language are stored across time, then transformed by new contexts into a living protest legacy. But more than this, he was taking control of time and space, and fusing both into a new space of historical memory. For example, the battle over time looms large in his autobiographies. In his *Narrative* of 1845, he notes the problem of having "no accurate knowledge of my age" and "no knowledge of the days of the month," remembers the sound of the driver's horn, the instructions to take less than five minutes for a meal. When Master Thomas instructs him to "lay out no plans" and instead achieve "complete thoughtlessness of the future," Douglass is denied *future* time as well. Or, in *My Bondage and My Freedom* (1855) he remembers the struggle to be "master of my own time" and the clash of slave time with the master's watch and horn. Again, there is no access to future time: he describes the denial of "progress" to the slave, who is "shut up entirely" without a "future."¹⁷

He translates these time-wars into a struggle for control over *historical* time. Time and history blend. The "order of civilization" is "reversed" by slavery, the plantation is a "full three hundred years behind the age," and Douglass feels the resulting pathology of wanting to remain "little forever." But in response to this denial of personal and historical time, Douglass attempts to seize control. He stays at a camp meeting longer than expected and eventually hires out his own time. Another victory is the slaves' music, which has no "time." Then, through his autobiographical act across three narratives, Douglass finally takes control of historical time.¹⁸

The battle for control over space rages with equal intensity. Wendell Phillips prefaces the *Narrative* with an assertion that space is unsafe for the slave ("there is no single spot . . . where a fugitive slave can plant himself and say 'I am safe'"), and Douglass goes on to describe slavery as a tomb and a pit. Covey controls all space through surveillance, he adds: "His work went on in his absence almost as well as in his presence and he had the faculty of making us feel that he was ever present with us . . . He was under every tree . . . and at every window." Equally, in *My Bondage*, Douglass describes the "holes and corners" around the plantation, the "out-of-the-way places" and the "'tabooed' spot . . . separated from the rest of the world," as opposed to the apparent "boundlessness of slave territory," its deliberately "vague and indistinct" geography.¹⁹

Space is confined and movement is circumscribed. While free men might "contemplate a life in the far west, or in some distant country," the "slave is a fixture; he has no . . . destination; but is pegged down to a single spot, and must take root here, or nowhere." Being sent away is to be "a man going into the tomb . . . buried out of sight and hearing" and slavery itself is "a stone prison." Douglass even notes that the Lloyd plantation is "a little nation of its own, having its own language, its own rules, regulations and customs." It is an entirely discreet space, "far away from all the great thoroughfares," so that no "foreign or dangerous influences" can disrupt the "natural operation of the slave system of the place." Controlling space, the slaveowners maintain power. In his third autobiography, *The Life and Times of Frederick Douglass* (1881), Douglass again took up the themes of confined space and constricted movement. Slavery is a "house of bondage," "a horrible pit," "a life of living death," a "dark corner" of a "dark domain."[20]

But just as he describes a series of resistances to controlled time, so Douglass lays out the transformation of slavery's controlled space. For example, he hides in the tight space of a closet and finds a vantage point from which to reverse the master's controlling gaze. Through the closet's "cracks" Douglass can see but not be seen: "I could distinctly see and hear what was going on, without being seen by old master." His descriptions of the underground railroad, and his own change in status by moving from one space to another, from Baltimore to New York, offer further spatial resistance, and his eventual decision to be "the thin edge of the wedge to open for my people a way in many directions and places never before occupied by them" reveals his sense that these pages themselves might seize control of slavery's space.[21]

In fact, Douglass's act of writing—and then repeatedly rewriting—his autobiography *was* another appropriation of space, as well as time. He found the self-creative space denied him by white abolitionists: "Give us the facts . . . We will take care of the philosophy," keep "a *little* of the plantation manner of speech," and don't "seem too learned," they had told him (trying to "pin" him down). The autobiographies' self-creative space was also a space of historical memory that challenged erasure; what he describes as silences around a "delicate subject," the silent presence of "unmarked" slave graves, the absence of "family records" for the slave, the things that are "speedily hushed up." Within his self-inscriptions, Douglass reveals these gaps in America's historical memory and insists upon the presence of counterhistory.[22]

For example, he imagines a different narrative altogether. In both the *Narrative* and *My Bondage* he notes that "circumstance" had liberated him from slavery, thereby embedding the voice of counterfactual history: "it is quite probable that, but for the mere circumstance of being thus removed . . . before my young spirit had been crushed under the iron control of the slave-driver, instead of being, today, a FREEMAN, I might have been wearing the galling chains of slavery." Or, again seizing control of historical memory, he makes his own writings a primary source. Updating the *Narrative* to *My Bondage*, he excerpted key novelistic passages (one about his grandmother, the Chesapeake passage, and a passage using the vernacular of white shipyard workers). Douglass's own younger voice is now the voice of a historical source.[23]

Equally important is that his autobiographies contain the persistent traces of a partially erased counterhistory: the "gashes" on his frost-cracked feet where he might lay his pen, the lines of a "diploma" written on his back by the whip, the traces of his brother's "footprints." And Douglass's narratives were *themselves* a form of historical trace. The slave might have to write in the "spaces left" between the lines, or find page space and "copy-book . . . [on] the board fence, brick wall, and pavement," as he explained in the *Narrative*, but there was room for a new history in the gashes and scars of the self under construction: revising his autobiographies, Douglass literally wrote between the lines of himself—in the "spaces left"—and crafted a layered history. A never-ending process of self-construction is apparent even in the frontispieces to his first two autobiographies. His image is unfinished in the *Narrative* and partially finished in *My Bondage*, where sketched, unfinished hands grip his jacket as though about to open it wide, suggesting an ongoing process of discovery or display that imitates the opening of the book (fig. 2).[24]

Far from accepting his space on the margins as an unbearable fixity, Douglass instead anticipated bell hooks's notion that "marginality [is] much more than a site of deprivation," rather "a central location for the production of counter-hegemonic discourse." It offers a "radical perspective from which to see and create, to imagine alternatives, new worlds," adds hooks. There was potentiality and possibility in history's crevice and Douglass dwelt there as a witness-participant and a liminal man in the making, his continuous evolution across three autobiographies a resistance to any fixed notion of character. This perpetual space making began to solve the problem of exclusion from history's space: his self-construction opened the boundlessness that he describes at the end of "What to the Slave," where there are no more "walled cities," the Pacific is at his feet, "[s]pace is comparatively annihilated," and there is hope for abolition. From the margins, abolitionist outsiders might now mold the center.[25]

Douglass also added fiction to his growing canon of historical reclamations. Like "What to the Slave" and his autobiographies, Douglass's *The Heroic Slave* describes battles for time and space. Madison Washington explains that slavery and flight has "turned day into night," and describes his punishment for staying "longer at the mill . . . than it was thought I ought to have done." But Washington seizes control of time by making it speed up and slow down: after a lengthy account of "two long hours," he skims over "five long years" in a mere phrase. And while Washington must make a swampy cave his home, the novella reverses the dynamic of confined space for slaves. Listwell—the white traveler—is trapped in a "hiding-place," and as Washington departs, Listwell remains "in motionless silence . . . fastened to the spot." Only upon declaring himself an "abolitionist" does Listwell recover his freedom of movement. Then, as in his other

Fig. 2. Frederick Douglass, frontispiece image to *My Bondage and My Freedom*, 1855. Courtesy of the Library of Congress, Prints and Photographs Division.

works, Douglass fuses time and space into the space of history. The tavern's space is under attack from "time and dissipation," its stables no longer a "comfortable shelter" for the "noblest steeds." Instead, however, it is a site of living history, surrounded by gossips who are as "good as the newspaper for the events of the day." The tavern's "history . . . is folded in their lips," and as folk historians they are "equal to the guides at Dryburgh Abbey."[26]

In contrast to the tavern's space of living history, Douglass presents the erasures of American historical memory: this time the absence of Washington from the "American annals." Taking up the particular codings of 1776 again, Douglass explains that "a man who loved liberty as well as did Patrick Henry—who deserved it as much as Thomas Jefferson—and who fought for it with a valor as high, and arm as strong, and against odds as great, as he who led all the armies for freedom and independence, lives now only in the chattel records of his native State." Here he creates a countermemory, making abolitionism the Revolution's legacy. But he also critiques those "annals," the erasures of which mean that "[g]limpses of [Washington] are all that can now be presented . . . a few transient incidents." Washington is visible by a "quivering flash of angry lightning," before disappearing, "covered with mystery . . . enveloped in darkness."[27]

Douglass continues this theme of partial history—what he terms "marks, traces, possibles, and probabilities"—throughout his novella. From his hiding place Listwell can only see Washington in brief glimpses, raising his head periodically to see "the sorrow-smitten slave," and during the slave revolt, Grant can only see "by the quick flashes of lightning that darted occasionally from the angry sky." Beyond critique, however, Douglass embraces these glimpses as an alternate, if fragmentary, history. From the trace of sorrow that lingers on a brow in the novella's first epigraph, to the "ineffaceable marks on the tavern" and the traces of Washington himself that are "daguerreotyped" on Listwell's "memory," Douglass gathers the "marks" and "traces" of a partially erased story. The traces of undocumented voices and folk history also emerge as rumors, hints, overheard snippets, and circulating stories in Douglass's historical romance. Washington eavesdrops on one man, and finds this private prayer to be "the most fervent, earnest, and solemn" he has ever heard. Listwell eavesdrops on Washington, and then on the men in the tavern: from a "private room" he hears "important hints." For both Washington and Listwell, the best stories exist beyond the space of public declaration.[28]

Making the archive's absences reveal as much as its selective inclusions, Douglass had adapted what was known about the *Creole* affair and endowed Madison Washington with a past. He had confronted the possibility that black people might be expunged from the official historical annals altogether and challenged the denial of personal history to the American slave. In the face of historical erasure, Douglass had written a different story in the spaces left.

HARRIET JACOBS'S LOOPHOLE

Along with Douglass, Jacobs gave literary abolitionism its most extensive hole story. *Incidents in the Life of a Slave Girl* has at its center a tiny garret space, measuring nine by seven feet, and three feet at its highest part. Jacobs hid in this space above her grandmother's house in Edenton, North Carolina, for seven years after escaping from her master in 1835. She fled North in 1842, and her freedom was purchased ten years later. She went on to work with abolitionists and early feminists, and to found a free school for blacks in Alexandria, Virginia. Now, writing her 1861 narrative as Linda Brent, she calls the garret space a "loophole of retreat."[29]

While a real site of confinement, this loophole becomes a metaphor for the slave's civic space—slavery's social death literalized. Slavery is a "living death," just as the garret is a "living grave" that makes Jacobs seem a specter to her friend Fanny: "Linda, can this be *you?* Or is it your ghost?" Slavery involves being beyond "the pale of human beings," makes the South a place where "the shadows are too dense for light to penetrate," where life is mere "stagnation," just as the garret is a "dismal hole." Slavery is a "cage of obscene birds," a "black pit," a "pit of abominations," and slaves live in the "house of bondage," each "tortured in his separate hell," just as Jacobs's resistance is a "plunge into the abyss." Others made the same connection. Noting Jacob's garret, Joshua Coffin, a member of the American Anti-Slavery Society, wrote to Child about the "edifice of slavery": "she was hidden for 7 years! in a small upper room of a house . . . The Vigilance Committee of this city are doing a fine business in weakening & delapidating the edifice of slavery. Success to them."[30]

If a literalization of the slave's social grave and their confined place within America's "house of bondage," the loophole is also a spatialization of time. To achieve this, Jacobs fashions the garret as a site where time blends with space. For example, she turns the hole's darkness into a sense of uncertain time: "I shall get out of this dark hole some time or other," writes Jacobs, adding that it sometimes appeared "as if ages had rolled away since I entered upon that gloomy, monotonous existence" and that the loophole's space disrupts time's passage ("Morning came. I knew it only by the noises I heard; for in my small den day and night were all the same"). Time is further spatialized because she juxtaposes her wait in the loophole, caught in an ellipsis between the states of slavery and freedom, with descriptions of temporal suspension: the "period of suspense" while waiting to know if she will be a slave, a later moment when the "suspense was dreadful" as she waited for "the truth" about her children's fate, an incident where she is "motionless as a statue," the possibility that Mr. Sands might "indefinitely postpone the promise he had made to give [William] his freedom." The loophole's space of suspension even echoes the liminal moments of night and day: slavery means "the very dawn of life is darkened by these shadows," and the slaves hope that as New Year arrives, "they might die before the day dawns."[31]

In fact, Jacobs repeatedly spatializes time throughout the narrative. Before entering the loophole, she feels one stage of life ending as she closes a gate: "With what feelings did I now close that little gate, which I used to open with such an eager hand in my childhood!" Later, while in another confined space, Jacobs's son makes time physical again—scratching a "mark for every day I have been here." Jacobs continued this temporal spatialization beyond her narrative, observing in a letter of 1867: "I am sitting under the old roof twelve feet from the spot where I suffered . . . there is no more need of a hiding place to conceal slave Mothers . . . the change is so great I can hardly take it all in . . . I was born here." Leaving a gap before the phrase that announces her own living time, Jacobs again makes the state of nonexistence (this time before birth, rather than life as a nonperson in slavery) into a textual hole that recalls her old "hiding place." Elsewhere in her letters she continued to use blanks rather than punctuation.[32]

Jacobs's retreat into time itself—by entering the loophole—is her greatest victory in the time wars that rage throughout her narrative. A clocked time binds the slaves: they must serve meals at an "exact time," experience the regularity of weighing provisions "three times a day," fear the "appointed hour" when their fate for the coming year is announced and the "daily . . . hourly occurrence" of slave children sold away from their mothers, follow instructions to be ready "to extinguish their pine knots before nine o'clock," and are punished for staying too "long . . . in the woods." Even the process of writing involved a battle with time: "I hope you will be able to read my unconnected scrawl—I have been interrupted and called away so often," observed Jacobs in a letter, adding in her preface to *Incidents* that she wrote "at irregular intervals, whenever I could snatch an hour from household duties."[33]

But, fighting back, the slaves conduct "midnight bakings" and hope to "hire our own time." They seize an "hour of singing and shouting" in an attempt to "sustain" themselves "through the dreary week," and hold onto "moments" that are "too precious to lose." Jacobs's brother refuses to beg his master's pardon, explaining: "I am waiting his time." And Jacobs imagines a different system of time, a "mystic clock," a time that is "counted by heart-throbs." Or, when asked by Dr. Flint to become his mistress, Jacobs responds with her own schedule: "I told him I was ready to give my answer now." (Flint is reluctant, replying that he "will not receive it now," and continues to impose a different clock—telling Jacobs's grandmother on another occasion: "I should like an answer tomorrow.") Then Jacobs wins the time war from her loophole. Sending letters to Flint, so that he sets out to look for her elsewhere three times, she dates them "ahead" and throws him into confusion.[34]

Jacobs's retreat into the loophole also enables her to seize control of time on a broader scale—time's movement into the future. Slavery means that slaves don't "know what a year may bring forth," that anything might "at any moment be wrenched away," that the future is uncertain: "Who knows what may happen?" Jacobs asks at one point. The only certainty is that there is "no prospect of being able to lead a better life." But in the loophole Jacobs ponders what she terms "the uncertain future." Returning to this phrase three times across fifty pages, she counters uncertainty with a chosen repetition. Equally, though her reassurance to William in chapter 2 that "brighter days will come by and by" is met with his belief that "we shall never be free," her friend Peter repeats the same words in chapter 25: "brighter days will come by and by," he tells Jacobs. On the level of the text, "brighter days" *have* "come by and by," appearing as promised and countering the impossibility of anticipating a future.[35]

Jacobs has spatalized time as the loophole, and entered that site to win the struggle over present and future time. And her act of temporal spatialization wins the struggle for *space* as well as time. This means physical space. Slaves are told by a minister to stay away from "the back streets . . . the bushes," not to "stop at the corners of the streets to talk, but go directly home, and let your master and mistress see that you have come." Jacobs fears that her son will be thrown into "a hole, as if you were a dog," and Flint seeks to control her through building a "lonely cottage" in a "secluded place, four miles away from the town." Even in the North she is banned from first-class train cars: "Colored people were allowed to ride in a filthy box, behind white people, at the south . . . It made me sad how the north aped the customs of slavery." As much as time, space is a necessary ingredient of freedom: observing that the "dream" of her life is "not yet realized," Jacobs locates this dream as one for space—"a home of my own."[36]

As with the battle over time, slaves fight back. While Mr. Litch is so effectually "screened" by his wealth that he is "called to no account for his crimes" against slaves, Jacobs's grandmother "screened herself in the crowd," and Jacobs is "screened behind a barrel" or put under the floor so that she "should hear what was going on." Or, though "constrained to listen" to Flint's proposal for the cottage, she decides that she will "never enter it," and later finds "a quiet nook, where no intruder was likely to penetrate" in order to teach a fellow slave to read. Then, in entering the loophole, Jacobs finally wins the battle for physical space. She inverts slavery's panopticon gaze, noting that "alone in my cell . . . no eye but God's could see me." Jacobs surveys the world from her "peeping-hole" and resists surveillance anticipating a moment in Philadelphia, where she sits at her window watching the "unknown tide of life." Equally important is her creation of a circular mail system from the garret space. Her letters to Flint lead him in circles, transforming the garret from a no-man's-land into a site of power.[37]

Yet the spatial battle is also waged beyond the level of physical space. Jacobs's garret is a literal and metaphorical space within the slave system, and she uses it to counter the erasure of *historical* space for slaves. Throughout, Jacobs is clear that slaves lack space in public history. One history needs to "tell quite a different story," and the "voices" of slaves are drowned out by the "thrilling voice of Jenny Lind in Metropolitan Hall" as well. Unless you visit the South as a "negro trader," Jacobs explains to her readers, "there will be . . . concealment." Slaves face the problem of people "making up stories about" them, and of one story about a runaway slave, Jacobs insists: "This whole story was false . . . She had never thought of such a thing as wishing to go back to slavery." As well, "whatever cruelties" are perpetrated simply pass "without comment," the letters on the grave of Jacobs's father are "nearly obliterated," Jacobs herself is threatened with death "if I was not as silent as the grave." Flint explicitly calls for amnesia. "Let the past be forgotten," he insists, and later repeats: "I wish the past could be forgotten." Equally complicit in this historical erasure are politicians. A senator tells Congress slavery is a "great moral, social, and political blessing," while, as Jacobs points out, the "secret memoirs of many members of Congress" would reveal "curious details" of their personal connections to slavery.[38]

This erasure of history means that the slave condition is not like the free, where history can be formally "handed down in the family, from generation to generation," explains Jacobs. Instead it is a "crime for a slave to tell who was the father of her child," and if a child has a black father, it is "sent where it is never seen by any who know its history."

Gaps in generations mean a grandmother can be "a mother to her orphan grandchildren"—"What tangled skeins are the genealogies of slavery!" observes Jacobs. Even beyond the family tree, history proceeds in the wrong order for slaves. Jacobs observes that the slave child will "become prematurely knowing" and one slave possibly begins disintegrating in the grave "before life was extinct."[39]

Jacobs sets out to counter these historical erasures and disorders, explaining in her preface that she wants to "convince the people of the Free States what Slavery really is," and in a letter that she will "write just what I have lived and witnessed myself." Historical erasure is hard to counter because memories are painful, useless, or interrupted. For example, while vivid ("that day seems but as yesterday, so well do I remember it," "How vividly does memory bring back that sad night!"), memory for Jacobs is painful. In a letter she describes her "painful rememberances" while beginning to write *Incidents*, and in the narrative itself she observes that telling her story was "painful for me." Many slaves still "shrink from the memory" of brutalities, she adds at another point, and she is "still pained by the retrospect." Of one incident she comments: "I would gladly forget if I could. The remembrance fills me with sorrow and shame." And, if not painful, slaves' memories are useless or interrupted: "we all know that the memory of a faithful slave does not avail much to save her children from the auction block," writes Jacobs, and later narrates a scene where her son is asked to "remember how mother looked" and is "interrupted" as he begins his description.[40]

Yet Jacobs does gain control of memory. While she opens the narrative by noting that she can only "try to think with less bitterness of . . . injustice," she closes it with a firm assertion of success in choosing her memories: "It has been painful to me, in many ways, to recall the dreary years I passed in bondage . . . Yet the retrospection is not altogether without solace; for with those gloomy recollections come tender memories of my good old grandmother." In between, she learns that her own act of writing brings with it an increased access to memory ("I had an opportunity to send a few lines home; and this brought up recollections"), and while writing her narrative she performed a "free" act of memory: in her appendix to *Incidents* Amy Post explains that "in talking with me, she wept so much, and seemed to suffer such mental agony, that I felt her story was too sacred to be drawn from her by inquisitive questions, and I left her free to tell as much, or as little, as she chose." Jacobs even becomes an embodiment of memory herself. Describing herself as a "ghost" and "spectre," she describes memory in the same terms ("the memory . . . haunted me," "[that] memory will haunt me").[41]

Then she enters the loophole, where time is spatialized and space itself is memory. "Uncomfortable as my situation was," writes Jacobs, "I had glimpses of things." The loophole is a space where the dead past comes alive—where she dreams "strange dreams of the dead and the living." It is also a space where the present enters history's narrative. She remembers in the garret "a chapter of wrongs and sufferings," a story of "how the poor old slave-mother had toiled," but also a story of "a poor, blighted young creature, shut up in a living grave for years." Slipping into a third-person voice to tell her own history, Jacobs moves that "blighted young creature" from history's "grave" into its living space. She repeats this third-person voice at another point during the garret sequence, calling herself a "helpless child" with "misery . . . brought upon her." And finally, the loophole is a space where a secret history is revealed. Jacobs sees a slave pass by, hears her secret mutterings, then learns "that woman's history." Or, on another occasion, she sees a slave "pursued by two men," and learns her history too.[42]

Jacobs gives further clues that the loophole is a site of memory. While living in the dark garret, she describes the past in the same terms: "My thoughts wandered through the dark past," or later the "great shadows from the mournful past." At one point she experiences "memories" while she has not "hooked the shutter," as though opening a real barrier can release a memory flood. Again spatializing remembrance, she describes "slipping through the trap-door" and entering "the room I used to occupy"—"how the memories crowded on me!" A parallel memory place is the slave's former church, for as she passes "the wreck of the old meeting house," she hears a voice of the past give instructions for her present and future: "I seemed to hear my father's voice coming from it, bidding me not to tarry till I reached freedom or the grave." A few pages later she translates her father's voice into the voice of protest history. Quoting Patrick Henry, she declares: "come what would, there should be no turning back. 'Give me liberty, or give me death,' was my motto." Or, in a small room within a white woman's house (where she takes refuge and waits for news of her children), she can tell yet another "different story": "A streak of moonlight was on the floor before me, and in the midst of it appeared the forms of my two children. They vanished; but I had seen them distinctly." Believing she witnesses an event that has already occurred to her children, Jacobs enters a site of memory.[43]

These transformations of confined, dark, or decaying space into usable sites of memory enable Jacobs to encounter and craft a counterhistory. Firstly, she appropriates the country's public history. Reading a newspaper by the light of a crack in the garret walls ("a piece of the

New York Herald"), she makes it "render" her "a service" by providing information of "streets and numbers." Then she turns the loophole into what she termed in a letter a "chrysalis," from which she and her different story might emerge. In its creative space, by the light of a crack in the walls, she reads books and creates her own "work" through sewing.[44]

Finally, and most notably, she remains in the South but sends a parallel self to freedom through her letters to Flint. Jacobs's loophole is here a literary space. She mixes slave narrative and sentimental novel, classic gothic and captivity narrative, then dwells in the space between and makes Flint a character in an epistolary novel. She appropriates the space of literary creation. But the letters to Flint, which explain that she is living in the North, are also a counterhistory. Beyond the fantastical counterhistory of one slave, which imagines "America . . . governed by a Queen, to whom the President was subordinate," Jacobs has found in her loophole a space of memory where she can write the ultimate "different story"—her own free papers.[45]

To examine the abolitionist literature of Jacobs and others for its spatialization of historical memory is therefore to respond to Liam Kennedy's charge that while "our common understanding of space is that it is simply there, intangible but given," we should instead consider space as an indicator of "embedded ideologies." For, in developing what Joseph Frank calls "spatial form," abolitionist writers affirmed that space is not "dead . . . undialectical," as Michel Foucault observes. As well, to examine the abolitionists' spatializations is to uncover the imaginative process by which they *overthrew* the confined space of America's civic and physical spheres and opened up spaces of agency instead. Literary abolitionists reimagined the no-place of America's margins as a space of resistance and freedom. Beyond the "negative utopia" was "a cultivation of alternative forms of life in the margins and cavities of the system."[46]

Finally, to uncover the abolitionist hole story is to reveal antebellum fusions of space and history that challenge Pierre Nora's famous formulations. Nora argues that *lieux de mémoire* have replaced *milieux de mémoire*. Whereas *milieux de mémoire* had provided "environments of memory," which were "positive, all-encompassing [and] explicative," *lieux de mémoire* offer mere "sites" of memory, which are "the ultimate embodiments of a commemorative consciousness." Memory is removed from its historical context, stripped of its living presence, and used for static commemoration. But abolitionist literature reveals a spatialized and "explicative" memory that "smoothes the transition from past to future [and] indicates what the future should retain from the past." In the abolitionists' different story was the ongoing presence of *milieux de mémoire;* a hole story that challenged America's swiss-cheese historical memory.

Notes

1. Harriet Jacobs, *Incidents in the Life of a Slave Girl. Written by Herself* (1861) (Chapel Hill: University of North Carolina Collection, 2003), 55; Jacobs, letter of 1852, in Jean Fagan Yellin, ed., *Incidents in the Life of a Slave Girl* (Cambridge: Harvard University Press, 2000), 232; Jacobs, *Incidents in the Life*, (1861), 114, 222.

2. Jacobs, *Incidents in the Life* (1861), 55; Jacobs, letter of 1852, in Yellin, *Incidents in the Life*, 232; Jacobs, *Incidents in the Life* (1861), 114, 222.

3. Jacobs, *Incidents in the Life* (1861), 114; Lydia Maria Child, "Introduction by the Editor," in Jacobs, *Incidents in the Life* (1861), 7–8.

4. Jacobs, *Incidents in the Life* (1861), 300; Jacobs, letter of 1853, in Yellin, *Incidents in the Life*, 235, my emphasis; Frederick Douglass, "What to the Slave is the Fourth of July?" (1852), in John Blassingame et al. eds., *The Frederick Douglass Papers, vol. 2* (New Haven: Yale University Press, 1987), 366. John Stauffer calls the abolitionists passionate outsiders: "They were passionate in their desire to reform America, and they were outsiders with regard to both their alienated status in society and the source of their values . . . Perhaps most important, they defined *themselves* as outsiders" (16). See *The Black Hearts of Men: Radical Abolitionists and the Transformation of Race* (Cambridge: Harvard University Press, 2002).

5. Frederick Douglass, *The Heroic Slave*, in *Autographs for Freedom* (Boston: John P. Jewett, 1853), 207, 192.

6. Walter Benjamin, *The Arcades Project*, "N 1, 9" (Cambridge: Harvard University Press, 1999), 458.

7. Frederick Douglass, "Pictures," holograph, n.d. [ca. late 1864], Frederick Douglass Papers, Library of Congress, unpaginated.

8. Houston Baker, "Richard Wright and the Dynamics of Place in Afro-American Literature," in Kenneth Kinnamon, ed., *New Essays on Native Son* (New York: Cambridge University Press, 1990), 85–116; John Michael Vlach, *Back of the Big House: The Architecture of Plantation Slavery* (Chapel Hill: University of North Carolina Press, 1993), 1, 5, 16.

9. Vlach, 16; bell hooks, "Homeplace, a Site of Resistance," in *Yearning: Race, Gender and Cultural Politics* (Boston: South End Press, 1990), 41–49; Vincent Harding, *There is a River: the Black Struggle for Freedom in America* (New York: Harcourt, 1981), 114; Eric Sundquist, *To Wake the Nations: Race in the Making of American Literature* (Cambridge: Belknap Press, 1993), 198.

10. Houston Baker, *Blues, Ideology and Afro-American Literature: A Vernacular Theory* (Chicago: University of Chicago Press, 1984), 202.

11. James W. C. Pennington, *The Fugitive Blacksmith* (London: Charles Gilpin, 1849), 44, 42, 3, 70, 72–73.

12. Harriet Beecher Stowe, *Uncle Tom's Cabin* (1852) (New York: Penguin, 1986), 597, 595, 564, 574, 566, 569, 566.

13. William Wells Brown, *The Black Man: His Antecedents, His Genius, and His Achievements* (1863) (New York: Johnson Reprint, 1968), 109–10.

14. William Wells Brown, *Clotel* (London: Partridge & Oakey, 1853), 224–25; Stowe, *Uncle Tom's Cabin*, 187; William Wells Brown, *The Narrative of William W. Brown* (1847; London: Charles Gilpin, 1849), 103.

15. Russ Castronovo, "Radical Configurations of History in the Era of American Slavery," *American Literature* 65, no. 3 (September 1993): 523–47. Castronovo cites Anthony Kemp's *The Estrangement of the Past* (1991), which uses the term "parenthesis" to "describe a temporal consciousness in which the immediate past stands as an abyss between the distant past and the present" (82–83).

16. Douglass, *The Heroic Slave*, 235.

17. Frederick Douglass, *Narrative of the Life of Frederick Douglass* (Boston: Anti-Slavery Office, 1845), 1, 29, 103; Frederick Douglass, *My Bondage and My Freedom* (New York: Miller, Orton & Mulligan, 1855), 328, 273.

18. Douglass, *My Bondage*, 51, 64, 44; Douglass, *Narrative*, 13.

19. Letter from Wendell Phillips, Esq., Boston, April 22, 1845, in Douglass, *Narrative*, xvi–xiii (xv); Douglass, *Narrative*, 60; Douglass, *My Bondage*, 101, 62, 64, 281.

20. Douglass, *My Bondage*, 177, 176, 301, 64, 62; Frederick Douglass, *The Life and Times of Frederick Douglass* (Hartford, CT: Park Publishing Co., 1881), 62, 78, 173, 27.

21. Douglass, *My Bondage*, 87; Douglass, *The Life and Times of Frederick Douglass* (Boston: De Wolfe & Fiske, 1892), 623.

22. Douglass, *My Bondage*, 361–62, 155, 60, 35, 127.

23. Ibid., 138–39.

24. Douglass, *My Bondage*, 132, 359; Douglass, *Narrative*, 102, 44, 43.

25. hooks, "Choosing the Margin as a Space of Radical Openness," in *Yearning*, 145–53; hooks, "What to the Slave," in *Yearning*, 388.

26. Douglass, *The Heroic Slave*, 195, 188, 178, 181–82, 206–8.

27. Douglass, *The Heroic Slave*, 175.

28. Ibid., 175, 176, 180, 236–37, 174, 206, 188, 197, 211.

29. Jacobs, *Incidents in the Life* (1861), 173.

30. Ibid., 82, 223, 238, 245, 58, 276, 224, 81, 6, 289, 58, 83; Joshua Coffin, letter of June 1842, in Patricia G. Holland and Milton Meltzer eds., *The Collected Correspondence of Lydia Maria Child, 1817–1880* (Millwood: Kraus Microfilm, 1980), 14:389, 4.

31. Jacobs, *Incidents in the Life* (1861), 198, 224, 173, 15, 165, 195, 206, 45, 26.

32. Ibid., 88, 181; Jacobs, letter of April 1867, in Yellin, *Incidents in the Life*, 249.

33. Jacobs, *Incidents in the Life* (1861), 22, 25, 27, 76, 75; Jacobs, letter of June 1857, in Yellin, *Incidents in the Life*, 242–43; Jacobs, 5.

34. Jacobs, *Incidents in the Life* (1861), 12, 19, 109, 212, 38, 40, 225, 128, 198, 194.

35. Ibid., 93, 58, 192, 117, 147, 177, 202, 19, 193.

36. Ibid., 106, 107, 118, 85, 82, 247–48, 302.

37. Ibid., 71, 37, 190, 67, 82, 112, 202, 175, 247.

38. Ibid., 278, 286, 81, 30, 68, 71, 138, 46, 127, 220, 185, 215.

39. Ibid., 20, 24, 81, 28, 121, 45, 76.

40. Ibid., 6; Jacobs, letter of 1853, in Yellin, *Incidents in the Life*, (1861), 236; Jacobs, *Incidents in the Life* (1861), 35–36; Jacobs, letter of 1852, in Yellin, *Incidents in the Life*, 232; Jacobs, *Incidents in the Life* (1861), 244, 46, 83, 15, 203.

41. Ibid., 16, 301, 132; Amy Post, "Appendix," October 30, 1859, in Jacobs, *Incidents in the Life*, 304–5; Jacobs, *Incidents in the Life*, 238, 140, 86.

42. Jacobs, *Incidents in the Life*, 184, 222, 223, 194, 184.

43. Jacobs, *Incidents in the Life* (1861), 202, 145, 190, 210, 138–39, 151, 164. Jacobs also summons protest history by referencing "Nat Turner's time" (138).

44. Ibid., 194, 177; Jacobs, letter of 1854, in Yellin, *Incidents in the Life*, 238.

45. Jacobs, *Incidents in the Life* (1861), 70.

46. Liam Kennedy, *Race and Urban Space in Contemporary American Culture* (Chicago: Fitzroy Dearborn Publishers, 2000), 8; Joseph Frank, *The Idea of Spatial Form*

(New Brunswick: Rutgers University Press, 1991); Michel Foucault, "Questions on Geography" (1976), in *Power/Knowledge: Selected Interviews and Other Writings, 1972–1977*, ed. Colin Gordon et al. (New York: Pantheon, 1980), 63–77, Lutz Niethammer, *Posthistoire: Has History Come To An End?* (New York: Verso, 1992), 4, 9.

Bibliography

Baker, Houston, Jr. Blues, Ideology and Afro-American Literature: A Vernacular Theory. Chicago: University of Chicago Press, 1984.

———. "Richard Wright and the Dynamics of Place in Afro-American Literature." In *New Essays on Native Son*. edited by Kenneth Kinnamon, 85–116. New York: Cambridge University Press, 1990.

Benjamin, Walter. *The Arcades Project*. Cambridge: Harvard University Press, 1999.

Brown, William Wells. *The Black Man: His Antecedents, His Genius, and His Achievements*. New York: Johnson Reprint, 1968.

———. *Clotel*. London: Partridge & Oakey, 1853.

——— *The Narrative of William W. Brown*. London: Charles Gilpin, 1849.

Castronovo, Russ. "Radical Configurations of History in the Era of American Slavery." *American Literature* 65, no. 3 (September 1993): 523–47.

Douglass, Frederick. "The Heroic Slave." In *Autographs for Freedom*. Boston: John P. Jewett and Company, 1853.

———. *The Life and Times of Frederick Douglass*. Hartford, CT: Park Publishing Co., 1881.

———. *The Life and Times of Frederick Douglass*. Boston: De Wolfe & Fiske, 1892.

———. *My Bondage and My Freedom*. New York: Miller, Orton & Mulligan, 1855.

———. *Narrative of the Life of Frederick Douglass*. Boston: Anti-Slavery Office, 1845.

———. "Pictures." Holograph, n.d. [ca. late 1864]. Frederick Douglass Papers, Library of Congress.

———. "What to the Slave is the Fourth of July?" In *The Frederick Douglass Papers Vol 2*, edited by John W. Blassingam, John R. McKivingan, and Peter P. Hinks. New Haven: Yale University Press, 1987.

Foucault, Michel. "Questions on Geography." In *Power/Knowledge: Selected Interviews and Other Writings, 1972–1977*, edited by Colin Gordon, 63–77. New York: Pantheon, 1980.

Frank, Joseph. *The Idea of Spatial Form*. New Brunswick, NJ: Rutgers University Press, 1991.

Harding, Vincent. *There is a River: the Black Struggle for Freedom in America*. New York: Harcourt, 1981.

Holland, Patricia G., and Milton Meltzer, eds. *The Collected Correspondence of Lydia Maria Child, 1817–1880*. Millwood: Kraus Microfilm, 1980.

hooks, bell. *Yearning: Race, Gender and Cultural Politics*. New York: Turnaround Press, 1991.

Jacobs, Harriet. *Incidents in the Life of a Slave Girl. Written by Herself*. Chapel Hill: University of North Carolina Collection, 2003.

Kennedy, Liam. *Race and Urban Space in Contemporary American Culture*. Chicago: Fitzroy Dearborn Publishers, 2000.

Niethammer, Lutz. *Posthistoire: Has History Come To an End?* New York: Verso, 1992.

Nora, Pierre. "Between Memory and History: Les Lieux de Mémoire." *Representations* 26 (1989): 7–24.

Nora, Pierre, and Lawrence Kritzman, eds. *Realms of Memory*. New York: Columbia University Press, 1996.

Pennington, James W. C. *The Fugitive Blacksmith*. London: Charles Gilpin, 1849.

Stauffer, John. *The Black Hearts of Men: Radical Abolitionists and the Transformation of Race*. Cambridge: Harvard University Press, 2002.

Stowe, Harriet Beecher. *Uncle Tom's Cabin*. New York: Penguin, 1986.

Sundquist, Eric. *To Wake the Nations: Race in the Making of American Literature*. Cambridge: Belknap Press, 1993.

Vlach, John Michael. *Back of the Big House: The Architecture of Plantation Slavery* Chapel Hill: University of North Carolina Press, 1993.

Yellin, Jean Fagan, ed. *Incidents in the Life of a Slave Girl*. Cambridge: Harvard University Press, 2000.

"Mirrors of hard, distorting glass": *Invisible Man* as Outsider Rhetoric
Ian Edwards

Perhaps the most crucial dilemma incumbent upon a cultural producer in the "margins" of society, is how she can critique or negotiate with the canonical discursive forms aligning her field, or with the hegemonic avatars of wider culture in general, without compromising her particular identity as marginalized subject. The African American novelist might therefore be said to be in a distinctly ambiguous position, relative to both the cultural mainstream and the literary traditions she inherits. Alongside its manifest heritage of white American and European literary antecedents, Ralph Ellison's *Invisible Man* also foregrounds several distinctly African American forms of expression—often, vernacular styles as opposed to strictly rhetorical modes—which serve to focalize Ellison's literary influences and imply a hybrid form of cultural production. The mythopoeia of Joyce and Eliot, the subterranean metaphor of Dostoevsky, and the left-existential aesthetic of Malraux thus dance cheek-by-jowl with African American folklore, urban slang, and religious idioms, underpinned by a melancholy blues tone and modulated by jazz cadences. Perhaps more notably, *Invisible Man* also interrogates fundamental precepts of the traditional rhetoric of U.S. society, such as "freedom" and "democracy." As such, in its virtuoso performance of these disparate voices, its profusion of rhetorical modes, and its nuanced portrayal of the dilemmas of African American subjectivity, *Invisible Man* is almost a definitive articulation of "Outsider Rhetoric" (a category which, incidentally, has helped to crystallize some of my own thinking on this text).

Though its prologue and epilogue both end on rhetorical notes ("what did I do, to be so black and blue?" and "who knows but that, on the lower frequencies, I speak for you?"), and it often has recourse to rhetorical gestures, *Invisible Man* embodies a degree of ambivalence toward rhetoric as traditionally conceived. Insofar as rhetoric might be seen, in the words of Rodolphe Gasché, as a totalizing gesture which "must perceive (its) object . . . as a singular or concrete object," with an "all-dominating motive of self-affirmation,"[1] we might oppose it to a notion of *style* that is "performative" in the sense used in Judith Butler's theories of gender. For Butler, gender identity is "citational" and is a "corporeal style, an *act* . . . where performative suggests a dramatic and contingent construction of meaning."[2] Just as the "parodic performances" outlined by Butler seek to "dramatize" the "contingency" of the gendered body, we might say that Ellison's combination of styles "cites" and recontextualizes a number of objects, undermining the putative fixity of the "singular" object addressed (and thereby essentialized?) by rhetoric. According to Fredric Jameson, the historical shift from rhetoric to style was constituted by the move away from "classical" forms of education, underlining the class-historical implications of the opposition between the two. They can, in his words, "be distinguished most usefully through the value and role they assign to the individual personality,"[3] implying that what is also at stake in the opposition between style and rhetoric is a conception of subjective agency, whereby agency is foregrounded in the use of style.

The contrast can be placed into further relief with an example from Ellison's own prose writing. In his essay "The Little Man at Chehaw Station," Ellison evokes a "light-skinned, blue-eyed Afro-American-featured individual" he beheld in New York, driving a Volkswagen Beetle "decked out with a gleaming Rolls-Royce radiator," clad in a combination of "English tailoring" and a "dashy dashiki" and exuding an air of "ultra-pukka-sahib haughtiness." His multi-cultural ensemble of "carefully stylized movements" and accessories is to Ellison a "clashing of styles" sounding "an integrative, vernacular note" that is intrinsically American, in its "compulsion to improvise on the given" and "willful juxtaposition of modes." Ellison's suggestion that this is a "freewheeling assault upon traditional forms of the Western Aesthetic"[4] may seem hyperbolic, but the analogue with his formal technique in *Invisible Man* —"improvising on the given" forms of Western literature—is particularly telling, and suggests a programmatic and strategic use of the pluralities of style within this text. At least apodictically, the congruence with Butler's idea of "parodic" gender performances is noteworthy here, as Ellison's "American Joker" similarly manipulates his bodily appearance with gestures that subvert essentialized notions of racial identity. The relationship of the "Joker" to the objects he employs is one which grants them no "concrete" qualities in themselves, but estranges them from their common cultural contexts and "performs" them in relation to one another at the same time as subverting their received meanings; my thesis in this paper is concerned with establishing a similar "performance" at work in *Invisible*

Man itself. The intention of this chapter is therefore to examine the dialogue between rhetoric and style as expressed in Ellison's work (particularly when read in concert with its predecessor, Richard Wright's *Native Son*) through the optic of cultural theory, a dialogue that is fundamental in maintaining a limited notion of creative agency for the subject within its culturally determinant contexts. Rhetoric, on the one hand, tends to totalize by means of objectifying, and can thereby serve to suppress difference, circumscribe audience response, and threaten the speaker's particular identity through its compromises with hegemonic discursive traditions. The uses of style, on the other hand and in Ellison's hands, imply an open-ended, dialogical statement of the expressive possibilities open to the outsider in fiction in general, and a "working-through" of the productive tensions implicit in the African American's position. As such I will be addressing Outsider Rhetoric in *Invisible Man* as a response, on two different if intimately related levels, to the various *discursive* and *subjective* problematics implicit in the marginalized agent's relations to hegemony.

Butler's work provides a compromise between a Foucauldean appreciation of the workings of power and the contingency of the psychic upon the social, and a psycho analytically informed grasp of the "psychic life of power." The delicate balancing act involved falls prey to neither a pessimistic pathos of the "constructed" nature of subjectivity, although its "constructedness" forms a significant limiting factor; nor, on other hand, does it espouse a voluntaristic, Marcusean utopia of the liberating effects of sexuality and the unconscious drives, although it should also be stressed that the psychoanalytic category of the "subject" and its excesses constitutes certain problems for the system of power, as much as the apparatuses of power pose problems for subjectivity. As the theory of gender performativity has been well documented I do not wish to rehearse her arguments at great length, but it is necessary to assert what I see as the key implications of Butler's work and the "transferability" of questions of feminine identity to questions of race, in order to establish the grounds of the arguments to follow. As Butler herself suggests, "race and gender should not be treated as interchangeable categories," and the fundamental question that arises with their juxtaposition in the context of performativity is "what happens to the theory when it tries to come to grips with race."[5] While it is necessary to delineate between racial and gendered stereotypes, it is difficult to do so without falling back on exactly the kind of essentialized notions through which hegemonic discourses grant them a false *a priori* status. Notwithstanding the differences in racial and gender identity in the border area between the biological and the cultural, it is at least plausible to suggest that both notions are *largely* constructed through discourse, and that the methods underpinning their construction can be similar or complementary. Bearing in mind that the subversive positions of the marginal figure often arise in response to the hegemonic fictions they seek to undermine, it would therefore seem pertinent to examine the ways in which these fictions constitute both limitations *and* potentialities for the praxis of marginalized subjects. Insofar as either gendered or racial norms subsist on false notions of "internal essences," it is possible to assert that similar practices exist whereby the "internal" nature of those fictions can be "externalized" and inverted.

Historically, blacks and females in the United States have both been disenfranchised, and also constrained by their status as units of exchange-value in the context of either slavery or domestic servitude. As, within the last century or so, socioeconomic changes have wrought a gradual (if limited) change in terms of black/female economic self-sufficiency, it might be suggested that their status has evolved to one of a combined exchange-value, and what Baudrillard terms a *sign-value*; normalized notions of "femininity" and "blackness" have therefore been as ubiquitous within culture in general, as the hegemonic white masculinity whose centered identity they serve to bolster. In a progressive sedimentation of historical discourses, the "essence" of black or female subjectivity has generally been expressed in monological terms that have naturalized them within the bounds of unquestioned assumptions of their bodily being. This process of naturalization has therefore been a means of perpetuating the very hierarchical structure it expresses, in the discursive embodiment of its hegemonic assumptions. In Butler's terms, the idea of performativity expresses a potential counterweight to these hierarchical fictions: "The view that gender is performative is sought to show that what we take to be an internal essence of gender is manufactured through a sustained set of acts, posited through the gendered stylization of the body."[6]

The "normative" practices which give rise to these unproblematized notions of femininity can therefore be challenged by "non-normative" practices which "call into question the stability of gender as a category of analysis."[7] A "gendered" act by a female such as the "butch dyke" pose brings a number of different conventions into dialogue. For Butler such an act is thereby utilizing the prescriptive injunctions that would seek to limit the subject *as the very grounds of her agency*, as the occasion to reiterate and transform gender norms into a gesture that subverts them, concurrently with an assertion of self-authorship. Accordingly, it is my intention in what follows to examine not merely what the theory of performativity implies for a reading of

Invisible Man, but to show also how the text anticipates and exemplifies the progressive implications of Butler's theory. As Butler implies, political practices intended to overturn gender stereotypes "will be conducted, in part, through contesting the *grammar* in which gender is given";[8] as a similar practice, we can posit Ellison's mode of fiction as one which "contests the grammar in which race is given" and which "opens up the field of possibility for (race) without dictating which kinds of possibilities ought to be realized."[9]

Although the critical spat initiated by James Baldwin's essay "Everybody's Protest Novel" and Irving Howe's piece "Black Boys and Native Sons" has been well documented, it seems to me the relationship between Richard Wright and his immediate successors has yet to be satisfactorily articulated in terms of Outsider Rhetoric. The debate was largely couched in terms of the artist's "responsibility"; in Howe's terms, the responsibility for "anger" and protest; in Ellison's and Baldwin's, the imperative to "celebrate the diversity of American life" (Ellison) and the "full, complex ambiguity of the human" (Baldwin). While this contrast reveals very different approaches to the novel form on the part of the antagonists, their grounds of disagreement occlude some fault lines of difference between them, and also some of the instructive ways in which Ellison works *with* and recites the cultural ontology implicit in *Native Son*. By reading the texts together, along with other key texts in the theorization of racial subjectivity, we can express the formal progression of the African American novel as critique in a way that refuses the *falsely* Manichean opposition generally imputed to Wright and Ellison. If *Invisible Man* is partly constituted, as Ellison states in a 1980 introduction, by "certain *problems* arising out of the pluralistic literary tradition from which [he] sprung,"[10] and if it is posited as an *answer* to those problems, it follows that Ellison sees them as the productive grounds for his own literary agency, as catalysts for the aesthetic of *Invisible Man*.

Wright himself articulated some of the contradictions specific to his black literary heritage in his essays, and *Native Son* is likewise conceived in response to them. Both texts are thus formed along the lines of an "iteration" of their normative contexts á la Butler, with the initial difference between them being that Ellison inherits the problems bequeathed by Wright, as well as those addressed by him. In his "Blueprint for Negro Writing," Wright outlines one such problem as being the "humble" attitude of the "prim and decorous ambassadors" (Booker T. Washington?) who preceded him in black letters, "pleading with white America for justice."[11] In its "servility" and "curtsying" to "prove" that the Negro was "human," Wright implies that the black writing which preceded him sought to "prove" a fact which should have been taken as a given, and thus foreclosed more powerful concrete demands for social change which might improve the condition of the black community. Three years later, after the publication of his collection of short stories *Uncle Tom's Children*, Wright identified a further problem as arising from his own work. Though the volume contained some of the most lacerating "protest" fiction of its time, Wright concludes in "How 'Bigger' was Born" that he made "an awfully naïve mistake," in that he had "written a book which even banker's daughters could read and weep over and feel good about." As such, he "swore" that his next book would be "so hard and deep that they would have to face it without the consolation of tears."[12] Insofar as black literature has the potential to interpellate a white audience, Wright sees that *Uncle Tom's Children* allows this relationship to subsist on the level of an emotive empathy with his embattled protagonists; a degree of consolatory rectitude is thereby supplied, which might allow the reader to elide their own participation in a racially oppressive society. As an ideological strategy at the level of content, *Native Son* therefore enacts its protagonist's subjectivity, his ignorance and the brutality of his actions, as the ultimate apogee of his status as Outsider in society. Further, the Naturalist form and emphasis on environmental conditioning, along with Wright's exposure of the socio-economic factors enveloping Bigger, returns a critique on a *systemic* level which indicts society as a whole in a way that is denied to the more limited purview of *Uncle Tom's Children*. The "dehumanizing" effects of the racial bar in America was thus given one of its most extreme and challenging expressions within U.S. literature, and though this in itself tended to bequeath further problems for black writing, on an interventional level Wright's stance was particularly trenchant.

In his eponymous text on the subject, Aristotle defines rhetoric as "the faculty of observing in any given case the available means of persuasion," and when "dealing with a popular audience," where the "scientific" knowledge necessary is lacking, it transpires as "the art of producing a semblance of demonstration where scientific demonstration is not possible."[13] Insofar as either the basis for wielding scientific knowledge, or the necessary social *platform* to persuade, have generally been denied to most African American citizens (and certainly were at the time of *Invisible Man*), we might assume that rhetoric as traditionally conceived has little relation to the black literary context out of which Ellison arose. A distinction should be introduced, however, between rhetoric's status as a form of persuasion or "performative" speech, and what Paul de Man (perhaps the limit-theorist of the rhetorical dimensions of literature) might term its status as a "system of tropes," its necessarily referential/metaphorical dimension. De Man's theory should not be read, though it is tempting, as implying that literature's efficacy is defined solely in terms of its tropological dimension. The performative sense of the literary act remains, indeed in Gasché's words "what de Man names 'rhetoric' . . . is precisely *the gap that becomes apparent between rhetoric as system of tropes and rhetoric as persuasion*."[14] While de Man considers rhetorical properties to be intrinsic to language itself and prior to the positioning of any particular "speaker," Kenneth Burke's position relates this "essential function" to a practical one that is "wholly realistic," namely the "use of language as a symbolic means of inducing cooperation in beings that by nature respond to symbols."[15] Rhetoric in Burke's view therefore necessarily implies a relationship between speaker and audience, in a *dialogical* model that nonetheless recognizes rhetoric's concern with "the manipulation of men's beliefs for political ends."[16] The particular set of symbols manipulated for this purpose, while grounded in the "magical" ability of language to sublimate its referential status as a set of symbols toward "spiritual" identifications within the audience that transcend the referent, must also therefore direct these spiritual identifications toward material ends. If rhetoric in its traditional sense, then, implies an instrumental relationship between speaker and audience, the fact of the inherently persuasive nature of language—of the "material" dimension of the signifier which must extend "tropologically" beyond its status as referent—would seem to be secondary to the particular ends toward which the speaker "intends" his audience.

Within the space created between these two, asymmetrical but complementary notions of rhetoric, the comparison between *Invisible Man* and *Native Son* provides an initial insight into the uses and pitfalls of rhetorical modes for the Outsider. In the cloying final section of the latter text, Wright uses the courtroom scene to ventriloquize his Marxian, determinist view of Bigger's fate, via the figure of the lawyer, Max. This recourse to unreconstructed European philosophical forms and a Jewish protagonist to articulate the text's fundamental polemical point, highlights the implicit ignorance of Bigger and the fact that, as Ellison suggests, Wright refused to credit his protagonist with the imagination or ability to understand and express his situation. Wright therefore returned a largely Eurocentric answer to the problems of the African American situation in a way that can hardly have had liberating possibilities for black consciousness. Further, and perhaps more pertinently, the lengthy courtroom speeches serve to suggest a third modality of rhetoric to add to the two above; namely, what we might term "mere" rhetoric, of the type that gets decried as "windy" in parliamentary debate, the dogmatic naturalization of discursive form and cultural content to the point of cliché. The location of the text's climactic scene within the courtroom suggests not only a juridical-legal stamp on Bigger's fate, but also Wright's desire to appropriate the gravitas and argumentative forms of extrafictional modes in order to reinforce his text's didactic stance. As such, the novel form ultimately assumes a position within, and as a subsidiary to, the "progressive ideas of the day" (i.e., Marxism) that Wright asserts should be "approached contemporaneously . . . (as) the primary prerequisite for collective work."[17] Thus, despite his proviso that "if the sensory vehicle of imaginative writing is required to carry too great a load of didactic material, the artistic sense is submerged,"[18] Wright's approach to critique in *Native Son* tends to obfuscate its literary specificity in order to conform to preconceived ideological-discursive strictures.

By way of contrast, an initial indication of what "Outsider Rhetoric" might mean in Ellison's context is that some of the key points in *Invisible Man*, and those which most strongly suggest a democratic reading of Outsider Rhetoric, are those at which the two "levels" of rhetoric identified already *intersect* in the "gaps" as implied above; where the "system of tropes" is commingled with a means of emotional, ethical, or moral persuasion, and the intimate interplay between them implies the chiasmatic structure of each modality and their codependency. In his framing narratives, Ellison's protagonist thus both alludes to and plays with "great American traditions" and his sly, subtle ironies carefully distance him from those traditions, just as his subterranean positioning places him physically at the margins of society. As opposed to the didactic compulsion evident in *Native Son*, and its centripetal tendency to envelop and subsume the discourses of the fictional and marginal, *Invisible Man* resists easy assimilation within its contemporary contexts.[19] Ellison's protagonist largely adopts the mode of suggestion or allusion rather than prescription, and more importantly at several points alludes directly to possible audience responses, keeping "open" the relationship that is very much circumscribed by *Native Son*'s dogmatic fervor. Put one way, if the artist on the margins is destined to enter the cultural mainstream on at least some level, thereby threatening her subversive particularity, Outsider Rhetoric provides a means of negotiating with the cultural "center" to which she is marginal without necessarily accepting its discursive strictures wholesale. Outsider Rhetoric might then be seen as mobilizing the particular (vernacular) traits of the outsider's position, and *re*-mobilizing the universal (hegemonic) signifiers of cultural canonicity.

As will be made clear in the course of this essay, it is crucial that a democratic Outsider Rhetoric privileges neither the "tropological" (in which case it merely embodies the "flash and filigree of the artist's craft"[20]), nor the "persuasive" (where the gap separating persuasion, and dogmatism or demagoguery is, as *Native Son* shows, ever slim) mode of rhetoric. If hegemony tends to work by means of monological fictions, *Invisible Man* demonstrates the counter-hegemonic implications of maintaining a more fluid notion of narrative. This open or dialogical notion of marginal creativity might be contrasted with *Native Son* at the level of discourse *and* subjectivity; the naturalist aesthetic espoused by Wright embodies a "closed" formal structure of fiction, and therefore enacts the essentialism of Bigger and black subjectivity in relationship to his environment, in the kind of functionalist *deus ex machina* which would hardly disgrace the most reductive theoretical excesses of Stalinist-era Soviet theoreticians. Wright's eventual estrangement from Marxist dogma proved in practice what his novel implied in theory, namely that the universalizing bent apparent in *Native Son* returns exactly the kind of monolithic discourse which perpetuated African American marginalization. We might note in this context Kenneth Burke's commentary on naturalist fiction, whereby the "scene-agent ratio" entailed in the scene "indicted" has a "brutalizing" effect "upon the people who are indigenous to this scene," and "in his humanitarian zeal . . . the novelist portrays characters which . . . are not worth saving."[21] The key problem engendered for Wright's literary successors was therefore how they might produce a critique of U.S. society which does *not* succumb to his fatalistic implications, and which maintains its literary specificity and the particularity of its African American heritage in doing so. In its polyvalence, I will argue, *Invisible Man* challenges essentialized notions of black identity as well as espousing a wider purview for black fictional creativity, enacting a pluralist form which is implicitly counterhegemonic as a consequence.

Another central figure within African American letters, Fredrick Douglass, sheds further light on the relationships between black discourse and the white tradition, and the particular constraints they place upon black subjectivity. Notoriously, Douglass was told by his white abolitionist sponsors such as Garrison to "give them the facts, and leave the philosophy to us" (significantly, Ellison's protagonist is also warned by his Brotherhood mentor that he "was not hired to think"[22]). The slave narrative was generally "framed" by a paternalist white gesture to verify its authenticity, in which context the prologue and epilogue of *Invisible Man* should be seen as asserting the narrator's choice to frame his *own* discourse. Strict boundaries were established between "proper" speech and African American dialect, and the former slave himself supposedly given very little rhetorical leeway. Despite, or perhaps because of this, Douglass's *Narrative* is an interesting example of Outsider Rhetoric. Proving to be at least as adept in the "philosophy" of abolition as his interlocutor-benefactors, Douglass appropriates many key symbols and registers of the U.S. mainstream of his day, including the language of Christianity, the U.S. Constitution and Declaration of Independence, and the American Jeremiad. As is commonly suggested by critics, it is his eventual mastery of, and self-fashioning through language, which proves to be the catalyst for Douglass's rejection of and escape from slavery. His sense of humanity is affirmed through education, leading to his resolve to resist Covey's physical oppression and the eventual "glorious resurrection" of his battle with the "slave-breaker." The *Narrative* therefore dramatizes both the liberatory potential of education, and the transformational power of physical struggle á la Frantz Fanon ("At the level of individuals, violence is a cleansing force. It frees the native from his inferiority complex"[23]). Both *Native Son* and *Invisible Man* similarly imply the foundational nature of rebellious violence, although as will be demonstrated later they accord to it a very different status. As well as providing an early example of the potential of the Outsider as critic of U.S. society, Douglass is central to the narrator's development in *Invisible Man*. He is given a picture of Douglass by Brother Tarp at the same time as his colleague gives him the link of chain which symbolizes his escape from bondage; Douglass becomes both a symbol of the horrors of the African American past, and a self-reliant, vernacular model for the narrator to emulate as his ties with the Brotherhood become progressively problematized by their myopia on the race question.

Having challenged the myth of African American inferiority and ignorance in his public displays of eloquence, Douglass condenses the act of self-assertion and the uses of rhetoric by putting his particular autobiographical narrative into the service of the universal discourse of abolition. His rhetorical technique undermines the institution of slavery in the idioms of the American tradition, and is particularly well represented in the incendiary (and highly rhetorical) address "What to the Slave is the Fourth of July?"

> What, to the American slave, is *your* 4th of July? I answer: a day that reveals to him, more than all other days in the year, the gross injustice and cruelty to which he is the constant victim. To him, *your* celebration is a sham; *your* boasted liberty, an unholy license; *your* national greatness, swelling vanity; *your* sounds of rejoicing are empty and heartless; *your* denouncing of tyrants, brass fronted impudence; *your* shouts of liberty and equality, hollow mockery; *your* prayers and hymns, *your* sermons and thanksgivings, with all *your* religious parade, and solemnity, are, to him, mere bombast, fraud,

deception, impiety, and hypocrisy—a thin veil to cover up crimes which would disgrace a nation of savages.[24]

Douglass's series of citations and inversions, intensifications and deflations, accumulates a "critical mass" against the system of slavery by articulating its inherent contradictions, especially in the astonishing accretion of clauses in the final sentence; the passage alludes to the self-congratulatory rites of U.S. culture as a series of mendacious and inflated *speech acts* ("celebration . . . boast . . . sounds of rejoicing . . . denouncing . . . shouts . . . prayers and hymns, sermons and thanksgivings") which are insidiously inverted into their own opposites. Perhaps more pertinently, the insistent personal pronouns of the above passage serve to indict the reader herself on an individual level, above and beyond the wider system represented by her "shouts of liberty" and so on. The point would seem to arise that, as Outsider Rhetoric, a critical discourse from the margins must embody a certain series of attitudes toward the anchoring tropes of its audience, situating its narrative as an *interpellative* act which encompasses the readers *within* the "center" (or behind the "veil") that is addressed; in Douglass's case it enforces a degree of empathy or *recognition* within the reader which might thereafter be used to political effect. It is this strategy of bringing both the establishment and his audience to account, *at the level of subjectivity and upon the rhetorical grounds of their own professed morality*, which is pertinent to Ellison's approach to critique in *Invisible Man*; this is clearly evidenced in the epilogue where his narrator resolves to "affirm the principle on which the country was built and not the men who built it, or at least not the men who did the violence."[25] Outsider Rhetoric becomes in this context a responsibility to illuminate the chasms between the system's self-representation and its real effects. Hence in *Invisible Man* the continual stress on the fissure between truth and appearance, or as Dr. Bledsoe says "between the way things are and the way they should be," the "veiling" of reality which is complementary to the text's fundamental trope of "invisibility."

Further, and once again in contrast with the directives of Garrison, Douglass in the above address eschews a critique based on a prosaic, factual approach; "At a time like this, *scorching irony, not convincing argument, is needed*. I would . . . pour out a fiery stream of biting ridicule, blasting reproach, withering sarcasm, and stern rebuke."[26] We should therefore note in this context the contrast between the ascetic vehemence of *Native Son* and Ellison's enigmatic, challenging irony, indeed attempting to "undermine 'em with grins" as per the deathbed imprecation of his grandfather which resounds throughout the text. While Wright's almost visceral anger was clearly effective as a tool of protest, so too, apparently, was Harriet Beecher Stowe's sentimentality. There is a sense in which, as Frantz Fanon implies, "Fervor is the weapon of choice of the *impotent*";[27] the element of Wright's text most lauded by critics such as Irving Howe might therefore be seen as a politically limiting factor hardly less regressive than Stowe's white-matriarchal sympathies. If in Butler's words "no political revolution is possible without a radical shift in one's notion of the possible and real,"[28] Ellison *refuses* the "self-castrating" gesture of fervor of *Native Son*, which absolutizes "real" conditions, in favor of expressing their "possibilities"; we can therefore read its formal technique as a series of "certain kinds of practices that precede their explicit theorization, and which prompt a rethinking of our basic categories."[29]

Bearing in mind the relative scarcity of black fiction in the United States prior to Wright and Ellison, it is also suggestive to situate their critiques within various discourses on the nature of black subjectivity; they inherit not only a certain set of problems concerning black writing, but also those concerning African American consciousness. W. E. B. Dubois, and his famous allusion to the black's "double-consciousness," provides a suitable starting point here. In Dubois's view, double consciousness was both a debt and a payoff for African American subjectivity, dramatizing the cultural conflict of the black's position, but also (and crucially) endowing African Americans with a privileged insight—"gifted with second-sight"—into the nature of society. Dubois's use of optical metaphors is particularly fundamental in much of the literature that followed him, as is his reference to the "veil," which is also adopted by *Invisible Man*. Further, Dubois locates within the duality of black consciousness, while it provokes a "waste of double aims, this seeking to satisfy two unreconciled ideals," a pluralistic opportunity to "develop the traits and talents of the negro, not in opposition to or contempt for other races, but rather in large conformity to the greater ideals of the American Republic, in order that some day on American soil two world races may give each to each those characteristics both so sadly lack."[30]

Opposed to the accomodationist stance of Booker T. Washington, and similarly to the secessionist rhetoric of black nationalists such as Marcus Garvey, Dubois sought to define the ways in which the black subject could enter U.S. society in terms that recognized her equality, assuaging Washington's overweening humility and Garvey's isolationism. It is in the sense of stressing the creative potential of African Americans *within* the "greater ideals of the American Republic" that Dubois's discourse most notably anticipates Ellison's. The black subject's status as Outsider to the U.S. mainstream is thus figured as inimical to her potentialities *within* it, implying the extent to which the "center" *relies* on the marginal for its own self-fashioning in discourse, and the extent to which the *exclusion* of the marginal is constitutive of the center. Dubois's oracular tones, and his delicate ideological and rhetorical tap dancing between antagonistic positions within African American discourse, foreshadow the critical stance adopted by *Invisible Man*, not least in Ellison's desire to provide a spiritual uplift for the black community *alongside* an improvement in social conditions; indeed, as opposed to Washington, Dubois saw the kind of betterment provided by higher education as fundamental to any future move toward social equality.

Despite its rectifying function in providing the African American with a special viewpoint from which to analyze society, it would be obviously and hugely remiss to suggest that "double consciousness" has not been, at least, as much a curse as a blessing. In the words of James Baldwin, it is the fact that "one is absolutely forced to make perpetual qualifications and one's reactions are always canceling each other out . . . that has driven so many people mad."[31] At the risk of perpetuating an idealist fallacy which projects the individual categories of psychoanalysis onto wider cultural structures, it might still be suggestive to speak of a particular *abjection* of black identity within white hegemonic society, provided the complex is approached as a descriptive (and not a normative) process. Frantz Fanon asserts that "the fact of the juxtaposition of the white and black races has created a massive psycho-existential complex,"[32] and makes the strong statement that "only a psychoanalytical interpretation of the black problem can lay bare the anomalies of affect that are responsible for the structuring of the complex."[33] Notwithstanding this interpretative remit, Fanon is sure to stress that the "double-process" which constitutes the complex is "*primarily* economic," and only "subsequently, the internalization—or, better, epidermalization—of this inferiority."[34] Hegel's apocryphal Master/Slave dialectic is recast by Fanon in the light of the real historical conditions of slavery; most notably, he empties the relationship of its "reciprocity" within the Hegelian rendering (of the reciprocity of recognition between master and slave), on the basis that "what the master wants from the slave is not recognition, but work."[35] As the "Negro steeped in the inessentiality of slavery was set free by his master," was "acted upon" and "did not fight for his freedom,"[36] Fanon asserts that the recognition of himself "as independent consciousness" is denied to the black subject. Similarly, as "the slave turns toward the master" for the locus of his identifications and "abandons the object" he is "less independent than the Hegelian slave,"[37] denied the restituting relationship to the object of work given in the Hegelian scene.

Fanon's arguments in *Black Skin, White Masks* are doubly suggestive, in implicating the formative power of the Occidentalizing white gaze upon black subjectivity, and also in indicating the need for identification, not with the "master" or the ideals he represents, but with the context of cultural objects in which the black subject is situated. The theme of recognition/misrecognition is taken up by Ellison in a similar manner. His protagonist tropes on his status as "invisible," firstly implying the *intentionality* of the gazes which "refuse to see" him, with a "peculiar disposition . . . [(a)] construction of their *inner* eyes, those eyes with which they look through their physical eyes upon reality."[38] "Aware of his invisibility," the protagonist "lives rent-free in a building rented strictly to whites," tapping electricity from the mains in a "fight with Monopolized Light and Power," who think their "power" is being tapped somewhere "in the jungles of Harlem." The protagonist's "joke" upon his antagonists is, "of course, that I don't live in Harlem, but in a border area."[39] In topographical terms, Ellison's prologue establishes his protagonist as *submerged* beneath a location that is strictly the preserve of whites (the modernist novel?), in a "border area" as opposed to the ghetto ("pulp" fiction?) in which the dominant discourse would place him. With regard to Burke's "scene-agent ratio," it might be said that Wright in *Native Son* "points up his thesis by too narrow a concept of scene; and this restricting of the scene calls for a corresponding restriction upon personality."[40] Ellison, by way of contrast, plays on the irony of his underground "scene" being "a world of possibilities," with the relationship to his "scene" providing the very *grounds* of his agency. The linear narrative which follows serves in one sense to explain how he came to be "aware of his invisibility," how he came to be disabused of the misrecognitions which characterized his relations to white power and its black proxies.

If the African American's position is in the above arguments defined by a certain trauma in the relation to white hegemony, a further twist is apparent if we consider the importance of language. As psychoanalytic theorists like Lacan and Kristeva point out, there is a fundamental ambivalence at the root of all signification, as language arises in the infant only when her nascent psyche apprehends itself as distinct from the maternal object; the "cry" of speech is thus initially the expression of the measure of this traumatic revelation. If the primary relation of subjectivity to language is in order to "replace" an ineffably lost maternal imago, in such views the use of language inevitably refers back to and recapitulates that originary trauma of loss on an unconscious level.[41] This ambivalence is surely intensified in the particular historical context of the imposition of the English language upon African American subjectivity. The black writer seeking to criticize U.S. society is thus in the paradoxical position of having to do so "in his master's voice," so to say. Though Ellison rightly points to the wide contributions of black vernacular patterns to American-English, the "melting-pot" effect he describes is still the grounds of a particular problem for African American writers, implying the need to make the American-English language "their own." Henry Louis Gates Jr.'s notion of black vernacular "Signifyin(g)" is developed in concert with many key examples, including Ellison, and demonstrates how the vernacular produces "repetition with a difference"; this implicates the black tradition in a "post-structuralist" style of deconstruction before the (theoretical) fact, whereby the arbitrary linkage of signifiers is dramatized and put into "play," and their universal claims undermined. A general conclusion that might be suggested is that the very existence of a distinct black vernacular dialect harbors subversive implications for the dominant U.S. discourse. All or any of the distinctive facets of African American speech might serve as memes which infiltrate and in-mix with the hegemonic body, rewriting its grammar, syntax, lexicon, and idiom: "On this level the melting pot did indeed melt, creating such deceptive metamorphoses and blending of identities, values and life-styles that most American whites are culturally part Negro American without even realizing it."[42]

With the above in mind, the juxtaposition of so many literary and cultural contexts in *Invisible Man* perpetuates multiple resonances. It is possible for the sake of convenience to identify two main strands in the history of the U.S. novel up to Ellison; on the one hand, a "vernacular" tradition running from Twain to Hemingway; on the other, a more "metaphysical" tradition following Melville. *Invisible Man* is distinctive in displaying an obvious set of relations to both traditions, and indeed to several beyond them. On an interventional level, Ellison simply demonstrates enormous chutzpah in assimilating and retranslating these traditions, in one fell swoop raising the formal bar not merely for African American fiction but for the U.S. novel as a whole. An interesting contemporary example is Mailer's *The Naked and the Dead*, also positioned between the two different paradigms. Mailer's linear rendering of the "Social Novel" within a wartime context is formalized by the Dos Passean conceit of the "Time Machine" interchapters, setting out the protagonists" class-historical backgrounds in order to posit their collectively representative status. The dominant strand, however, posits an Ahab-esque irrational "will" in the figure of Croft, whose quest for self-transcendence becomes the focal point of the text's climax. The vernacular paradigm is thus subsumed within the metaphysical to the detriment of the former, implying that Mailer saw the problems of the individual as more compelling than those of the social collectivity, as is demonstrated by much of his subsequent writing. Ellison's technique, however, with its adherence to a jazz aesthetic, is more "democratic" in placing the contradictions of his literary inheritance into *dialogue*; in the jazz group, for Ellison there is an "art of individual assertion *within and against the group* . . . as a member of the collectivity and as a link in the chain of tradition."[43] The different modalities of narrative are placed on an equal footing in *Invisible Man*, and insofar as the narrator's journey entails an answer to the fundamental question of being, "Who am I?," it is posited on both philosophical and vernacular levels. Classical existential notions of "freedom" and "responsibility" are alluded to and developed, as is a Kierkegaardian "sickness unto death," but the narrator cannot even begin to answer them until he has reconnected with his vernacular roots, a process initially instigated by the distinctly less philosophical question, "WHO WAS BUCKEYE THE RABBIT?"

While he adopts several of the keynotes to the Melvillean symphonic style—not least, in *Invisible Man*'s considerable scope, as well as its probing of the metaphysical dimensions of the novel, and its democratic potential—Ellison's adherence to the vernacular is maintained at the level of form in several ways. In terms of his status as Outsider, the inclusion of various white paradigms within his text might place it in danger of the kind of accomodationist gesture that sanctifies hegemonic forms at the expense of marginalized ones. *Invisible Man* not only asserts its "right" to use the high-cultural material of Great Dead White Male writers, but the propriety of placing slang, African American folklore or jazz singers alongside them on an equal footing, and the possibility of their being *reinvented* through the black vernacular optic. Ellison's wide-ranging formal remit thus constitutes a self-empowering intervention of partial mastery over his literary antecedents, and a close examination of some of his iterative performances demonstrates the way Outsider Rhetoric can work with and upon the standards of cultural canonicity. One such canonical source, Dostoyevsky's *Notes From Underground*, presents a splenetic narrator who the text's "editor" assures us in an epigram is "a representative figure from a generation still surviving." This self-confessed antihero provides a model for Ellison's protagonist, and the latter provides illuminating differences at the levels of content and form. Dostoyevsky's protagonist is the epitome of misanthropy, who ends the text admitting he "missed life through decaying morally in a corner . . . losing the habit of living, and carefully cultivating my anger underground."[44] The narrator assumes a hectoring, interpellative tone and eventually affects to have "carried to a logical conclusion in my life what you yourselves did not dare take more than half-way." The Underground

Man's glimpse at the existential void anticipates its audiences" denial ("I know that you will be angry with me for saying this") that he "daren't speak for 'all of us!',," and in his refusal of "cowardice" and "self-deception," moreover, he suggests he has "turned out to be more alive than you." This outward projection of self-loathing promotes the conclusion that "we find it difficult to be human beings, men with real flesh and blood," and that we are "content" with this state of decorporealization to the extent that "soon we shall invent a method of being born from an idea."[45] While he ends saying he will "write no more," the narrative is framed by an epitaph to balance the earlier epigram: "This is not the end, however, of the "Notes" of this paradoxical writer. He could not help going on. But to us too it seems that this would be a good place to stop."

While Ellison's rendering of the underground man sometimes displays a similar degree of spleen, his knowing irony is its dominant mode. As opposed to the movement described by Dostoyevsky *away* from the corporeal, Ellison's narrator immediately alludes to his bodily being of "substance, of flesh and bone, fiber and liquids," *before* the ironic aside that he "might even be said to possess a mind." Further, while Dostoyevsky's text is capped by the closure of the editor's statement, implying that the narrator's compulsion to keep "going on" holds no further significance, Ellison's adoption of the form of the question and his orientation toward the future makes the text truly open-ended. In direct contrast to the Underground Man's belligerent insistence on "speaking for" his assumed audience at the same time as "cultivating his anger underground"—ultimately positing his own condition as symptomatic of man's alienation from society—*Invisible Man*'s representative stance comes in the suggestive mode of "*Who knows, but that . . . I speak for you?*" His representative status is based on the insinuation of inclusivity or commonality, echoing Burke's notion that "only those voices from without are effective *which can speak in the language of a voice within.*"[46] In Burke's view, rhetorical language is "inducement to action (or to attitude, attitude being an incipient act),"[47] whereby the speaker might use hortatory speech to induce identification between himself and his audience. In terms of the persuasive dimension of rhetoric, part of *Invisible Man*'s particular acuity lies in its ability to *imply* its ideological ends *without* enacting a scission between "without" and "within" the speaker/audience relationship, as with Dostoyevsky's narrator. Most notably, while the former is resolved to stay "underground," Ellison's narrator concludes *Invisible Man* with his resolve to *end* his "hibernation," which was in any case a "preparation for a more overt action," with implications to be discussed shortly.

If the relation to *Notes From Underground* demonstrates a more dialogical rendering of one of *Invisible Man*'s sources, the text's most notable play on Melville shows a particularly African American translation of canonicity. The "Whiteness of the Whale" chapter in *Moby Dick* is "signified upon" in Ellison's prologue, in the reefer-dream sequence that enacts the text, "The Blackness of Blackness" in a preacher's dialect and mode of address. Melville's chapter is characteristically rhetorical and elliptical, multiplying questions and qualifications to circle around its central theme. The "whiteness" addressed by the philosopher-manqué Ishmael is characterized by the heavy repetition of etherealized terms such as "mystical," "sublime," "divine," "ghastly" or "supernatural." This recourse to terms of reification reflects the way whiteness "shadows forth the heartless voids and immensities of the universe," and the Albino whale therefore symbolizes a "colorless, all-color of atheism from which we shrink."[48] Language itself might be represented here in its chiasmic structure, with the "ghastly" qualities of whiteness implying the abyss at the core of signification. As opposed to the ineffably referential nature of whiteness, and the "void" it "shadows forth," Ellison's "blackness" is representative more of *plenitude*, and is shown as a *self*-referencing or performative trope: "In the beginning . . . there was blackness . . . Now black is . . . an' black ain't . . . Black will git you . . . an' black won't . . . It do . . . an' it don't." Ellison opposes the ethereal presentation of Ishmael's whiteness to a more visceral language of the "bloody red sun," implying an originary blackness "in the beginning" that is thereafter veiled by the "colorless, all-color of atheism." Further, the dense allusiveness of Ishmael's speculations is replaced by the definite articles and active properties of black dialect, notably interspersed with the responses of the preacher's audience. A similar rewriting is undertaken to modulate another Melvillean source of *Invisible Man*, as the protean ghetto everyman Rhinehart represents a form of Melville's "Confidence Man." As opposed to the varying *rhetorical* modes of persuasion undertaken by the latter, with varying degrees of good and bad faith, Rhinehart's identity is "performed" by the outer *styling* of his ghetto uniform of hat and shades. *Invisible Man* seems to imply in this context that "persuasion" within society is undertaken on extraverbal as well as verbal levels, with the difference that physical styling performs its persuasion in a much more insidious and unquestioned manner.

The call-and-response pattern embodied in "The Blackness of Blackness" is fundamental to Ellison's democratic technique and to his protagonist's "rabble-rousing" speeches, and enacts a dialogical form in which, unlike that of *Native Son*, audience response is not circumscribed in advance by an ideological straitjacket. Most pertinently,

"The Blackness of Blackness" demonstrates a reversal of the notion that "white is right" which pervades the protagonist's psyche at the beginning. Being positioned between the *Bildungsroman* and the picaresque style of fiction, *Invisible Man* undercuts some of the bourgeois notions of self-development implicit in the *bildungs* with its implications of a morally relative universe (as implicit in the picaresque). The "education" of the protagonist is enacted in a negative sense, whereby the mythologies and mystifications surrounding his false consciousness are gradually rejected. The protagonist's initial belief that "white is right," suggested by the deranged veteran early in the text, serves as the "quilting point" or "master signifier" which knits together his misrecognition of hegemony.[49] Once this ruling trope is undone, *Invisible Man* then uses its linear progression to demonstrate the protagonist's moves *away* from other, related, hegemonic fictions, and it is instructive to consider both the scene in which the "veil" is removed for the protagonist, and the primary features of hegemony which are subsequently disavowed. After the accident in the Optic Paints factory ("If it's Optic White, it's the right white") the protagonist is ensconced in the factory hospital, where he undergoes electroshock therapy and hears the "waggish" racism of the doctors attending to him. Returning to consciousness, their questions such as "what is your name?" or "'what is your mother's name?" elicit no response. It is their random recourse to African American folklore that eventually catalyzes the protagonist's search for identity—"WHO WAS BUCKEYE THE RABBIT?'"—as well as his irreverent attitude toward his white interlocutors ("he was your mother's backdoor man, I thought"[50]). Thereafter, the orienting factors of the protagonist's being are derived from black vernacular sources, and the ameliorating aspects of his condition illuminated by black figures such as Mary Rambo, the "devil's son-in-law" Peter Wheatstraw, and Frederick Douglass; the "old, down home" approach of his first speech, though wildly successful in eliciting an audience response, incurs the disapproval of several "Brotherhood" colleagues due to its "backward and reactionary" nature. The speech ends with his declaration that he is becoming "more human," in distinct contrast with the pseudoscientific credos of the Brotherhood, and their inevitable break is catalyzed by the Brotherhood's refusal to acknowledge the particular problems of the "race issue." This contretemps is dramatized in the scene in which Brother Jack removes his glass eye, a scene heavily imbued with metaphors of sight, from which the protagonist reaches the conclusion that "he can't even see me." At this point the protagonist adopts his metaphor of "invisibility," and the climactic Harlem riot occasions his "descent" into the "world of possibilities" underground.

The linear progression of the narrator's vernacular education therefore dramatizes the move *away* from, firstly, Washingtonian notions of accommodation and gradualism (embodied by Dr. Bledsoe), and secondly, the "scientific" universalizing explanations of theory. Both stances are shown to obfuscate white hegemony, and Ellison's narrative rejects further implications that ensue. He states that a particular problem occupying him at the time of writing was the "problem of Black leadership," and *Invisible Man* dramatizes its contradictions. The protagonist's ambition to be a "leader of his people" is initially couched in the kind of self-aggrandizing tones repeated in Brother Jack's insistence that he is the "leader" of the people in Harlem. *Invisible Man*'s reversal of this trajectory of ambition implies that both are pervaded by the kind of "top-down" theory of political organization that cannot *but* result in the totalization and marginalization ultimately perpetuated by the Brotherhood upon "its" people in Harlem. Ellison replaces this false ethos of leadership with one of *cooperation;* his narrator marvels at the torching of a "deathtrap" tenement building: "I was seized with a sense of exaltation. They've done it, I thought. They organized it and carried it through alone; the decision their own and their own action. Capable of their own action . . ."[51] *Invisible Man* therefore valorizes spontaneous, "bottom-up" group praxis over-above centralized "leadership"; in answer to his "problem" of black leadership, the solution is posited as localized and pluralistic. The adoption of an *instrumental* relationship, on the part of the speaker *toward* his audience, implies in traditional rhetoric a hierarchical attitude and the perpetuation of hegemony; it is this assumption which is subverted and superseded in *Invisible Man*. Ellison replaces the hortatory and declamatory modes of rhetoric in favor of a politics of critical analogy, a pluralistic sense of "division" in place of the monolithic positions of hegemony.

In answer to the aesthetic problems alluded to already, the solution is equally pluralistic. Ellison's vernacular style arises as an expressive compromise between his high-modernist literary and African American folklore antecedents, mediating between them to produce a more inclusive dialogue, moderating modernism's elitism and folklore's antiquity. In *Invisible Man* the uses of style are posited at the level of *demonstration,* as opposed to the sense of "persuasion" implicit in rhetoric. While modernist style tended toward an elitist stance, often embodying an aesthetic devoid of class-political significance, naturalist fiction often overemphasized its pedagogical function. Ellison is clearly distrustful of demagoguery, but he also seeks a path more progressive than his modernist forebears. The attitude toward "tradition" as exemplified by T. S. Eliot's "Tradition and the Individual Talent" suggests a relationship between artist and tradition in purely formal-aesthetic terms. This relationship is opened out into a dialogue by *Invisible Man*, toward a conception of style *as* artistic agency, as defined by and in opposition to tradition. Similarly, Ellison's call-and-response style actually mediates *between* the dogmatic stance of *Native Son*'s "clenched militancy" (Howe) and the kind of "willed affirmation" Howe ascribes to *Invisible Man;* insofar as the text *has* an "affirmative" level, it is one which we might say involves an "optimism of the will," but also a "pessimism of the intellect." Ellison is therefore far from espousing the kind of naively voluntarist position ascribed to him by Howe. Cementing his status as something of a deconstructionist *avant la lettre*, the writerly intervention embodied by Ellison takes on the mode of the *double-negative affirmation*. His stance can be compared with that of Fanon, who says that "man is a *yes* that vibrates to cosmic harmonies";[52] "*Yes* to life. *Yes* to love. *Yes* to generosity."[53] But Fanon says that man is "*also* a *no. No* to scorn of man. *No* to degradation of man. *No* to exploitation of man. *No* to the butchery of what is most human in man: freedom."[54] Ellison's narrator puts it in remarkably similar terms:

> So it is that now I denounce and defend . . . I condemn and affirm, say no and say yes, say yes and say no. I denounce because *although implicated and partially responsible*, I have been hurt to the point of abysmal pain, hurt to the point of invisibility. And I defend because in spite of it all I find that I love . . . I *have* to love. I sell you no phony forgiveness . . . but too much of your life will be lost, its meaning lost, unless you approach it as much through love as through hate. *So I approach it through division*. So I denounce and I defend and I hate and I love.[55]

The return to a questioning of "responsibility" is central to the narrator's decision to emerge from his "hibernation"; in his prologue, he asserts that "responsibility rests on recognition," and of course the body narrative comes to apprise him of the *lack* of recognition which constitutes his state of "invisibility." In a Sartrean sense the protagonist "assumes his freedom" as a *consequence* of the willed refusal of recognition which constitutes his "invisibility" ("when I discover who I am, then I'll be free"[56]), in Fanon's terms realizing that his "duty" is one "of not renouncing his freedom through his choices."[57] His "hibernation" is thus "a *covert preparation for a more overt action*," before he assumes the responsibility to *reverse* his state of "invisibility" through an engaged artistic stance, suggesting (in typically equivocal fashion) that there is "a possibility even an invisible man has a socially responsible role to play."[58] Ellison's instantiation of the self-authoring existential figure progresses from the *performative* register of "I denounce and defend and I hate and I love" to the *suggestive* dimension of the final sentence, "*Who knows but that*, on the lower frequencies, I speak for you?" His mode of position taking thus promotes a "scene-agent ratio" which invites the "you" of the address to *assume* the comparison *as distinct from* the "scene" she is indigenous to, implying both the potentially marginal status of *any* U.S. subject, *and* their democratic potential as "agents."

Though *Invisible Man* displays a marked distrust towards "political" action, its frame narratives indicate a future direction toward a kind of vernacular guerilla-aesthetic. The ever-present possibility of violence in African American life is a concern shared by Wright, Ellison, and Baldwin. While Ellison's prose writing generally embodied a "reasonable" stance more palatable to the white establishment in the radicalized sixties, the Rabelaisian tones of the Harlem riot in *Invisible Man* imply a textual charge in excess of the measured urbanity of Ellison's prose. Compared with *Native Son* and the pathos of Bigger's individual rebellion (and *contra* Fanon), Ellison's portrayal of violence suggests that it can only be in any way redemptive in a *collective* context, if it arises in response to wrongs directed at the community as a whole. The spontaneous group uprising in *Invisible Man* demonstrates a level of humanity that cannot be circumscribed by power, and a subaltern violence that "boomerangs" back at a violent, oppressive society. Ellison's mode of Outsider Rhetoric thus articulates the disavowed or rejected portions of U.S. hegemonic fictions in order to lay bare their contradictions, holding up "mirrors of hard, distorting glass" to the audience to show the inverted relationship of African American subjectivity and U.S. "democracy." Insofar as the system cannot *but* produce "bad subjects," Ellison implies the "bad nigger" is a reverse-mirrored image of the wider system oppressing him. The metaphor of the "boomerang," which the protagonist initially uses to describe the trajectory of "contradiction" which is "how the world works,"[59] develops into a motif of Ellison's literary technique; having been "boomeranged" by circumstances which remove the "veil" from society, Ellison's protagonist says he "boomeranged a long way from the point in society to which I originally aspired,"[60] *becoming* himself the rebounding object of contradiction. *Invisible Man* equally becomes the "boomerang" aimed back at white America by its author, embracing the contradictions of his subjective and discursive position as the grounds for his subversive agency.

In terms of the next chain of research implicit in this trajectory, I would point to the example of the contemporary black writer Walter Mosley. Having established a sizable oeuvre of crime fiction based in the black ghettoes, Mosley has progressed to produce fiction with a genuine sociopolitical and ethical scope. In his protagonist Socrates Fortlow (see *Always Outnumbered, Always Outgunned* and *Walkin' the Dog*) Mosley represents the development of an ethical subjectivity in response to the problems of black urban life. A murderer released from prison after thirty-five years, Fortlow is portrayed as struggling under the daily pressures *not* to seek recourse to violence, and to make some sense of the problems that beset him. The climax of *Walkin' the Dog* is Fortlow's exposure of a racist, murderous police officer. Inspired by the self-styled "rebel" Lavant Hall, Socrates parades the facts of the officer's brutality in front of his police station, causing a riot (much like Ellison's Harlem riot) and eventually exposing the killer. The character of Hall is directly linked by the text to Ellison; he says of himself that he is "invisible like Ralph Ellison,"[61] spreading handmade posters advertising the iniquity of "Amerikka." Socrates, having in the course of the two novels become something of an ethical vigilante on an individual level, uses Hall's example to assert his indignance on a wider scale. The conclusion to his intervention is somewhat equivocal, however. In Fortlow's own words: "We had the whole city scared . . . but nothin' changed. No-one said, 'hey lets get together an' vote or strike or just get together and say somethin' true.' Me complainin' to some newspaper is like me tellin' the warden I don't like his jail."[62]

Combining a Wrightian emphasis on the dehumanizing factors of environment with Ellison's more celebratory and sympathetic mode, Mosley pulls few punches in his depiction of ghetto life, while evoking a constant (if underplayed) philosophical/ethical frame of reference (as indicated by the naming of his protagonist). In the novels, these issues are played out through the sumptuously restrained vernacular quality of Mosley's prose, which is entirely embedded in the rhythm of black street dialect and which places the sometime-urbane prose of Ellison at a distance; the vernacular is still, in this sense, a powerful tool for the expression of marginal subjectivity *contra* the system. As an intervention this essay is intended to outline and theorize modalities of counterhegemonic modes of literary agency, and perhaps, as an adjunct, to gesture toward marginal agency in general (hence Mosley's lesser concern for literary self-consciousness in favor of the portrayal, in Socrates, of an evolving ethical and oppositional subjecticity). Mosley rejects Ellison's focus on traditional mythemes such as "democracy" and "freedom," however; his mode of "responsibility" is posited at the level of opposing the system *as a concrete ensemble* (rather than Ellison's more abstract allusiveness). Due to the proliferation of the power of capital, and its ability to rhetoricize its inequities as owing to the imperatives of the profit margin, the problems addressed by Ellison are far from having receded from American society. Mosley's is, to be sure, a more combative worldview than that of Ellison, though he retains the utopian register of the latter, what Thomas Pynchon calls "a kindness instinct that survives extinction." Mosley seems to be in favor of more constructive and organized responses to repression than is shown in response to Socrates' intervention (or than is shown in Ellison's Harlem riot). His faith in the ties of community, the potential for dialogue and cooperation, and the enduring capacity of the human spirit for independence and freedom, are clear in the texts.

What is perhaps less clear, without recourse to Mosley's prose writings, is exactly what he denotes the primary problem to be, a problem that seems to be infinitesimally out of the grasp of Socrates. In his nonfiction *Workin' on the Chain Gang*, Mosley stresses the *systemic* problems posed to subjectivity in contemporary America: "Whites, blacks and all other groups face the same problems today."[63] Most notably, racial and gender differences are to Mosley subsumed within the differences instantiated by the inequality of wealth and opportunity in American society; "desiring comfort is not a race thing, a gender thing."[64] It is the particular basis of this cooperative imperative that is most strikingly asserted in Mosley's nonfiction; the emblematic "naming and shaming" of the police officer by Socrates Fortlow is transmuted into a "naming of the system" in *Workin' on the Chain Gang*. For, as suggested above, one of the key implications of *Invisible Man* is of the "*potentially marginal* status of *any* U.S. subject, *and* their democratic potential as agents" (or: the way all agents can be made Outsiders). Mosley's purview in *Workin' on the Chain Gang* is to address the nature of *what* it is exactly in American society that imposes this marginalization. His conclusion is clear from one particular chapter heading: "Defining the Great Enemy: the Margin of Profit," from which I append the following: "The verb, then, is *marginalize*. We are marginalized by the profit of capitalism. We are the footnotes to Citibank and the Mobil Oil Corporation and Chiquita Brands International. We are the edges that form the outline of the behemoth that tells us he is the only way."[65]

Mosley "signifies" upon the word "margin" to denote the way "profit" ineffably contributes toward "marginalization"; we might say, in the face of capital, all forms of agency are *made* "marginal." So, while Mosley suggests (with Ellison and *contra* the Brotherhood) that the "race question" is still key, he also gestures toward a coalitional politics established primarily on the basis of class and relation to capital. His ideal response to the problem of the profit margin is that of "speaking out, then by shouting out, and finally by action,"[66] circumventing a democratic process he feels to be fatally flawed by directing his response at the corporate structure that subtends it. Hence another "boomerang" is aimed at American (capitalist) culture, in this case positing opposition to the system *on the very grounds by which the system seeks to define us*. Once again, the idea is that the "marginal" position of the social agent provides the very grounds for her opposition to the system. Mosley's utopian gambit is that there is more that unites us, in the face of the "behemoth" of capital, than there is that divides us. The primary divides to be breached, then, are those *between* marginalized subjects in recognizing their grounds for common interest, and between marginalized subjects and the system that denies them opportunity. The means by which this can be achieved—"the only way out is to be crazy, to imagine the impossible and ridiculous"[67]—is set by Mosley in *Workin' on the Chain Gang* in the context of human creativity and invention: "In order to celebrate a new age we must create a new age. And creation is the hardest act of all."[68] Socrates, similarly, says that "you gotta dream it up. You got to make it up. And when you get it right, it'll be there."[69] As with Ellison, Mosley promotes a parallel between artistic agency and social protest, suggesting that oppositional forms of cultural production may contain the germs for oppositional forms of political practice. Despite the factors limiting black and ghetto agency, the "world of possibilities" implied in *Invisible Man* is not yet wholly circumscribed, as is indicated by Socrates' progress from convict, to tramp, to relative financial and social comfort. And, despite the absence of Wright's self-neutering stance of "fervor," Mosley implies, as Ellison does, a "responsibility" for black writers. This responsibility is, very much along the lines of *Invisible Man*, to portray the "possibilities" of black/ghetto existence and opposition to the system, every bit as much as to represent their limitations.

Notes

1. Rodolphe Gasché, *The Wild Card of Reading: On Paul de Man* (Cambridge: Harvard Univsersity, 1998), 48.
2. Judith Butler, *Gender Trouble* (London: Routledge 1999), 177, emphasis original.
3. Fredric Jameson, *Marxism and Form* (Princeton: Princeton University Press, 1971), 335.
4. Ralph Ellison, *Going to the Territory* (New York: Random House, 1987), 24.
5. Butler, *Gender Trouble*, xvi.
6. Ibid., xv.
7. Ibid., xi.
8. Ibid., xix.

9. Ibid., viii.
10. Ralph Ellison, *Invisible Man* (London: Penguin, 2001), xxxviii, emphasis added.
11. Richard Wright, 1937, collected in Winston Napier, ed., *African American Literary Theory* (New York: New York University, 2000), 45.
12. Ibid., 23.
13. Gasché, *The Wild Card of Reading*, 106.
14. Gasché, *The Wild Card of Reading*, 19, my emphasis.
15. Kenneth Burke, *A Grammar of Motives and a Rhetoric of Motives* (New York: Meridian, 1962), 567.
16. Ibid., 565.
17. Wright, collected in Napier, *African American Literary Theory*, 52.
18. ibid.
19. "Human existence, created as it is *in* many languages, presents two opposing tendencies. There is a "centrifugal" force dispersing us into an ever greater variety of "voices," outward into a seeming chaos ... And there are various "centripetal" forces preserving us from overwhelming fluidity and variety. The drive to create art works that have some kind of coherence—that is, formal unity—is obviously a 'centripetal' force ... but we are always tempted to follow that drive too far in the direction of imposing a monologic unity." Wayne Booth, introduction to *Problems of Dostoevsky's Poetics*, by Mikhail Bakhtin, trans. Caryl Emerson (Manchester: Manchester University, 1984). It is my contention that along similar lines, Wright's "centripetal" tendencies are "followed too far in the direction of a monologic unity" and that Ellison's dialogical technique acts as a corrective to this; perhaps not coincidentally, insofar as Dostoevsky, an acknowledged source for Ellison's style, performed the same kind of corrective in the context of Tolstoy's "monological" mode of fiction.
20. Ellison, *Going to the Territory*, 7.
21. Burke, *A Grammar of Motives and a Rhetoric of Motives*, 9.
22. Ellison, *Invisible Man*, 469.
23. Frantz Fanon, *The Wretched of the Earth*, trans. Constance Farrington (London: Penguin, 1990), 74.
24. Fredrick Douglass, collected in Paul Lauter, ed. *Heath Anthology of American Literature*, (Boston: Houghton Mifflin, 2002), 1889, emphasis added.
25. Ellison, *Invisible Man*, 574.
26. Douglass, "What, to the American Slave, is the 4th of July?," collected in Lauter, *Heath Anthology*.
27. Frantz Fanon, *Black Skin, White Masks*, C. L. Markman (London: MacGibbon and Lee, 1968), 11, emphasis added.
28. Butler, *Gender Trouble*, xxiii.
29. Ibid.
30. W. E. B. Dubois, *The Souls of Black Folk* with an introduction by Donald B. Gibson; and with notes by Monica M. Elbert (New York: Penguin, 1996), 16.
31. James Baldwin, *The Price of the Ticket* (London: Michael Joseph, 1985), 144.
32. Fanon, *Black Skin, White Masks*, 14.
33. Ibid., 12.
34. Ibid., 13, emphasis added.
35. Fanon, *Black Skin, White Masks*, 220.
36. Ibid., 219.
37. Ibid., 221.
38. Ellison, *Invisible Man*, 3, emphasis original.
39. Ibid., 5–6.
40. Burke, *A Grammar of Motives and a Rhetoric of Motives*, 9.

41. "Mourning for the Thing [the maternal object]—such a possibility comes out of transposing, beyond loss . . . the imprints of an interchange with the other articulated according to a certain order . . . Verbal sequences turn up only if a trans-position is substituted for a more or less symbiotic primal object . . . being a true reconstitution which retroactively gives form and meaning to the mirage of the primal Thing. . . . The negation of that fundamental loss opens up the realm of signs for us, but the mourning is often incomplete. It drives out negation and revives the memory of signs by drawing them out of their signifying neutrality. It loads them with affects, and this results in making them ambiguous, repetitive or simply alliterative." Julia Kristeva, *Black Sun: Depression and Melancholia*, trans. Leon S. Roudiez (New York: Columbia, 1989), 52.

42. Ellison, *Going to the Territory*, 108.

43. Ralph Ellison, *Shadow and Act* (New York: Random House, 1964), 234.

44. Fyodor Dostoyevsky, *Notes From Underground*, trans. Jessie Coulson (London: Penguin, 1972), 122.

45. Ibid., 123.

46. Burke, *A Grammar of Motives and a Rhetoric of Motives*, 563, emphasis added.

47. Ibid., 566.

48. Herman Melville, *Moby Dick* (London: Penguin, 1992), 204–13.

49. The "quilting point" is a Lacanian concept defined by Dylan Evans as "the fundamental attachment-points between the signifier and the signified where this slippage [between signifier and signified] is temporarily halted. A certain minimum number of these points are necessary for a person to be called normal, and when they are not established, or when they give way, the result is psychosis." Dylan Evans, *An Introductory Dictionary of Lacanian Psychoanalysis* (London: Routledge, 1996), 149. On a more ideological level, Slavoj Zizek defines the "master-signifier" as an "empty" signifier which is the focus of sociopolitical struggle in order to "fill in the master-signifier with a particular content" (in the case of *Invisible Man* the "empty" signifier "whiteness" is "filled in" with the discourse of white racial hegemony), i.e., the imposition of particular values upon a universal signifier. "White is right" is in this context the "fundamental attachment-point" that allows the protagonist to assume the "normality" of segregated U.S. society. Slavoj Zizek, *The Parallax View* (London: Verso, 2006), 37.

50. Ellison, *Invisible Man*, 242.

51. Ellison, *Invisible Man*, 548.

52. Fanon, *Black Skin, White Masks*, 10.

53. Ibid., 222.

54. Ibid.

55. Ellison, *Invisible Man*, 580, emphasis original/<u>emphasis added</u>.

56. Ibid., 243.

57. Fanon, *Black Skin, White Masks*, 229.

58. Ellison, *Invisible Man*, 581.

59. Ellison, *Invisible Man*, 6.

60. Ibid., 573.

61. Walter Mosley, Walter *Walkin' the Dog* (New York: Little, Brown, 1999), 153.

62. Mosley, *Walkin' the Dog*, 172.

63. Walter Mosley, *Workin' on the Chain Gang; Shaking off the Dead Hand of History* (New York: Ballantine Books, 2000), 52.

64. Ibid., 106.

65. Ibid., 83.

66. Ibid., 114.

67. Ibid., 102.
68. Ibid., 114.
69. Mosley, *Walkin' the Dog*, 259.

Bibliography

Baldwin, James. *The Price of the Ticket* London: Michael Joseph, 1985.
Burke, Kenneth. *A Grammar of Motives & A Rhetoric of Motives*. New York: Meridian, 1962.
Butler, Judith. *Bodies That Matter*. London: Routledge, 1993.
———. *Gender Trouble*. London: Routledge, 1999.
Dostoyevsky, Fyodor. *Notes From Underground*. Translated by Jessie Coulson. London: Penguin, 1972.
Douglass, Frederick. "What, to the Slave, is the Fourth of July" In *Heath Anthology of American Literature*, edited by Paul Lauter. Boston: Houghton Mifflin, 2002.
Ellison, Ralph. *Going to the Territory*. New York: Random House, 1987.
———. *Invisible Man*. London: Penguin, 2001.
———. *Shadow and Act*. New York: Random House, 1964.
Fanon, Frantz. *Black Skin, White Masks*. Translated by C.L. Markman. London: MacGibbon & Kee, 1968.
———. *The Wretched of the Earth*. Translated by Constance Farrington. London: Penguin, 1990.
Gasché, Rodolphe. *The Wild Card of Reading. On Paul de Man*. Cambridge: Harvard University Press, 1998.
Jameson, Fredric. *Marxism and Form*. Princeton: Princeton University Press, 1971.
Mosley, Walter. *Walkin' the Dog*. New York: Little, Brown, 1999.
———. *Workin' on the Chain Gang; Shaking off the Dead Hand of History*. New York: Ballantine Books, 2000.
Wright, Richard. "Blueprint for Negro Writing" (1937). In *African American Literary Theory*, edited by Winston Napier. New York: New York University Press, 2000.
———. *Native Son* London: Vintage, 2000.

Historical Moments, Historical Words: The Continuing Legacy of Malcolm X and Huey P. Newton in Common's Rap Music
Coretta Pittman

Racial and ethnic groups who have been marginalized often use rhetoric to rebel against and challenge oppressive conditions. For black Americans specifically, using "rhetoric, the faculty of observing in any given case the available means of persuasion,"[1] is one way they have historically contested institutional racism. Using oratory and song as their means to persuade, black American activist-rhetors demanded equality by delivering powerful sermons, speeches, songs, and raps to express individual and communal discontent with unfair democratic practices. Black activist-rhetors such as Frederick Douglass, Sojourner Truth, Marcus Garvey, Malcolm X, and Huey P. Newton used oratory to argue that marginality and racial oppression were not forms of domination black people were willing to deal with continuously. In our current society, rap artists also challenge lingering racism, sexism, and classicism aurally. Presently, Common, formerly known as Common Sense, is an emcee-activist-rhetor who uses rap music to argue for black empowerment.

This chapter focuses on Malcolm X's black nationalist rhetoric, Newton's Black Panther Party rhetoric (BPP), and Common's black consciousness rhetoric. I have chosen to examine sections from Malcolm X's speeches, Newton's BPP rhetoric, and Common's rap lyrics to historicize the relationship between the black liberation struggle of the 1960s and black consciousness in the 2000s. Each speech act utilized by Malcolm X, Newton, and Common essentially argues for the empowerment of the collective black population. That is to say, each activist-rhetor concentrates his rhetorical efforts to ensure that black Americans are empowered to lead a more economically, socially, and intellectually rewarding life. Understanding the dynamic relationship between oratory and enacting the principles and philosophies inherent within the speech acts and raps of men such as Malcolm X, Newton, and Common is of vital importance. Because rhetoric has been the guiding force that has helped the oppressed believe in the promise of equality, this examination of their words and the ideological connections between them brings to light that historical continuity for equality lives today in the artistic expression of rap music.

To lay out the historical trajectory between Malcolm X, Newton, and Common, I begin this chapter with an assessment of Malcolm X's contribution to the black liberation struggle of the 1960s. Where Malcolm X is unfortunately killed in 1965, I take up an examination of Newton and his BPP rhetoric in 1966. Finally, I turn to Common, a socially conscious rapper, who invokes, borrows from, and adapts Malcolm X's black nationalist rhetoric and the BPP rhetoric to "spit modern rhymes" that deal with historical and contemporary issues affecting black people in urban America. While my assessment notes the successes each activist-rhetor had and has on the collective psyches of black and white people in the twentieth and twenty-first century, this chapter will also address their rhetorical limits. Their limits as activist-rhetors are connected to racial problems but also to their rhetorics. Because debates about race are tied to America's complicated racial history and because blackness has fundamentally been seen as inferior, black activist-rhetors sometimes face hostile crowds inside and outside their own "home communities."[2] Thus, their bodies and their words define them as racial and rhetorical outsiders.

Outsider Status

In many ways, Malcolm X, Newton, and Common are outsiders within and outside their "home communities." As racial outsiders in the broader American society, Malcolm X's, Newton's, and Common's physical bodies are marked. More to the point, there is no denying the fact that as black men living in America, their black male bodies are "othered." Furthermore, as activist-rhetors fighting for the rights of black women and men, Malcolm X's black nationalist rhetoric and Newton's BPP rhetoric and the "rhetoric of the gun" often alienated them from the black middle class and white society generally. Common's sociopolitical infused rhymes have alienated him from mainstream rap fans. For example, Malcolm X's early separatist speeches, his attacks on white supremacy, and his condemnation of black Southern Christian leadership imposed additional outsider status onto his black body. Newton's BPP rhetoric, his rhetoric of the gun, his imprisonment, and his erratic behavior also left physical and ideological barriers between himself, the black middle class, and white society, thereby ensuring that an outsider status would inevitably occur. Common's early condemnation of gangsta rap, his sociopolitical commentaries, his rock-influenced rap, and his expositions on love have helped to contribute to his outsider status.

On the one hand, Malcolm X's marginalization and outsider status were self-imposed. His open and fervent condemnation of white supremacy made him an outsider in black and white communities. His critique of black Southern Christian leadership marginalized him as well. On the other hand, his outsider status was imposed on him. For example, black and white people unfamiliar and uncomfortable with his rhetoric were intimidated by his boldness. For instance, Malcolm boldly described white people as "blue eyed blond haired devils." He mocked famous black civil rights leaders by referring to them as Uncle Toms. Writing about Malcolm X's critique of Dr. Martin Luther King, Jr., John Lucaites and Celeste Condit write, "Malcolm X repeatedly scoffed at the civil rights movement represented by King. He nagged that all King and his people wanted was to be able to share a cup of coffee with a 'cracker.'"[3] His vociferous indictment of the failures of democracy caused many to turn away from his black nationalist rhetoric. Yet, in many ways, what Malcolm X said to black and white people in his speeches "was" true. Some members of white society had inflicted extreme psychological trauma on the black psyche. Black people had allowed white people's perception of their black bodies to destroy their self-esteem and thus their self-worth. When he blamed enslavement and Jim Crow for the emotional and economic ills affecting black people, he was not telling lies; he was merely "calling out" white people for the damage they had inflicted on the collective spirit of black people.

In some ways, Newton suffered a similar outsider status to Malcolm X. There was a self-imposed outsider status but there was also one that was imposed on him and the BPP members (though many would argue the BPP caused their own trouble). First, Newton's racial heritage, identity, and BPP rhetoric did not please the "establishment." The gun-toting, police-checking, "thug" mentality of Newton scared many people. Like Malcolm X's black nationalist rhetoric, the larger public misunderstood Newton's rhetoric and his strategies to help black urban communities. For instance, protecting the black community from police brutality was an important part of the BPP's platform. One of the ways Newton and party members sought to protect the black community was to arm themselves with guns. For many in black urban communities in the 1960s and 1970s, the police represented an intrusive and sometimes abusive presence in their communities. In order to be physically and psychologically on par with the police force,

Newton adopted the "gun" as the means to equalize the power differential between the white police force and black members in the BPP and the black community the police were patrolling. While his intentions to "police the police" may have been sincere, the long-term repercussions caused a great deal of consternation between the "state," the white public, and the black middle class. Thus, Newton's outsider status was further entrenched in the psyches of the American public and, more specifically, the federal government.

Although it is much easier to examine the rhetoric of Malcolm X and Newton and to study the historical legacy of their body of work, Common is an important contemporary and unique figure too. He is not connected to a religious or sociopolitical movement nor does it appear that he will create one in the near future. But, his eight albums and numerous interviews give us a great deal of information about his political, spiritual, cultural, and economic beliefs, many of which he has borrowed and adapted from the liberation struggle of the 1960s and 1970s. In fact, in his music one can hear the echoes of Malcolm X's black nationalist rhetoric and Newton's BPP philosophy. In effect, I would call Common a figurative son of Malcolm X and Newton. In some ways, like them, Common is an outsider.

In the hip-hop world, Common is considered a socially conscious rapper. This means that his music typically deals with sociopolitical or economic issues specific to the empowerment of the black community, particularly empowerment in urban communities. While supporters of "good" rap music, (although good rap music is relative) might consider it good to talk about real issues affecting the lives of American citizens, talk about politics does not do much to sell his records. In fact, while Common is a fantastic lyricist, his music is great, he is often outsold by people such as 50 Cent, T. I., Lil Wayne, Young Jeezy, and others who rarely if ever make political statements. Thus, to some inside and outside the rap community, he is a rhetorical and "commercial" outsider. His messages of black love, the strength of black women, and the critique of the status quo often places him at odds with the marketing of the hypermasculine black male. But, Common knows he is an outsider in the commercialized world of rap.

While all men are outsiders to a degree, I do not want to suggest that Malcolm X, Newton, and Common failed to have any influence in the broader society. Pre-Mecca Malcolm X forced America to reconcile its oppressive treatment of urban blacks. Post-Mecca Malcolm X internationalized race politics. Newton's BPP created programs for underprivileged black children and brought much needed attention to police brutality. In the face of the gross commercialization of rap music, Common's black consciousness rhetoric illustrates that artistic expression can be both edifying and entertaining. Additionally, Common's contribution to hip-hop and the broader American society demonstrates that black maleness is not always hypermasculine and hypersexual.

Meeting Malcolm X

In the following pages, I address the successes and limits of each activist-rhetor's words. I also link rhetorical theories between each figure when appropriate. Viewed as outlandish, loud, and racist, Malcolm X, unlike his contemporary King, spoke for a population of people most others wanted to dismiss. Released from jail in 1952, Malcolm X entered civil society poised to tackle the evils of white supremacy. Former hustler, pimp, and criminal, Malcolm X, formerly Malcolm Little, stunned the world with his depiction of white Americans as "blue-eyed pale-face devils." Under the tutelage of Elijah Muhammad, Malcolm X rose in the ranks of the Nation of Islam (NOI) to become its premier spokesperson from 1959 until his departure in 1963. The NOI was a religious organization focused on uplifting black people from "mental darkness." "The theology of the Nation of Islam created a mission of racial redemption for its followers primarily defined in terms of psychological rehabilitation from self-hatred and its corresponding anti-social behavior."[4] The NOI followers, particularly Malcolm X, exercised rigorous self-discipline and transformed other former criminals into more mature and focused people.

Before Malcolm X exited prison to become the premier spokesperson for the NOI, he sharpened his oratorical skills in jail and later became a masterful speaker and one of America's greatest social critics of the twentieth century. Often maligned for challenging white supremacy with what his opponents called black supremacy, Malcolm X openly condemned "the blue-eyed pale-faced devils" and their brand of vigilante "injustice." Americans wanted to know why Malcolm X spoke so boldly and loudly about black people's problems. Interestingly, America's racist practices helped to shape Malcolm X's fury. He was a product of his society, an outsider who was embittered by the racial oppression he suffered long before he ever went to prison. If his racial heritage and prison time made him an outsider before he joined the NOI, his racial identity and black nationalist speeches further entrenched his marginalized position in American society.

His rhetoric was considered by many on the conservative right as too inflammatory and by the liberal left as too radical. However, he transformed the way urban black Americans' problems were addressed publically. Urban blacks in the mid-twentieth century, largely ignored by Southern activists, came into the public's view when Malcolm X, spurred on by his own sense of alienation, led urbanites to understand their specific concerns as part of a larger discussion of rights talk. As a son of urban America, Malcolm X experienced hardships and disappointments like his fellow urban brothers and sisters. However, unlike them Malcolm X was bold, self-righteous, and unabashedly open. While pre-Mecca Malcolm X may have spread fear into and alienated the hearts and minds of some blacks and many whites, his black nationalist rhetoric did alter the way American society talked about urban blight and community despair in the 1950s and 1960s.

Malcolm X's radical rhetoric was situated between his experience in the North and his eyewitness account of urban decay. Like Malcolm X, many blacks believing in the hospitality in the North soon realized that something was terribly wrong with racial politics in Northern cities. James Cone in *Martin and Malcolm and America: A Dream or a Nightmare* observes that "the contrast between what blacks expected to find in the 'promised land' of the North and what they actually found there was so great that frustration and despair ensued, destroying much of their self-esteem and dignity."[5] Hence, Malcolm X's rhetoric sought to rebuild black Americans' self-worth in a climate that was hostile to the collective black population. Reiland Rabaka in "Malcolm X and Critical Theory: Philosophy, Radical Politics, and the African Americans Search for Social Justice," embraces his radical rhetoric. Rabaka writes:

> For Malcolm X (1992), political institutions and social organizations and movements were relevant only insofar as they were "radical". . . . the "present struggle," and ultimately the preeminent "struggle" for Malcolm X–and we could aver most freedom fighters throughout human history–has ever been the struggle for human rights. In exploring Malcolm's contributions to critical theory, it is important to keep in mind his commitment to radicalism, and Black radicalism in particular.[6]

Thus, Malcolm X's black nationalist rhetoric came to symbolize for both Cone and Rabaka a radical reformulation of ideas that would drastically alter black Americans' positions as second–class citizens. Malcolm X's radicalism was evident in his speech "The Ballot or the Bullet":

> No, I'm not an American. I'm one of the 22 million black people who are the victims of Americanism. One of the 22 million black people who are the victims of democracy, nothing but disguised hypocrisy. So, I'm not standing here speaking to you as an American, or a patriot, or a flag-

saluter, or a flag-waver–no, not I. I'm speaking as a victim of this American system. And I see America through the eyes of the victim. I don't see any American dream; I see an American nightmare.[7]

The American nightmare Malcolm X referred to was a direct response to the hypocrisy of American democracy, which he then turned into a vehement attack on the idealism of American citizenship. Such radical rethinking of American idealism led impoverished black Americans to rethink their positions as second–class citizens.

Malcolm X and Northern Racial Politics

In reality, Malcolm X was probably no different from other black men and women in America who had to bear witness to the failed promises of democracy. Unemployment, lack of educational opportunities, and poor housing was the code of the day. Malcolm X was talking about all the issues that affected working-class black people. The world had ignored far too long the plight of urban blacks. It was understood by many that urban cities provided black people economic opportunities that were denied to them in the agrarian South. Such assumptions were partly right. Jobs in Northern factories did give black people a chance to earn more money but the racial climate was no less harmful in the North than in the South. Some blacks did find employment; however, the jobs offered little upward mobility. Malcolm X knew that Northern racial politics had halted black Americans' ability to gain economic independence. Cone writes, "As Martin Luther King's dream was developed in the context of black people's fight against segregation in the South, Malcolm's nightmare was shaped in the context of their fight for dignity and respect in the North."[8] In one sense, Malcolm X spoke to and for Richard Wright's timely protagonist, Bigger Thomas.

Wright's 1940 novel, *Native Son*, set in south Chicago exemplified the harsh conditions poor inner city blacks experienced in America. Unable to fulfill his dream to become a pilot, Bigger Thomas is forced to find menial work in the home of a benevolent wealthy white couple. Bigger is apprehensive about his role as a black man working in their home. His skepticism is not without merit. He ultimately makes terrible decisions that send his life spiraling downward, which eventually leads to his imprisonment. He mistakenly kills the daughter of the wealthy couple. Given little choices educationally and economically, Bigger Thomas, like many other Bigger Thomases of the world, is left to fend for himself. Few public figures better understood the plight of black Americans than Malcolm X who, like Bigger Thomas, was given little opportunity to advance in America's urban cities. Malcolm X, upon telling his seventh grade teacher he wanted to be a lawyer was flippantly told, 'Malcolm, one of life's first needs is for us is to be realistic. . . . You've got to be realistic about being a nigger. A lawyer–that's no realistic goal for a nigger.'"[9] Even though Bigger Thomas is a fictional character, his characterization is a testament to the oftentimes cruel and harsh realities of ghetto life in the inner city, a life Malcolm X knew to be real for the majority of black people living in cities like Chicago, Cleveland, Detroit, and Philadelphia.

Malcolm Speaks: Public and Private Voice

Because Malcolm X's experiences taught him to despise racial oppression, he became a passionate opponent of American racism. Throughout his years as a leader inside and outside the NOI, Malcolm X was a spokesperson for black Americans, particularly poor black urbanites. His powerful oratory gave black people hope. His willingness to confront racism head-on taught them that they did not have to fear reprisals from white Americans. In fact, in an audacious speech Malcolm X proved how courageous he was as a NOI spokesperson. Instead of situating black Americans' hope for economic freedom within an integrated American society, Malcolm X argued that separation would work better for their sovereignty. In "The Chickens Come Home to Roost" speech, Malcolm X argued that black people needed a separate geographical space within the United States border. He remarked, "We want no integration with this wicked race that enslaved us. We want complete separation from this race of devils. But we should not be expected to leave America and go back to our homeland empty-handed. After four hundred years of slave labor, we have some back pay coming, a bill owed to us that must be collected."[10] Even though Malcolm X later revised his separatist ideas, many black people residing in the North and in the South did not have the courage to openly express rage at white people. They also did not have the courage to demand from the federal government separate land to move away from white people. Although many black people felt the same way as Malcolm X and members of the NOI, they did not dare express their feelings in a public forum. However, Malcolm X's outsider status as a racially, religiously, and rhetorically marginalized public figure allowed him to speak vehemently against racism. Malcolm X's speeches gave a public voice to black Americans' most private thoughts.

Black people have always used a private and public voice to survive in American society. The public voice masked their private pain and their private voice gave voice to their public shame. Because enslavement taught black people that language was so important, they recognized its potential for harm or liberation. In a postslavery America, it was not at all unusual, generally speaking, for black Americans' public voice to be subservient to white Americans' demands, that is, fail to openly rebuke white supremacy. However, in the 1950s and 1960s, Malcolm X gave black Americans' private voice a public expression. Malcolm X said to white racists what blacks said privately. Michael Eric Dyson explains part of Malcolm X's appeal. Dyson remarks, "It was Malcolm's unique ability to narrate the prospects of black resistance at the edge of racial apocalypse that made him both exciting and threatening. Malcolm spoke out loud what many blacks secretly felt about racist white people and practices, but were afraid to acknowledge publicly."[11] Malcolm X made public statements that frightened many black and white people but he also made some black people feel good. Finally, a black person was standing up to white Americans. It was through his speeches that his public voice gave the black American man and woman what they desperately needed, reason to love themselves. Historically, black Americans had been taught that everything black was inferior, including their physical bodies and intellectual capabilities. Whether black people publicly or privately acknowledged their profound sense of self-hate, Malcolm X taught them that black did not equal inferior. Celeste Condit and John Lucaites, in "Malcolm X and the Limits of the Rhetoric of Revolutionary Dissent," describe Malcolm X's contribution to history. They write, "perhaps Malcolm X's most powerful rhetorical weapon was his recharacterization of Blacks through a revisionary Black history."[12]

It was not because Malcolm X's speeches rebuked white supremacy that made black people happy; it was "how" he spoke about slavery, oppression, and discrimination. Cone suggests that the "black poor reveled in his courage to be 'blunt speaking' and 'frank talking.'"[13] Unafraid, bold, and charismatic, Malcolm X told white people they were morally wrong for treating black Americans like they were second-class citizens. Certainly, other leaders talked openly about slavery, racial discrimination, and inequality, but Malcolm X's rhetoric was different. Condit and Lucaites suggest, "Malcolm X was the herald of the revolution of Black consciousness in the 1960s. He helped to give Black America the self-confidence to scare White America into negotiating with it."[14] He was a black man who exclaimed to the world that the collective black population must receive fair treatment in their own country. Simply put, Malcolm X's rhetoric gave black men and women their manhood and womanhood back. Unfortunately, Malcolm X was killed in the Audubon Ballroom in 1965. Even though Malcolm X's physical body was laid to rest in 1965, his speeches were not. They continue to be discussed and analyzed in scholarly articles, books, and in classrooms all across America. In fact, then and now, Malcolm X reminds us all that outsider status does not necessarily mean one's messages go unheard or unheeded.

Huey P. Newton's Black Panther Party Rhetoric

One year after Malcolm X's death, Huey P. Newton and Bobby Seale formed the Black Panther Party for Self-Defense in Oakland, California in 1966. Both Newton and Seale were students attending Merritt Junior College in Oakland, California. They were disenchanted with King's nonviolent rhetoric and other liberal-minded civil rights leaders. They therefore decided that a different rhetoric was needed to address the concerns of black people. The BPP would address in theory and in practice the immediate needs of black people in urban cities. Newton expressed the need for the party's formation in the following lines. "We had seen Martin Luther King come to Watts in effect to calm the people, and we had seen his nonviolence rejected.... We had seen the Oakland police and the California Highway Patrol begin to carry their shotguns in full view as another way of striking fear into the community.... One must relate to the history of one's community and to its future. Everything we had seen convinced us that our time had come."[15] King's nonviolent rhetoric and protest action had helped black people gain some legal rights; however, unemployment, housing discrimination, and poor education remained serious problems affecting black communities all over the United States. As Newton so aptly thought, the time was ripe for the BPP to address the urgent needs of black Americans.

Newton and Seale created a Ten Point Program in October 1966 to represent what they saw as immediate concerns of the BPP. Too long to quote here, I present points 7 and 10 as important in locating the early success of the BPP but also to link Malcolm X's black nationalist rhetoric with Newton's BBP rhetoric. "[Point] 7. We want an immediate end to POLICE BRUTALITY and MURDER of Black people. [Point] 10. We want land, bread, housing, education, clothing, justice, and peace."[16] In the early formation of the BPP, Newton's organization concentrated on police brutality. It was no secret that white police officers patrolling black neighborhoods did not always provide the inhabitants with kind and respectful treatment. Newton and other black people viewed the police presence in their neighborhoods with contempt and they wanted to curtail police brutality by patrolling the police. Point 7 of the Ten Point Program caused much consternation in the police force. Armed with law books and weapons, Panther members watched police as they questioned individual blacks on the streets of Oakland. Like the police who could bear arms legally, Newton used the Second Amendment of the Constitution as his reason to bear arms to protect local black communities from renegade police. Newton talked about the success of the police patrols in his autobiography *Revolutionary Suicide*. He remarked, "At first, the patrols were a total success. Frightened and confused, the police did not know how to respond, because they had never encountered patrols like this before.... With weapons in our hands, we were no longer their subjects but their equals."[17]

Point 7 in the Ten Point Program was an effective way of integrating the revolutionary rhetoric of the BPP into the lives of the black community in Oakland and inserting their machismo into the faces of city-state governments. Gun toting black men was not a sight the establishment wanted to see or experience on a firsthand basis. Newton and other party members openly carried weapons to protect their communities from legalized and sanctioned protection from the police. The activities of Point 7 received the attention of the American public, but more importantly, Point 7 received the attention of the American government. Point 7 also helped to impose an outsider status onto Newton and the BPP.

Point 10 in the BPP's program, though seemingly idealistic and indisputable, was a request many who labored for civil rights made time and time again. Yet, black people living in the United States had to beg, demand, and finally protest in order to acquire basic rights. Until black people received all the demands requested in Point 10, Newton and other BPP members organized programs to improve the lives of black citizens. According to JoNina M. Abron, "[The] Panthers established a network of community service projects designed to improve the life chances of African American people.... The Party's survival programs aimed to help Black people overcome the devastating effects of racism and capitalism."[18] The Panthers organized free breakfast, health, educational, and criminal justice programs. The programs sponsored by the BPP were designed to alleviate the unmet needs of black people in Oakland and other branches of the BPP. Many black people in large urban areas were suffering economically and Newton and his organizers wanted to help feed them literally and figuratively. The projects involved turning revolutionary rhetoric into practical action. "[The] programs, which cover such diverse areas as health care and food service as well as a model school, the Intercommunal Youth

Institute, are meant to meet the needs of the community until we all can move to change social conditions that make it possible for the people to afford the things they need and desire."[19] The survival programs were part of the glory years for the BPP. The success of the survival programs helped to uplift the spirits of local community citizens who benefited from the work of BPP members. The survival programs provided much-needed credibility to the BPP. The complex behavior of party members and Newton's own erratic behavior had ascribed a renegade quality to the organization which often placed it at odds in the communities they were trying to help. With the survival programs, the BPP could make a case that it was a useful and important organization.

Newton's rhetoric of self-empowerment was present in the BPP's survival programs. His rhetoric was not simply polemical attacks against the American government, it was rhetoric turned into action. To combat empty political rhetoric, Newton and BPP members organized programs to address the intellectual deficiency, the social need, and the political development of impoverished black communities. This need to revitalize the black community against a nation unwilling to do so was revolutionary. Errol Henderson explores Newton's revolutionary rhetoric. He writes, "These 'poor people's programs' provided a cultural reorientation for participants allowing for the political transformation envisioned by the BPP. The cultural reorientation was toward the best in African American culture. Because the opposition between this national culture and the dominant White supremacist culture, the result was a very revolutionary *process*, as opposed to the revolutionary *act* of organizationally picking up the gun for a political objective."[20] Newton always envisioned the leadership of the BPP not simply as rhetorical leadership but also active leadership. In *Revolutionary Suicide*, Newton promoted rhetoric and action. "The Black Panthers have always emphasized action over rhetoric. But language, the power of the word, in the philosophical sense, is not underestimated in our ideology. We recognize the significance of words in the struggle for liberation. . . . Words are another way of defining phenomena, and the definition of any phenomenon is the first step to controlling it or being controlled by it."[21] Newton's revolutionary rhetoric continued to be shaped by the desires and the needs of the community. When Newton organized the BPP, he recruited the "street" brothers and sisters. Newton considered himself part of the street, and he realized the revolutionary potential of the street brothers and sisters. Thus, when other social movements had distanced themselves from "the brothers on the block," Newton and other party members embraced them. What Newton did was to revise Marxist ideology regarding the underclass. Judson Jeffries summarizes Marx's critique of the underclass when he writes "Marx called this segment [underclass] of society the lumpenproletariat. He argued that the lumpenproletariat was the most undisciplined and untrustworthy segment of society, and that, because of these characteristics, it was ill equipped to contribute significantly to the revolution. Marx claimed that this group was more likely to be coopted and converted into informants."[22] Newton disagreed with Marx's claims that the underclass could not be possible revolutionaries. In fact, Newton was successful at organizing the "brothers on the block." Henderson describes his success, "One is reminded that the BPP's attempt to organize the most disorganized group in the United States, the lumpenproletariat . . . . is impressive."[23] The brothers on the block served in many capacities in the BPP.

Like Malcolm X, Newton believed and understood that individuals who were marginalized by race, social class, and gender had something positive to offer the world. He did not want to throw individuals away because they had criminal backgrounds. Newton thought he could teach the outsiders to channel their energies in a positive direction. After all, Newton was an outsider too. The initial rhetoric of the BPP caused Newton and other members of the BPP to be outsiders within their home communities. The early rhetoric of the gun scared many people. The deaths of key BPP members further isolated the BPP and made them a renegade group inside and outside their home communities. Yet, their marginalized status outside the BPP failed to stop them from positively influencing the lives of black people.

Common

After the death of Malcolm X, the eventual demise of the BPP, and Newton's downfall, national black leadership suffered. Although Jesse Jackson and older members of the civil rights movement were still involved in mobilizing the black community in the 1980s and 1990s, the fervor with which Malcolm X and Newton galvanized the minds and spirits of their respective communities certainly did not happen in the same way for Jackson and other civil rights leaders. However, an unlikely and controversial new genre of music catapulted black issues onto the national scene in a way that Jackson's Rainbow Push Coalition did not. The new genre of music is called rap and the culture associated with rap is known as hip-hop. Common is part of a hip-hop community of socially conscious rap artists who focus their lyrical content and activism on raising the awareness of and need for a positive black consciousness. His lyrics are imbued with a deep appreciation and love for the rhetoric of black power and black nationalism. In "Voices Underground: Hip Hop as Black Rhetoric" Marcia A. Dawkins argues that "the functional nature of rhetoric uncovers the symbols and labels rappers use, and mediates realities of the African American community. As rhetoric, hip hop allows for the manipulation of symbols to create worldviews and evidence an intellectual stance. As part of a historical legacy, hip hop provides a place for its music (i.e., jazz and the blues) and a kaleidoscope through which to view the past, present, and future of black intellectual movements."[24] Common is one socially conscious rapper who addresses the concerns of urban citizens rhetorically and in practice. Although less popular than rappers like Snoop Dog, T. I. and Nelly, who receive more air play and media exposure, Common remains an important figure in rap. Though Common does not have a religious or political organization like Malcolm X or Newton (he does have a youth organization which is called the Common Ground Foundation), he uses his albums to serve as a catalyst to spark much-needed dialogue on the subject of black subjectivity, black love, and black consciousness. With urban decay, despondency, joblessness, and poor housing remaining essential problems in the lives of poor and working-class blacks, Common's music is a fresh reminder that subtle and overt forms of racial oppression continue to haunt black people.

For all of Common's successes—he has released eight albums—he remains a peripheral but important figure in the rap world. Common's black consciousness rhetoric is not necessarily popular in a market economy that is driven by album sales rather than lyrical content. This places Common in a peculiar position as an artist. While two of Common's albums have been called classics and one has earned critical acclaim (*Resurrection* 1994,[25] Like Water For Chocolate 2000[26] and *Be* 2005[27] respectively) he lacks the national exposure that his more radio friendly peers receive. Because their albums (50 Cent, Nelly, T. I.) appeal to a broader range of people and their lyrics are infused with references to violence, sex, and materialism they sell more records. Selling more records has not stopped Common from commenting and contesting the gross materialism of the day.

Common is a unique and lyrically powerful rapper from Chicago, Illinois. A product of the 1970s, he witnessed the moral decay and decadence of the 1980s and 1990s. Upon finding himself enmeshed in a society without iconoclastic figures to speak for the collective black population, Common's music and hence his black consciousness rhetoric attempts to fill the gaping hole left by the deaths of key freedom fighters. Speaking about his artistic contribution to society in an interview in *Recoil*, Common admits his role is "to be progressive, to be the deliverer of messages, to be the reporter of what's going on and ways to get out. To be the enlightener, to be the escape sometimes from our situations, to be the life-giver in different ways, to be the teacher, to be the entertainer."[28] Dropping his first album in 1992 and his latest album in 2008, Common continues to be a mainstay in the music industry. His unique blend of jazz, R&B, and funk has failed to give him "platinum" sales but that does not deter Common from rapping.[29] Politically and socially astute, Common's music delves into the psyches of the black working class. Writing about Common's need to stay connected to the people, in a review of *Like Water for Chocolate*, Mark Anthony Neale restates Common's conscious links to his community, "In a recent appearance on BET Tonight with Dead Prez and Kevin Powell, Common related to host Tavis Smiley. . . . his need to continue to connect with the folks as he states, 'Somedays I take the El to gel with the real world.'"[30] Though Common is not the only socially conscious rapper in the game, his staying power is what sets him apart from others. For sixteen years, Common's music has blurred the line between entertainment and education.

This is no easy feat for Common who is a member of a special group of socially conscious rappers: KRS-One, Mos-Def, and Talib Kweli. That Common has two classic rap albums and reasonable rap sales says as much about the music industry as it does about his album content. However, sales alone cannot be used as a barometer to measure his importance (he was recently a guest on the Oprah Winfrey show to talk about misogyny in rap lyrics). Serious rap fans know that album sales are not an indicator of talent or substance. Common's albums are full of substantive material. In Common's own words, he argues that rap sales are not his main focus. In a 1998 interview, he reflected on his moderate album sales, 'I ain't looking like Yo man, I gotta go double platinum' or anything. Of course it would be a blessing but I ain't falling victim to that shit. I want longevity y'know.'"[31]

Common is not a marginal figure in the rap game because he cannot rap. In fact, platinum selling artist Jay-Z rhymes, "Truthfully I wanna rhyme like Common Sense, But I did five-mil'—I ain't been rhymin' like Common since."[32] His position in rap is complex. It has more to do with marketing, lyrical content, acceptability, and American culture. Common raps about self-empowerment, self-esteem, community involvement, and personal responsibility. These are not the only topics in Common's rhymes but they do represent a moderate portion of his work. Nevertheless, his topics are serious, sensual, and spiritual. Thus, the kind of black consciousnesses rhetoric that comes from his albums has not always received radio and video play on television's major music networks like BET or MTV.

To emphasize Common's outsider status in the commercialized rap world but to highlight his contribution to black consciousness, I examine four songs from four different albums to illustrate his unique approach to music. The songs are not a total representation of his talent or lyrical content. I have chosen these songs to make a larger point about the power of his rhetoric, how it connects to Malcolm X and Newton, and his outsider status. His second album, *Resurrection*, released in 1994 has been called a rap classic. The fifteen-track album is a compilation of male bravado, street poetry, and sociopolitical commentary. The song "Chapter 13 (Rich Man vs. Poor Man)" is a collaboration featuring Ynot. Rapping back and forth over drumbeats and synthesized instrumentals, Common and Ynot discuss the complex interactions between black, Asian, and white citizens' relationships relative to the way money and power are exchanged between the powerful and the powerless. Common raps:

> Okay it was a black man a white man and a Chinese man
> The black man of course he was po' (yeah)
> The white man. . . . he was rich (uh-huh)
> And the Chinese man, he owned a sto' (aight c'mon)
> Okay the black man livied on Beat Steet
> The white man lived on Wall Street
> And at the Chinese man's store is where they all meet
> Not really on the good foot
> Cause the white man kept stepping on the black man's toes! (damn)[33]

Common describes the social and economic interactions between three types of American citizens. As they each encounter one another, impositions are made on the least of them, black people. The encounter is a historically rooted problem but also a contemporary one as Asians and black Americans have recently had negative interactions in urban communities. One only needs to view Spike Lee's film *Do the Right Thing* or Allen and Albert Hughes's movie *Menace to Society* to see real life imitated on the big screen. In each film, tempers flare as the black and Asian characters are agitated by the presence and behavior of each other. More to point, there is real cultural misunderstanding between the black and Asian characters but no one in the film attempts to empathize with each other's pain. Thus, it becomes easy to shoot the Asian storeowner in *Menace to Society* or hurl insults at one another in *Do the Right Thing*.

Common's "Chapter 13 (Rich Man vs. Poor Man)" reiterates Malcolm X's and Newton's critique of black economics. For instance, Malcolm X frequently criticized the white power structure because it had denied black men and women the right to access economic opportunities it had afforded white males. For example, Malcolm X often argued that it was economically debilitating to black communities when they did not own the businesses in their communities. If black people were ever going to be free from domination, they would have to acquire capital. Point 10 of Newton's BPP manifesto made a similar argument. Newton understood that land ownership would give black people the power they needed to control their material conditions. Common takes up the argument again in his song "Chapter 13 (Rich Man vs. Poor Man)." The white man has a job on Wall Street, which indicates high income, the Asian man owns a store, which means he can amass wealth, but the black man has no income, which means he has no power. Similar themes are addressed in black nationalist rhetoric, BPP rhetoric, and Common's black consciousness rhetoric.

Common's third album, *one day it'll all make sense*, was released in 1997. What makes *one day it'll all make sense* an interesting and unique album is Common's willingness to rap about abortion, personal responsibility, and spirituality. The rap song, "G.O.D. (Gaining One's Definition)" is an amalgamation of black history, spirituality, and cultural mythology. Harkening back to the mythology of the white man as devil, made popular by Malcolm X and NOI members, both Common and Cee-Lo reflect on the belief in whiteness as evil and blackness as inferior. Relying on mythology and focusing on the failures of education, Common and Cee-Lo also spit verses that locate underachievement and self-hate in the cultural lore perpetuated in the American school system. Common raps:

> Understanding and wisdom became the rhythm that I played to
> And became a slave to master self
> A rich man is one with knowledge, happiness and his health
> My mind had dealt with the books of Zen, Tao the lessons
> Koran and the Bible, to me they all vital
> And got truth within 'em, gotta read them boys.
> "G.O.D. Gaining One's Definition"[34]

In order to rid oneself of the belief in personal inferiority, Common rhymes that people must take it upon themselves to locate truth in various contexts. Instead of relying on one religious doctrine as a way to define and understand oneself, Common suggests that revelation occurs when people read multiple texts to understand their place in the world. Like Malcolm X and Newton before him, Common recognizes that enlightenment is a process. Unlike more mainstream contemporary rappers, he does not argue that enlightenment happens because one has material wealth. In other words, wealth does not presuppose happiness and knowledge.

Moderate airplay has not stopped Common from releasing albums. In 2000 *Like Water For Chocolate* was released. Common's fusion of R&B, rap, politics, and social commentary is a breath of fresh air. One song in particular, "A Song for Assata," is a riveting tribute to Assata Shakur, a BPP member imprisoned for a crime she argues she did not commit, though she later escaped in 1979 and is currently an exile living in Cuba. Assata is for many a symbol of government repression but for Common, she represents freedom. In "A Song for Assata" Common re-transcribes Assata's life from text to song, detailing her interaction with the police. In the subtext of the song, Common also reveals the often contentious relationship between party members, the police force, and state repression. His compelling description is a convergence of lyrical innovation, intellect, and inquiry. Over beats and background vocals, Common rhymes about Assata's imprisonment and his freedom. Common raps:

> There were lights and sirens, gunshots firin'
> Shot twice wit her hands up
> Police questioned but shot before she answered
> One panther lost his life, the other ran for his
> Scandalous the police were as they kicked and beat her. . . .
> I wonder what would have happened if that woulda been me?
> All this shit so we could be free, so dig it, y'all.[35]

Paying homage to Assata was for Common an important historical moment. Like the BPP before him, Common recognizes the abuse of power the police used against party members. In an interview with Matt Sonzala, he reveals what it was like to meet Assata Shakur. He remarks, "To meet Assata Shakur . . . . was one of the most special moments of my life . . . . She's like a living martyr really, like somebody who sacrificed their life for freedom for all people. It was like meeting history, like meeting the revolution right there."[36] In living flesh, Assata reminds Common that gaining freedom for black Americans caused much internal and external pain for party members. In fact, Assata teaches him that his individual freedom is not to be taken lightly. At the end of the verse when Common rhymes "I wonder what would have happened if that woulda been me," he reveals the extent to which personal sacrifice requires courage and fortitude, characteristics he is not so sure would motivate him to do the just and righteous thing in the face of racism.

In his 2005 album *BE*, Common continues to rhyme about "the struggle." *BE*, a self-reflexive record, revisits personal pain, joyful triumph, love, and politics. A special collaboration with the Last Poets, Abiodun Oyewole and Umar Bin Hassan, makes Common's black consciousness rhetoric all the more historically significant. The Last Poets were a group of young men who used spoken word to challenge racial oppression during the Liberation Movement of the 1970s. They were a precursor to socially conscious rappers in the 1980s. Abiodun Oyewole and Umar Bin Hassan, two present members of the Last Poets rap on Common's song "The Corner." Identifying the street as both a manifestation toward crime and a possible deterrent against crime, Common bemoans the corner and the Last Poets applaud the corner. Common raps:

> Bang in the streets the police is Greeklike
> Its steep like coming up where niggers is sheeplike
> Rappers and hoopers we strive to be like
> G's with 3 stripes seeds that need light
> Cheese and weaves tight needs and thieves strike
> The corner where struggle and greed fight[37]

While Common recognizes the dangers of the street, a street both Malcolm X and Newton knew to be dangerous for black men and women, the Last Poets highlight the corner's past glory in Common's song "The Corner." They rap:

> The corner was our magic, our music, our politics, Fires raised as tribal dancers and war cries broke out on different corners Power to the people, black power, black is beautiful.[38]

The juxtaposition of the corner as both confining and liberatory is made manifest in the past nostalgia spoken of by the Last Poets and in the present observation of street life by Common. That Common chooses to collaborate with the Last Poets is a testament to his abiding faith in the historical legacy of the freedom struggle of the 1950s–1970s. In an interview with *PopMatters*, Common explains his collaborative efforts with the Last Poets, "They gifted at writing. . . . they took my song to a higher level. And that's what hip-hop was about to me. It would have a message. It would take you to the next place."[39] Always a politically minded rapper, Common understands that language is a reflection of geographical time and place and as such, his song "The Corner" reflects his penchant for historical truth, politics, and black consciousness.

I have examined four songs from Common's albums to highlight why he is a rhetorical and musical outsider in mainstream society. Common's music is rooted in an oratorical and musical legacy that pays homage to the Liberation rhetoric of the 1950s and beyond. Such a legacy has made his music highly political but also less commercial. His music and activism is an extension of the work Malcolm X and Newton were doing in the 1960s and 1970s. His Common Ground Foundation specifically harkens back to Newton's survival programs which attempted to serve the unmet needs of impoverished black urban communities. Common's foundation "strives to implement and assist programs that broaden the life experiences, build life skills, encourage healthy living, promote cultural awareness and emphasize self-empowerment in youth."[40] Workshop sessions such as "Sex and the City," "All about the Benjamins," "Owning Our Images," and "Media Literacy," all contribute to the rhetorical and practical history of black consciousness and black power rhetoric.

Malcolm X's, Newton's, and Common's outsider status never stopped their activism or influence. However, Malcolm X's critics like to note that his black nationalist rhetoric never fundamentally changed laws or public policies that altered material conditions for black Americans. Opponents of Newton and his BPP rhetoric argue that his disgraceful behavior and other BPP members overshadowed the collective good of the survival programs in America's urban cities. Common's lack of institutional and organization ties to prominent institutions may also be problematic. Despite the criticisms leveled against Malcolm X, Newton, and rap music in general (this includes Common), their messages are still important and resonate with segments of the American population most people have forgotten. In spite of their outsider status, each man's rhetoric continues to influence international and national audiences. We can look at Common's music as one example of the influence of Malcolm X's black nationalist rhetoric and Newton's BPP rhetoric.

Notes

1. Aristotle explains rhetoric's persuasive appeal in his text *Rhetoric*.
2. In *Traces of a Stream*, Jacqueline Jones Royster defines the spaces African American women writers occupy as members of different racial and writerly communities.
3. John Lucaites and Celeste Condit's essay "Reconstructing: Culturaltypal and Counter-Cultural Rhetorics in the Martyred Black Vision," *Communication Monographs* 57 (1990): 5–24 examines the philosophical differences between key freedom fighters of the 1960s.
4. For more information about Martin and Malcolm's philosophical differences

and similarities, read James Cone's *Martin and Malcolm and America: A Dream or a Nightmare*. New York: Orbis Books, 1991.

5. In Cone's text, he describes the hopes, fears, and realities of black life in America's urban centers.

6. For a fuller discussion of Malcolm X's ideas about radicalism, read Reiland Rabaka's essay "Malcolm X and Critical Theory: Philosophy, Radical Politics, and the African American Search for Social Justice." *Journal of Black Studies*. 33 (2002): 145–65.

7. To see Malcolm X's "radicalism" at work rhetorically, read "The Ballot or the Bullet" in *Malcolm X Speaks: Selected Speeches and Statements*. Edited by George Breitman. New York: Grove Press, 1965. 23–44.

8. See Cone's *Martin and Malcolm and America: A Dream or a Nightmare*.

9. Alex Haley and Malcolm X. The *Autobiography of Malcolm X*. New York: Ballantine Books, 1999.

10. In the "Chickens Come Home to Roost Speech," Malcolm X challenges integrationist ideals. "The Chickens Come Home to Roost." *The End of White World Supremacy: Four Speeches by Malcolm X*. Edited by Benjamin Goodman. New York: Merlin House, 1971. 67–80.

11. Michael Eric Dyson explains Malcolm X's appeal to black Americans in *Making Malcolm: The Myth and Meaning of Malcolm X*. New York: Oxford University Press, 1995.

12. Malcolm X's Black Nationalist rhetoric was often criticized for its lack of direct political action even though his rhetoric forced America to reconcile its negative treatment of black Americans. Celeste Condit and John Lucaites write about the limits of his rhetoric in their essay "Malcolm X and the Limits of the Rhetoric of Revolutionary Dissent." *Journal of Black Studies*. 23. (1993): 291–313.

13. Read James Cone's *Martin and Malcolm and America: A Dream or a Nightmare*.

14. Read Celeste Condit and John Lucaites's essay "Malcolm X and the Limits of the Rhetoric of Revolutionary Dissent."

15. Huey Newton explains the impetus for the Black Panther Party in *Revolutionary Suicide*. Huey P. Newton. *Revolutionary Suicide*. New York: Harcourt Brace Jovanovich, Inc., 1973.

16. For a complete list of the Black Panther Party's Ten Point Program, read Huey Newton's *Revolutionary Suicide*.

17. Ibid.

18. In "Serving the People": The Survival Programs of the Black Panther Party," Jo Nina M. Abron describes the positive outcomes of the survival programs created by the BPP. Such a description is necessary in light of the sometimes negative legacy of the BPP. *The Black Panther Party Reconsidered. Edited by* Charles E. Jones. Baltimore: Black Classic Press, 1998. 177–92.

19. Ibid.

20. Errol Henderson explains the success of the survival programs. "The Lumpenproletariat as Vanguard? The Black Panther Party, Social Transformation, and Pearson's Analysis of Huey Newton. *Journal of Black Studies*. 28 (1997): 171–99.

21. See Huey Newton's *Revolutionary Suicide*

22. Judson Jeffries describes Huey Newton's foundational philosophy for organizing the "brothers on the block." *Huey P. Newton: The Radical Theorist*. Jackson: U of Mississippi Press, 2002.

23. See Errol Henderson's essay "The Lumpenproletariat as Vanguard? The Black Panther Party Social Transformation, and Pearson's Analysis of Huey Newton."

24. Rap music continues to have its critics. Yet, there are many in the academy who

view rap music as a serious art form. Marcia Dawkins's essay, "Voices Underground: Hip Hop as Black Rhetoric." *The Literary Griot.* 10.2 (1998): 62, describes how rap music is a rhetorical practice utilized by today's rap musicians.

25. Common's second release, *Resurrection*, is considered a rap classic. In fact, one of his songs on the album, "I used to love h.e.r." remains an important song in history of rap music. *Resurrection*. Relativity Records, 1994.

26. Common's 2000 release *Like Water for Chocolate* is a significant album for him. Its release showcased his lyrical virtuosity. In fact, Mark Anthony Neale calls *Like Water* "a brilliant album." *Like Water for Chocolate*. MCA Records Universal, 2000.

27. ALLHIPHOP.com gave *BE* five stars. *BE*, Geffen Records, 2005.

28. In this interview, Common defines his artistic purpose. Like many socially conscious rappers, Common is serious about his role as a social observer and critic. http://www.recoilmag.com/interviews.common_0303.html *(accessed by August 3, 2005)*.

29. The Recording Industry Association of America provides data on gold and platinum albums. www.riaa.com *(accessed by April 28, 2007)*.

30. Read Mark Anthony Neale's album review for *Like Water for Chocolate* for more information on Common's connection to his community. http://www.popmatters.com/columns/criticalnoire/000505.shtml. *(accessed by March 13, 2007)*.

31. Common talks about the importance of longevity in this interview. http://www.nochaser.com/interviewCommon.htm *(accessed by August, 2, 2005)*.

32. On the song "Clarity," from Jay-Z's *The Black Album*, he rhymes about the complex relationship between integrity and album sales. "Clarity." *The Black Album*. DEF JAM, 2003.

33. Common's socio-political commentary is evident in the song "Chapter 13 (Rich man vs. Poor Man)" from his album *Resurrection*.

34. This song from *Like Water for Chocolate*, "G..O.D. (Gaining One's Definition)" could easily be entitled The Mis-eduction of the Negro (the title of which I have borrowed from Carter G. Woodson's book *The Mis-eduction of the Negro*. In the song, Common and Ce-Lo rap about the perils of misinformation.

35. "A Song for Assata," from Common's *Like Water for Chocolate* album is a riveting tribute to Assata Shakur, a Black Panther Party member currently living in exile in Cuba. Common interviews Assata and subsequently transcribes her life in a tribute to her in "A Song for Assata."

36. Common talks about his interview with Assata Shakur. "Rapper Common Hasn't Lost His Sense," Matt Sonzala, http://www.alphabeats.com/interviews/artists/common.htm.

37. "The Corner" from *BE* highlights Common's connection to like-minded spoken word artists from the 1970s. In this song, Common raps with two members from the Last Poets about the complex duality of America's street corners.

38. Ibid.

39. In this interview with PopMatters, Common explains why he used The Last Poets in his song "The Corner."

40. Common's website http://www.commongroundfoundation.org explains the history and purpose of his foundation.

Bibliography

Aristotle. *Rhetoric*. Translated by Robert W. Rhys. New York: Modern Library, 1984.
Carpenter, Tim. "Common." http://www.recoilmag.com/interviews/common_0303.html.

Condit, Celeste, and John Lucaites. "Malcolm X and the Limits of the Rhetoric of Revolutionary Dissent." *Journal of Black Studies* 23 (1993): 291–313.

Cone, James. *Martin and Malcolm: A Dream or a Nightmare*. New York: Orbis Books, 1991.

Dawkins, Marcia A. "Voices Underground: Hip Hop as Black Rhetoric." *Literary Griot* 10, no. 2 (1998): 62–84.

Dyson, Michael Eric. *Making Malcolm: The Myth and Meaning of Malcolm X*. Oxford: Oxford University Press, 1995.

Goodman, Benjamin. "The Chickens Come Home to Roost." *End of White World Supremacy: Four Speeches by Malcolm X*. New York: Merlin House, 1971. 64–84.

Haley, Alex and Malcolm X. *The Autobiography of Malcolm X*. New York: Ballantine Books, 1999.

Hamilton, Pierre. "Resurrection: Common Walks." http://www/popmatters.com/music/interviews/common.htm.

Henderson, Errol. "The Lumpenproletariat as Vanguard? the Black Panther Party, Social Transformation, and Pearson's Analysis of Huey Newton." *Journal of Black Studies* 28 (1997): 171–199.

Jeffries, Judson. *Huey P. Newton: The Radical Theorist*. Jackson: University Press of Mississippi, 2002.

Jones, Charles E., ed. "Serving the People: The Survival Programs of the Black Panther Party." *The Black Panther Party Reconsidered*. Baltimore: Black Classic Press, 1998.

Lucaites, John, and Celeste Condit. "Reconstructing: Culturaltypal and Counter-Cultural Rhetorics in the Martyred Black Vision." *Communication Monographs* 57 (1990): 5–24.

Malcolm X. "The Ballot or the Bullet." *Malcolm Speaks: Selected Speeches and Statements* ed. By George Breitman. New York: Grove Press, 1965.

Neal, Mark A. "Like Water for Chocolate: Common's Recipe for Progressive Hip Hop." http://www.popmatters.com/columns/criticalnoire/000505.shtml

Newton, Huey P. *Revolutionary Suicide*. New York: Harcourt Brace Jovanovich, 1973.

Rabaka, Reiland. "Malcolm X and Critical Theory: Philosophy, Radical Politics, and the African American Search for Social Justice." *Journal of Black Studies* 33 (2002): 145–65.

"Recording Industry Association of America." www.riaa.com.

Royster, Jacqueline Jones. *Traces of a Stream: Literacy and Social Change among African American Women*. Pittsburgh, PA: University of Pittsburgh Press, 2000.

Sonzala, Matt. "Rapper Common Hasn't Lost His Sense." http://www.alphabeats.com/interviews/artists/common.htm.

Spoon T, QUIZative, Terry Malko, and V Unique. "Common." http://www.nochaser.com/interviewCommon.htm.

www.commongroundfoundation.org

Discography

Common. "A Song for Assata." *Like Water for Chocolate*. 2000. MCA Records Universal.

———. "Chapter 13 (Rich Man vs. Poor Man)." *Resurrection*. 1994. Relativity Records.
———. "G.O.D. (Gaining One's Definition)." *one day it'll all make sense*. 1997. Relativity Records.
———. "The Corner." *BE*. 2005. Geffen Records.
Jay-Z. "Clarity." *The Black Album*. 2003. DEF JAM.

Outsider Rhetoric in Italian American Immigrant Autobiographies
Ilaria Serra

Unexpected voices

THE MAJORITY OF ORDINARY ITALIAN IMMIGRANTS TO THE UNITED States seems to have remained voiceless. Thousands arrived in the United States from big towns and small villages in the last century. They were farmers, miners, carpenters, tailors, and bricklayers. Some were college graduates and a few were doctors. But they all passed into this country in silence. They have left almost no accounts of their lives, no firsthand written trace of their existence. The story of Italian immigration is filled with these "silent" lives and deaths, consumed without words, between work and nostalgia. Giuseppe Prezzolini, an Italian intellectual who settled in New York City between 1929 and 1962, laments that "our immigrants left only sweat and tears, not words."[1] He even tries to gather a few testimonies of their experience, but is deeply disappointed: "I once asked through the local Italian-language press to gather memories of immigration. I had no answer. Nobody preserved memories of his own or his parents' migration. Instead, they tried to forget it."[2] He calls first-generation immigrants "a lost generation," and immigration "a great mute tragedy:" "Its victims did not know how to write, and almost did not know how to express themselves. The survivors do not want to remember. Whoever interrogates them finds a wall of reticence sometimes covered by the paint of pride. The good success of some covers the disgraces of many."[3]

In this bleak landscape, I was able to unearth over sixty forgotten texts, autobiographies by ordinary Italian immigrants of the twentieth century, texts that are considered neither literature nor history, and are buried in archives and in the drawers of private houses.[4] They prove that Italian immigrants were far from being reticent and victims, some of them at least. Some of them *wanted* to remember and *to be remembered*. They wanted to cut out for themselves a little corner in the history of big people for their small stories. The little resources they had, they used to write impervious memories and bony life stories. Like the immigrant doctor Previtali who scribbles on his deathbed, "il libro," as his last word to his son, these authors are all almost obsessed with creating what must appear to them as an "object of intellect": the "book." There are several immigrants who want to see their writings become books. There are copies of such books published at the writer's expenses by the so-called "vanity press" or by cheap and provincial printers, sometimes read only by relatives, sometimes disregarded even by close friends. Now that financial and technological means have become available, it is impossible not to notice the determination of these old writers to have their lives contained in a book. It seems that immigrants who come from a "productive," "material" background absolutely need the objective, material consistence of paper and cardboard. Only the shape of the book matters. It is life itself, packaged between two cheap covers, which calls for recognition.

These numerous testimonies of immigration must be considered rhetoric on the margins. Autobiography has traditionally been a genre of great men and women, "men or women of outstanding achievement in life" writes Roy Pascal.[5] It was written by illustrious men, "first generals and 'governors' of the earthly kingdom, and then since the beginning of the Christian era, those of the celestial kingdom (the saints)."[6] Our writers belong instead to a cultural and social class that is not supposed to write. They are authors with tired hands and little familiarity with pen and paper. They belong to a working class, which has "often been erased by the generic byline 'Anonymous.'"[7] These writers are outsiders at many levels: they are immigrants, a foreign minority; they are little educated or almost illiterate; and they are ordinary, uninfluential men and women.

In this essay, I will describe how inconsequential people can transform themselves into "authors," through their generative, creative rhetoric. These Italian authors overcame obstacles such as a poor education, little time to write, jobs that sucked all their energy often in manual work. These immigrants had to strengthen their stuttering voice, and pin down the insecurity of their space in society. They wrote to gain acceptance and blow away prejudice (often a very harsh one). They did so through a rhetoric of indirect resistance. They never attacked American society, or the mainstream culture, but they cut a little space in history. They indirectly gave themselves a line in the history books that would ignore them. Their critique is mild, never offensive, but quietly defensive. Here, I will read several representative pieces of their texts through rhetorical categories, such as the strength of performance (J. L. Austin and Kenneth Burke), the power of assertion that makes them transcend their working/lower class (Pierre Bourdieu and Paulo Freire), and the democratizing potential of writing (Walter Ong). I will also propose for them new rhetorical terms because, being new subjects of discourse, they call for a different description: they give voice to the *self in history*, they resent the *ethos of the survivor*, and they are examples of *quiet individualism*.

Generative Rhetoric

By writing, these immigrants bring us close to a conception of rhetoric as a performative act, according to the definition of "speech act theory" by the language philosopher J. L. Austin. In *How to Do Things with Words*, he gives the name of performative to any utterance that performs an action by virtue of being delivered. Our immigrants' utterance-books are productive, strong stimulations of a particular effect: the effect of literally writing themselves into existence. By writing these authors put an end to their being written, to their being numbers in statistics or passive objects of someone else's description, and they do give birth to themselves. Perhaps the most urgent of such performative acts is the autobiography of the fisherman Bartolomeo Vanzetti who writes his story, *Una vita proletaria*, literally in order to save his life from the electric chair. For all the others, writing brings forth a reaffirmation of their human existence, but also a reversal of an existing social condition and a crossing of cultural boundaries.

These immigrants belong to a class of people who is not supposed to write. For centuries cultural capital has coincided with economic capital. For Pierre Bourdieu's *Distinction*, art and cultural consumption are "predisposed, consciously and deliberately or not, to fulfill a social function of legitimating social differences."[8] Writing is also set to distinguish between classes. Bourdieu signals the trap of exclusion and self-exclusion, according to which those who feel incompetent, unentitled, and impotent are also indifferent to art, culture, and creative writing.[9] In the same way, "personal opinion" is a bourgeois invention and an acquired right, according to Bourdieu: our authors thus cross a social line when they feel entitled to produce their own personal opinion, perhaps the most personal of all opinions, their own version of their life. Therefore, our autobiographical material takes us to the "borderland," on the boundaries between cultural classes. By writing, our authors take a step toward a hierarchically superior cultural class. Even when using faltering words they cross over the line, and are often aware of the length of their stride. They appropriate literacy in the most productive sense, as writing. In so doing, these immigrants are reversing concepts of magical comprehension practiced by their class for centuries.

Italian peasants and lower classes often suffered from what Paulo Freire calls a "magic consciousness" that "simply apprehends facts and attributes them to a superior power," that "is characterized by fatalism, which leads men to fold their arms, resigned to the impossibility of resisting the power of facts."[10] They are powerless because they live and accept a worldview constructed from above, by the capricious "fortuna," fate or destiny. For Freire, who speaks of illiterate South American peasants, literacy is what can gain them back the possibility of their agency. But there is a passive literacy, which enables people to read while it keeps them in the same subservient position, and an active literacy. William Covino highlights the first type of literacy calling it "false magic" that, with formulaic incantation, attempts to suspend or control the possibilities of human action (he is hinting to scandalous newspapers and sensational journalism). Instead, Covino describes true magic as the real rhetoric, as "action that creates action, words that create words."[11] Borrowing from Kenneth Burke, he asserts that "true-correct magic is *generative*, practiced as constitutive inquiry or the coercive expansion of the possibilities of human action."[12] This true magic is proper of our writers' autobiographies. As we have said, by taking writing in their own hands, by daring to dream to produce a "book" (the insignia and accessory of a superior cultural class), by delivering their personal opinion, by becoming subjects and not objects of description, through their generative rhetoric, our authors perform a cultural leap.

For these particularly unorthodox authors it is necessary to propose an alternative history of rhetoric. The explanations that have been made for immigrant autobiography do not satisfy our category of authors: these autobiographies are not merely repetitions of the "success story" or the "passage to Americanization" of the immigrants. They are only marginally "narratives of conversion," and many of them care little for the "American model of Americanization."[13] They are instead completely self-absorbed in their own immigrant model, their own particular story of immigration, their own ethos of the *quiet individual who survived History*. I have to suggest, therefore, different critical terms that overturn traditional concepts. If canonical autobiographers, those great men and women, produce "histories of the self," our autobiographers chronicle the adventures of *self in history*. If the canon speaks of the birth of individualism through firsthand accounts, for our authors we have to speak of *quiet individualism*, not shouted but softly whispered. And, finally, if traditional autobiographical rhetoric copes with the ethos of the hero, we have instead to deal with the *ethos of the survivor*.

Entering History through the Back Door

However unexpectedly, these authors loudly speak their first and last names, and refuse the destiny of anonymity. They "speak themselves into textual existence."[14] They write because they are urged on by a pressing need, that of saving their lives from the oblivion of History and of immigration. Their strong rhetorical acts are the first sign of a will to speak out, to proclaim individuality, and to create a voice for traditionally voiceless people. Many of these ordinary autobiographers are conscious that they are going against expectations, they are breaking rules. They practice rhetoric with a sense of political and social purpose.

It is the case, for example, of the Sicilian Antonio Margariti who voices his dilemma when he says that writing makes him enter the world of "Ipossente" ("Thepowerful" collapsing the space between article and noun) who never listen to "ipoverette" ("thewretched" also without spacing). A stonecutter for the Erie Canal and a factory worker in Philadelphia, Antonio Margariti leaves his native Ferruzzano (Reggio Calabria) in 1914 when he is twenty-two. After the last member of his family dies, the need to defy oblivion pushes him to write a masterpiece of literature of the impoverished, *America! America!* His broken Italian is witty and sharp, ironic and cutting, a powerful yet rough tool to express his pointed ideas and clear conceptions of history as "seen from below." His fascinating world is clearly divided between "Thepowerful" (*Ipossente*) and "thepoors" (*ipoverette*): "the youth of the village they were divided in two groups Thepowerful and thepoor and it goes without saying I was with thepoor."[15] The same division remains in America, where he describes his anger toward injustices in terms of "land," terms that the immigrant understands: "the homeland is for the rich ones, the homeland of the poor is still to be made."[16]

Margariti is perhaps the most conscious and the most pungent in repeating that writing is his vengeance against history. In the very beginning of his autobiography he claims his place in History with these effective words:

> I don't write for the art and neither for the glory / I write what boils in my brain / I write and I revolt against the old world . . . I remember my long existence not very happy, or life if life it can be called that is my hard past,

the life of the big people is written by the great historians and remains in History, but [not] for me who am nothing else than a little grain fallen from the space and outside my neighborhood nobody knows I Exist and perhaps one can think I write for Ambition without Ambition one can't do anything.[17]

By crossing the border of silent peasantry, Margariti reacts to the elitism of history written by few. Knowing to be only "a grain fallen from the space," he uses his only weapons—a cutting tongue and a shrewd brain—to make his story known beyond the fence of his garden, his neighborhood.

The "pick and shovel poet" Pascal D'Angelo, like Margariti, is perfectly conscious that writing his story is the last effort to symbolically uproot himself and step outside his assigned territory into "the upper world." Born in Introdacqua (Sulmona) in the region of Abruzzi in 1894, Pascal D'Angelo arrives at Ellis Island in 1910 as a sixteen-year-old boy. He becomes a man in America, where his desire to learn also makes him an outsider. He endures his companions' derision as "that queer Italian laborer"[18] who memorizes Webster's dictionary and writes "jokes" for his friends. He spends his days in the public library and nights in a malodorous room that had been a chicken coop: "At least if my body was living in a world of horror I could build a world of beauty for my soul," he remembers.[19] At the end of his relatively famous autobiography, *Son of Italy*, he praises his own triumph, shown though the eyes of Italian working men: "More sincere and dearer to my heart were the tributes of my fellow workers who recognized that at last one of them had risen from the ditches and quicksands of toil to speak his heart to the *upper world*. And sweeter yet was the happiness of my parents who realized that after all I had not really gone astray, but had sought and attained a goal from the deep-worn groove of peasant drudgery."[20]

D'Angelo's rhetoric remains that of the outsider because he pays dearly for it. He constructs his portrait through the ethos of work, as an immigrant worker who struggles for an education and raises himself from the gutters. He never denies his humble origin, and stresses his struggles and not his success. To his literary satisfaction he dedicates only one page. His ethos as a pick and shovel worker, far from being an embarrassment, becomes strength for him: "I always was and am a pick and shovel man."[21] He does not shy away from his laborer's roots, remembering all the derogatory epithets attached: "I was a poor laborer—a dago, a wop or some such creature."[22] Such ethos is so striking that it is picked up by a reviewer of the 1922 issue of *Il Carroccio*, who writes about the man "who passed to lyre from the shovel";

"the poet of the shack."[23] But even if not bringing money and glory, writing is for him what makes a man a man; D'Angelo writes: "A dog is silent and slinks away when whipped, while I am filled with the urge to cry out."[24] Writing becomes the antidote to dispersion and oblivion for an immigrant who will die young (at thirty-eight) and without money for a proper burial: "Who hears the thuds of the pick and the jingling of the shovel. All my works are lost, lost forever. But if I write a good line of poetry—then when the night comes, and I cease writing, my work is not lost. My line is still there. It can be read by you to-day and anyone else to-morrow. But my pick and shovel work cannot be read either by you to-day or by anyone else to-morrow."[25]

Walter Ong states that the alphabet is a democratizing script, easy to learn, and soon available for all. People who have never really had a voice in the social world, do immediately notice this "democratizing" aspect of writing. The Sicilian Calogero Di Leo, for example, opens his book of memories with the claim that everybody writes books today. If even Monica Lewinsky wrote one, he can do the same:

> Ladies and Gentlemen if today anybody can write the book of his life, or his past, or his adventures, or his romantic past, of any kind. . . . Now another writer has arrived Mrs Monica Luewinkie, with her love novel her dolce vita of some years with Mr. President of the United States Bill Clinton, and a book of a few years of love romance and she is already famous in all the world, she too and the president come from an ancestry of emigrants and if she has written a book why can't I write one too.[26]

Calogero Di Leo writes "Vita di un emigrante turista milionario" in 2000. This is a fresh piece of writing by a sixty-three-year-old short man born in Lucca Sicula who looks back at his accomplishments and defeats with an ironic smile. His same title is a half-joke: the "Life of a Millionaire Immigrant Tourist" is actually the life of an immigrant, not that of a tourist even if he lives in Fort Lauderdale, Florida, and certainly not that of a millionaire, having lost the money of his failed restaurants. The text is a bright example of the bittersweet irony of the "normal immigrant." Its pages shape the "immigrant philosophy" made of a thousand new departures, defeats, and renunciations: "the one that suffers is always the poor immigrant."[27] Nevertheless, this sense of resignation is softened by an undying optimism that permeates the narrative: "Everything [that] is part of life is necessary to learn, like Noah who was nine hundred and still learned."[28] Besides, the immigrant has no other alternative: "Either going directly back to Italy I have to die of hunger. I say no, Calogero, be brave, because he who endures wins."[29]

The obsession with remaining unknown scours the immigrant Gabriel Iamurri, who arrives in the United States as a boy in 1895. At sixty-three, during the time free from his confectionery shop, Iamurri is compelled to write in order to ransom back all those lives of ordinary immigrants who have been worked to death and thus to silence. He tells horrific stories of unskilled laborers who tried to commit suicide under a train to escape from beastly work, and of others who died and nobody paid their insurance, and nobody cried over them. Their lives were worthless: "A shovel, a pickaxe, any kind of tool had more value for them than one of us; for if a man lost his life for them he could soon be replaced without any cost to them, but if a shovel or a pick was broken, it was a different story, it cost them something."[30] These worthless lives would be forgotten, if it were not for Iamurri's writing: "Nothing is ever recorded of their suffering, their tears, of their hunger, and, especially of the injustice they suffered at the hands of their employers. They are indeed the forgotten man, the unknown soldier who gave much for the prosperity and greatness of the country but received very little in return."[31]

We can see how these outsiders' rhetoric becomes all the more urgent. They are writing an almost invisible social class into existence.

Chronicles of the Self in History

In contrast to autobiographies of great people or autobiographies of Americanization, which are "histories of the self," these immigrants' works are accounts of the "self in history." While successful immigrants tell the adventures of the self as rising against the background of history, common immigrants tell of the misadventures of a self constantly wrestling with it.[32] For common immigrants, history, not the self, prevails. Virginia Yans-McLaughlin introduces these contrasting terms, "history of the self" and "self in history." Drawing a comparison between the oral stories told by Jewish and Italian laborers in New York, she notices a different sense of self and a different sense of history in Italian and Jewish immigrants. She maintains that Italians hold an "atomistic" sense of history that "does not perceive the self or society as an unbroken, linear development";[33] for them fate, not will, dominates, and resignation, not fight, is their remedy. This "atomistic" sense of history can be found in many of our autobiographies: they are a succession of facts, and these facts push the person to act and decide his/her actions, not the opposite. History shapes the man. Luigi Barzini also stresses the importance of history in shaping Italian behavior: "[The Italian] is powerless to deflect the tides of history. He can only try to defend himself from their blind violence, keep his mouth shut and mind his own business."³⁴

The *ethos of the survivor* is another key word for ordinary immigrant autobiographies. It is shared by all social classes, especially the poor ones, and refers to the sensation nourished by the "man in history" of having escaped from destruction, having survived through the stampede of life. Immigrants normally feel it because they have escaped the bites of hunger and misery, but often also specific events, like earthquakes, wars, Fascism, laws (like the 1924 Quota Act that limits the number of Italian entrances), or accidental deaths. They all feel it. They are all aware that they have survived America itself and a deterministic social structure for the purpose of making themselves. From the poor worker who survives the explosion of the coal mine of Cherry, Antenore Quartaroli, whose struggling ethos is obviously the high point of his *memoire* ("Yet we had to fight until the last moment even if sure to die");³⁵ to the doctor, Michele Daniele, who also adopts the ethos of the struggling immigrant: "The truth of the matter is that I shall be quite content to be able to say about the years to come what I have been able to say about those that are past: *I lived through them.*"³⁶

The rhetoric of survival in these writers is a struggle against the "circumstances of life." It is not an heroic struggle, accompanied by war horns, but a defensive, quiet movement. What life has brought to them in spite of themselves, at destiny's whim, they try to mend with their writing. The postman Michael Lamont is perfectly aware of the constructive possibilities of telling a story in first person, because only he who lived it knows "how it is." He regrets that his friends do not write down their life, and says: "it's too bad because the tales they will tell will die with them, it's a shame because they really tell it how it is."³⁷ Born in West Virginia, Lamont is a simple man who worked as a shoemaker and a postal worker. His biography is a succession of endings (many attempts and many failures). He was profoundly transformed by the experience of immigration, and his name changing proves it. Life renamed him, despite himself. He sarcastically ends his autobiography with a lapidary: "Michelangelo Lomanto now known as Michael Lamont due to circumstances beyond my control. Thank you" (54).

In these autobiographies, the trauma of immigration is sometimes sublimated in metaphors such as name changing. The first name is extremely important for the autobiographers (as underlined by Lejeune's concept of the "autobiographical pact" and also by Boelhower),³⁸ and its change is always annotated in writings. It takes the form of a surgical removal in Oreste Fabrizi's words: this stone carver from Sandonato (Frosinone) explains the cut in his name (Fabrizio) as an "amputation," the result of immigration: "The change to the actual Fabrizi happened, non requested, when I was given my American citizenship in 1934. For a mistake of transcription in the certificate my name resulted amputated of its 'o' vowel."[39]

Many of these firsthand accounts try to mend a failure or a forgetfulness of history. Thus sadness creeps into Michele Pantatello's description of his triumphal return to Italy. Even if economically satisfied, this seventy-year-old blacksmith knows the price of his success. In his *Diario-biografico, l'ultimo immigrante della Quota, 25 nov. 1922* (self-published in 1967), he describes his 1960 trip back to his hometown where he pays his respect to a lost name, and honors the disappearance of his entire family: "to renew a stone at the cemetery of my town where the bones of my Father rest, it was faded, and this time it was made in marble with bronze letters to remind the future generations, always, the name of a family disappeared from the Village, for the circumstances of life."[40] In this final paragraph of Pantatello's book we find the main characteristics of subaltern autobiographers: the sheltering gesture against the adverse "circumstances of life" that wiped out a whole family, and the act of writing a name on a tombstone, or the story of a life, not accompanied by trumpet sounds but by the soft whisper of death.

The same mourning idea is present in Giovanni Veltri's last words that are marred by the idea that his Italian name will be lost forever because his two grandsons in Canada have inherited the anglicized name of Welch. "Finally," he writes, "I built a decent chapel in the cemetery where I hope my bones will be laid to rest. However my soul is tormented by the thought that my name will end with me because there is no one who will pass it on."[41] Called John Welch in America and Giovanni Veltri in Italy, this immigrant lives his identity as a worker with intense pride and assumes it as his primary ethos. Not only does he work for himself but, through his railroad company, the Welch Company (founded with his brother Vincenzo), he starts a chain migration from his hometown of Grimaldi in Calabria. "A ghenga e Veltri" (Veltri's gang) is the common name for these laborers. Giovanni leaves Calabria in the 1880s for the American Northwest, and is ninety years old when he dictates his story to his niece in Italian. His *Memories* cover the years 1867–1954, and with the typical ability of an oral teller, he recovers hundreds of names from oblivion.

Remembering names as a saving act is also the main feature of Gregorio Scaia's story. A simple worker from the mountains of Trentino, he is conscious of cutting out a space in history, not only for himself, but for his entire immigrant group. Scaia grabs the working-man ethos as a flag that he plants on the territories colonized by Italian immigrants. He is seventy-two in 1953, when he writes his memories in Seattle: "this little story written in the free time on the Pacific coast," a little typewritten booklet full of mistakes.[42] This autobiography becomes a real collective exaltation of the entire group of immigrants traveling with him, all of whom "merita di esere ricordati" ("deserving to be remembered"). In his "Prefazio" we find a rhetorical appeal to the goodwill of his readers, as also the consciousness that the worth of his little booklet lies in saving his companions' lives from oblivion:

> I believe this is the only book to this day written about our foreign colonies, the only and unique reason of writing this book is telling and informing and conserving in the heart and in the mind of our people and future generations, the works and obstacles and struggles that our Trentini had to fight in their trips on land and sea, and the sacrifices they had to endure, in any part of the world, in unknown countries so far from home, all to gain a piece of bread with seven crusts, so our poor ancestors used to say once upon a time.[43]

What the factory worker Pietro Greco tries to save is the poetry hidden in humble immigrant life. His unpublished and apparently unfinished autobiography, "Ricordi d'un immigrato, Brooklyn, 3 Maggio 1965," describes a cultural Little Italy that finds its highest moment in the description of the Barberia di Mastro Gaspare. Gaspare was illiterate, with silver hair and an upright character; even his steps are rhythmic and his hands light as snow. His little barbershop is presented as the unexpected kingdom of poetry that is destined to disappear, if it was not for the saving power of Greco's writing: "Mastro Gaspare's poetry was not put on paper to be preserved; it had the lifetime of some combinations of clouds that appear beautiful and suggestive in the blue immensity of space, but a sudden wind destroys and dissolves, and they only remain in the memory of those who saw them."[44]

These writers are filled with a sense of rhetorical urgency. They are running against time because first-generation immigrants are on the verge of oblivion, often sacrificed to the second generation: "The immigrant parents would be more or less a 'lost generation,'"[45] writes Bruna Pieracci, the daughter of a miner who died of too much work to give his children the possibility of a better life. Immigrant mothers and fathers never had the time or the means to write, and they left the pen to their children. We have in fact many accounts of second-generation immigrants, torn souls, split between two worlds, home and country. As for the first generation, it is fading away, and the poet

Lawrence Ferlinghetti salutes it in "The Old Italians Dying," a beautiful poem that resounds with the tolling of bells and describes old immigrants in a striking verse, as "waiting . . . for their glorious sentence on earth / to be finished."

Quiet Individualism

All critics agree that autobiographies are born with a new discovery of a sense of individuality. Autobiography appears in times of crisis, when an "earthquake" of any sort gives birth to a new person, an individual, a fragment severed out of a whole. Georges Gusdorf individuates the birth of autobiography in the age of the Copernican revolution.[46] Immigration works as a kind of Copernican revolution, which destabilizes the sense of self of man: he is severed out from the rest of the universe, he is only one particle in it and not its center. The effect is a new sense of loneliness and responsibility. Pushed to the limit of the universe with its rotating planet, man is called to act with a stronger sense of responsibility, but also with a growing sense of individualism. This discovery of individualism links immigration to the Copernican revolution. As a Renaissance man/woman, the immigrant feels the ground shifting under his feet, and autobiography becomes the tool to build his/her own centrality, his/her own identity as a particle of this chaotic universe.

Ordinary immigrant autobiographies are no exception: they also accompany a revaluation of the individual. But a particular type of individual, a "quiet individual." *Quiet individualism* is a middle-way conception of individualism, valid for most of our immigrants who are not entirely successful, even if they "made it"; who are decent, but not admired in American society (and more often than not scorned for their accent and ethnicity). These immigrants have, yes, learned the meaning of individualism because they have *detached* themselves from the mass that remained at home. Nevertheless, being "common men," they do not put themselves on a pedestal, they cannot say "look at me and do as I did because I have been the best" (like the "arrived" Lee Iacocca or Jerre Mangione or Constantine Panunzio do). Writing for their family and not for the general public, they cannot say "Listen to me all of you people because I have an interesting life to tell you" (like Henry Adams or Benvenuto Cellini). Being geared to the past and not to the future, they cannot say "look at my life and use it as a model" (like Benjamin Franklin). To the exceptionality of the individual they substitute the normality of experience, to the representative life they substitute a common life, to the listening audience they substitute the few interested ones.

These writers belong to the category of simply decent people. Philippe Lejeune invokes a place for them (autobiography), when he realizes how many autobiographies have been written not only by deviant personalities (stories of crime or madness) or successful people (success stories), but also by "honest people": "I propose a new space, at the center of the target (if I may dare say), that of honest people."[47] The authority of our "decent" authors cannot come from their standpoint in life, not from their education, but from the sincerity and the value of firsthand experience they can boast. So, Emanuele Triarsi, a bricklayer from Sicily who arrives in the United States in 1949, sighs his humbleness at the end of his booklet: "Ah—if I were a writer!" He nevertheless sets to write a "little story" that is the final gift to his dead wife. The effectiveness of his prose is not marred by its roughness, and he makes up for the lack of education with his authenticity by testifying that this book is written with his heart. "I do not have instruction and so I cannot write a novel, but only a little story, the best I can."[48]

Far from being a mere rhetorical topos, modesty is not feigned in these writers who know perfectly well they are normal people, hard-working immigrants. Aldobrando Piacenza, a janitor who settles in Chicago in the first decade of 1900, admits his smallness: "without a language, little school and no apprenticeship,"[49] he was able to carve a little niche for himself: "with honest work I built my decent refuge here in America."[50] He tries a variety of jobs before settling with a tobacco and newspaper shop in Highwood, a suburb of Chicago, but he makes himself out of his own hands and with some unexpected help from *paesanos*.

The tailor Pio Federico, born in Abruzzo in 1891 and migrated to America in 1909, pours his modest apology at the beginning of his *An Autobiography* (typewritten, 1960): "In this story I will try to describe in the best way possible all I remember of my past, from childhood till now. If anyone came into contact [with this papers], do not expect to read 'My Prisons' by Silvio Pellico; this is a simple story written by a man who is sixty-nine, a tailor, with minimum instruction of fifth grade, therefore. I will be grateful if not teased. Pio Federico Los Angeles 1960."[51]

Quiet individualism does not mean minimalism or plainness. There is a dignified strength in their being simple. The bricklayer Antonio De Piero, for example, writes to affirm himself as a man. Born in the small town of Cordenons in northeastern Italy in 1875, he writes his autobiography, *Le mie memorie scritte nell'isola della quarantina*,[52] in 1922. For him writing is a productive, *performative* activity that makes man become agent and maker of history. His last words in justification of his work resonate in capital letters (in the manuscript), and pronounce his belief in man as a creator: "I ALSO HAVE ACCOMPLISHED THE CHARACTERISTIC DUTIES OF A MAN: THE PHILOSOPHERS COUNT FOUR: 1) BUILD A HOUSE 2) WRITE A BOOK 3) HAVE A CHILD 4) PLANT A TREE."[53]

The Rhetoric of Graphics

De Piero writes his declaration of humanity in capital letters. In fact, graphics play an important part in these writings. New to the pen, these authors use it as a sacred instrument and its signs are particularly significant. I have been lucky to see these texts in their original form: its materiality is as important as its content. Elisabeth Evans, for example, a fragile woman who writes her horrific experience in a myth-less, naked America of the Seventies, writes her memories on a notebook with a pencil. Even her writing, with an ephemeral pencil, corresponds to her sensation of inadequacy: "I feel like I have to apologize for my existence."[54]

Unfamiliar with words, these authors mold their words and written signs as they would mold a hot iron or a piece of wood. These workers-writers play with the materiality of writing. Antonio Margariti uses punctuation to express irony by inserting a sequence of question marks, or gives words visual importance when he writes them in capital letters: LIBERTA (freedom), PEPPINO (his lost immigrant brother), or AMERICA or the visible meaning of *Ipossente* (the powerful) and *ipoverette* (the poor). Margariti makes his almost a sacred alphabet, a hieroglyphic where all signs have a meaning. This strong assertion finds a graphic translation also in the last words of Paul Ricciardo's autobiography. He literally underlines it: "I have remained alone as a scarecrow, and thus ends the life of a poor *man*."[55] Also the tailor Pio Federico bends orthography to his will and the effect is ingenious, such as when he inserts a period to enhance the last phrase as a rhyming lapidary saying: "percio'. Ve ne sono grato, se non sbeffegiato" ("therefore. I will be obliged if not mocked"). The beginning of his story also demonstrates the wit often hidden in the humble prose. The insertion of graphical signs as commas and periods and capital letters play an important part in shaping the meaning on the author's will: 'In a little town, of the strong and gentle Abruzzo, on March 11th 1891, I came to be a part, of this world. Baptized, PIO Nicola Camillo Giuseppe."[56] Those two commas breaking the sentence in unorthodox places only magnify the poetry of the antithesis "forte e gentile" (strong and gentle) and the sense of belonging in "venni a far parte, di questo mondo" (I came to be a part, of this world) heightening the "being a part" and the isolation of "this world" as the Other at the same time. The importance of the individual's first name is shown in the capitalization of the letters of his name, Pio, a short name that most needs highlighting.

The Rhetoric of Outsiders

As we have seen, these autobiographies relate to traditional rhetoric in a particular way. They call forth new critical terms that I have explored above, such as *man in history, quiet individualism,* and *ethos of the survivor.* Here are some further rhetorical considerations.

The attachment to facts is a characteristic of the rhetoric of these writers. Having their first-hand experience as the main justification for their ethos as writers, they make large use of anecdotes which they swear to be true. They dip their hands into the bucket of "non-artistic proofs," as Aristotle calls them: they bring facts as their testimonies, real facts, "fatti veri," as Calogero Di Leo says repeatedly. The stress on the authenticity of their words is always strong and it is what gives them the authority to speak: they gain authority thanks to being first-hand witnesses and protagonists of the facts they describe. As for their "artistic proofs" these authors naturally appeal to *logos, ethos,* and *pathos.* First of all, they create their own ethos, the ethos of the immigrant, the survivor, the fighter against an adverse destiny, the poor that bends but never breaks. Then, they make large use of pathos: their stories drip sufferance and hardship. Pathos is their first source of ethos, because their lives of sorrow make them heroes. The narrations of the difficulties of emigration, their arduous integration, their complex process of identification are many elements of their pathetic path. Finally, being authors *in limina* between orality and literacy, these writers create logos by largely drawing from folk culture. They rarely use enthymemes or syllogisms, but often play with maxims and examples. They repeat the maxims of their youth, the words of their ancestors with which they have grown up, and they retell "examples" from the oral tradition, stories of the past that everyone in the village knows. Maxims and examples give to their stories the flavor of eternity, the echo of timeless knowledge. Proverbs are a constant presence. For example, the ice-cream maker Calogero Di Leo colors his narration with many oral proverbs: "there are more days than sausages;"[57] "we say who lives hoping dies in despair"; "the old proverb does not err that the satiated does not believe the hungry";[58] "the old proverb says if there is life there is hope";[59] "you know the old proverb everything is good for broth";[60] "an old Sicilian proverb says the jug brings the water until it breaks."[61]

A final remark about the language that many of our authors elect as their language of writing: Italian, which is their mother tongue but a minority speech in the United States. This same means of expression keeps some of them marginal in the literary landscape, excluding English readers. Italian is for many immigrants not a choice but a necessity. Many, like Antonio Margariti and Calogero Di Leo, do not master English enough to write in it, some of them having already much difficulty scribbling in their own language. Naturally, the author's mastery of English goes alongside with their level of integration in American society. The poet Pascal D'Angelo and the educated pastry maker Gabriele Iamurri are, for example, two writers that most consciously struggle to gain acceptance and appreciation, and subsequently write in English. For a few of them instead, Italian has been a conscious choice because their writing is directed to their immediate family and to close friends, thus reinforcing the unity of their subcommunity but also cutting out the larger public of America. Pietro Greco and Gregorio Scaia, for example, write and give honor to their own small group of fellow immigrants, which are their protagonists and their audience. We have to conclude that for many of these authors marginality is a second skin that they cannot, or do not want to shed away even when trying to make the big leap and crossing the boundary of their status. Marginality is the necessary pedestal from which they spring forth, by becoming authors of their lives.

Notes

1. Giuseppe Prezzolini, *I trapiantati* (Milano: Longanesi, 1963), 409. My translation.
2. Ibid., 242.
3. Ibid., 403.
4. The entire research has been published in my book, *The Value of Worthless Lives. Writing Italian American Immigrant Autobiographies* (New York: Fordham University Press, 2007). The archives in which these texts are preserved are the Immigration History Research Center in Saint Paul, MN, the Center for Immigration Studies in Staten Island, and the Archivio Diaristico Nazionale of Pieve Santo Stefano (Arezzo, Italy). A similar study has been done in England by David Vincent, in his monumental research *Bread, Knowledge and Freedom*. An important difference between British autobiographers and our immigrants is that ours are very aware of the novelty of their work while British "authors were secure in the knowledge that in different ways and in different contexts the common people had always been historians of their own lives" (xiii).

5. Roy Pascal, *Design and Truth in Autobiography* (Cambridge: Harvard University Press, 1960), 10.
6. Luca Scarlini, *Equivoci e miraggi. Pratiche d'autobiografia oggi.* (Milano: Rizzoli, 2003), 10. My translation.
7. Anne Goldman, *Take my Word. Autobiographical Narratives of Ethnic American Working Women* (Berkley: University of California Press, 1996), ix.
8. Pierre Bourdieu, *Distinction: A Social Critique of the Judgement of Taste* (Cambridge: Harvard University Press, 1984) 7.
9. Paulo Freire develops this idea in his political concept of "selective democracy," a tricky democratic system shunned first of all by those who refuse what they are refused. In this system the impoverished ones who are not supposed to vote also refuse to get involved and interested in politics (*Education to Critical Consciousness*).
10. Paulo Freire, *Education for Critical Consciousness* (New York: Seabury Press, 1973), 44.
11. William Covino, *Magic, Rhetoric, and Literacy: An Eccentric History of the Composing Imagination* (Albany: State University of New York Press, 1994), 92.
12. Ibid., 93.
13. See William Boelhower's *Autobiographical Transactions* and James Holte's "The Representative Voice."
14. Goldman, *Take my Word*, xvii.
15. Antonio Margariti, *America! America!* (Salerno: Galzerano, 1983), 103. "I giovanotti del paese erano divisi in due gruppi Ipossente e ipoverette e io senza dirlo era coi ipoverelle." (My translation).
16. Ibid., 12. "La patria E' dei padroni, La patria dei poveri sideve fare ancora." (My translation).
17. Ibid., 87. "Io no scrivo per L'arti O' per La gloria / scrivo per quello che bolle nel mio ciriviello / scrivo e miribello al vecchio mondo.... ricordo la mia lunga esistenza poca felice o' vita se vita sipuo chiamare cioe il mio duro passato, la vita dei grandi viene scritta dai grandi storici e remane nella Storia, ma per me che sono come un granello cascato nello spazzio e fuore del mio vicinato nessuno sa che io Esisto e forse sipuo anche pensare che io scrivo per Imbizione senza Imbizione non si fa niente."
18. Pascal, *Son of Italy* (New York: Macmillan, 1924), 146.
19. Ibid., 169.
20. Ibid., 185, emphasis mine.
21. Ibid., 145.
22. Ibid., 138.
23. *Il Carroccio. Italian Review* 16, no. 1 (July 31, 1922): 56. "[Il poeta] che dalla vanga passa alla lira"; "il poeta del tugurio." (My translation).
24. D'Angelo, *Son of Italy*, 137.
25. Ibid., 74–75.
26. Calogero Di Leo, "Mai Biuriful Laif (Vita di un emigrante turista milionario)" (typescript, 2001 Archivio Diaristico Nazionale Pieve S. Stefano (AR) Italy), 1. "Signori e Signore se oggi qualsiasi persona puo' scrivere un libro della sua vita, o del suo passato, o delle sue avventure, o del suo romanzo amoroso, di qualsiasi genere.... Adesso si e aggiunta unaltra scrittora la signora Monica Luewinkie, col suo romanzo amoroso la dolce vita di qualche anno col signor Presidente degli Stati Uniti di America Bill Clinton, e un libro di pochi anni di avventura amorosa e gia' e famosa in tutto il mondo, anche essa e il presidenti vengono di discentenza di emigrante e se essa a scritto un libro perche' non lo posso scrivere anchio uno."
27. Ibid., 117. "Quello che va per il mezzo e il povero emigrande." "Lemigrante passa tante ingiustizie e umiliazione e delle volte non si puo' difendere."

28. Ibid., 167. "Tutto e parte della vita serve per imparare come Noe che aveva novecento anni ancora imparava."

29. Ibid., 118. "O ritornare intietro diretto in Italia anche mi tocca morire di fame. Dico no Calogero coraggio che chi la dura la vince."

30. Gabriel Iamurri, *The True Story of an Immigrant* (Boston: Christopher Publishing House, 1951), 48.

31. Ibid., 49.

32. Angelo Pellegrini, a successful immigrant, notices this shift in mode between Italy and America: "Had I remained in Italy, my childhood experience would have prepared me to accept frustration with patience and humility; in America they have matured as habits of work, thrift, and self-reliance as are necessary in the achievement of a certain measure of self-realization" (Angelo Pellegrini. *Immigrant's Return* [New York: Macmillan, 1951], 28).

33. Virginia Yans-McLaughlin, "Metaphors of Self in History: Subjectivity, Oral Narrative, and Immigration Studies," in *Immigration Reconsidered: History, Sociology, and Politics*, ed. Virginia Yans-McLaughlin (New York: Oxford University Press, 1990), 274.

34. Luigi Barzini, *The Italians* (New York: Atheneum, 1965), 157. Gabriel Iamurri gives another inflection to the immigrant as "man in history." In an un-American way, he asserts that personal talent alone is never sufficient to attain realization, but that history and the outer conditions are instead determinant: "I said at the beginning of the introduction to my TRUE STORY OF AN IMMIGRANT when I talked about my destiny that one in order to succeed not only has to have certain talents, but also the *soil* wherein they can develop, where they can grow to their full size, for if not they will die with him and *nothing will ever be known*" (Iamurri, *True Story*, 21, my italic).

35. Antenore Quartaroli, *Grande Disastro della Mina di Cherry, Ills. 13 Novembre 1909 scritto da Quartaroli Antenore, Uno dei Superstiti, Otto giorni Sepolto vivo nella Mina* (n.p, n.d. Archivio Diaristico Nazaionale, Pieve S. Stefano (AR), Italy), 16. "Ma eppure bisognava lottare fino all'ultimo momento anche sicuri di morire." (My translation)

36. Michele Daniele, *Signor Dottore. The Autobiography of F. Michele Daniele, Italian Immigrant Doctor (1879–1957)*, ed. Victor Rosen (New York: Exposition Press, 1959), 237.

37. Michael Lamont, "Michael Lamont," in *Italian American Autobiographies*, ed. Maria Parrino (Providence: Italian Americana Publications, University of Rhode Island, 1993), 54.

38. "According to ethnic semiotics, in the beginning was the name. In order to discover who he is, in order to begin, the subject must interrogate the beginning of his name. Ethnic discourse is a discourse of foundations" (*William Boelhower. Through a Glass Darkly: Ethnic Semiosis in American Literature* (Oxford: Oxford University Press, 1984), 81.

39. Oreste Fabrizi, "Memorie (1897–1923)" (typescript, Immigration History Research Center, Minneapolis, MN, 1987), 125. "Il cambio all'attuale Fabrizi e' avvenuto, non richiesto, quando nel 1932 mi fu concessa la cittadinanza americana. Per uno sbaglio di trascrizione nel certificato di cittadinanza il mio nome risulto' amputato della vocale 'o.'" (My translation) Fabrizi does not really care too much about this change, but he is instead incredibly attached to his past in the town of Sandonato and his whole book is a description of how it was then, from the priest to the last midwife. His memory is amazing, and the time freezes in his words.

40. Michele Pantatello, *Diario-biografico, l'ultimo immigrante della Quota, 25 nov.*

1922 (privately printed, 1967), 124. "Per rinnovare una lapide al Cimitero del mio paese dove riposano le ossa del mio Genitore, che era sbiadita e, questa volta venne fatta in marmo con lettere di bronzo per ricordare ai posteri, per sempre il nome di una famiglia scomparsa dal Paese, per le circostanze della vita." (My translation)

41. Giovanni Veltri, *The Memories of Giovanni Veltri* (Ontario, Can.: Multicultural History Society Ontario Heritage Foundation, 1987), 76.

42. G. Poletti, ed., "Un pezo di pane dale sete cruste. Diario di Gregorio Scaia (1881–1971)," *Judicaria* (May–August, 1991): 1–71. The page numbers refer to the original in the Archive of Trento.

43. Gregorio Scaia, "Un pezo di pane dale sete cruste. Diario di Gregorio Scaia (1881–1971)," *Judicaria* (May–August, 1991): 1–71. "Credo che questo sia l'unico libro che sia mai stato scritto al giorno d'ogi in riguardo ale nostre colonie cominciate al estero, l'unico e sol motivo di scrivere questo mio libro, e di narare et informare e conservare nel cuore e nela mente, dei nostri popoli e dele nostre future generazioni, i lavori ostacoli e lote che hano dovuto combatere nei viagi di mare e di tera, e sacrefici che hano dovuto afrontare e soportare i nostri Trentini, in qualunque parte del mondo, in paesi sconosciuti cosi lontani dai paesi nativi, tuto per guadagnare un pezo di pane dale sete cruste, cosi dicevano i nostri poveri avi da una volta." (My translation).

44. Pietro Greco, "Ricordi d'un immigrato, Brooklyn, 3 Maggio 1965" (typescript, 1965 Immigration History Research Center, Saint Paul), 141."La poesia di Matro Gaspare non veniva posta sulla carta per essere conservata; aveva la durata di certe combinazioni panoramiche di nuvole che, nell'immensita' azzurra dello spazio, appaiono belle e suggestive, ma che subito il vento scompagina e dissolve, e possono rimanere solo nella memoria di chi le vede." (My translation).

45. Bruna Pieracci, "Bruna Pieracci," in *The Immigrants Speak*, ed. Salvatore LaGumina (New York: Center for Immigration Studies, 1979), 33–47, 38.

46. See Georges Gusdorf's "Conditions and Limits of Autobiography." *Studies in Autobiography.* James Olney (New York: Oxford University Press, 1988).

47. Philippe Lejeune *On Autobiography* (Minneapolis: University of Minnesota Press, 1989), 167.

48. "Ah, if I were a writer!"; "Non ho istruzione e di conseguenza non penso di scrivere un romanzo, ma solo una piccola storia, il meglio che posso." (This and next, my translation)

49. "Senza lingua poca scuole e senza nessuno innizio di un mestiere."

50. Emanuele Triarsi, "La solitudine mi spinge a scrivere" (typescript, 1986 Arcivio Diaristic Nazionale, Pieve S. Stefano (AR), Italy.), 55. "Con onesto lavoro mi sono edeficato un discreto ricovero qui in America." (My translation).

51. Pio Federico, *An Autobiography*, ed. and trans. Helen Federico (privately printed, 1966), 1. "In questa storia, cerchero' di descrivere, nel miglio [*sic*] modo possibile, tutto cio' che ricordo del mio passato, dall'infanzia fino ad oggi. Se qualunque venisse a contatto, non si aspettasse di leggere 'Le mie Prigioni' di Silvio Pellico; e' una semplice storia, scritto da un 'uomo [*sic*] all'eta' di sessantanove anni, di professione sarto, con la minima istruzzione [*sic*] della quinta classe elementare, perciò.' Ve ne sono grato, se non sbeffegiato. Pio Federico Los Angeles 1960. (My translation) Silvio Pellico's book *Le mie prigioni* was known to boys like Pio who went to school right after the Italian Risorgimento.

52. The original is in Ellis Island but a photocopy of it is also in the Archive of Pieve Santo Stefano. In 1993 it won the IX Edition of the Prize Pieve-Banca Toscana, and was thus published by Giunti Gruppo Editoriale, Florence, in 1994.

53. Antonio De Piero, *L'isola della quarantina. Le avventure di un manovale friulano*

nei primi decenni delle grandi emigrazioni. (Firenze: Giunti, 1994), 72. "IO PURE HO COMPIUTO I DOVERI CARATERISTICI DELL'UOMO: I FILOSOFI NE CONTANO QUATRO: 1) FABRICARE UNA CASA 2) SCRIVERE UN LIBRO 3) E FARE UN FIGLIO 4) IMPIANTARE UN ALBERO." (My translation).

54. Elisabeth Evans, "Un attimo una vita." (typescript, 1996 Archivio Diaristic Nationale, Pieve S. Stefano (AR), Italy.), 3. "Ho la sensazione di scusarmi di esistere." (My translation)

55. "Io sono rimasto solo come uno spaventapasseri, e così finisce la vita di un povero *uomo*." Quoted in L. Faranda and L. M. Lombardi Satriani, "Memoria e autorappresentazione" in *Per una storia della memoria*, ed. C. Pitto (Cassano Ionico: Jonica Editrice, 1990, my translation). 177.

56. Federico, *An Autobiography*, 6. "In un piccolo paesello, del forte e gentile Abruzzo, l'undici marzo del 1891, venni a fare parte, di questo mondo. Battezzato. PIO Nicola Camillo Giuseppe." (My translation)

57. Di Leo, "My Biuriful," 80. This and the next ones are my translations.

58. Ibid., 175. "E per questo il vecchio proverbio non sbaglia che il sazio non crede al digiuno."

59. Ibid., 47. "Il vecchio proverbio dice finche ce vita ce speranza."

60. Ibid., 81. "Sapete il vecchio proverbio tutto fa brodo."

61. Ibid., 122. "Un vecchio proverbio Siciliano dice che tanto la brocca va all'acqua e si rompe."

Bibliography

Austin, J. L. *How to Do Things with Words*. Cambridge: Harvard University Press, 1962.

Barzini, Luigi. *The Italians*. New York: Atheneum, 1965.

Boelhower, William. *Autobiographical Transactions in Modernist America: the Immigrant, the Architect, the Artist, the Citizen*. Udine: Del Bianco, 1992.

———. *Through a Glass Darkly: Ethnic Semiosis in American Literature*. Oxford: Oxford University Press, 1984.

Bourdieu, Pierre. *Distinction: A Social Critique of the Judgement of Taste*. Translated by Richard Nice. Cambridge: Harvard University Press, 1984.

Covino, William. *Magic, Rhetoric, and Literacy: An Eccentric History of the Composing Imagination*. Albany: State University of New York Press, 1994.

D'Angelo, Pascal. *Son of Italy*. New York: Macmillan, 1924.

Daniele, Michele. *Signor Dottore. The Autobiography of F. Michele Daniele, Italian Immigrant Doctor (1879–1957)*. Edited by Victor Rosen. New York: Exposition Press: 1959.

De Piero, Antonio. *L'isola della quarantina. Le avventure di un manovale friulano nei primi decenni delle grandi emigrazioni*. Firenze: Giunti, 1994.

Di Leo, Calogero. "Mai Biuriful Laif (Vita di un emigrante turista milionario)." Typescript. Pieve Santo Stefano, Archivio Diaristico Nazionale, 2001.

Evans, Elisabeth. "Un attimo una vita." Typescript. Pieve Santo Stefano, Archivio Diaristico Nazionale, 1996.

Fabrizi, Oreste. "Memorie (1897–1923)." Typescript. Minneapolis: Immigration History Research Center, 1987.

Federico, Pio. *An Autobiography.* Edited and translated by Helen Federico. Self-printed, 1966.

Ferlinghetti, Lawrence. "The Old Italians Dying." *From the Margin. Writings in Italian Americana.* Edited by Anthony Tamburri, Paolo Giordano, Fred Gardaphe. 135–38.

Freire, Paulo. *Education for Critical Consciousness.* New York: Seabury Press, 1973.

Goldman, Anne. *Take my Word. Autobiographical Narratives of Ethnic American Working Women.* Berkley: University of California Press, 1996.

Greco, Pietro. "Ricordi d'un immigrato, Brooklyn, 3 Maggio 1965." Typescript. St. Paul, MN: Immigration History Research Center, 1965.

Gusdorf, Georges. "Conditions and Limits of Autobiography." In *Studies in Autobiography*, edited by James Olney, 28–48. New York: Oxford University Press, 1988.

Holte, James Craig. "The Representative Voice: Autobiography and the Ethnic Experience." *Melus* 9, no. 2 (1982): 25–46.

Iamurri, Gabriel. *The True Story of an Immigrant.* Boston: Christopher Publishing House, 1951.

Il Carroccio. Italian Review 16, no. 1 (July 31, 1922).

Lamont, Michael. "Michael Lamont." Parrino, Maria, ed. *Italian American Autobiographies*, edited by Maria Parring 41–54. Providence: Italian Americana Publications, University of Rhode Island, 1993.

Lejeune, Philippe, Annette Tomarken, and Edward Tomarken. "Autobiography in the Third Person." *New Literary History. Self-Confrontation and Social Vision* 9, no. 1 (Autumn 1977): 27–50.

Margariti, Antonio. *America! America!* Salerno: Galzerano, 1983.

Ong, Walter. *Orality and Literacy.* London: Metheun, 1981.

Pantatello, Michele. *Diario-biografico, l'ultimo immigrante della Quota, 25 nov. 1922.* Self-published. St. Paul, MN: Immigration History Research Center, 1967.

Pascal, Roy. *Design and Truth in Autobiography.* Cambridge: Harvard University Press, 1960.

Pellegrini, Angelo. *Immigrant's Return.* New York: Macmillan, 1951.

Piacenza, Aldobrando. *Memories.* Typescript. St. Paul, MN: Immigration History Research Center, 1956.

Pieracci, Bruna. "Bruna Pieracci." In *The Immigrants Speak*, edited by Salvatore LaFumina, 33–47. New York: Center for Immigration Studies, 1979.

Pitto, Cesare, ed. *Per una storia della memoria. Antropologia e storia dei processi migratori.* Cassano Ionico: Jonica Editrice, 1990.

Previtali, Giuseppe. *Doctor Beppo. An Italian Doctor in America.* N.p.: Giovanni Previtali, 1984.

Prezzolini, Giuseppe. *I trapiantati.* Milano: Longanesi, 1963.

Quartaroli, Antenore. *Grande Disastro della Mina di Cherry, Ills. 13 Novembre 1909 scritto da Quartaroli Antenore, Uno dei Superstiti, Otto giorni Sepolto vivo nella Mina.* N.p.: Pieve Santo Stefano, n.d. Archivio Diaristico Nazionale.

Scaia, Gregorio. "Un pezo di pane dale sete cruste. Diario di Gregorio Scaia (1881–1971)." *Judicaria* (May–August 1991): 1–71.

Scarlini, Luca. *Equivoci e miraggi. Pratiche d'autobiografia oggi.* Milano: Rizzoli, 2003.

Serra, Ilaria. *The Value of Worthless Lives: Writing Italian American Immigrant Autobiographies.* New York: Fordham University Press, 2007.

Triarsi, Emanuele. "La solitudine mi spinge a scrivere." Pieve Santo Stefano, Archivio Diastico Nationale. Typescript, 1986.

Vanzetti, Bartolomeo. *Una vita proletaria*. Salerno: Galzerano, 1987.

Veltri, Giovanni. *The Memories of Giovanni Veltri*. Edited by John Potestio. Ontario: Multicultural History Society Ontario Heritage Foundation, 1987.

Vincent, David. *Bread, Knowledge and Freedom. A Study of Nineteenth-Century Working Class Autobiography*. London: Europa Publication Limited, 1981.

Yans-McLaughlin, Virginia. "Metaphors of Self in History: Subjectivity, Oral Narrative, and Immigration Studies." In *Immigration Reconsidered: History, Sociology, and Politics*, edited by Virginia Yars-McLaughlin, 254–90. New York: Oxford University Press, 1990.

"To Live Outside the Law, You Must Be Honest": Words, Walls, and the Rhetorical Practices of *The Angolite*

Scott Whiddon

On January 15, 2005, Wilbert Rideau was released after forty-four years behind bars at the Louisiana State Penitentiary at Angola.[1] Rideau's retrial—his fourth since 1961– rekindled the divisions over race and rehabilitation that have contextualized his case since his initial arrest for the killing of Julia Ferguson in Lake Charles, Louisiana. Rideau's retrial also once again brought national attention to *The Angolite*, the award-winning prison-based news magazine that he edited for over three decades. Since the early 1950s, *The Angolite* has provided journalistic and creative accounts of prison life to an audience both inside and outside the walls of the penitentiary. *Angolite* articles such as "The Deathmen," "The Sexual Jungle," "Conversations With the Dead," and "Prisonomics" allow readers on both sides of the walls, bars, and concertina wire to get a glimpse of prison life. It has been featured in the *New York Times, All Things Considered, Nightline*, and other popular media venues. In 1979, *The Angolite* won both the Robert F. Kennedy Journalism Award and the Silver Gavel Award from the American Bar Association; the following year, Rideau and coeditor Billy Wayne Sinclair won the coveted George Polk Award for Special Interest Reporting—one of the most prestigious journalism prizes next to the Pulitzer. *The Angolite* is also a seven-time finalist for the National Magazine Award.

Of course, neither Rideau—a former death row inmate—nor any staff member of the *Angolite* was able to accept any awards in person, despite the fact that in each case, it was the first time that an inmate had won any of these accolades. Yet *Angolite* staffers continued to attract attention in the public sphere despite their positioning as outsiders who lack the usual access to sites of participation such as in the academy or the mainstream press.[2] Rideau was also a coproducer for *The Farm: Life Inside Angola Prison*, a Sundance Award-winning and

Oscar-nominated documentary. His article "Why Prisons Don't Work," featured in the March 21, 1994, issue of *Time*, helped popularize both *The Angolite* itself and the claim that he was "the most rehabilitated prisoner in America."[3]

The tangled history of Louisiana State Penitentiary is well documented in Mark Carlton's *Politics and Punishment: The History of the Louisiana State Penal System*.[4] In 1939, a national news story by Harnett Kane dubbed Angola "the Alcatraz of the South." In 1951, in the wake of an inmate protest against harsh working conditions where thirty-one prisoners slashed their own heel tendons, *Collier's* labeled the facility "America's Worst Prison." Despite improvements by various wardens and governors, especially Gov. Robert F. Kennon, the massive budget reductions throughout the 1950s and 1960s along with the high number of inmate assaults and murders led Angola to be known as "the bloodiest prison in the South." During the 1970s, many inmates took to the practice of sleeping with Sears Roebuck catalogs tied to their chests to protect them from late-night knifings. In 1974, a U.S. district court judge ordered the state of Louisiana to end such violence and improve conditions for inmates. Within two years, Angola was desegregated and Rideau became the first black staff member of *The Angolite*. Already fairly famous for his efforts with *The Lifer*, another prison newspaper circulated by black churches, Rideau helped turn *The Angolite* into a credible, well-known publication.[5]

While many readers and scholars of prison journalism might see *The Angolite* and Wilbert Rideau as synonymous, the power of this publication goes beyond the accomplishments of a single man. Considering such theorists as Goffman and Foucault, the work of the generations of *Angolite* writers is a highly politicized literacy practice that works against what might be called "institutionalization." *The Angolite*'s success is fairly miraculous considering that prisons, in the words of activist and scholar Angela Davis, are an absent-presence, "a black hole into which the detritus of contemporary capitalism is deposited."[6] Prisons, especially in the American South, are placed elsewhere, far away from our daily consciousness. Furthermore, Americans rarely think of inmates (aside from the rare exceptions) as highly literate, rational beings. As noted by literacy theorist and prison ethnographer Anita Wilson, "There is almost a universal theory that illiteracy and criminality are synonymous. National literacy surveys around the world inevitably focus on the lack of literacy ability among the world's prisoners, and statistics are frequently linked to educational shortcomings."[7]

The aim of this essay is to both introduce *The Angolite* to the scholarly community and to analyze the rhetorical strategies that are typically featured in current issues via the lens of contemporary literacy studies. While literacy studies is certainly not a new field, it might be easy for some readers to simply associate "literacy" with "the ability to read and write."[8] However, as noted by James Paul Gee, the focus of literacy studies "should not be language, or literacy, but *social practices*."[9] It is not simply reading or writing that is paramount, but rather how such practices determine *insiders* and *outsiders*. Gee defines discourses as "ways of being in the world; they are forms of life which integrate words, acts, values, beliefs, attitudes, and social identities as well as gestures, glances, body positions, and clothes."[10] In short, a discourse "is sort of an identity kit."[11] Scholars connected with the New Literacy Studies, including Brian Street, David Barton and Mary Hamilton, Roz Ivanic, and the aforementioned Anita Wilson, take a "situated" view of literacy/ies, "where multiplicities of reading, writing, and literacy-related activities are contextualized within day-to-day life."[12] Barton and Hamilton provide a succinct explanation of such an approach to literacy that radically departs from a traditional, "autonomous" model: "Literacy is primarily something that people do; it is an activity, located in the space between thought and text. Literacy does not just reside in people's heads as a set of skills to be learned and it does not just reside on paper, captured as text to be analyzed. Like all human activity, literacy is essentially social, and it is located in the interaction between people."[13]

Gee provides the link between "literacy" and "discourse/s." As he argues in "What is Literacy?," "Discourses are inherently 'ideological.' They crucially involve a set of values and viewpoints in terms of which one must speak and act, at least while being in the discourse; otherwise one doesn't count as being in it."[14] Therefore, "literacy," among the range of definitions we attach to it, is *social;* it is a method of identification and membership status. As recent scholars such as J. Elspeth Stuckey have noted, literacy can be violent, divisive, controlling; while we might always position literacy as "emancipatory" (and, at times, most prison writers understandably tend to perpetuate this notion), literacy—as a social device—separates the center from the margins, the insiders from the outsiders. Although *Angolite* writers are certainly outside the realm of traditional discourse, they use their long-standing publication as an attempt to enter larger conversations on punishment.

One tool that can be used to connect the New Literacy Studies' concerns with ideology and community to *The Angolite*'s primary considerations of penal culture is James Boyd White's discussions of "constitutive rhetoric." White sought to reshape how law is typically understood away from a system of fixed rules and procedures and toward a branch of rhetoric: "the central art by which community and culture are established, maintained, and transformed."[15] Drawing upon Gorgias's classical definition of rhetoric "as the art of persuading people about matters of justice and injustice in public places of the state," White emphasizes the rhetorical aspects of legal discourse that extend beyond mere persuasion and, instead, "creates, or proposes to create, a community of people, talking to and about each other."[16] "Every time one speaks as a lawyer," White argues, "one establishes a character, an ethical identity."[17] Although White's argument is mainly targeted toward traditional legal argumentation (within the courtroom, for example), his concern with how language—and, specifically, language that is concerned with punishment—constitutes how human agents are viewed in the public sphere seems right at home with the daily work of a newspaper completely written and edited by inmates in a historically troubled penitentiary.

The various staff members of *The Angolite* collectively attempt to compose a counter-identity against the American conception of the prisoner, a conception that has been masterfully traced by John M. Sloop in *The Cultural Prison: Discourse, Prisoners, and Punishment*.[18] Rather than focusing on individual prisoners, reform polices, or even punishment itself, Sloop's study is centered on how prisoners and punishment have been represented in mainstream American media during the past half century. Sloop provides a comprehensive account of one set of discourses—"all articles from popular journals under the heading of prisoners (or relevant subheadings) in the Reader's Guide to Periodical Literature from 1950 to 1993."[19] He notes that "studying the articulations that surround a term like prisoner aids us in understanding the cultural definitions of institutional discipline."[20] This work extends Foucault's genealogical practice to our own era and place; in short, he attempts to describe not only how we as a culture have "seen" prisoners within particular historical moments, but also how such representations are indeed part of punishment himself. "We cannot understand the enacted meaning of the term 'prisoners'" Sloop argues, "by looking only at what philosophers and sociologists mean by it unless such philosophers and sociologists have taken their discourse into the public forum and made claims in the ideological struggle over its meaning."[21] While Americans' notions of prisoners have changed over the course of one hundred years in varying, complex ways, and while the popular representation of female inmates over the past fifty years is relatively stable—"positioned along the lines of the gendered roles of motherhood and protector of cultural morality"—representations of male inmates during the past thirty years have become radically violent and Africanized.[22] As Sloop notes toward the end of his discussion of 1975 to 1993 (in which most rehabilitation-oriented programs were removed from federal and state facilities), "Male African-American prisoners (and, to a degree, other nonwhite male prisoners) are constrained by their past representations."[23]

Yet *Angolite* writers take on the identity of journalists, historians, critics, photographers, and lawyers; by learning and practicing these roles, they practice literacy in a radically different way than what is usually associated with the faceless, nameless millions of Americans living under surveillance as part of the prison-industrial complex.[24] By writing in genres that are recognizable to mainstream readers (or, as White posits, "by speaking the language of his or her audience, whatever it may be"),[25] these outsiders attempt to enter discourses that are normally as sealed and closed as the prison itself.[26] In light of Barton and Hamilton as well as James Boyd White, an issue of *The Angolite* is essentially an interaction between writers and readers (both inside and outside the boundaries of the penitentiary) who collaboratively reassess the cultural conception of prison and prisoners. As an example of constitutive rhetoric, *Angolite* staff members attempt to reshape commonly held assumptions of the prisoner, to grow beyond a marginalized status, to become something other than *other*.

The Angolite exists and has always existed in what Wilson (drawing upon Bhaba and others) calls a "third space"—a position between the institution of the prison and the various literacies of the "free world":

> In order to "win the battle" [against becoming "prisonized" or "institutionalized"] people in prison construct a space between inside and outside worlds where they can "occupy their minds" while living out their everyday prison lives. Bounded by a consensual experience—in this case the experience of prison—such a space can accommodate a whole community with a membership that can include both central and peripheral players, prisoners and staff, and those who live both inside and outside the prison walls.[27]

In a similar manner, Adela C. Licona, drawing on the mestiza consciousness work ("which refuses fixed dichotomous structures and their implications for matters of (self) representation"[28]) of Gloria Anzaldua, sees third space as "a location and/or practice."[29] "As a location," Licona argues, "third space has the potential to be a space of shared understanding and meaning-making."[30] Rideau himself has argued that *The Angolite* office is one of the few "neutral spaces" within LSP—a space where writers work to construct an account of the world of Angola and the larger discourse of the penitentiary.[31] While the actual "neutrality" of *The Angolite* as site and publication is a complicated issue (which will be discussed later in this essay), this "third space" allows for the long-standing connection between *Angolite* writers and both their inmate and non-inmate audiences; by drawing on genres and modes that are recognizable to non-inmate readers, and by presenting themselves in a tone that reflects both candor and credibility, *Angolite* writers create a third space that reaches out to both inmates and "freemen." As writers, they attempt—and, as noted by the letters to *The Angolite* from non-inmate readers, are somewhat successful—in offering an alternative to the unredeemable convict. Tommy Tarr, a former assistant editor in the late 1960s, offers a succinct articulation of what *The Angolite* means for both its writers and readers:

> [The *Angolite*] is the voice of the convict far removed from the centers of influence. It is dedicated to the men it represents, and the women too, though they are some distance from us in point of space. Though such a journal has a limited sphere of influence, it reaches those whose words are heeded, and if it can ever, at any time engage or ally one man, it has done a great deal. There are few people aware of or concerned with the state of corrections. . . . When an editorial staff puts together a magazine, it does so in the hope that someone will realize . . . that convicts are real people, just like the guy next door. . . . The truth about prison is an untold story—we doubt it can be told. But every member of the Penal Press, who is allowed to, makes an effort at telling that story.[32]

As of this essay, the *Angolite* has only been briefly discussed in a scholarly context by James McGrath Morris in his *Jailhouse Journalism: The Fourth Estate Behind Bars*, who argues that it is a success in the rapidly vanishing world of prison journalism. I am indebted to Morris's foundational historical study of the penal press and his chapter on *The Angolite* in particular; what I will add here is yet another context, that of current studies of literacy. As outsiders, *Angolite* staff writers appropriate rhetorical strategies that are common in mainstream texts and discussions in order to position their own resistance and to provide a counteridentity that challenges contemporary notions of prisoners and prison culture; for these writers, literacy is a sociopolitical practice.

For the purposes of this essay, and because Wilbert Rideau's writing is fairly well known despite the absence of *Angolite*-centered rhetorical studies in academic publications, I have mainly limited my sources to only the issues published during 2003, allowing for a closer look at the actual writing within each issue. In 2003, *The Angolite* published a series of combined issues to make up for gaps in publication during the previous year. At the time, the staff included Kerry Meyers, Lane Nelson, Douglas Dennis, Clarence Goodlow, Jeffery Hillburn, and Ronald Walker. Other LSP inmates as well as "free" writers also contributed occasional articles and creative works. Such contributions further the collaborative nature of this publication; in a sense, *The Angolite* functions as a space where staff members, LSP officials, non-inmate writers and readers, and inmates from both LSP and other institutions come together through the act of writing to renegotiate what it means to be an inmate in a maximum security penitentiary.

As noted by Kendall R. Phillips, resistance and political engagement through writing might seem improbable considering the complex nature of power in Foucault's model of discourse. Phillips's thorough exploration of rhetoric and Foucault locates a space for invention and even resistance to the totalizing power of discourse and the seeming implausibility for a free agent participating in emancipatory politics.[33] White, in his work on constitutive rhetoric, also notes the role of power and dominance: "The establishment of comprehensible relations and shared meanings, the making of the kind of community that enables people to say 'we' about what they do . . . involves persuasion."[34] In this manner, *The Angolite*—as a body of writing by inmates, a group of marginalized rhetors, a physical space within a historically troubled institution—is an impressive rhetorical act in both its longevity as a publication and the power of its prose. Despite its physical and ideological marginalization, *The Angolite* works as a site of resistance by maintaining an ethos of responsible journalism and by using genres and methods that are valued by both the inmates at LSP and non-inmate audiences. It recognizes the complex nature of power that marks their hours as writers and inmates, yet it continues to enact contemplation and potential social change from the unlikeliest of locations.

"DOWN AT THE PENITENTIARY . . ."—PHOTOGRAPHS AND COVERS

While quite different from those mimeographed, typewritten pages of the early years and even up until the 1970s, the current issues of *The Angolite* maintain many of the generic features that have always been part of its structure. All issues begin with a striking photograph or pen-and-ink drawing on the cover: a lone inmate mops down "The Walk," a long concrete sidewalk that connects the main building to cellblocks and dorms; an exaggerated skull draped by the state flag of Texas and surrounded by headlines from Texas newspapers ("Karla Faye Tucker dies by lethal injection; first woman to be executed in

U.S. in 15 years"; "Texas kills 33rd inmate this year; accounts for nearly half of all executions in U.S."); a stark, black and white photograph of Point Lookout, the prison cemetery. The cover from May/June 2003 portrays inmate Eugene Tanniehill at work as a preacher—offset in the photo by hand-drawn and photographic clips of shackles, nails, and the old "white stripe" uniforms of the penal farm; the July/August/September issue announces the new education center at Angola, underscored by a passage from Judge Henry A. Politz: "Every person deserves to be treated fairly, with respect.... There ought to be no short cuts with people's rights."

Such covers are worthy of their own analysis; yet it is the photographs, pictures, and covers that often draw readers into the world of both Angola and *The Angolite*. Each cover is either the work of a staff member or a contributor from within the prison system. The covers of *The Angolite* as well as the photographs that are a staple of each issue draw readers into the world of Angola; the articles that accompany these images provide evidence for how inmates understand the context of the prison. The difficulty of interpreting photographs that center on incarceration and punishment has been taken up in several critical texts. Diana George and Diane Shoos, for example, explore the complicated nature of lynching photographs and how they seem to articulate a mere historical event and not a site for continued inquiry; the reader/viewer is placed in a tangled position between witness and voyeur, and George and Shoos conclude by noting how both positions have a role in "eclipsing" the political aspects of such photographs.[35]

Yet *Angolite* staff members are aware of the rhetorical power of such images; photographs *of* inmates *by* inmates and published within an inmate magazine that calls attention to their position as outsiders are a strong representational force and work as an incentive for readers to peruse pages and vicariously "enter" the gates of Angola Prison with an inmate as their guide. Consequently, *Angolite* photographs have been the impetus for other published writings, such as Jane Officer's *If I Should Die: A Death Row Correspondence*. Officer, who corresponded with death row inmate Andrew Lee Jones, presents their letters along with *Angolite* photographs of the electrocuted body of Robert Wayne Williams; the brutal images show the first- , second- , third- , and fourth-degree burns on Williams's face and head and were used to argue against the use of the electric chair as a means of execution for failing to meet evolving standards of decency. In one of the letters, Williams states that "these people here . . . they want us dead and forgotten . . . they are trying to break our spirit but I won't let them break mine.... We are lost to the outside world.... The way it seem, they are just going to take us completely off the map."[36] Clearly, one

"TO LIVE OUTSIDE THE LAW, YOU MUST BE HONEST" 173

purpose of *The Angolite* and specifically the photographs contained within is to combat such erasure.

As part of the back cover, each *Angolite* issue carries a subscription form for outside readers, framed by the masthead: "Curious . . . about the world beyond bars?" This question reverberates with the difficult viewer status as voyeur or witness, and such a position is further complicated with the printed claim in each issue that *The Angolite* has "the freedom to publish whatever it desired, subject to the same standards governing professional journalism." Proclaiming that *The Angolite* is "America's boldest experiment in journalism and freedom of expression in the world behind bars," the advertisement is scaffolded by praise from such acclaimed writers as Peter Jennings ("considered the best prison journalism in the country") and Elmore Leonard ("fascinating samples of prison life . . . The real stuff"). Such claims, along with similar passages from *The New York Times*, the New Orleans *Times-Picayune*, the *Baltimore Sun*, and other publications, work to show that the writings contained within *The Angolite* are seen as worthy and laudable by mainstream, "insider" institutions.

The photograph in the subscription advertisement in the case of four of the five 2003 issues—a group of inmates working on the penal farm in the blistering Louisiana sun while an armed guard on horseback, positioned in the foreground, looks on – reminds us that these men are certainly outsiders who lack access to traditional forms of rhetorical, physical, and social participation. As with all of the photographs printed in each issue, this strategy is consciously deployed as a legitimizing discourse that both acknowledges their perceived untrustworthiness and shows that *The Angolite* is indeed, as Leonard notes, "the real stuff" and a force that can spur action and even reform.

"NOW I BEEN IN JAIL WHEN ALL MY MAIL SHOWED . . .": *ANGOLITE* EDITORIALS

During the years of Rideau's editorship, each *Angolite* issue began with an editorial entitled "Getting it Together." Such a phrase seems fitting considering both the purposes of *The Angolite* as well as the themes of rebirth, self-reliance, and rehabilitation that are hallmarks of prison writings: "Redemption, second chances, change—it's a thread woven into the fabric of our society. If there is no such thing as change or redemption, then we might as well fire all the preachers, counselors, social workers. . . . If redemption isn't possible, then we are lost to perdition, we are lost."[37]

In 2003, editor Kerry Meyers changed the name of the editorial column to "Wire to Wire," and the above passage is from his first installment under this new title; drawings of barbed wire and a guard tower again cue readers to the outsider position of *The Angolite* staff. The January/February issue specifically assured readers on both sides of the wire that "Wilbert Rideau's legacy with *The Angolite* is assured" and that the column will "continue to provoke thought, encourage dialogue, and stir the conscience"[38] of *The Angolite* audience. Meyers's editorials highlight key features of each respective issue, introduce readers to new staff members, and offer thoughtful reflections on topics that are central to the larger conversation about prison culture.

In five editorials in 2003, Meyers discusses such topics as the removal of college courses and Pell Grants for inmates, the rapidly aging prison population in Louisiana, the failures and successes of inmates who have left Angola, and the range of legislation passed in 2003 that affect prison life such as reforms for juvenile justice and the execution of the mentally retarded. In each of these editorials, Meyers—like his predecessor Rideau—attempts to show that, in his words, "There is no such thing as a typical prisoner. Each is an individual whose path and circumstances are unique."[39] Meyers's claim in the July/August/September editorial also offers a similar appeal: "No, Angola is not some warped fusion of television and Hollywood—Oz, Shawshank Redemption, Cool Hand Luke, or an old gangster film. As titillating as it sounds, sweaty, muscle bound, tattooed and hygienically challenged monsters rattling bars and howling sexual insults . . . waiting to pounce at the first opportunity, do not populate this prison."[40]

While Meyers notes that prison is "a societal necessity,"[41]—a claim that runs counter to the work of such activists as Angela Davis who call for the complete abolition of the prison as an international institution—his writing in each editorial articulates that prisoners can indeed be ethical, literate, intelligent, and worthy of attention. Instead of an unfocused rant, each editorial introduces an organized collection of writings centered on inmate issues. Meyers's voice would be right at home with any editorial column in a major newspaper. Such a practice—a practice that is recognizable by most readers as an established genre in journalism and as a dialogical act, inviting responses via reader mail—continues the traditions established by previous *Angolite* editors. *The Angolite* positions prisoners as outsiders who accept their punishment but still work toward improving their daily lives behind bars via a range of social practices. Meyers represents himself and his fellow staffers as ethical rhetors, providing a balanced, reasonable account of Angola-centered events and concerns.

"You forgot to leave me with the key": *Angolite* Columns

Like most magazines, *The Angolite* features several regularly appearing segments that focus on specific issues. Such divisions help give a sense of organization and continuity to the *Angolite* as a whole. Again, considering Sloop's assessment of contemporary representations of American prisoners, one might expect *The Angolite* to merely be an all out assault with no sense of rhetorical balance or restraint. Instead, the subdivisions—such as "Inside Angola," "Religion in Prison," "Legal Spectrum," "Straight Talk," "News Briefs," "Sports Front," and "Club News"—offer cues as to how *The Angolite* functions for both inmate and non-inmate readers. Such divisions employ recognizable journalistic genres: they report events, explain issues, profile figures of interest, summarize data, and narrate stories. Several of these regularly occurring columns are strong examples of source-based writing, drawing upon legal rulings, newspaper articles, scholarly books, and other mainstream texts. The meaningful use of such materials helps *Angolite* writers—again, positioned by the dominant sphere as outsiders—to gain a further sense of credibility. For example, "Legal Roundup"—a collaboratively composed column– provides clear explanations of state and federal rulings and developments. Although *The Angolite* is not completely centered on legal issues like *Prison Legal News* (another popular inmate-written publication based in Washington state), this column not only directly connects to *The Angolite*'s inmate audience but also helps to represent *Angolite* writers as journalists who can present source materials effectively and ethically.

Douglas Dennis, a forty-four-year veteran of Angola, is the key writer behind "News Briefs," "Straight Talk," and the regularly appearing book review section. While "Straight Talk" simply provides a two- to four-page list of various passages from current media organized by topics such as "Prison Life" or "The War on Drugs" (each with a full citation and occasional brief commentary), "News Briefs" functions more like a traditional roundup of recent developments interconnected by Dennis's riveting prose style. In the issues published during 2003, Dennis discusses such topics as the Prison Rape Elimination Act, exorbitant phone rates for families calling their loved ones in prison, voting restrictions on ex-prisoners, "boot camps" for juvenile inmates, state-level clemency, sports therapy, DNA testing, and restorative justice. Each sub-column provides full source materials and a balanced account of each topic. Dennis's book reviews are also an excellent example of an inmate who has become an expert in a range of penal issues. For example, in his review of *Aging Prisoners: Crisis in*

American Corrections, Dennis shows how author Ronald Aday's conclusions strike on a local level: "With half its total population 40 and older, Angola has become far more peaceful than in its bloody past and far more needy of medical attention. Health services will consume more than $14 million during the 2003/2004 fiscal year, or 14.6 percent of Angola's $97 million budget."[42] Such connections not only help develop his reviews but also provide further implicit arguments against popular conceptions of Angola and prison culture in general. While book reviews are common in mainstream journals and magazines, the mere fact that these reviews are composed by a long-term inmate shows how an outsider can use mainstream genres to articulate a voice that might be deemed as valid by non-inmate, "insider" readers. In a 1993 interview with the *Caucus Quarterly,* Dennis offers the following comment about the need for media accountability and calls attention to *The Angolite*'s sense of responsibility; such claims seem far from the popular representations of prison life traced in Sloop's study: "I think the media, including us, print media and electronic media, have a responsibility to the public. They're always so quick to holler about freedom of the press, and I'd be in the front ranks waving the placard, too, but where you have a freedom you have a responsibility, and in my opinion I see a major shirking of responsibility."[43]

While many of these regularly appearing columns initially appear to be written specifically for inmate readers, these writings often offer cues for non-inmate audiences and even readers who aren't so familiar with *The Angolite* or the troubled history of Angola. In the January/February issue, a feature in the "Inside Angola" series entitled "Doing Their Part" begins with a brief description that is clearly unnecessary for Angola inmates; such a move, however slight, shows how *Angolite* writers are aware of their position and how they wish to include readers from both sides of the wire: "Isolated in the northwestern corner of West Feliciana Parish, 20 miles from the nearest town and surrounded on three sides by the Mississippi River, the deep ravines of the Tunica Hills on the fourth, Louisiana State Penitentiary at Angola is considered the middle of nowhere. Though the prison is isolated, its more than 1,800 employees are not."[44]

"Inside Angola" typically covers a wide range of topics, such as graduation ceremonies from technical education programs, deaths of inmates, outsider visits to LSP, and updates on inmate programs. The inclusion of events such as graduations, deaths, visits, etc., serve to represent Angola to non-inmate readers as a functional social space—perhaps more like the outside world than like popular depictions of prison life. Still, there are obvious differences; one segment, also from the January/February issue, discusses the results of DNA testing which led to the release of an inmate who had already served sixteen years behind bars as an innocent man. Another reports how the "Red Hat Cellblock"—"a concrete block of 30 five-by-seven foot cells with solid steel doors, no heat, [and] a 12-inch square barred, windowless and screenless hole ... in each cell for ventilation" with only "a concrete slab ... as a bed, and a hole in the floor for a toilet" and used to break the most incorrigible of inmates from 1934 until 1973—is now designated as a historical landmark and listed in the National Registry of Historic Places.[45] As a legacy to the cruel history of Angola—at times, each tiny cell held 5 to 6 men and was sometimes used as a holding cell for inmates bound for death row—current Warden Burl Cain argued that it was necessary to save the building "so we don't go back there."[46] Such topics seem to serve the rhetorical purpose of presenting prisoners as victims themselves.

The article "Doing Their Part," quoted above, focuses on a call-up of reservists and National Guard members in late 2002 and how Angola employees and their families—as well as Angola inmates—were affected. *Angolite* staffers interviewed prison employees who either had children deployed for the Persian Gulf or were called up themselves, focusing on the "anxiety of those left behind."[47] This article also notes that many Angola inmates have sons and daughters in active duty or in the National Guard or reserves. What is crucial here is that the article closes by noting that because of this event, "prisoners and employees, who work and live together, will have one less thing that separates them."[48] While not all "Inside Angola" articles explicitly try to establish a connection between staff and inmates—or, furthermore, inmates and "freemen"—such tactics that attempt to challenge audience conceptions of prisoners and of what constitutes the Angola community are quite common, as seen in another "Inside Angola" article from that same issue titled "Angola Blues": "Warden Burl Cain says nine out of ten Angola prisoners will die here. Given that, and the yearly reduction of numbers of Angolans being released, one would expect this maximum security prison, packed to the gills with killers, rapists, and armed robbers, to be a maelstrom of desperation and violence.... In truth, Angola is safer than a typical shopping mall. This is no accident; it is Cain's plan.[49]

This example brings up the question of *Angolite* representations of authority figures such as wardens, guards, and other LSP employees. In 1974, Warden C. Paul Phelps publicly stated that *The Angolite* was free to publish whatever it wanted, as long as the newsmagazine was held to the same standards as any other news publication; *The Angolite* would be "a credible vehicle of information in a place traditionally ruled by rumor."[50] Such a statement pushed the publication into the public sphere and eventually led to Rideau's popularity as a writer. All wardens since Phelps, including Cain, have held to this position. Still, this question of editorial control merits some discussion. Eleanor Novek, in her ethnographic study of a more recently created inmate newspaper at a women's facility, posits the notion of "the devil's bargain": "administrators extend inmates the privilege of creating a newspaper that gives them voice but can revoke that privilege suddenly and arbitrarily."[51] Morris offers a similar concern in his history of the penal press: "A prison journalist who is unwilling to go along with the censor's capricious blue pencil may find the description 'uncooperative, disrespectful of authority' in his parole application file."[52]

While in-house murder rates are certainly quite low under Cain's administration and while his championing of what he calls "moral rehabilitation" is popular with religious groups that volunteer at LSP, Cain has not always been shown in a favorable light by the popular press. As noted by *Christianity Today* writer Chris Frink, Louisiana senator Don Cravins (who chaired a Senate committee overseeing prisons) was unimpressed with the Cain-era Angola and noted that Cain and his staff "do what they want . . . There is no accountability."[53] Warden Cain was also accused of bribery by *God of the Rodeo: The Search for Hope, Faith, and a Six-Second Ride in Louisiana's Angola Prison* author Daniel Bergner, who argued that Cain tried to "wrest editorial control of the book and charge him $50,000 for continued access to the prison."[54] While Cain denied the allegations, the Department of Corrections settled out of court. Cain has also been held in contempt by a federal judge in a lawsuit filed by an inmate "who claimed he was punished for blowing the whistle on the prison's canned-food relabeling business, run with inmate labor."[55] Furthermore, a 1998 Senate committee chaired by Senator Cravins accused Cain of "allowing a businessman to keep horses at the prison and of squelching . . . *The Angolite*."[56] Although Cain admitted to the first charge, he denied any attempt at censorship.[57]

While Warden Cain has become quite the public figure, considering his role in the Angola Prison Rodeo (see below) and his participation in documentaries such as *The Farm*, it is both impossible and outside the scope of this essay to determine the exact level of influence that wardens and staff members play in the daily life of *The Angolite*. As noted by photographer Deborah Luster, whose *One Big Self: Prisoners of Louisiana* captures the images of several Angola inmates and earned praise from the *New York Times*, wardens "are only going to let you see what they want you to see."[58] Luster's claim seems quite similar to a comment Rideau made in a recent speech at the Medill School of Journalism at Northwestern University: "Let's face it—if you want to continue publishing you can't alienate the authority."[59]

Despite the above claims against Cain, one could easily argue that he is a vast improvement from Angola wardens of the past and that LSP is certainly a better place it was during the first half of the twentieth century. For example, educational opportunities for inmates at LSP have drastically increased despite the loss of federal grants for college courses for inmates, as noted in several *Angolite* articles as well as accounts within popular Louisiana newspapers. In another "Inside Angola" article, Cain is praised for his participation in a prison cemetery program; Point Lookout, a cemetery for inmates whose families cannot afford to bury their inmate-relatives, is supported by two inmate self-help organizations. The project "replaced a 'get it over and done with' approach . . . with a group of volunteers who gave dignity to the occasion by providing a small interment service at the gravesite."[60] Cain is quoted in the article as wanting "dignified burials that family members . . . would find appropriate."[61] "When a prisoner dies," Cain states, "his sentence is over. . . . He's served his time." Such a practice plays a strong role in the lives of the inmates at LSP: "It makes a difference, not only to [family members] but to us," states project coordinator Checo Yancy; "It helps us deal with what, eventually, will be all our fates."[62]

Such programs, as reported in "Inside Angola" and "On the Farm," another short, inmate-written column that appears near the end of every *Angolite*, reflect well on both the prison administration and the inmates themselves; Cain and other Angola staff members are frequently represented in *The Angolite* as integral participants and even collaborators in LSP events. Furthermore, the mere notion that *The Angolite* still exists while dozens of prison publications have folded speaks volumes about Warden Cain and his staff.[63] In fact, Warden Cain made several public statements before the release of Wilbert Rideau supporting his rehabilitation and his abilities as a journalist. While academic writers and prison activists might wish to portray all Southern prison wardens as similar to figures in popular films such as *Cool Hand Luke*, the representation of power figures within prison publications is a much more complicated issue.

Instead, the matter at hand is how *Angolite* writers offer a representation of what occurs "Inside Angola," and such articles as "Doing Their Part" reflect a keen sense of the delicate situation between inmate journalists and prison authority figures. In several instances, *Angolite* writers accentuate positive changes made by wardens throughout its history as a publication. While *The Angolite* does not exist to merely represent Louisiana State Penitentiary as "safe," the tactics in the above examples reflect how these outsiders deliberately use rhetoric to gain a sense of access to mainstream discussions of prisons and to represent themselves as responsible, ethical journalists. While we, as readers, might not ever physically see "Inside Angola," *Angolite* writers position themselves as honest, trustworthy, and able to give us a glimpse of life behind bars.

Two other regularly occurring *Angolite* columns—"Sports News" and "Club News"—also attempt to give readers a sense of the day-to-day activities of life at LSP. Programs such as organized football and basketball as well as inmate organizations such as the Human Relations Club, Veterans Incarcerated, the Angola Special Civic Project, and the Angola Lifers Association are incredibly important to the lives of LSP inmates; such programs allow inmates to take leadership positions and to succeed in ways that are antithetical to the popular national conception of long-term inmates. While this coverage might be more important to *The Angolite*'s inmate audience, stories that discuss football championships, fund-raising efforts, educational opportunities, and other inmate club and sports team related activities are a prime component in the rhetorical positioning of *The Angolite* as a publication read by both non-inmates and prisoners alike; as readers, we are shown men taking part in activities that are normally considered as character building and philanthropic and, recalling Gee, as "ways of being in the world" despite the prisoner's exile status, as opposed to the aforementioned "maelstrom of desperation and violence" that might be associated with such a place as Angola.

"I CAN TAKE HIM TO YOUR HOUSE BUT I CAN'T UNLOCK IT": *ANGOLITE* FEATURE ARTICLES

Generally, each issue of *The Angolite* includes two to four longer articles—anywhere from nine to fifteen pages long—that take a close look at a single concern. While the earliest *Angolite* issues touched on several of the concepts discussed in these articles, such as sex in prison or legal developments or Angola-centered events, the issues published under Rideau's leadership brought such concerns to center stage and gave room for these topics to be developed at length. Morris argues that at the time, *The Angolite* became "the single most influential inmate force within the Louisiana prison system" although Rideau repeatedly noted that the *Angolite* staff cannot be seen as "power brokers in the traditional sense . . . What we have is the ability to influence people."[64]

Still, it is easy to see how *Angolite* writers have used their rhetorical strategies to enact change despite their marginalized position as inmates within the prison system. For example, a Rideau-era article about long-term inmates highlighted the case of Frank Moore—an inmate who had served thirty-three years and had been overlooked by prison officials and state-level bureaucrats. The publicity generated by the article led the Louisiana Board of Pardons to review his case and to eventually release him. Such influence is unheard of within the history of the penal press. Former Warden C. Paul Phelps once stated that it would be almost impossible to "describe this scene to any correctional officer in the nation. They would never understand it, much less relate to it."[65] While Phelps hoped that *The Angolite*—and perhaps, specifically, the insightful nature of the feature articles that brought to light both the brutal history of Angola and the difficulties of current, day-to-day prison life for both inmates and staff members—would act "as a vehicle of communication between the inmates and the administration,"[66] it should be clear by this point that the *Angolite* also works as a medium for discussion and even identity reformation between *Angolite* writers and non-inmate readers. The current staff of *The Angolite* continues the tradition established during the Rideau era of covering topics that are central to the conversation about prisoners and punishment. For example, Lane Nelson's "Death Watch" articles are an excellent introduction to the lengthy, tangled history of the death penalty in the United States, and many of these articles have been collected in *Death Watch: A Death Penalty Anthology*. An eight-year veteran of death row, his work discusses how capital cases often differ within the same legal process, the problems in providing competent legal counsel for capital cases, the selective application of the death penalty in light of racial and gender differences, and reflections of death row inmates.

During 2003, *The Angolite* featured lengthy articles that covered a wide range of prisoner-related issues: the difficult history of the Louisiana Criminal Code; the landmark commutation of 171 death row inmates by former Illinois governor George Ryan; the case of Herbert Welcome, a mentally retarded Angola inmate; the gritty history of Texas's stance on executions; the legislative overhaul of juvenile justice policies in Louisiana. *Angolite* feature articles in 2003 have also centered on issues, events, and figures that are specific to Angola: a report on a visit by former heavyweight boxing champion George Foreman; a discussion of armed robbers held at Angola prison (and how Louisiana is "in overkill mode with its sentencing,"[67] citing how one inmate is serving ninety-nine years for robbing thirty-five dollars from a snow-cone stand); an account of Longtermers's Day, a social gathering for inmates who have served time for over twenty-five years. Such articles, like Meyers's editorials and the photographs included in each issue, are meant to give readers a sense of life inside Angola prison and to challenge popular perceptions of inmates and sentencing policy.

Granted, some *Angolite* representations of Angola events might seem rather confusing or even apologetic. Every Sunday in October, thousands of visitors pay to witness the Angola Prison Rodeo, with events such as bull riding, bareback riding, and bulldogging. However, rodeo participants are Angola inmates; while some are seasoned cowboys who work the livestock held on Angola Farm, many "had never seen livestock of any kind until they entered the Angola arena."[68] The first rodeo was held in 1965, and by 1967 the event was opened to the general public. Currently, the rodeo takes place in an eight-thousand-seat arena that is almost always sold out weeks before rodeo season. Inmate participation is voluntary, but such rodeo events as Convict Poker (a "chicken game" where inmates attempt to remain seated at a poker table while surrounded by agitated bulls) and "Guts and Glory" (in which participants attempt to grab a chip from between the horns of a charging bull) are hardly the stuff of typical rodeos and, to some, seem to merely perpetuate a theater of violence veiled as a tourist spectacle. Melissa Schrift, in her ethnographic-based discussion of the Angola Rodeo and "institutional tourism," offers the following critique: "The presentation of inept cowboys is bound with the promise of injury and violence. When asked why the rodeo is such a popular tourist destination, inmates do not hesitate to acknowledge the warped appeal of their inexperience. A small group of inmates laugh self-consciously as an inmate bluntly describes the appeal of the rodeo: 'They here to see somebody get stomped. They here to see us get hurt.'"[69]

Considering the power dynamic between inmates and prison officials, it is impossible to imagine such a critique published in the pages of *The Angolite*—despite the magazine's history of cutting-edge journalism; *Angolite* rodeo articles provide a narrative account of events, a list of winners for both rodeo and hobby-craft events, profiles of select participants, and allusions to the positive implications that the rodeo has for inmates, as offered in the October/November/December issue:

> Rodeo [concession] sales help Angola's 32 inmate self-help and religious organizations to provide social, rehabilitation, and education programs for the inmate population. Programs such as CPR training, the Point Lookout Project . . . the Angola Hospice program, and other services provided . . . by inmate organizations could not exist to the extent they do without rodeo revenue. With corrections funding getting tighter and tighter, even the prison fire department and other groups have come to depend on rodeo concession monies to purchase much needed equipment.[70]

Angolite articles that cover the rodeo also help publicize the hobby-craft show that is part of every rodeo; inmates spend all year creating woodwork, paintings, pottery, jewelry, clothing, and other items as "a creative outlet to kill boredom" and to feel useful. The sale of their wares allows inmates to reinvest in their own work, and many participate "for no other reason than the opportunity to interact with the public and, for those few hours, to once again feel like human beings."[71] Like rodeo participants, hobby crafts are judged in a contest that also allows inmates a sense of fulfillment, and such awards are published in *The Angolite*. At times, *Angolite* articles echo Warden Cain's comments about the rodeo and rehabilitation: "The ones who change their lives and try and rehabilitate themselves are the ones you see out here. And we must give the opportunity for change. . . . The inmates know that if they were to act up and mess up and cause something to happen . . . then I wouldn't have the rodeo. . . . There's tremendous peer pressure to bring out the best in everyone. . . . It's a safe prison."[72]

Again, this is not to say that *The Angolite* functions only as an argument in support of any warden's particular policies or to merely show the best sides of Louisiana's only maximum security prison. Obviously, in this case, the fact that inmate rehabilitative activities are mainly supported by rodeo concession sales offers an implicit argument for funding needs. Nelson's "Death Watch" features, by that same notion, offer strong appeals for fairer sentencing and a re-examination of the contradictions that are inherently bound to capital punishment laws. Other features highlight specific needs of the prison population, such as "The Door to Opportunity," also published in the October/November/December issue. Jeffery Hilburn, a former prison librarian, documents the high traffic that the current prison library sees on a daily basis, profiles a member of its staff, and implicitly argues for more donations. Most importantly, Hillburn argues against dominant representations of prison life: "A walk into an Angola dormitory or cellblock on any given day will find prisoners escaping in a way that doesn't entail digging under walls or scaling razor-topped fences. Their escape comes through the quiet and peaceful reading of books, magazines, and newspapers. It is a simple search for freedom. . . . Though most are paying for poor choices, they haven't abandoned the quest for knowledge or given up on the hope of improving themselves."[73]

This representation of literacy as salvation—a trope described by Sylvia Scribner via her own ethnographic/literacy work[74]—is contextualized by a lack of traditional literacy at LSP and within all prisons; as noted by Hillburn and others, a recent Test of Adult Basic Education "showed the average reading level was 5.8, or just slightly below sixth grade."[75] Yet Hillburn profiles several inmates who are engaged with the act of reading and writing: "The image of prisoners peacefully reading, at odds with the image of the Angola of the past, is not one that Hollywood can translate into box office revenue.... Educational opportunities are important if [prisoners] are to be provided avenues of release and any hope of living a productive life if released."[76] Granted, such hope of release is slim; at the time of this article, 3,500 of the 5,108 inmates were serving life or natural life sentences.

It is worth noting here that occasionally non-inmate writers contribute large articles to *The Angolite*. Many of these contributors come from academia, such as Burk Foster, a professor of criminal justice at University of Louisiana-Lafayette who collaborated with Rideau and Dennis on *The Wall is Strong: Corrections in Louisiana*.[77] Other writings come from legal professionals, such as the reprint of Judge Ginger Berrigan's explanation of the pardon board process, "Straining the Quality of Mercy."[78] Berrigan's article, originally featured in *Louisiana Law Review*, shows how and why the chances of a Louisiana convict getting clemency are quite slim. Keith Nordyke, a Baton Rouge attorney who has successfully represented several Angola prisoners before parole and pardon boards, is also a frequent contributor; like Berrigan's 2002 *Angolite* article, Nordyke takes the pardon/parole issue to task, explaining the twists and turns of such procedures for both inmate and non-inmate audiences. Including these non-inmate contributors performs a number of rhetorical functions. Obviously, as shown by the few examples above, these writers offer professional accounts and explanations of topics that are of key interest to the inmate audience; likewise, they offer expertise for non-inmate readers who wish to educate themselves on penal procedures. But more importantly, one might argue that such inclusion allows *The Angolite* to be seen as a collaborative text; even the simple, physical connection of including an article written by a "freeman" in the same space as a piece by an inmate helps readers see *Angolite* writers—and perhaps inmates in general—as something other than the illiterate and brutally violent figures that we often conceptualize. As a rhetorical act, the presence of non-inmate professionals gives *The Angolite* yet another way of portraying themselves in a range of roles that seem far from the world of the "prisoner." Such writings provide yet another level of legitimacy for *The Angolite* and an alternative method for these writers to enter mainstream, centralized discussions of penal issues and prisoner concerns.

Features such as Hillburn's give readers a chance to get detailed, in-depth accounts of inmates and inmate life at Angola prison. Like the other sections of *The Angolite*, they provide a counteridentity that works against "the portrayal of prison life in movies and television, which often show men who do nothing but plot and plan to prey on the weak and helpless."[79] While the few remaining inmate magazines and newspapers aside from *The Angolite* mainly act as information-based newsletters aimed mainly at an internal audience, as Morris notes in his history of the penal press, *The Angolite* and the features it offers in each issue represents these inmates as something other than the identity that is imposed by dominant prison narratives.

"He knows my fate": Religion in Prison

It has often been noted that society's outsiders find agency via religious writing and speech practices. Anne Stockdell-Giesler has written on the rhetorical power of spirituals within the African American slave community, and Susan Cahill's introduction to *Wise Women: Over Two Thousand Years of Spiritual Writing by Women* notes "spirituality itself is a fertile source of . . . human liberation."[80] Obviously, religion played a strong part in the civil rights movement of the 1960s, where such speakers as Dr. Martin Luther King, Jr. and the young Jesse Jackson, among others, incorporated traditional Christian tropes into the rhetoric of liberation and freedom for all. While religion, like literacy, has often been used as a method of exclusion, it can also act as a force for social change and a venue for outsider voices, such as prisoners, to find a place within a larger discussion.

"Faith-based" rehabilitation has been part of the rhetoric of Angola since the late 1990s. The underlying concept for such a structure can be found in Louisiana Revised Statute 15:828.2: "The Legislature finds and declares that faith based programs offered in state and private correctional institutions and facilities have the potential to facilitate inmate institutional adjustments, to help inmates assume personal responsibility, and to reduce recidivism." In recent years, the concept of faith-based prison programs has become increasingly popular, leading to both support and criticism.[81] At Angola, the most active program within the faith-based agenda is the Angola Extension Campus of the New Orleans Baptist Theological Seminary (NOBTS). In light of the removal of Pell Grants and the majority of college-level opportunities for inmates that took place during the Clinton administration, NOBTS provides the only four-year degree program at LSP; however, its concentrations of study are limited to such subjects as Christian counseling and ministry. In terms of other religious programming, revivals and gospel music concerts are quite common at

LSP, and several different Christian denominations send volunteers to aid with counseling, worship services, and healing ministries.

Such activities are covered in the regularly appearing column "Religion in Prison." Even before this column officially began, religious activities were a common theme for *Angolite* articles. Again, like the representation of wardens and staff members, the role of religion—specifically, traditional/fundamentalist strains of Christianity—is quite complicated. Novek, in her own study mentioned earlier, admits that some articles in prisoner-written publications, especially those that espouse self-improvement, "may be an attempt to perform the newly 'corrected' identity to prison authorities in gain respect or privileges, or they may demonstrate that some internalize the images of themselves fed back by the prison system."[82] Yet such publications are still incredibly important to participants: "They recognize their ability to inform, educate, and comfort, and may reframe their identities as advocates for others. These experiences lead some [inmate] journalists to express a sense of empowerment, self-awareness, or agency that inspires confidence and directs action."[83]

The coverage offered in "Religion in Prison," like the other regularly appearing columns, is divided into subheadings and offers accounts of events sponsored by such groups as Full Gospel, Cowboys for Christ, Catholic Ministries (over one thousand inmates are Roman Catholic, as to be expected in a Louisiana prison), St. John's Institutional Baptist Brotherhood, and the Students of Islam. Again, while such a column might seem to be aimed only at an inmate audience, these reports that narrate events ranging from music programs and church meetings to facility expansion continue one of *The Angolite*'s main rhetorical functions: the presentation of a counteridentity that can challenge preconceived notions of inmates.

Articles such as those from the October/November/December issue relate services as "filled to near capacity" with "a large number of outside guests" where inmates can often "be with their families."[84] A Catholic volunteer is quoted as saying, "Each year I come up to Angola trying to lift their spirits . . . they always end up lifting mine."[85] Pastors and lay ministers are shown offering solace to prisoners in population (able to work and take part in activities such as clubs), in lockdown, on death row, and in the prison infirmary wards. The work of inmate ministers is also represented: "It just takes a minute of our time," one states, "to stop and talk to a brother in the dorm or yard and invite him to mass. . . . Sometimes they say no and walk away. But sometimes, they appreciate me taking time to ask and show up for mass."[86] Inmates are also shown as involved with committee duties, such as keeping a newsletter for Catholic inmates, restoring a dilapidated chapel, and educating other inmates as to the nature of religious practices that are less known in the Angola prison community such as Islam. Other issues profile such events as a reunion of prisoner missionaries who were trained at LSP but sent via NOBTS to other prisons for ministry work, dramatic presentations by Christian theatre organizations, and an interfaith gathering that brought together over three hundred inmates together in a call for Christian unity.

Because of the increase in faith-based programming at LSP, such coverage seems to be right in line with *The Angolite*'s explicit goal of reporting activities that take place at Angola. "Religion in Prison" might not be surprising or as cutting edge as other current columns or features, but as a regularly appearing segment it offers yet another angle to the argument implied within each issue of *The Angolite*. If religious activities are valued as noble pursuits by both readers and prison staff members, and if such activities actually provide both a literal and metaphorical sanctuary for LSP inmates, then it makes sense to give such practices a featured presence in the pages of *The Angolite*.

"Sometimes it gets so hard, you see . . .": *Angolite* Prose and Poetry

While *The Angolite* features a staff of regularly contributing writers, each issue concludes with sections of poetry and prose writing submitted by Angola inmates as well as prisoners from other institutions. The majority of these poems and prose pieces (which even occasionally include short dramatic works and pieces that sound like current hip-hop lyrics) employ similar tropes, such as end-rhyme, fixed stanzas (much like gospel and blues music), and themes such as redemption, choices, pathways, and a living connection with the divine. One could argue that such writings act as a web that connects prisoners in various locations. More importantly, a writer who sees his work published within *The Angolite* gets the same satisfaction as any writer working toward recognition. Each section is introduced by noting that such writings are published "in the name of freedom of expression"; while most work draws upon the physical space of the prison as inspiration, it is important to remember that this work has the ability to go beyond the gates of LSP and into the hands of non-inmate readers.

As noted by Wilson, "prison is spatially constructed as a total institution (Goffman 1961), controlled by physical and metaphorical demarcation (Cressey 1961), where hierarchies of power rule the establishment (Sykes 1970)."[87] While writing poetry or creative prose might not be "necessarily high on the literacy-related agenda of people"[88] in the world outside the prison, the literacy acts represented in these sections of *The Angolite* are a high commodity amongst Angola inmates. Such written work shows inmates creating their own space and, like *Angolite* writers, working against the numbing power of the total institution. By including such creative work, *The Angolite* becomes even more of a collaborative effort among inmates.

Like the articles from non-inmate writers, the poems offered at the end of many *Angolite* issues by Aaron Neville—a Grammy Award–winning vocalist and member of the Neville Brothers, an immensely popular R&B vocal group from New Orleans—can be seen as a deliberately deployed rhetorical strategy. While the writing of "experts" plays a variety of roles, Neville's poetry allows a certain type of identification for inmate readers. Neville served six months for automobile theft at the age of eighteen, and became addicted to heroin during his sentence. A frequent contributor—"*The Angolite*'s Honorary Staff Poet"—who has performed both solo gospel music and with the Neville Brothers at Angola, Neville's poems are placed between the "Sounding Off" prose responses and "Expressions," the section reserved for inmate-written poetry. While including prison poems from sites other than LSP might allow inmates to feel a connection to others in their situation, Neville's submissions fall right in line with one of the main themes of *The Angolite*—that a prisoner can redeem himself via a multiplicity of literacies such as songwriting or poetry.

By including Neville—a name known by most Louisianans—and by explicitly noting his troubled past in a sidebar to each piece, inmate readers not only see his poetic work as perhaps "equal" to the inmate-written poetry included in *Angolite* issues, but also see another example of a man from among their own ranks who has become a success story, who is freed of the prison chains and bars that define the existence of every Angola inmate. As seen in this passage from a recent issue, Neville's words reverberate with the themes of survival, resistance, and redemption that are prime motifs of *Angolite* writing:

> All I have is today, 'cause yesterday is already gone
> I'm not promised tomorrow and, like I said, the days aren't very long
> So I gotta do all I can before the sun goes down tonight
> And say a prayer that I open my eyes to see the morning light.[89]

"To live outside the law": Some concluding remarks

At the conclusion of the second chapter to *Literacy Matters: Writing and Reading the Social Self*, Robert P. Yagelski discusses the oft-cited chapter "Saved" from *The Autobiography of Malcolm X*—perhaps "the quintessential American fable about literacy" as self-improvement and even as redemption.[90] Considering Malcolm X's narrative, Yagelski argues: "Literacy is about possibility and power, a means of writing a way into a society that had written him off and working toward changing that society. . . . It is an entrance to worlds of knowledge that were closed off to him . . . And it is a means of constructing identity and claiming agency." [91]

Like Wilbert Rideau and the staff members of *The Angolite* from its first issue to its current status as one of the few long-surviving members of the penal press, Malcolm X wrote "within and yet against" the dominant ideology in their respective historical moments.[92] Both Malcolm's autobiographical self-fashioning and the various texts that make up the collective history of *The Angolite* are firmly rooted in an attempt to enter a discourse that is beyond the street or the prison cell. One could easily posit the assumption that like the transformed Malcolm X that is offered in "Saved," *Angolite* writers are prime examples of self-made men, literate and powerful by their own means. One might also argue that *The Angolite* is simply Bedlam with a printing press—a freak show of sorts that asks readers to gaze upon the implausibly literate inmates positioned in a space that evokes connotations of rape and extreme violence. But such claims flatten the work of *The Angolite* into just a mere success story—and perhaps one that simply reiterates that the current penal system works and works well. For the over two million Americans living under state surveillance, such claims are absurd and insulting. Like Martin Luther King's "Letter from Birmingham Jail" – perhaps his most poignant civil rights document—*Angolite* writers transform the southern penitentiary into a site of identity formulation and a rallying point for freedom.[93]

The subheadings for this essay are taken from Bob Dylan's 1966 song "Absolutely Sweet Marie." As a former volunteer and researcher at Angola, I listened to this song repeatedly as I drove north from my home in Baton Rouge to work with an inmate-tutoring group at LSP and to meet with *Angolite* writers during six months in 2004. While these men might be considered "outside the law," their collective work as writers is an inspiring attempt to express a counteridentity that is far from the one imposed on them by dominant narratives. As "outsiders," their journalistic honesty and integrity allows them, if only in glimpses and moments, to be seen as ethical and responsible, with voices that are worthy of recognition. As noted by Rideau and as seen in the work of the current *Angolite* staff, such writing functions as sociopolitical action and as a call to reconsider our national understanding of prison culture: "*The Angolite* is one of the few instruments left us through which to convey realities and to chip away at the monstrous image the public has conceived of us. . . . In that context, *The Angolite* and its achievements must be regarded as a symbolic hoisting of the flag for those prisoners struggling to transcend their tragic mistakes, their personal problems and the pain of their life-situation in search of something better and decent in life."[94]

Notes

The staff members at Hill Memorial Library/Special Collections, especially Gina Costello, have been incredibly gracious and helpful with my research throughout this project. I must also thank those who have given me their own reflections on LSP, especially the current staff of the *Angolite*, Dr. John Robson of the New Orleans Baptist Theological Seminary, and former University of Louisiana-Lafayette faculty member Burk Foster. Finally, much thanks goes to Drs. Katrina Powell, Susan Weinstein, and Anne Stockdell-Giesler, my colleague Jessica Ketcham, and my wife Carrie Green, who have all lived with this project as long as I have.

1. Louisiana State Penitentiary is often referred to as "Angola" or "LSP." In this chapter, they are used interchangeably.

2. Nancy Frasier offers a succinct explanation of Habermas's concept of the public sphere: "a theatre in modern societies in which political participation is enacted through the medium of talk. It is a space in which citizens deliberate about their common affairs, hence, an institutionalized area of discursive interaction." Distinct from both the state and the official economy, Frasier finds that Habermas's idea of the public sphere is "indispensable to critical social theory and to democratic political practice" but is not "sufficiently distinct from the liberal model of the bourgeois public sphere to serve the needs of critical theory today." "Rethinking the Public Sphere: A Contribution to the Critique of Actually Existing Democracy," *Habermas and the Public Sphere*, ed. Craig Calhoun. (Cambridge: MIT University Press, 1992), 109–42. See also Houston A Baker, Jr., "Critical Memory and the Black Public Sphere," *Public Culture* 7 (1994): 3–33.

3. George Howe Colt, "The Most Rehabilitated Prisoner in America," *Life*, March 1993: 68.

4. Mark T. Carleton, *Politics and Punishment: The History of the Louisiana State Penal System* (Baton Rouge: Louisiana State University Press, 1971). Carleton's account provides a narrative from the earliest days of the prison, through the violence of prisoner leasing and dramatic shifts in administration, to its continued focus on "legitimate profit making" rather than rehabilitation. "If Louisiana's penal history is unique in any respect," writes Carleton, "the uniqueness may be found in the total politicalization of the system since it was initially leased in 1844." See pages 195 and 199. For other historical accounts of Angola, see Anne Butler and C. Murray Henderson's *Angola: A Half Century of Rage and Reform* (Lafayette, LA: University of Southwestern Louisiana University Press, 1990) and *Dying to Tell: Angola—Crime, Consequence, Conclusion at Louisiana State Penitentiary* (Lafayette, LA: University of Southwestern Louisiana University Press, 1992).

5. Those interested in a more detailed account of Rideau might turn to Amy Bach's "Unforgiven," *Nation*, January 16, 2005, as well as Michael Perlstein's "Wilbert Rideau is Freed," *Times-Picayune*, January 16, 2005. *Life Sentences: Rage and Sur-*

vival Behind Bars (New York: Times Books, 1992) is an excellent collection of *Angolite* articles that features Rideau's work.

6. Angela Y. Davis, *Are Prisons Obsolete?* (New York: Open Media Series, 2003), 16.

7. Anita Wilson, "'Speak Up—I Can't Write What You're Reading': The Place of Literacy in the Prison Community," *Journal of Correctional Education* 47, no. 2 (June 1996): 95.

8. For an excellent review of literacy studies as a field, see James Collins and Richard K. Blot, *Literacy and Literacies: Texts, Power, and Identity* (Cambridge, MA: Cambridge University Press, 2003), especially chapters 2 and 3.

9. James Paul Gee, "Literacy, Discourse, and Linguistics: Introduction," in *Literacy: A Critical Sourcebook*, ed. Ellen Cushman et al. (Boston: Bedford/St. Martin's Press, 2001), 525.

10. Ibid., 526.

11. Ibid.

12. Anita Wilson, "'Four Days and a Breakfast': Time, Space, and Literacy/ies in the Prison Community," in *Spatializing Literacy Research and Practice*, ed. Kevin M. Leander and Margaret Sheehy (New York: Peter Lang, 2004), 70.

13. David Barton and Mary Hamilton, *Local Literacies: Reading and Writing in One Community* (London, Routledge Press, 1998), 3.

14. James Paul Gee, "What is Literacy?," In *Literacy: A Critical Sourcebook*, ed. Ellen Cushman et al. (Boston: Bedford/St. Martin's Press, 2001), 538.

15. James Boyd White, "Law as Rhetoric, Rhetoric as Law: The Arts of Cultural and Communal Life," *University of Chicago Law Review* 52, no. 3 (1985): 684.

16. Ibid., 684, 690.

17. Ibid., 690.

18. John Sloop, *The Cultural Prison: Discourse, Prisoners, and Punishment* (Tuscaloosa: University of Alabama Press, 1996).

19. Ibid., 7.

20. Ibid., 13.

21. Ibid., 6.

22. Ibid., 126.

23. Ibid., 159.

24. See Eric Schlosser, "The Prison Industrial Complex," *Atlantic Monthly*, December 1998, 51–77.

25. White, "Law as Rhetoric," 688.

26. Granted, one could argue that Angola is quite the "open" institution, in light of such practices as tours, craft fairs, the Angola Prison Rodeo, documentary filmings, the presence of volunteer organizations, etc. However, as argued by Melissa Schrift, whose work is discussed later in this chapter, "the prison is a space that defines itself by its ability to conceal." See Schrift, "The Angola Prison Rodeo: Inmate Cowboys and Institutional Tourism," *Ethnology* 43, no. 4 (2004): 331.

27. Wilson, "Four Days," 74.

28. Adela C. Licona, "Borderlands' Rhetorics and Representations: The Transformative Potential of Feminist Third-Space Scholarship and Zines," *NWSA Journal* 17, no. 2 (2005): 104.

29. Ibid.

30. Ibid., 105.

31. James McGrath Morris, *Jailhouse Journalism: The Fourth Estate Behind Bars* (New Brunswick, NJ: Transaction Publishers, 2002), 160.

32. Tommy Tarr, "Viewpoint," *The Angolite*, June 1971, 3, 12.

33. Kendall R. Phillips, "Spaces of Invention: Dissention, Freedom, and Thought in Foucault," *Philosophy and Rhetoric* 35, no. 4 (2002): 328–44.
34. White, "Law as Rhetoric," 693.
35. Diana George and Diane Shoos, "Deflecting the Political in the Visual Images of Execution and the Death Penalty Debate," *College English* 67, no. 6 (2005): 607.
36. Mark Dow, "How the Body Be Burn: Letters Inside and On Death Row," *Texas Observer*, November 10, 2005, www.texasobserver.org/article.php?aid=287.
37. Kerry Meyers, "Wire to Wire," *The Angolite*, January/February 2003, 1.
38. Ibid.
39. Kerry Meyers, "Wire to Wire," *The Angolite*, May/June 2003, 1, 2.
40. Kerry Meyers, "Wire to Wire," *The Angolite*, July/August/September 2003, 1, 2.
41. Ibid., 1.
42. Douglas Dennis, "Angola Blues," *The Angolite*, July/August/September 2003, 48.
43. "About TV: A Conversation From Inside Prison Walls," *Caucus for Television Producers, Writers, and Directors*, September 1993, www.caucus.org/archives.93 fal_abouttv.html.
44. "Inside Angola," *The Angolite*, January/February 2003, 10.
45. "Inside Angola—Doing Their Part," *The Angolite*, March/April 2003, 11.
46. Ibid.
47. Ibid.
48. Ibid.
49. "Inside Angola—Angola Blues," *The Angolite*, March/April 2003, 13.
50. Morris, *Jailhouse Journalism*, 160.
51. Eleanor Novek, "'The Devil's Bargain': Censorship, Identity, and the Promise of Empowerment in a Prison Newspaper," *Journalism* 6, no. 1 (2005): 20.
52. Morris, *Jailhouse Journalism*, 10.
53. Chris Frink, "Controversial Cain," *Christianity Today*, May 7, 2004, http://christianitytoday.com/ct/2004/005/5.39.html.
54. Ibid.
55. Ibid.
56. Ibid.
57. It seems interesting that all of these passages come from a *Christianity Today* article, in light of Warden Cain's explicit use of Christian tropes in his public statements. See also Daniel Bergner, *God of the Rodeo: The Search for Hope, Faith, and a Six-Second Ride in Louisiana's Angola Prison* (New York: Crown Publishers, 1998). For a different viewpoint, see Dennis Shere, *Cain's Redemption: A Story of Hope and Transformation in America's Bloodiest Prison* (Chicago: Northfield Publishing, 2005).
58. Charlotte Bruce-Harvey, "Nesting in Razor Wire," *Brown Alumni Magazine*, March/April 2004, 53.
59. Katherine Nugent, "Award Winning Inmate-Journalist Wilbert Rideau Visits Medill," *Inside Medill News*, April 20, 2005, http://medill.northwestern.edu/medill/inside/news/awardwinning_inmate_jour nalist_wilbert_rideau_visits_medill.html.
60. "Inside Angola," *The Angolite*, March/April 2003, 15.
61. Ibid.
62. Ibid.
63. See Morris, *Jailhouse Journalism*, chap. 19, concerning the decline in prison newspapers and magazines.
64. Morris, *Jailhouse Journalism*, 163.
65. Ibid., 166.

66. Ibid., 160.
67. Lane Nelson, "The Armed Robber," *The Angolite*, October/November/December 2003, 34.
68. Lane Nelson and Jeffery Hillburn, "It's Not Your Father's Rodeo," *The Angolite*, October/November/December 2003, 26.
69. Melissa Schrift, "The Angola Prison Rodeo: Inmate Cowboys and Institutional Tourism," *Ethnology* 43, no. 4 (2004): 339–40.
70. Nelson and Hillburn, "It's Not Your Father's Rodeo," 24.
71. Ibid.
72. Schrift, "The Angola Prison Rodeo," 336.
73. Jeffery Hillburn, "The Door to Opportunity," *The Angolite*, October/November/December 2003, 18.
74. Sylvia Scribner, "Literacy in Three Metaphors," *American Journal of Education* 93, no. 1 (1994).
75. Hillburn, "The Door to Opportunity," 20.
76. Ibid., 21.
77. Burk Foster, Wilbert Rideau, and Douglas Dennis, *The Wall is Strong: Corrections in Louisiana* (Lafayette: Center for Louisiana Studies, 1995).
78. Ginger Berrigan, "Straining the Quality of Mercy," *The Angolite*, September/October 2002, 33–37. Originally "Executive Clemency, First Offender Pardons: Automatic Restoration," *Louisiana Law Review* 62 (2001): 49.
79. Hillburn, "The Door to Opportunity," 20.
80. Susan Cahill, *Wise Women: Over Two Thousand Years of Spiritual Writing by Women* (New York: W. W. Norton, 1996).
81. For a discussion of faith-based prison programming, see Jacqui Goddard, "Florida's New Approach to Inmate Reform: a 'Faith-Based' Prison," *Christian-Science Monitor* (online version), December 24, 2003, http://www.csmonitor.com/2003/1224/p01s04-usju.html.
82. Novek, "'The Devil's Bargain,'" 15.
83. Ibid., 8.
84. Ronald Walker, "Religion in Prison—Full Gospel," *The Angolite*, October/November/December 2003, 56.
85. Dale Gaudet, "Religion in Prison—Catholic Ministry," *The Angolite*, October/November/December 2003, 57.
86. Ibid., 58.
87. Wilson, "Four Days," 72.
88. Ibid., 71.
89. Aaron Neville, "When the Sun Goes Down," *The Angolite*, January/February 2003, 61.
90. Robert P. Yagelski, *Literacy Matters: Writing and Reading the Social Self* (New York: Teachers College Press), 1999, 54.
91. Ibid., 45.
92. Ibid., 46.
93. See Baker, "Critical Memory."
94. Wilbert Rideau and Billy W. Sinclair, "Getting it Together," *Angolite*, March/April 1979, 3.

Bibliography

"About TV: A Conversation From Inside Prison Walls." *The Caucus for Television Producers, Writers, and Directors*, September 1993. http://www.caucus.org/archieves.93fal_abouttv.html.

Bach, Amy. "Unforgiven." *The Nation* (online version). January 3, 2002, http://www.thenation.com/doc/20020121/bach.

Baker, Jr., Houston A. "Critical Memory and the Black Public Sphere." *Public Culture* 7 (1994): 3–33.

Barton, David and Mary Hamilton. *Local Literacies: Reading and Writing in One Community*. London: Routledge Press, 1998.

Bergner, Daniel. *God of the Rodeo: The Search for Hope, Faith, and a Six-Second Ride in Louisiana's Angola Prison*. New York: Crown Publishers, 1998.

Berrigan, Ginger. "Straining the Quality of Mercy," *The Angolite*, (September/October 2002): 33–37.

Bruce-Harvey, Charlotte. "Nesting in Razor Wire." *Brown Alumni Magazine* (March/April 2004): 53.

Butler, Anne and C. Murray Henderson. *Angola: A Half Century of Rage and Reform*. Lafayette, LA: University of Southwest Louisiana Press, 1990.

———. *Dying to Tell: Angola—Crime, Consequence, Conclusion at Louisiana State Penitentiary*. Lafayette, LA: University of Southwest Louisiana Press, 1992.

Cahill, Susan. *Wise Women: Over Two Thousand Years of Spiritual Writing by Women*. New York: W.W. Norton and Company, 1996.

Carleton, Mark T. *Politics and Punishment: The History of the Louisiana State Penal System*. Baton Rouge: Louisiana State University Press, 1971.

Collins, James and Richard K. Blot. *Literacy and Literacies: Texts, Power, and Community*. Cambridge: Cambridge University Press, 2003.

Colt, George Howe. "The Most Rehabilitated Prisoner in America." *Life* (March 1993): 68–75.

Davis, Angela. *Are Prisons Obsolete?* New York: Open Media Series, 2003.

Dennis, Douglass. "Angola Blues." *The Angolite* (July/August/September 2003): 13.

Dow, Mark. "How the Body Be Burn: Letters Inside and On Death Row." *The Texas Observer*, November 10, 2005. http://www.texasobserver.org/article.php?aid=287.

Foster, Burk, Wilbert Rideau, and Douglass Dennis. *The Wall is Strong: Corrections in Louisiana*. Lafayette, LA: Center for Louisiana Studies, 1995.

Frasier, Nancy. "Rethinking the Public Sphere: A Contribution to the Critique of Actually Existing Democracy." In *Habermas and the Public Sphere*, edited by Craig Calhoun, 109–42. Cambridge: Massachusetts Institute of Technology Press, 1992.

Frink, Chris. "Controversial Cain," *Christianity Today*, May 7, 2004. http://christianitytoday.com/ct/2004/005/5.39.html.

Gaudet, Dale. "Religion in Prison—Catholic Ministry," *The Angolite* (October/November/December 2003): 58–59.

Gee, James Paul. "Literacy, Discourse, and Linguistics: Introduction." In *Literacy: A Critical Sourcebook*, edited by Ellen Cushman et al, 525–37. Boston and New York: Bedford/St. Martin's Press, 2001.

———. "What is Literacy?" In *Literacy: A Critical Sourcebook*, edited by Ellen Cushman et al, 537–44. Boston and New York: Bedford/St. Martin's Press, 2001.

George, Diana and Diane Shoos. "Deflecting the Political in the Visual Images of Execution and the Death Penalty Debate." *College English* 67, no. 6 (2005): 587–609.

Goddard, Jacqui. "Florida's New Approach to Inmate Reform: a 'Faith-Based'

Prison," *The Christian-Science Monitor* (online version), December 24, 2003. http://www.csmonitor.com/2003/1224/p01s04-usju.html.

Hillburn, Jeffery. "The Door to Opportunity." *The Angolite* (October/November/December 2003): 18–21.

"Inside Angola—Doing Their Part." *The Angolite* (January/February 2003): 10–12.

"Inside Angola—Doing Their Part." *The Angolite* (March/April 2003): 10–12.

"Inside Angola—Angola Blues." *The Angolite* (March/April 2003): 13.

Licona, Adela C. "Borderlands' Rhetorics and Representations: The Transformative Potential of Feminist Third-Space Scholarship and Zines." *NWSA Journal* 17, no. 2 (2005): 104–29.

Morris, James McGrath. *Jailhouse Journalism: The Fourth Estate Behind Bars.* New Brunswick, NJ: Transaction Publishers, 2002.

Meyers, Kerry. "Wire to Wire." *The Angolite* (January/February 2003): 1.

———. "Wire to Wire." *The Angolite* (May/June 2003): 1–2.

———. "Wire to Wire." *The Angolite* (July/August/September 2003): 1–2.

Nelson, Lane. "The Armed Robber," *The Angolite* (October/November/December 2003): 32–37.

Nelson, Lane and Jeffery Hillburn. "It's Not Your Father's Rodeo." *The Angolite* (October/November/December 2003): 22–31.

Neville, Aaron. "When the Sun Goes Down." *The Angolite* (January/February 2003): 61.

Novek, Eleanor. "'The Devil's Bargain': Censorship, Identity, and the Promise of Empowerment in a Prison Newspaper." *Journalism* 6, no. 1 (2005): 5–23.

Nugent, Katherine. "Award Winning Inmate-Journalist Wilbert Rideau Visits Medill." *Inside Medill News,* April 20, 2005.http://medill.northwestern.edu/medill/inside/news/awardwinning_inmate_journalist_wilbert_rideau_visits_medill.html.

Perlstein, Michael. "Wilbert Rideau is Freed." *Times-Picayune*, January 16, 2005.

Phillips, Kendall R. "Spaces of Invention: Dissention, Freedom, and Thought in Foucault." *Philosophy and Rhetoric* 35, no. 4 (2002): 328–44.

Rideau, Wilbert and Billy W. Sinclair. "Getting it Together," *The Angolite* (March/April 1979): 2–3.

Rideau, Wilbert and Ron Wikberg. *Life Sentences: Rage and Survival Behind Bars.* New York: Times Books, 1992.

Schlosser, Eric. "The Prison-Industrial Complex." *Atlantic Monthly*, December 1998, 51–77.

Schrift, Melissa. "The Angola Prison Rodeo: Inmate Cowboys and Institutional Tourism." *Ethnology* 43, no. 4 (2004): 331–45.

Scribner, Sylvia. "Literacy in Three Metaphors." *American Journal of Education* 93, no. 1 (1994): 6–21.

Shere, Dennis. *Cain's Redemption: A Story of Hope and Transformation in America's Bloodiest Prison.* Chicago: Northfield Publishing, 2005.

Sloop, John. *The Cultural Prison: Discourse, Prisoners, Punishment.* Tuscaloosa: University of Alabama Press, 1996.

Tarr, Tommy. "Viewpoint." *The Angolite* (June 1971): 3, 12.

Walker, Ronald. "Religion in Prison—Full Gospel." *The Angolite*(October/November/December 2003): 56.

White, James Boyd. "Law as Rhetoric, Rhetoric as Law: The Arts of Cultural and Communal Life." *University of Chicago Law Review* 52, no. 3 (1985): 684–702.

Wilson, Anita. "'Speak Up—I Can't Write What You're Reading': The Place of Literacy in the Prison Community." *Journal of Correctional Education* 47, no. 2 (1996): 94–100.

———. "'Four Days and a Breakfast': Time, Space, and Literacy/ies in the Prison Community." In *Spatializing Literacy Practice and Research*, edited by Kevin M. Leander and Margaret Sheehy, 67–90. New York: Peter Lang Publishing, 2004.

Yagelski, Robert P. *Literacy Matters: Writing and Reading the Social Self.* New York: Teachers College Press, 2000.

"Protect yourself at all times": *Million Dollar Baby*, Boxing, and Feminine Agency
Ian Edwards

> Gender is the repeated stylisation of the body, a set of repeated acts within a highly rigid regulatory frame that congeal over time to produce the appearance of substance, of a natural sort of being. A political genealogy of gender ontologies, if it is successful, will deconstruct the substantive appearance of gender into its constitutive acts and locate and account for those acts within the compulsory frames set by the various forces that police the social appearance of gender.[1]

THERE ARE SEVERAL BASIC PROBLEMS ATTENDING THE FEMALE SUBject's participation in traditionally masculine, public spheres, and her assertion of agency within them. Insofar as the assumption of agency is itself projected within culture as something of a masculine prerogative, and insofar as a sport like boxing is so suffused with the masculine ethos, the representation and participation of women in boxing provides a particularly vexed field in which questions of female agency can be worked through. When a woman participates in boxing as a means of constructing the self, does this entail a denial of her femininity and an acceptance of the "masculine" norms that govern the field (though I intend to call into question the necessarily masculine status of those norms), thus reinforcing patriarchal structures (making of herself a "masculinized" woman)?[2] Is a specifically feminine reiteration of those norms possible? Or is the gendered status of boxing itself merely provisional, its putatively masculine status merely a contingent fact based on the gender of the vast majority of its participants to this point? The aim of this essay is to assess the film *Million Dollar Baby* as illustrative of the problems posed to those females who attempt to assert themselves in traditionally masculine spheres, and as a partial (if flawed) answer to those problems. Further, it will be assessed in the light of some critical responses to the film, insofar as they exemplify the theoretical ambivalences of addressing issues of gender and marginalized forms of agency. If boxing seems an incongruous arena in which to demonstrate feminine agency, one of the masculine preserves least likely to cede to the equality of women, it is surely also an opportunity for women to reverse gender norms most spectacularly and unexpectedly (and therefore with a certain subversive force). The spectacle of a woman boxing, I will argue, is one whose very nature makes of it a contestatory narrative running counter to the patriarchal norm, in Butler's terms above providing an alternative "stylisation of the body." Implicit in this assumption is the need to "formulate a project that preserves gender practises as sites of *critical agency*,"[3] with the dual emphasis on both the "agency" of the female subject, and its potential to serve as a "critical" practice.

Within the film studies canon (as expounded by Stephen Heath and the *Screen* "school" in the 1970s), film has often been seen to objectify and paralyze the feminine body by means of the (masculine) camera/ gaze. Even in some prominent films promoting a more proactive relationship between (and a more progressive view of) the female subject and her body—I think particularly of Linda Cameron in *Terminator 2*, Sigourney Weaver in the *Alien* trilogy, or Angela Bassett in *What's Love Got To Do With It?* —there were distinctly less progressive agendas and reactions to emerge. The general trend was to view the physiques of Hamilton and Bassett as impressive expressions of method acting, in a similar sense to the extreme dieting of models; ultimately, the act of bodily shaping itself serving as secondary to the objective filmic end to which the female subject submits. Further, each of these apparently progressive, self-mastering female subjects was set very much in the context of traditional domestic roles as spouse and/ or mother. While Hamilton's character is somewhat "kickass," she is entirely subordinate to her role as mother; similarly, Bassett's portrayal of Tina Turner largely centers around her turbulent relationship with Ike; even that most feminist of action heroines, Weaver's Ripley, battles in the seminal scene of the trilogy a gigantic, monstrous evocation of the mother-figure, in defense of her own surrogate child.[4] Even when the female agent in film transgresses by enacting "masculine" norms of agency through the body, the tendency would seem to be to continually refract (and literally domesticate) this sense of agency through more traditional feminine roles.

The women's bodybuilding documentary, *Pumping Iron II: The Women*, provides an interesting insight into the perils surrounding feminine assumption of masculinised norms (I will use "masculinized" from this point onward, as opposed to "masculine," to indicate that these are norms which are open to contestation and have been *constructed* as masculine, rather than being inherently so). The film's basic contrast is between the "conventionally prettier and sexier" Rachel McLish, and Bev Francis who "looks and moves like a man" (Chris Holmlund). The film imposes in Adrienne Rich's words "a compulsive heterosexual orientation" on the female bodybuilders, continually portraying them in tandem with their male spouses, whereby the potential "gender trespass" of women in bodybuilding is mediated by the copresence of traditional feminine roles and attitudes.[5] As Holmlund notes, while bodybuilding in men does not lead to anxiety over the nature of masculinity, the question of "what is woman?" is ever-present in *Pumping Iron II*. It is significant, then, that the eventual winner of the competition is neither the "conventionally pretty" McLish, nor the "gender-trespassing" Francis. The winner, Carla Dunlap, is both an articulate spokesperson for progressive feminist politics and the only contestant who is not portrayed with men. In Holmlund's words, "Despite her autonomy and despite the fact that she is more muscular than many of the other women, she never poses a threat of homosexuality the way Bev does because, by comparison with Bev, she still looks and moves like a woman." *Pumping Iron II* therefore posits a particularly feminine articulation of bodybuilding, or a rearticulation of the relationship of femininity and muscularity, without departing too far from (heterosexual) gendered norms.

Despite the highly masculinized status of bodybuilding as a sport, there are ways in which we can actually see it as articulating an objectifying tendency in which the body is conceived as static, and existing on an entirely formal/aesthetic level, as with the petrified status of so many female bodies in film. In training, the immense work that goes into the bodybuilder's physique is almost entirely unrelated to practical purposes; bodybuilders are comparatively weak for their great size, and by most measurements lack physical fitness (I once knew a national-class bodybuilder who could barely run around the block). In competition, the body-as-image is frozen in a series of "poses," foreclosing its potential for movement. In the words of Butler, within those terms, "the body" appears as a passive medium on which cultural meanings are inscribed."[6] As a field, then, bodybuilding would seem to be particularly suited to returning the same kind of regressive, objectifying portrayals of women bemoaned by generations of feminist film critics. The spectacle of the sculpted bodies in the bodybuilding arena, parading before judges who impose subjective criteria upon highly objectified, nonfunctional bodies-as-images, is perhaps the apogee of the "depthlessness" imposed upon the body in postmodernity, an implication all the more pertinent for its female participants insofar as this spectacle mirrors the way female bodies have been represented for centuries. By way of contrast, the body of the boxer is entirely related to *function*, and the body is mastered not as an end in itself, but with a view to developing its *kinetic potential;* the boxer's body is a vehicle for movement which demands continual re-interpretation, rather than an empty vessel upon which static meanings can be imposed. It is in this sense that I see the representation of women in boxing (or other combat sports/martial arts) as a particularly effective arena for promoting progressive gender politics, insofar as the body is very much a vehicle for individual *agency*, defying attempts to confine it within static norms.

With the above concerns in mind, my own (aesthetic) approach to *Million Dollar Baby* was by way of its portrayal of feminine self-authorship through the body, assessing the extent to which it falls prey to, or avoids, the objectifying and domesticating tendencies so often apparent in the filmic presentation of women acting out even apparently "nonfeminine" roles. In viewing any boxing film, however, my own approach is always, already colored by my status as a very keen fan and follower of boxing. While some interesting feminist criticism has emerged around *Million Dollar Baby*, I feel it has lacked somewhat in boxing-specific knowledge and orientation, and in relating the female boxing film to the already-existing "traditional" canon of boxing films. With a greater emphasis on the vicissitudes of boxing as a whole, of its fundamental precepts and paradoxes, we can see how the film dramatizes certain contradictions at the heart of boxing, the cultural contradictions they issue from, and an extent to which these issues *transcend* (or precede) "mere" gender. The critic who addresses the issue of women in boxing solely through a gendered perspective risks both the elision of nongendered implications of the sport, which are several and weighty, and the return of the same kind of gender binaries that would ostensibly omit women from boxing (or male-dominated spheres in general) altogether. Before addressing the films directly, then, I wish to articulate some of the more pertinent aspects of boxing as a cultural phenomenon.

In several senses, we can see boxing in America as a particular modality of outsider discourse; it is notable, then, that Eastwood refers to boxing in interviews on *Million Dollar Baby* as a sport of "people at the fringes of society . . . oddballs . . . people at the periphery of society."[7] Boxing has no central franchising body as with the NFL, NBA, or NHL, and has no collegiate structure. Not only do the vast majority of professional fighters come from marginal positions in terms of class, but also in terms of ethnicity. The relative paucity of "white" boxers in the modern era as compared with the period to 1950—the Jewish American, Italian American, and Irish American communities have largely been assimilated within the American middle class—is expressed all the more strongly by the furor that erupts over the emergence of each generation's "great white hope." Italian American boxers (or other fighters of European heritage) are now mainly subsumed within the rubric of "white hopes," with the implication being that boxing is nowadays largely the preserve of African Americans and Hispanics. The Mexican community, for one, is famous for its near-fanatical love of boxing, and the opportunities for the expression of Hispanic pride it provides (major Mexican and Puerto Rican festivals, for example, are nearly always dovetailed with fights involving the respective nations' premier fighters). Without wishing to minimize the different cultural heritages attached to boxing for different communities, the common denominator is very much that of class, and boxing in some ways dramatizes the class system as a whole in America. The hierarchy of boxing is almost tragically weighted toward the "top" end, the most visible (or, to most people, the *only* visible) sphere of boxing— world championship fights at expensive casinos—and ineffably works toward the marginalization of the many less glamorous contests, in less glamorous venues, which dwarf the former in number. This "tip of the iceberg" of the visible media spectacle of boxing in relation to the greater mass of its unacknowledged participants, is a gestalt that embodies Marx's comments on the exploitation of labor and its effacement in the system of commodities, and the disproportions of wealth and opportunity operative in American society as a whole.

A further paradox comes to light when we assess the relationship of the fighters and the spectators. On the one hand, the cliché of "bloodlust" holds some truth. When a fighter is hurt and seems "ready for the kill" (particularly the opponent of a hometown boxer or favorite), or especially when she is cut, there is a tangible increase in the intensity of the crowd's reaction; "baying for blood" is hardly an overstatement. However, in the event of a particularly heavy knockout, the transformation wrought upon the crowd is perhaps surprising in view of this "bloodlust" (which it would be naive and fruitless to deny). A palpable hush, literally a deathly silence, will descend upon the hall. The event that many in the crowd were cheering for, when it transpires in particularly brutal form, produces a stunned sense of complicity in the onlookers. I cannot have been alone in thinking, in the three minutes or so waiting for one badly poleaxed boxer to arise from the canvas, I would be in a deeply ambivalent situation, should *the very worst* occur. When my friends asked "how the boxing was" last night, and I had to tell of a person killed or crippled in front of my eyes, while I or my neighbor shouted it on, how would I feel? In a sport where fatality is a rare, but necessarily highly charged result, death and the spectators" complicity in it form an ever-present undercurrent. For my own part, the ultimate stakes that underlie boxing form a part of its irresistible appeal, despite the great ambivalence that attaches to it. If courage is indeed "grace under pressure"—and boxing in the hands of its most virtuoso exponents is, among many other things, a supreme exhibition of grace—the appeal of boxing to its spectators is surely related to the extreme pressure, perhaps unparalleled in sports, that an omnipresent potential for paralysis or death place on the participant. Part of the equalitarian viewpoint of *Million Dollar Baby*, however ambivalent the film as a whole might be, lies in its stressing that women boxers share exactly the same risks as their male counterparts. The risk entailed for the participants is, of course, wholly at the root of the ambivalent and complicitous relationship between the spectators and the boxers. I wonder, however, if the rather unique position this places the spectator in—of passively consuming a spectacle entailing pain and suffering and possibly even death—is one of a difference in *degree* rather than a difference in *kind* to other, less visible relationships of complicity.

While the antiboxing lobby cite this chilling subtext as ample reason for the redundancy of boxing in modern society, suggesting that a sport so brutal has no place in a civilized culture, I wonder if this condemnation is not naive, if not paradoxical. We might certainly have cause to wonder whether indeed our society, with the real threat of violence ever present in many areas and symbolized violence ever present in the media, is as yet so "cultured" as to make the "brutality" of boxing inimical to it. Many boxers will wax phlegmatic on the dangers posed in the ring, as compared with those they faced in their lives outside of the ring; ghetto existence (which, it cannot be stated enough, forms the horizon of possibilities for most boxers) thus provides the proper context for appreciating the very different relation to danger that boxers have, compared with their (largely middle-class) would-be advocates in the abolitionist lobby. Beyond the potential of violence for subjects in underclass life, the employment "opportunities" open to them often serve to make boxing seem comparatively easy. The Olympic champion Michael Spinks unusually did not turn professional having won his medal, opting instead for employment in a factory. The chemicals, machinery, and abject safety standards in this working environment threatened illness, disfigurement, and death to the extent that Spinks began a professional boxing career as *less* threatening to his health. In a strong sense, then, boxing as a discourse of the socially marginal can be seen as simply externalizing the contradictions of the outsider's position, the naturalization of violence in everyday life, and the foreclosure of so many forms of cultural self-authorship. While to many writers, boxing seems an epic arena for the playing out of existential truths—what Loïc Wacquant terms the "pre-fabricated exoticism" common to depictions of the sport—in relation to their cultural position most boxers simply consider it their *job*. Contrary to more high-blown representations, Wacquant—a Bourdieu-influenced sociologist who devoted an ethnographic study to boxing in Chicago and ended up training with the boxers in the gym[8]—asserts that boxing is more usefully seen as a craft or job than as an art form. It might be suggested, then, that a key difference between boxing and other equally or more dangerous (but socially sanctioned) occupations, is that boxing *externalizes* the kind of complicity developed in arguments above, through its dimension as spectacle, in a way that (say) coalminers maimed or killed in accidents simply cannot. The boxer enforces on the spectator a sense of the social inequality and immobility that are fundamental to his choice (and the choices of so many like him) to box professionally, in the absence of any preferable (or even any other) options. I wonder, then, if boxing is repulsive to some people as much for its dramatization of social inequality—to which many would respond by placing their heads in the sand—as for its perceived brutality. If boxing (like coalmining) is merely perceived as a tough and dangerous job, one that ("surely. . . .," to the uninitiated) "no-one in their right mind would do if they had much of a choice," the complicity of society as a whole in the inequities that contribute to boxers' choices must be considered.

The gendered status of boxing as supposedly "masculine" also bears some investigation along these lines, particularly with regard to the idea of "aggression" (which is actually in any case an ambivalent virtue in boxing). In the words of Joyce Carol Oates, "raw aggression is thought to be the peculiar province of men," and entails the channeling of destructive urges into spectacles; "the contemplation of ruins is a masculine specialty."[9] While Jose Torres (former World Champion Light-heavyweight) states that the "*machismo* of boxing is a condition of poverty," Oates questions if it is a condition "uniquely of poverty," pointing instead to its roots in "adolescence" and "the denial of the feminine-in-man that has its ambiguous attractions for all men, however "civilised.'"[10] That Oates can point with such confidence to "all men" bespeaks a somewhat essentializing viewpoint on her part, which invites a counterview in the interest of a more progressive gender politics. The insidious cultural myth that perpetuates supposedly feminine ideals of nurturing (and passivity/submission) over/above "masculine" aggressivity (implicitly: agency) clearly serves to limit female agency. It does so, moreover, at the expense of ignoring the fundamental structures of subjectivity, where aggressivity might be seen as every bit as normal (and healthy) as nurturing or empathy. Part of the problem might be in the assumption that the act of aggression articulates a position of power or strength. In an opposing view, we might suggest that the more power*less* an individual feels, the *greater* the propensity for violent acting out. Further, it can be seen as problematic to view aggressivity as purely "destructive'; surely it can be equally empowering (think of Frederick Douglass's battle with the "slave-breaker, Covey"?[11]) I would therefore seek to locate the particular resonance of any individual "powerlessness" and its corollary aggressivity within a frame that accounts for factors beyond the gendered. In the words of Natalie Angier, "Of course (women) are aggressive. They're alive, aren't they?"[12] In the face of a cultural prohibition against female aggression, "other ways of redirecting or sublimating female aggression" manifest themselves, such as "anorexia, self-injuring, and depression."[13] The key contrast, it seems to me, between boxing and the inverted forms of female aggressivity/self-authorship mentioned above, is again in the means/end relationship promoted between the female subject and her body. All of these alternative models of feminine demarcation of the body turn around an *introversion* of sorts, where the static female body is signified upon as an end in itself. With the boxer's body attuned to ends (i.e., motions, actions) *beyond* itself, we can suggest a disruption of the insidious, annular cycle of (say) anorexia, insofar as the body's passive, submissive modalities that are promoted in the latter, as opposed to its *active* properties being developed in boxing.

Oates's reference in the citation above to "adolescence" provides a key segue-point here, between a (regressive) view of aggressivity as inherently "masculine," and one which sees aggressivity as fundamental to the transition of *any* "adolescent" from the world of children to that of adults (this is a key implication of another female boxing film, *Girl Fight*). Which is to say that the assumption of "adult" norms on the part of the adolescent is unthinkable without a certain minimal aggressivity, which in the Developmental school of psychology (as practiced by D. W Winnicott or, from a more feminist perspective, Jessica Benjamin)[14] is in the first place crucial in "individuating" the infant as a child/subject relating to the adult world of signs and affects; individualism is first attained by the "aggressive" negotiation with, and casting off of, parental influence. Further, developmental sociology views see a similar minimal aggressivity as fundamental to the assertion of the would-be adult's right to take her place in the adult sphere: "If conflict is necessary for growth, if one needs not only empathy and attunement but the ability to oppose others and express one's will, then healthy aggression is mandatory to the development of self and to positive connection.'"[15]

Bearing in mind the idea that a certain aggressivity is necessary for the subject's transition into adult life, I wonder if Torres might not be correct in his assessment of machismo as, if not "uniquely" (pace Oates) a phenomenon of social position and/or poverty, then *primarily* so. Insofar as subjects of the ghetto milieu that dominates boxing assess their lives as lacking potential access to many of the forms of gratification within culture, perhaps the "aggression" of their attempts to make the transition into adult culture—by way of boxing, gangs, crime, "gangsta rap," for example—is strictly correlative to this sense of impotence. It is significant, then, that the protagonist (Maggie) in *Million Dollar Baby*, in seeking to persuade the predictably cynical (male) trainer to teach her to box, is only successful when she enlists her class position and its associated miseries as the justification for her desire and "need" to box: "I'm here celebrating the fact that I've spent another day scraping dishes and waitressing, which I've done since thirteen . . . my brother's in prison, my sister cheats on welfare pretending that one of her babies is still alive, my daddy's dead and my momma weighs 312 lbs; if I was thinking straight I'd go back home, find a used trailer, buy a deep fryer and some Oreos. Problem is, this is the only thing I ever feel good doing. If I'm too old for this, then I've got nothing."

This is cemented by the consistent class marking of Maggie as protagonist, her calling Frank "boss" despite his telling her not to, her promises of diligence (to be a good worker), and her deferential mannerisms toward him. What is interesting in the above is that as with the boxers described by Wacquant, it is less the financial poverty of her background that Maggie seeks to transcend, but the poverty of *opportunity* afforded to her theretofore.

The means by which Clint Eastwood's trainer eventually accepts her request is emblematic of the ambivalent gender politics of the film as a whole. Maggie is initially portrayed as proactive in the face of gender norms. She *actively* solicits Eastwood's trainer and can only win him round by showing the requisite stubbornness and desire, in the face of his assertion that he "doesn't train girls." Upon accepting her, however, he insists on a return to unquestioning acquiescence ("You don't say anything, you don't question me, you don't say, maybe. . . . Don't argue with me, that's the only way we're doing this"). The gender implications are clear; while the female agent wishes to gain mastery of her body (a seemingly progressive move) in a male-dominated sphere (a transgressive move), she must enlist the services of a male expert (with clearly regressive implications). It is crucial to note, however, that Frank's services are placed very much in a commercial as well as paternalistic light, since as Maggie pays her "dues" to the club he is as much employee as indispensable provider of masculine knowledge and techniques. He is therefore partially her "boss," as in her insistent use of the word, but also partially in thrall to the talent and potential of this woman who ultimately fights for a $500,000 purse (and who becomes the only fighter he has taken to a "title shot"). This seesaw relationship between an embryonic feminine agency and a repressive paternalism continues throughout the film, indeed is structurally repeated on several occasions. I would like to concentrate first on the aspects of the film that I judge to carry progressive implications less tainted by its masculine directorly bias. Uppermost of these is the initial presentation of the female body, which, in line with my expectations, contrasts with more traditional representations of the female body-as-image. At almost all times Hilary Swank's body is portrayed as performing some form of boxing-related motion. As opposed to the montage scenes in the *Rocky* series (which have rightly passed into culture as parody now, see *Team America: World Police*), where the functional utility of the "training" performed by Stallone is often seemingly secondary to its display of his physique,[16] the training portrayed in *Million Dollar Baby* is admirably concerned with the mundane, quotidian skills of boxing. Swank, by the way, throws a much more technically correct punch than Stallone does in any of his films; the relative boxing "realism" of *Million Dollar Baby* compares favorably with any boxing film I have seen, and brings to light not only the "unrealistic" aspects of *Rocky* et al., but their primary concern for "display" over function. Stallone's punches are thrown "for the camera," they are heaved at the opponent with maximum visible muscular effort and movement (and therefore minimum efficiency). *Million Dollar Baby*'s relative "realism" perhaps implies, in its rejection of display and muscular form in favor of function and motion, that the genre of mainstream boxing films is actually *burdened* by the symbolic baggage of the muscular male form. In overturning cultural misconceptions that muscular size necessarily equals power, the *female* boxing film returns the body to its "natural" status in boxing, shorn of the generic obligation to display the kind of bodies that are functionally near useless in the "real" world of the sport. Thus, perhaps somewhat paradoxically, the woman's boxing film proves in some ways to be a more appropriate vehicle for articulating boxing on a "realistic" level, and to form a critique of extant (male) boxing films.

As a corollary to the film's representation of Swank in almost perpetual motion, and the progressive implications this carries for feminine self-authorship, a major part of *Million Dollar Baby*'s impact lies in its ability (or more accurately Swank's ability) to provide a convincing portrayal (even to this critical eye) of a woman as a *competent* boxer. To contextualize this on an anecdotal level, only a couple of months before I saw the film, I was a spectator of a women's boxing match for the first time. My own gendered reactions to this bout were part of a shift in attitude enforced upon me by the event. Despite my putatively progressive gender politics—I had no problem with women boxing if they wished to—I must confess an abiding suspicion that I very much doubted, as a boxing fan, that they would be any *good* at it. I am pleased to have been disabused of this misconception by one of the female boxers, a twenty-eight-year-old named Lindsey Scragg who happens to be from my hometown. Perhaps fifteen seconds of the bout had elapsed before it was overpoweringly obvious that she "could box a bit,"[17] despite its being her debut displaying all of the hallmarks of the well-schooled fighter (the most obvious ones being the neatness of her footwork, the solid compactness of her stance, the correctness of her punches, and her balance and guard while delivering them). Only another fifteen seconds were required to indicate also, firstly, that at a mere 126 pounds she carried a punch like a mule's kick, and secondly, that her (more experienced) opponent was woefully outmatched against her. This provided a dual source of ambivalence for me, initially insofar as I was genuinely shocked by her punching power, which was advertised by a resounding series of thuds that could be heard right to the back of the hall, as they say. The further cause of ambivalence for me was that her opponent, accordingly, was taking a fearful beating. I couldn't help but wonder, as I sat there all but shouting "stop the fight" out loud, if my concern for her opponent was a purely gendered reaction. The simple fact of a woman being hit and hurt repeatedly was too viscerally shocking for any intellectualized ideas of equality I had. Upon further reflection after the event, it occurred to me that being a spectator of *any* particularly one-sided boxing match is a profoundly ambivalent and uncomfortable experience (perhaps because, as with the heavy knockout, the spectator's complicity is called into question by the very emotions that attend it); it is as though the pain and effort entailed can only seem justified to the average spectator in the context of a relatively even bout. Notwithstanding this pregendered aversion to *any* one-sided beating, I found it impossible to deny that the particular source of my discomfiture was the spectacle of a woman on the receiving end of a physical thrashing. Until I see Lindsay fight again I feel bound to say that the reeducation of my gendered expectations in boxing has only, as yet, gone so far as to reconcile me with the fact that some women might be able to "box a bit," and indeed "punch a bit." Whether or not I will reconcile myself to the sight of women getting hurt remains to be seen, although my comment to Lindsay in our interview ("I look forward to seeing you fight someone at your own level," i.e., someone good enough to test her) suggests that I at least have the desire to test that emotive barrier. Lindsay's skills will be better showcased against someone with at least comparable skills. This coheres with the reactions of the audience as a whole, insofar as once a woman boxer proved to be competent, the predominant reaction seemed to be to sit back and admire her skills and talent, just as we would any male boxer.[18] In the kind of blue-collar masculine environment hardly known for its progressive gender politics, I was surprised to see just how quickly the audience acclimatized itself (if indeed the rest of the audience *needed* to do so) to the idea of a woman fighting.

I would imagine, then, that the section of society *least* likely to be surprised and impressed by Swank's dexterity in impersonating a boxer would be boxing fans, or at least those who have seen women box (if so, I find the irony almost delightful). I would also hope, to a certain degree, that the gender expectations of many male and female viewers of the film were challenged and altered; the key misconceptions being that, firstly, women would/should have no desire to box, and secondly, no ability to do so. In providing a relatively convincing portrayal on both levels, *Million Dollar Baby* can be seen as at least partially progressive.[19] In the words of Butler, to some degree Maggie represents "the unanticipated agency, of a female 'object' who inexplicably returns the glance, reverses the gaze, and contests the place and authority of the masculine position."[20] However, I do not wish to assume that progressive implications can be taken from the simple fact of women's transgressing the traditional gender boundaries of sports—that a woman's presence in the boxing ring is necessarily progressive—insofar as the act of transgression involves bringing herself continually into dialogue with masculinized norms and masculine figures. As has already been indicated, the trajectory of the film's implicit gender politics undergoes a series of progressive-regressive shifts, and it is necessary to break these cycles down in some detail, to approach the specific problems entailed in the female's act of transgression. Most notably, the relationship between Maggie and her trainer—and its implicitly patriarchal undertones—can be seen as problematizing any naive notion of the female boxer as a protofeminist figure. Just as her initial assertion of agency in badgering Frank to train her is equivocated by his demand for submission to his authority, Maggie's development as a boxer is characterized by an oscillation between voluntarism and submission. As Morgan Freeman's voice-over indicates, the trainer must extend his will over the body and mind of his charge: "You show them how to stand, keep their legs between their shoulders . . . you strip them down to bare wood, make them so tired that they only listen to you and nothing else." The submission itself, however, is ultimately only performed by the boxer's *ego* on her own, sometimes unwilling, flesh (and this is by far the most profound—and progressive—revelation of participation in any combat sport; the realization of the astonishing extent to which the body can be made to submit and endure). The submission of her ego is also therefore implicit—to an extent—in the relationship between fighter and trainer. For, as Freeman's voice-over goes on to opine: "All fighters are pigheaded, one way or another. Some part of them always thinks they know better than you. Truth is, even if they're wrong, even if that one thing is going to be the ruin of them, if you can beat that last bit out of them, they ain't fighters at all."

The boxer's relationship with the trainer, then, is fraught with ambivalence. On the one hand, the boxer is unlikely to fulfill her potential without paying full heed to the trainer, and submitting her body (and a good portion of her mind) to his regime. On the other hand, the true fighter's mind is, if we believe Freeman's dictum, definitively resistant to total submission, and while as the boxer's body *is* subject to the control of the trainer while in training, it is (doubtless maddeningly, for many trainers) autonomous during the bout itself.[21] It would seem to be this area of ambivalence, between voluntarism and submission, that is addressed by the recurring power shifts between Maggie and Frank in the film, and is significantly an ambivalence that might well exist between most (or any) trainers and most (or any) boxers; *the "patriarchal" overtones attending to the relationship between Maggie and Frank in a way transcend gender, or at least exist in very similar forms between all-male partnerships of trainer and fighter.* I stress this particularly, as much of the film might carry the appearance of distinctly patriarchal biases, of the male (father) figure imposing his will upon the female subject.[22]

A patriarchal attitude might also be read into Frank's desire to "protect" Maggie. However, this must again be qualified. Frank is firstly portrayed as being overprotective of *all* of his fighters; his protégé Big Willie leaves him to pursue a title bout with another manager, having been told by Frank for a couple of years that he will be ready "with another couple of fights" (Freeman's sardonic comment being "oh, so it's a *Championship* you're protecting him from?"). Further, the rule that is given by Frank to Maggie as the sine qua non of boxing stresses her *own* agency; the rule is to "protect her*self* at all times." Perhaps, then, the potentially patriarchal stress on "protection" actually dramatizes the *trainer's* submissive position and the ambivalences that attend it—giving the best of his knowledge to the fighter but ultimately having to stand by and watch them perform—as much as it stresses the fighter's submission. Frank's relationship with Big Willie brings out another contradiction that attends the position of the "master" in the "master/pupil" dialectic. Upon Big Willie's leaving him for another trainer, Frank's assertion that "he can't teach you anything" is returned with the devastating response "you already taught me everything I need to know." Hence, in many martial arts films, the "student" ultimately ends up surpassing the "master," in a move which stresses not only the emergent properties of youth over/above experience and age, but the contingency of received knowledge and technical skills upon the creative and improvisatory capacities of the succeeding generations needed to embody and enact them. To cite Butler again, we can read in Eastwood's figure, and his relationship to the burgeoning agency of Maggie, "the radical dependency of the masculine subject on the female 'Other' (which) suddenly exposes his autonomy as illusory."[23] Perhaps surprisingly, in a film where the knowledge of the trainer is often seemingly foregrounded, the implication is that the trainer's knowledge (the knowledge of the cultural dominant) has limits, and can become obsolescent, in a way that the potential of the fighter (the emergent agent) does not.

In a series of events in the film, this oscillatory cycle is confirmed, bringing with it myriad ambivalences. Frank initially agrees to train Maggie only until she is ready to fight, at which point they will find her a "proper" manager (i.e., one who is prepared to take risks on her behalf). He quickly intercedes however when, watching from the wings, her first bout is going badly (naturally, after Frank's intercession, she wins the fight, having carried out his instructions to the letter). His intrusion is the first of several strategic uses of the one-minute interval between rounds, a scenario in which the trainer's agency is repeatedly—perhaps somewhat unrealistically—shown to be instrumental in changing the pattern of the fight for Maggie.[24] In one instance, then, having had her nose broken in the first round, Maggie returns to the corner in a physical mess and in danger of having the fight stopped due to the injury. While Frank at first suggests that the injury is too dire to treat, it is at Maggie's insistence—"you can fix it. I've seen what you can do"—that he manipulates the broken nose with his hands, enough for her to continue (and, naturally, win) the fight. Once again the cycle of the female agent's voluntary submission to a male figure's manipulation and control of her body is instantiated. This cycle is, however, often reversed in the film, lest we begin to suspect it carries little but patriarchal overtones. For instance, then, after a run of spectacular first-round knockouts, Frank chastises Maggie for finishing the fights too quickly; she will not gain the necessary experience, and will find it difficult to find managers willing to match their fighters with her, by displaying such devastating power. Maggie seeks to go up in class from the four-round fights that mark the novice fighter, and in the words of Freeman's voice-over "Frank made her fight another four-rounder, just to let her know who was boss." Maggie, of course, knocks her opponent out in the first round again. *The film's cycle of voluntary submission to the (male) law is thus supplemented by one of voluntary transgression of that law in a way that should preclude our reading purely patriarchal implications into it.* In Butler's words, "Power [seems] to be more than an exchange between subjects and an Other; indeed, power [appears] to operate in the production of that very binary frame for thinking about gender." In this view it is the "production" via "exchange" that delimits gender along the lines of hierarchical relationships, but this mode of production is fluid and appears in the gaps, as it were, between notional poles of "subject" and "other." Insofar as multiple positions obtain within this matrix: "Because certain kinds of "gender identities" fail to conform to those norms of cultural intelligibility . . . [their] persistence and proliferation . . . provide critical opportunities to expose the limits and regulatory aims of that domain of intelligibility . . . [and] open up within the very terms of that matrix of intelligibility rival and subversive matrices of gender disorder."[25]

Insofar as Frank's knee-jerk response that he "doesn't train women" represents an insistence on masculinized norms, and this insistence is ultimately overridden, we are thus presented with a certain "resignification of norms [which] is thus a function of their *inefficacy.*"[26]

None of the above is intended to obfuscate the senses in which we can denote an unreconstructed masculinist/patriarchal narrative at the heart of *Million Dollar Baby*. The implications of the lost father/lost daughter subplot might indeed serve to anchor the film as a whole. Frank is shown to write letters weekly to his estranged daughter—these letters are returned to sender every time—and the film ends with Freeman's character writing to her, narrating the events surrounding Frank's relationship with Maggie, and suggesting that it is *his* development that is central to the film. In the words of one contributor to the women's studies forum WMST-L, Maggie's "purpose" in the film is "to provide Eastwood's character with a second chance at parenting a daughter." Maggie, equally, is shown to be seeking a father figure, and the mirroring of these two plotlines undoubtedly casts a patriarchal pall over the proceedings. This regressive trajectory is exemplified by Frank's "naming" of Maggie; for her first big fight, he acquires a fancy-looking robe for her walk to the ring, with the Gaelic legend

"Mo Cuishla" (he is teaching himself Gaelic in a move which emphasizes his own and Maggie's Irish heritage) emblazoned on the top. He doesn't tell her what this means, and it is not until the end of the film when she is on her death-bed that we find out it means "my darling, my blood." Frank exercises firstly the masculine imperative to name the female subject, demonstrated by the possessive "my," from which obviously patriarchal conclusions follow. The resonance of his "fathering" Maggie is heightened still further with the combination of the diminutive "darling" and the genitive "blood." This pales into insignificance, however, in the light of the film's ending. Maggie is crippled by a cheating opponent who hits her after the bell and, completely paralyzed, she is placed in the hospital, and ultimately has to entreaty Frank to end her life for her. Not only does this equivocate the film's progressive tendency to grant the female subject agency through her bodily potential, but more pertinently, alludes to decades of filmic punishments visited upon transgressive female figures in Hollywood. To cite one of the (many) critical assertions on the WMST-L forum to this effect: "if you step too far out of bounds as a woman, something terrible will happen to you." Even women who loved the film tended to be repelled by the ending which not only *immobilizes* the formerly active body of its female subject, but moves thereafter toward its *dismemberment* (Maggie's lower legs have to be amputated as they become gangrenous through her immobility). In the context of Hollywood history it seems almost impossible to read past the implication that female transgression will (or should) be punished.

As is usual in this film, however, this skein of repressive masculinity imposed upon female agency is mollified, at least somewhat. It is perhaps the most shocking exhibition of agency in the film when the immobilized Maggie, having had her request to end her life turned down by Frank, bites off her own tongue in a failed attempt at suicide. In the words of a WMST-L contributor, *contra* unequivocal assertions of the film's unreconstructed paternalism, "What of the fact that Maggie took control of her own life/death desire by biting her tongue?" And while the moral dilemma of Maggie's "right-to-die" is taken on by Eastwood's character, it is undeniable that this is a dilemma *forced* upon him—against his will (as with the initial dilemma of whether he should train a girl)—*by* Maggie. Similarly to her attaining acceptance from Frank as a boxer, Maggie demonstrates the will to define and control her *own* body in order to compel his assistance in her goals for it. In her final speech the film's motif of embryonic agency and self-determination, however equivocal, is fully dramatized: "I can't *be* like this . . . not after what I've *done. People chanted my name* —well, not my name, some damn name you gave me—I *got* what I needed. I *got* it all." Maggie's "acceptance" of her fate comes through having earned recognition on a wider cultural level—"people chanted my name"— and despite its not being her name but "some damn name [Frank] gave" her that was chanted, the film asks us as an audience to validate her satisfaction. Maggie's repulsion toward her disabled state of "being" is contrasted by her with what she had "done," again rejecting passive modes of being in favor of active modes, and the final statements provide a double emphasis on "getting"; the female subject is in this context in an *appropriative* relationship with cultural norms, having "gotten" (largely) through her own agency the recognition that had eluded her theretofore.

There are other contexts that should be assessed before coming to a conclusion about the admittedly ambivalent ending of *Million Dollar Baby*. Perhaps foremost among these are the cloyingly triumphalist "happy" endings that betoken (and indeed beset) the traditional boxing film. In this regard the ending of *Million Dollar Baby* can be seen as both a realist corrective and critique, a deepening of the frame of reference of the boxing film to include its ultimate consequences; while it may be less than edifying to the average filmgoer's taste, it is perhaps indicative of a lack of moral and ethical depth that so many filmmakers, when approaching the subject matter of boxing, totally occlude the very real dangers that attend the sport. As already indicated, I feel that the ending stresses an equality of risk for women boxers, a risk that is made all the more poignant insofar as boxing films in general utterly foreclose it. And while the ending might be read as an allegory of the *limitations* of female agency, it is crucial to note that, as already suggested, *Million Dollar Baby* is very much a *masculine* cultural production. Maggie's enforced paralysis can thus be seen as indicative of "the injurious effects of [male] discourse" upon the relationship between the female body and subjectivity.[27] In Butler's words: "A materialist feminist approach shows that what we take for the cause or origin of oppression is in fact only the *mark* imposed by the oppressor; the "myth of woman" plus its material effects and manifestations in the appropriated *consciousness* and *bodies* of women."[28]

While we can see Maggie's *body* as ultimately "marked" by the masculine discourses that envelop it, "what we take for the cause of oppression (i.e., a mutable sense of female agency) is in fact only the *mark* imposed by the oppressor" (i.e., the desire of masculine cultural production to keep that agency within certain bounds), and her *consciousness* remains self-assertive nonetheless. In gender terms, the ending of *Million Dollar Baby* can be read as an embattled, challenged masculinity effecting a symbolic denial of emergent female agency that it has given form to, almost in spite of itself, and the very violence of this process of "marking" as a corollary to the depth of (male) insecurities that female agency gives rise to. Mapping the ending onto culture in general, we can see that progressions in feminine self-assertiveness occasion grudging concessions within the masculinized sphere, and a subsequent turning away from or refusal of male consciousness to adjust to the fact of increased (if not yet perfect) gender equality.

In this reading, the "emergent" level of *Million Dollar Baby* as a narrative is thus the female, class-marginalized subject's "need" to assert herself within the cultural manifold, expounding an ethic of activity in the face of its norms, however dire the consequences. While Maggie must therefore enter into dialogue with patriarchal norms, "to operate within the matrix of power is not the same as to replicate uncritically relations of domination. It offers the possibility of a repetition of the law which is not its consolidation, but its displacement."[29] It seems that while Maggie cannot "displace" the law (that boxing is wholly a masculine preserve), she can at least hold it to account on the grounds of inclusivity (boxing is a largely masculine preserve in which some women can find fulfillment). We might therefore read Maggie's fate not just as that visited upon the gender *transgressor*, but also as that willingly accepted by the *pioneer* of alternative forms of gender expression, whose intervention creates the conditions for the franchise of that form of self-expression to be widened. As stated earlier, however, if we read the film solely at the level of its gender politics, we risk essentializing the cultural field it addresses, basically ceding the field to the "masculine" and occluding pre/nongendered elements that can be seen as equally pertinent (and, indeed, equally regressive). To cite an essay by David Walsh:

> Aside from its three central characters, who are given some kind of special dispensation, Eastwood's work expresses nothing but contempt for humanity, especially for working class humanity. The black and latin kids in the gym are malevolent louts; the one decent "gym-rat" is mentally handicapped and a rather pathetic figure. . . . Most telling of all, and most grotesque, is the portrayal of Maggie's family in Missouri, as lazy, selfish monsters, caricatures of "poor white trash."[30]

As Walsh's remarks imply, it might be suggested that the sometimes-dubious gender politics of *Million Dollar Baby* pale into insignificance next to its regressive class and racial politics. The film's treatment of Maggie's family is indeed startlingly condemnatory, although I feel it is more productive to assess the significance of this within the film and its contexts as a whole, rather than to dismiss it wholesale on those grounds. On one level, we can again see the film as rejecting some of the more formulaic conceits of the boxing film. The *Rocky* films and *Cinderella Man*, to name but two examples, are in a sense domestic/family narratives that merely happen to have boxing as their accidental subject. Thus, a great deal of time is spent in the domestic environments of *Rocky, Cinderella Man,* or even *Raging Bull,* as opposed to the almost total exclusion of this sphere in *Million Dollar Baby*. The home environments of all the protagonists of the film, when indeed they are represented, are represented as claustrophobic spaces, devoid of light (indeed, *Million Dollar Baby* seems almost pathological in the elision of light from its shots). The risk entailed in representing Maggie in a more "traditional" domestic environment would be to "domesticate" her own role in more traditional terms, and it is interesting that Eastwood almost totally rejects this move. The domestic environment is in this sense foreclosed, in order to *foreground* the gym environment. In a similar sense to James Jones's war novel *The Thin Red Line*, from which all factors unrelated to the battleground it portrays are excluded (in order to stress the unique horrors and all-encompassing nature of war), we might suggest that the domestic sphere is minimized in *Million Dollar Baby* in order to imply the intenseness and uniqueness of the gym and boxing. Maggie's family are doubtless portrayed in such an unflattering light in order to stress the singularity of her determination and the scope of her self-assertive journey, a case of the particular (individual) being promoted at the expense of the universal (class) that is denigrated. While I do not wish to minimize the regressive class politics at stake here, I feel Walsh fails to denote the partially utopian impulse that is operative in the film on behalf of the (female) "individual," even if this does come at the expense of her class.[31]

Walsh's particular ire is also therefore directed at what he terms "an attitude that would have been scorned by the filmmakers of another era—relentless individualism," although it is crucial to note that he only discerns this "individualism" mainly in the character of Frankie: "Eastwood's persona consciously takes the law into his own hands . . . the characters Eastwood plays are not answerable to anyone, except themselves. . . . Eastwood's characters take matters into their own hands and then go about their business, *convinced of their essential rightness* [emphasis original].

An interesting repetition of the film's directorly bias is made by Walsh here. While we can discern many elements of the film that are adduced to emphasize Eastwood's role as star/director—the influence of the trainer in the intervals between rounds, the foregrounding of his search for a surrogate daughter, the focus on his moral dilemma in acceding to Maggie's request to end her life—Walsh's critical focus on the "Eastwood persona" ultimately serves to solidify it ("the effort to identify the enemy as singular in form is a reverse-discourse that uncritically mimics the strategy of the oppressor instead of offering a different set of terms").[32] It should be considered, also, that the focus on the figure of the trainer, and the masculine bias that might be read into it, are features of the source text from which *Million Dollar Baby* was taken, a series of short stories called *Rope Burns* by F. X. O'Toole, a former trainer himself who narrates all of the stories in the collection from that perspective. We should appreciate as a balance to the "relentless individualism" that is, admittedly, *one* strand of the film's ideological underpinnings, firstly, that Frank's "individualism" is rendered as an alienated, detached quality that is actually close to a burden. Hence Freeman's sardonic chidings, the austerity of Frank's domestic surroundings, and hence particularly the ending that is given to *him*; he is effectively sent to the margins of the text, and as with so many Frankenstein's monsters and "difficult" figures this can be seen as playing out a form of textual banishment.[33] It is debatable, also, that Frankie is indeed "convinced of his essential rightness," insofar as the deathbed request from Maggie occasions clearly labeled soul-searching on his part, and insofar as shocking measures must be undertaken by Maggie in order to enlist his assistance in her suicide.

To put it one way, Walsh takes the film at its (final, symbolic) word, so to say, and addresses its "dominant" strand at the expense of its "emergent" strand. As a representation of certain dogmatic leftist tendencies to denigrate the category of "individualism" as idealist and ideological, Walsh serves to downplay the sense in which the film's nascent agency (as represented by Maggie) is set in the context of her social background and put into dialogue with a more traditional, masculine notion of "individualism" (represented by Frank). Boxing is, in any case, nowhere near as "individualist" a sport as might be supposed. As suggested in earlier paragraphs we should see the boxer's development in the light of a dialogical relationship with the trainer. Most boxers, accordingly, when talking of their preparation and strategies for a fight, will insistently use the collective pronoun—e.g. "*we* were expecting a tough fight, *our* strategy was to . . . etc."—which amply indicates the cooperative basis of their efforts (to cite one phrase from *Rope Burns* "you can't be the horse *and* the jockey and win"). Apropos of the history of Marxist theory, we might suggest that the dogmatic rejection of the category of the individual is a particular blind spot; without a theory of the subject, how can we locate the particular efficacy of the transmission of ideologies from social collective to "individual"? Further, Walsh seems to address the individual purely at the level of the isolated *ego;* the dilemmas of the individual he addresses are moral, and he fails to take into account the *bodily* dimension of subjectivity that is given a progressive slant in the first two-thirds of the film.[34] In the words of Butler, "We need to understand that the "viability" of a woman's life depends upon an exercise of bodily autonomy and on social conditions that enable that autonomy."[35] While Maggie's "viability" is curtailed by the film's ending, as the foregoing has hopefully shown, her development shows the negotiability and plasticity of the borders within which she exercises her "bodily autonomy," implying that repressive paternalism (whose presence in society it would be naive to deny) is continually open to challenge.

The contradictions issued forth in *Million Dollar Baby* serve to illuminate those facing women involved in masculine spheres in general and, I feel particularly, those facing women who participate in combat sports and other, masculinized sports. The rewards to be gained from these exercises in gender transgression are, it seems to me, strictly related to those contradictions, and should thus be embraced as opportunities for the "rewriting of the grammar" (Butler) that subtends received gender norms. To cite a contributor to WMST-L on the subject of women in combat sports:

> Most theorists . . . tend to be dismissive of physical projects in general: they regard them as a form of disciplining the body, and hence, negative. If I wish to teach about this in class, I have few resources that explore the productive dimension of women's physical aggression and strength . . . most importantly for women, this training (in combat sports) involves learning to move the body in ways that have been socialised out of them. . . . Feminists have been great at getting women to yell, be aggressive, and put their anger into appropriate projects in the political and social sphere. Why, then, do we reject appropriate expressions of aggression in the physical sphere?

In this view, the schooling of the female body in "aggressive" techniques acts as a corollary to female self-empowerment within the social sphere. We must appreciate that the female subject has a bivalenced relationship to her own body; firstly, as a medium of self-authorship, but secondly and concurrently, as a form of expression *pro* or *contra* social norms ("the personal is the political," so to say). A woman's sense of self-authorship can be perpetuated by participation in sports—"physical training, and learning to express physical power and aggression in appropriate ways, literally changes their life in other areas" (WMST-L contributor)—and to deny the efficacy of the improved self-image that follows from this would be to deny that patriarchal hegemony functions largely through the control of female bodies and body images.³⁶ In terms of the sport of boxing itself, insofar as women's boxing has only been sanctioned in the United States since 1997, and insofar as the trainers in boxing are predominantly male, there is an inevitable potential for masculine biases to be superimposed over the female agents in this field. However, as women gradually enter the field and the technical know-how relative to it passes into female hands, this imbalance can be righted somewhat. The spectre of women teaching other women to box (or practice other combat sports), possibly within all-female environments, presents much more empowering possibilities for women seeking to develop a relationship to their own bodies without male intercession. As Leah Hager Cohen's book suggests,³⁷ this is a prospect becoming more feasible, if not at a particularly frenetic pace, then in line with current demand (although the impact of *Million Dollar Baby* may yet alter this).

As is hopefully clear, I view *Million Dollar Baby* as a fascinating illustration of the dialectics of gender and the problems of female self-authorship, one that has some progressive implications almost in spite of itself. It is on this basis that I would strongly recommend teaching the film in any gender studies courses, and especially those that focus on the representation of the female body.³⁸ The film's more regressive moves are exactly those features most interesting in the teaching of this subject area, and its ambivalences particularly productive in illustrating the progressive-regressive (or vice versa) trajectories that mark advances in female empowerment. To cite Butler on early Hollywood explorations of gender transgression (such as *Some Like it Hot* or *Victor, Victoria*), we can see *Million Dollar Baby* as displaying:

> *anxiety over a possible gender transgression [that] is both produced and deflected within the narrative trajectory* . . . a film which produces and contains the transgressive excess of [Swank's] performance . . . and though these texts are important to read as cultural texts in which gender transgression is negotiated, I would be reticent to call them subversive. Indeed, one might argue that such films are functional in providing a ritualistic releases for a heterosexual economy that must constantly police its own boundaries against the invasion of feminine agency, and this displaced production and resolution of [masculine] panic actually fortifies the regime in its self-perpetuating task.³⁹

In order to *prevent* a film such as *Million Dollar Baby* becoming a text that "fortifies the regime in its self-perpetuating task," it seems to me that there are several tasks incumbent upon us as cultural critics. The first, it seems, is not to overstate critique at the expense of utopian potential. While the film's regressive gender politics cannot be effaced, indeed may be so glaring as to make that impossible, I would be equally reticent to reject it solely on those grounds, as I would to champion it uncritically for its "individualism" or its *frisson* of feminist agency. The very real shifts in consciousness that can be occasioned by women performing difficult physical tasks or participating in combat sports—on a minor level, my own reaction to Lindsay Scragg is testament to this—are at least partially exemplified by *Million Dollar Baby*. In a film that could have fallen prey to so many of the clichés that attend the representation of women, and which rejects so many of the clichés of the boxing film, I find it hard not to pay some heed to its residual progressiveness, indeed feel it would be regressive to do so. Most pertinently, I feel it would be a simple misreading of *Million Dollar Baby* as a text, not to recognize its *dialogical* frame of male female relations, and the challenges presented to the masculine positions in that frame.

As already indicated I find much of the criticism directed at the film on the WMST-L forum and by David Walsh to be pertinent. However, I feel that in their various singular focuses (paraphrased simply, *Million Dollar Baby* "has a wholly regressive portrayal of women/class, therefore it is to be rejected") they not only occlude the film's genuinely utopian strand (however compromised it is), but also possibly the most devastatingly regressive element of all. The assumption that disabled life is not worth living merits not a word from Walsh and little on WMST-L, despite the fact that, unlike the portrayals of gender and class, there are no mitigating/mollifying factors whatsoever in the portrayal of disability. As with the representation of Maggie's family, perhaps this is supposed to intensify the uniqueness of the boxer and the extent to which she has to rise above her givens, identify totally with her position, and therefore make any alternative to this lifestyle choice appear inane or meaningless. *The inherent risk that is dramatized is that the extension of one particular marginal lifestyle, the promotion of one particular outsider discourse, threatens to demote, denigrate, or marginalize others.* This is a process that can be perpetuated by cultural criticism as well as by cultural production. Within the vocabulary of *Million Dollar Baby*, it seems as though we are asked to see any underclass figure that shows dedication and discipline to the extent required of the boxer to be almost miraculous. It is as though the film has to take away with one hand what it has given with another: the "gym-rats" and the Fitzgerald family must be boorish and objectionable in order to lionize Maggie, Frankie, and Dupris (Freeman); Frankie's masculine ethos must necessarily suffer at the expense of Maggie's agency; disability must necessarily be rejected in order to elevate the status of the boxer (or to provide Eastwood with a sufficiently weighty dilemma and the film to provide a suitably shocking "twist").[40]

The problem here, it seems to me, and one which I have not seen addressed suitably by other critics, is not specifically or solely the film's gender/class/disability politics, *but its almost unquestioning (and unquestioned) adherence to a binary logic of zero/sum.* The primary task for cultural critics, having outlined this binary mode of cultural production, is to reject or challenge that binary frame. This can be done by problematizing and expanding upon the ostensible oppositions of the text, as this essay has attempted to do in terms of the film's gender politics, demonstrating the *interplay* (and thus reciprocity) between the polarities set out in the text and refusing to take them as static norms, and thereafter gesturing toward the overturning of those norms. Accordingly, it may be incumbent upon us as cultural critics to advance textual readings in terms of *plural* contexts, in order to disrupt the binaries of the text, to avoid perpetuating yet another binary frame, and to avoid marginalizing other subject-positions. It is on this basis that Butler's championing of gender "parody" comes into its clearest light. While *Million Dollar Baby gestures* toward a questioning of gender boundaries at the level of *content,* these boundaries are ultimately left undisturbed in the film's *formal* frame. As opposed to the parodic practice such as transvestitism that melds different generic aspects in order to estrange them from their given contexts—subverting the formal frame of the grammar of gender—Eastwood's mode of cinematic form is so steeped in the mainstream tradition that its most subversive implications are partially "domesticated." It might therefore be appropriate to distinguish between, firstly, the film's sociocultural context at the level of content, and secondly its mode of *reproducing and relating to that context/content.* This gap between form and content can be seen in the presentation of Maggie's progress through training. While the *content* displayed is relatively nontraditional in terms of the boxing film—as stated earlier, it represents the development of the more mundane *skills* of the sport—the manner of shooting falls wholly in the remit of the mainstream modes of the genre (i.e., "time-lapse" shots to show progress through repetition). In other words, it is essential to remember that this is a film which comments both on the issue of women in boxing and on its own means of representing it, *and it is those means of representation that transpire as derogatory toward feminine agency.* My own future direction in terms of the issues raised in this essay is thus, firstly, to teach the film within the context of a gender studies course, whereby a greater range of response can be elicited at the level of its gender politics. Similarly, on an empirical level I intend to conduct questionnaires and interviews at future boxing shows; I will be most interested to gauge the reaction of "average" boxing fans, both to the film and to "real life" women boxers, insofar as they conform to or breach traditional stereotypes. As a counterweight to the masculine bias of *Million Dollar Baby*, another women's boxing film, *Girl Fight* (dir. Karyn Kusama), makes for some fascinating contrasts, and points toward a much less equivocal portrayal of feminine agency; I intended to include analysis of *Girl Fight* within this essay, but that must be postponed for a future undertaking. On that basis, the myriad of issues raised in both of these films lend themselves well to a collection of essays devoted to them at the level of their representation of marginalized gender, class, race, and disabled agency, a project I would be happy to superintend.

Notes

1. Judith Butler, *Gender Trouble* (London: Routledge, 1999), 43–44.
2. In the words of Judith Butler: "One question that feminists have raised . . . is whether the discourse which figures the act of construction as a kind of imprinting or imposition is not tacitly masculinist, whereas the figure of the passive surface . . . is not tacitly, or perhaps quite obviously, feminine." Judith Butler, *Bodies That Matter* (London: Routledge, 1993), 4.
3. Ibid., emphasis added.
4. Although this stress on the maternal is given an interesting slant in *Alien 3*, in which the climactic fight for Ripley is to *prevent* her own conception of the alien within her.
5. Adrienne Rich, "Compulsory heterosexuality and lesbian existence," *Signs: Journal of Women in Culture and Society* 5 (Summer 1980): 631–60.
6. Butler, *Gender Trouble*, 12.
7. Interview is included as an extra on the *Million Dollar Baby* DVD.
8. Loïc Wacquant, *Corps et âme: Carnets ethnographiques d'un apprenti boxeur* [Body and soul: ethnographic notebooks of an apprentice boxer] (Oxford: Oxford University Press 2007). Despite his admirably pragmatic bent, Wacquant still asserts that what "binds" boxers to the gym, over/above "poverty, fame or the possibility of occupational mobility," is "how gripping it is . . . the sheer sensuous, aesthetic and moral experience of being embedded in that universe" (interview, 2007). It seems that even when assessed by an academic sociologist, to whom Norman Mailer's comparison of two boxers fighting to a "metaphysical discussion" is anathema, and who seeks to define boxing as a "trade or craft," the fundamental questions of "aesthetics" or "morality" have a tendency to seep back into his discourse. Poverty, then, seen in purely financial terms, is secondary to a poverty of *opportunities for self-expression* and/or self-authorship that can be seen as the primary "answer" boxing gives for the problems associated with ghetto life.
9. Joyce Carol Oates, *On Boxing* (London: Harper Collins, 2006) 73, citing Erik Erikson.
10. Ibid., 76.
11. See the reference to Frantz Fanon in my other essay in this volume, "Mirrors of hard, distorting glass . . ."; "at the level of the individual, violence is a cleansing force, etc." While clearly the valorization of aggression over (say) passivity carries its own problems, it seems to me it is essential to cite the act of aggression in its specific context. In terms of the history of repressive norms of female submissiveness, then,

we might ask how they are to be contested and turned around *without* recourse to actions that carry with them at least a notional level of violence (these could be physical or symbolic)? Or, in terms of the cultural position of the marginalized ghetto male, bearing in mind his lack of access to most forms of communication, is it not likely that his means of expression are likely to be implicitly, if not explicitly, violent? So, while I find 50 cent's album title *Get Rich Or Die Tryin'* repellent on several levels, it does at least seem to me an understandable response to mainstream society, insofar as it invokes society's own dominant capitalist ethos, and (in the marginalized agent's lack of access to riches) the violence needed to bridge the financial divide.

12. Natalie Angier, *Women: An Intimate Geography* (New York: Anchor, 2000), 76.

13. Leah Hager Cohen, *Without Apology: Girls, Women and the Desire to Fight* (New York: Heidenfield and Dixon, 2005), 69.

14. D. W. Winnicott, *The Maturational Process and the Facilitating Environment.* London: Karnac, 1990. Jessica Benjamin. *The Bonds of Love: Psychoanalysis, Feminism and the Problems of Domination.* London: Pantheon, 1988.

15. Dana Crowley Jack, *Behind the Mask: Destruction and Creativity in Women's Aggression* (Boston: Harvard University, 2001) 132.

16. I think of the sequels here rather than the original film, which showed a series of improvised training props in line with its blue-collar ethic and aesthetic.

17. This was my (obviously quite surprised) comment to my (male) neighbor at the end of the first round, which received a nod of agreement that seemed to reproach me for sounding so surprised (perhaps he had seen women box to this level before, or his gender politics were simply more progressive than mine). Note, while there was certainly surprise implicit in my comment that she could "box a bit" ("a bit" actually means "quite a lot" in the understatement characteristic of many boxing phrases, "he can punch a bit" implies a punch that would stop anything short of a bull elephant, for example), the qualifier "for a girl" was definitely not implicit; my meaning was "she could box a bit," full stop.

18. The respect shown for both participants, by the way, was exemplary throughout the audience. There were no wolf whistles or catcalls, and if anyone had any wisecracks to make, they kept them quiet (perhaps wisely in view of Lindsay's hard hitting).

19. As with this comment on the women's studies forum WMST-L: "I know several athletic young women. They all saw *MILLION DOLLAR BABY*. They all hated the ending. But what they loved, and what they took home from the film, was the very rare mainstream portrayal of an athletic woman making her way in the world with determination and spirit. . . . These young women . . . find boxing inspiring and empowering. They like being strong, looking strong, and feeling strong. They rarely see "themselves" portrayed in the mainstream media."

20. Butler, *Gender Trouble*, xxvii–xxviii.

21. With the exception, of course, of the one-minute intervals between rounds, in which the trainer gets to dispense technical advice, moral support, and to control cuts if necessary ("cutman" is Frank's particular speciality).

22. I am grateful to the woman's studies forum at WMST-L.org (www. research.umbc.edu/~korenman/wmst/Million Dollar Baby.html) for a long and interesting discussion on the film. The main feminist criticisms raised on the forum that I wish to address are as follows: "Her success depended on a male's decision to condescend to her and help her"; and "Maggie is clearly punished for her forceful trespassing by the most severe sentence of all . . . admittedly stretching it, but it feels more of a threat like 'stay where you belong, girlie-or else!'"

23. Butler, *Gender Trouble*, xxviii.

24. While it cannot be denied that fights *can* be won and lost by the efficiency (or lack of it) in a fighter's corner—especially in the fixing up of cuts and other injuries—it seems that this aspect is particularly stressed due to Eastwood's starring role.
25. Butler, *Gender Trouble*, 24.
26. Judith Butler, *Bodies That Matter* (London: Routledge, 1992), 236.
27. Butler, *Bodies That Matter*, 224.
28. Butler, *Gender Trouble*, 34, emphasis original/<u>emphasis added</u>.
29. Butler, *Gender Trouble*, 40.
30. "The absence of democratic sensibility in American film-making," World Socialist Web site, www.wsws.org.
31. I find it odd that Walsh states "Nothing about her life . . . angers the ever cheerful and ebullient Maggie . . . (she) accepts her destiny without a murmur." In the minirant that wins Frank over (see page 243, above), Maggie's sarcastic "celebration" refers firstly to "scraping dishes," before moving onto a litany of stereotypical trailer-park clichés, returning to sarcasm via the rather funny reference to deep-fried Oreos. While Swank's demeanor is indeed stoical other than in this instance, it can only be suggested that in the context of her complaints, boxing *is* Maggie's form of protest.
32. Butler, *Gender Trouble*, 19.
33. Though, of course, it could be read as merely allowing Frank to escape from his responsibility.
34. In a view such as Judith Butler's, then, the individual is interpellated, and subjectivity formed, via the body as a terrain of ideological inscription and demarcation. Lacking a theory of either the body or subjectivity, dogmatic and reductive leftist approaches such as those of Walsh are ill-suited to address the ambivalences of the particular location of subjects within particular fields.
35. Judith Butler, *Undoing Gender* (London: Routledge, 2004), 12.
36. For essays on the relationship of sports and gender, see the following: Joli Sandoz and Joby Winans, eds., *Whatever It Takes: Women on Women's Sport* (London: Farrar, Straus & Giroux, 1999); Susan K. Cahn, *Coming on Strong: Gender and Sexuality in Twentieth-century Women's Sport* (New York: Free Press/Macmillan International, 1994; Shelia Scranton and Anne Flintoff, *Gender and Sport: A Reader* (New York: Routledge, 2001); Michael Messner, *Taking the Field: Women, Men, and Sports* (Minneapolis: University of Minnesota Press, 2002); Leslie Heywood, *Pretty Good for a Girl* (New York: Free Press, 1998); D. Sabo, K. E. Miller, M. J. Melnick, and L. Heywood, *Her Life Depends On It: Sport, Physical Activity, and the Health and Well-Being of American Girls* (East Meadow, NY: Women's Sports Foundation, 2004); Susan Birrell and Mary G. McDonald, eds., *Reading Sport: Critical Essays on Power and Representation* (Chicago: Northeastern University Press, 2000); Pat Griffin, *Strong Women, Deep Closets: Lesbians and Homophobia in Sport* (Champaign, IL: Human Kinetics, 1998); and Nancy Theberge, *Higher Goals: Women's Ice Hockey and the Politics of Gender* (Albany, NY: SUNY Press, 2000).
37. Leah Hager Cohen, *Without Apology; Girls, Women and the Desire to Fight* (London: Weidenfield & Nicholson, 2005). A writer who originally introduced herself to a group of women boxers, trained by a woman, to research and write about them, Cohen was "seduced" to the extent that she herself became an enthusiastic participant.
38. It would be fascinating, for example, to teach the film in tandem with another Swank vehicle dealing with gender transgression, *Boys Don't Cry*.
39. Butler, *Bodies That Matter*, 126, emphasis added.
40. I scare quote the word strategically. I found it hard not to laugh when Maggie's

nemesis is described upon her introduction in the film as "the most dangerous woman in the world . . . notoriously dirty . . . she doesn't even care if she kills someone in there." On which grounds the "twist" of Maggie's crippling can hardly be described as subtle or surprising.

BIBLIOGRAPHY

Birrell, Susan, and Mary G. McDonald, eds. *Reading Sport: Critical Essays on Power and Representation*. Chicago: Northeastern University Press, 2000.

Butler, Judith. *Bodies That Matter*. London: Routledge, 1993.

———. *Gender Trouble*. London: Routledge, 1999.

Cahn, Susan K. *Coming on Strong: Gender and Sexuality in Twentieth-century Women's Sport*. New York: Free Press/Macmillan International, 1994.

Cohen, Laura Hager. *Without Apology; Girls, Women and the Desire to Fight*. London: Weidenfield & Nicholson, 2005.

Griffin, Pat. *Strong Women, Deep Closets: Lesbians and Homophobia in Sport*. Champaign, IL: Human Kinetics, 1998.

Heywood, Leslie. *Pretty Good for a Girl*. New York: Free Press, 1998.

Messner, Michael. *Taking the Field: Women, Men, and Sports*. Minneapolis: University of Minnesota Press, 2002.

Sabo, D., K. E. Miller, M. J. Melnick, and L. Heywood, *Her Life Depends On It: Sport, Physical Activity, and the Health and Well-Being of American Girls*. East Meadow, NY: Women's Sports Foundation, 2004.

Sandoz, Joli, and Joby Winans, eds. *Whatever It Takes: Women on Women's Sport*. London: Farrar, Straus & Giroux, 1999.

Scranton, Shelia, and Anne Flintoff. *Gender and Sport: A Reader*. New York: Routledge, 2001.

Theberge, Nancy. *Higher Goals: Women's Ice Hockey and the Politics of Gender*. Albany, NY: SUNY Press, 2000.

(Still) Calling Out from the Closet?: The Rhetoric of Visibility in Queer TV and Film
Rebecca Ingalls

Introduction

On April 30, 1997, ABC aired the coming out episode of the show *Ellen*. While many audience members viewed this episode and Ellen as groundbreaking for the mainstreaming of queer rhetoric in TV and film, others criticized the construction of the event as a reification of homosexual stereotypes and the silencing of queer identity. In her essay, "What's Wrong with this Picture?" Susan Hubert argues, "Ellen's supposedly controversial attempt to push the limits of acceptability actually reinscribes conventional sexual politics,"[1] asserting that because Ellen DeGeneres does not identify herself in a political way, she misses a valuable opportunity to stand up against "the structures of social injustice."[2] The coming-out episode, Hubert suggests, actually keeps both Ellen Morgan's and Ellen DeGeneres's homosexual identity in the closet, and "provides a good measure of what the entertainment industry considers to be both within limits and off-limits for prime-time television portrayals of gays and lesbians."[3]

Before we extend Hubert's argument, let us give credit where credit is due. It's important to note that Laura Dern, who played the character of Susan—a sort of Platonic gatekeeper to guide Ellen from the closet she didn't know she was in and "out" into her sexual awareness—has claimed ten years later on Ellen's talk show that she was out of work for a year and a half after appearing on the episode. On the show, which aired April 23, 2007, Ellen (explaining that this was her first discussion of the episode on her talk show) suggests to Dern and to her studio audience that Dern's decision to appear on the episode was a "risky" choice that few other actresses would have made. Acknowledging to Ellen the "extraordinary experience and opportunity

... really an honor" of her appearance on the show, Dern also explains to the audience the "backlash" that followed in the "terrifying" lack of acting work available to her after the show, as well as the "not-so-nice letters" from viewers. One might argue, thus, that the show had plenty of political fallout, even if Ellen appeared to be apolitical in her execution of the project.

Furthermore, the coming-out episode succeeded as one effort in the global endeavor of the gay community to claim space in a culture where either no space has been provided, or where the public has been—sometimes violently—resistant to gay rights. In visual media, where the public eye is the well-trained customer, and the values of the public are so often on the table when it comes to programming, it has been especially critical for the gay community to be rhetorically savvy. Integrating token gay characters, let alone gay relationships, into mainstream media has been a delicate business. And, in many ways, we have succeeded in creating an audience that is not only tolerant, but that will also laugh and even invest in a gay actor or character (the success of *Will & Grace* is a prime example). Even if one does believe that Ellen has not politicized herself enough, there can be no question that she is, indeed, a gay icon, one that can now be seen on national television every afternoon on a highly successful talk show. And this act of claiming space—of making an argument for legitimacy and creating an audience for that argument—is at the heart of the constitutive rhetoric of gay culture.

However, nearly ten years later, Hubert's point deserves our attention. The complexities of rhetorically constituting a marginalized community are vast, and, as I will argue below, the gay community and its audience still seems to be holding on to the closet as a rhetorical shelter in the margin—its role as a metaphor in the construction of an argument for hetero-normativity is still critical and troublesome. In her interview with Ellen, Dern makes a claim that should give us all pause. She describes the "backlash" of the coming out episode as "radical": "it was radical because we look now at something that would be completely the norm on television, which is the great news." And yet, it is important to recognize the fact that it is *not* completely the norm; though it is interesting that she believes that it is, or, perhaps, believes that saying so will make it true.

It goes without saying that queer identities have surfaced more significantly in "mainstream" television and film in recent years, and yet we ought to be both optimistic and troubled by the continued rhetorical presence and purpose of the closet in these media. We can acknowledge the progress made in the media to create an argument for homosexuality that constitutes it as an identity, a legitimate love story, even a physical practice that may be accepted in mainstream culture. Despite these positive movements, however, we must follow the path that Allen and Faigley forge as they continue to ask whether or not certain "discursive strategies for social change" have "led or not led to actual material change,"[4] or ask what continues to hold a movement back. In constructing media-based arguments that aim to legitimize homosexuality, we still find—without much difficulty—that the closet, for so long a part of the gay story, is ever present. I argue that the closet, which Sedgwick has described as "the defining structure of gay oppression in [the twentieth] century" and which is intimately connected to many of the "epistemologically charged pairings" that we find in culture today (e.g., "secrecy/disclosure and public/private"),[5] continues to serve as both a hideout for gay actors and characters, as well as a place of separation of "gay" from "straight" that even progressive heterosexual culture still utilizes for comfort. As I will assert below, we must attend to the rhetorical presence of the closet, especially as it undermines the visibility of gay identity in the media.

Who's Who in Queer Culture

In doing this analysis, it is useful to acknowledge where we do not want to begin. In his introduction to the collection *Out Takes: Essays on Queer Theory and Film*, Ellis Hanson marks the 1980s and '90s as a time of burgeoning scholarly attention to intersections between queer theory ("a very new coinage peculiar to the 1990s")[6] and film. He argues that academic exploration of homosexuality in film has taken a turn away from "the politics of representation," which aims to type images of gay and lesbian identity and the individuals who go with those images (rather like the game of Memory—match the gay "characteristic" to the gay person/character). He describes such efforts as the documentary *The Celluloid Closet*, which seems to offer its viewers a tidy delineation of the who-is and who-isn't gay in the cast of characters, as vastly limiting in its inability to examine the queer intricacies of the films it highlights; it merely addresses the obvious—that there is a gay person in the house. Likewise, Hanson criticizes the cinematic "ideological machinery" that tries too hard to construct "positive" or easily definable gay images of homosexuality and ultimately makes for both "bland" film and resistant members of the activist queer audience who experience the aggravation of homophobia that can result from a film that misrepresents.[7]

What intrigues Hanson more, and what this article will further examine with respect to the rhetoric of gay visibility in the media, is the "promising backlash against this preoccupation with 'positive images' [with] . . . a political call for new representations, preferably by, for, and about minority communities who have been excluded from the mainstream." Credit is due, claims Hanson, to the intellectually critical collision between queer theory and cultural studies, which "seeks to define the significance of filmmaking and other social practices in the broader history of political struggle and capitalist production. . . . cultural studies most overlaps with queer theory in its efforts not merely to valorize or vilify, but to analyze and critique, to theorize the process of production and consumption rather than simply to expose it, and to question the very paradigms through which the cinematic and the political are said to be allied."[8]

Hanson urges his readers, however, to question the typing that some queer cultural studies critics can do to film (this film is good, that film is bad), and instead to approach film with a critical eye that examines the ways in which film undermines, reaffirms, or complicates the "identity politics of representation."[9]

Heeding Hanson's advice, we can see that, while Hubert seems to assert Ellen's ultimate failure to properly out herself on her TV show back in 1997, we do not do the show the critical justice it deserves by identifying the episode as "wrong" (as the title of her article articulates it). Ellen was, indeed, a pioneer, in the most literal sense of the word. As a woman who was not completely "out" in her own industry, Ellen DeGeneres accomplished an impressive double play when she asserted what she called "my own truth."[10] As I mention above, it can be argued that she *has* paved the way (to use a term as cliché as "pioneer") for the visibility of homosexuality in the media. Though she rarely makes her sexuality the political focus of her talk show, Ellen is a highly paid, successful TV personality who can be seen more than once a day rowing down (or up?) the mainstream. The rhetorical power of her one-word name, which was also the name of her '90s comedy show—the one in which she let the world know she was gay— shifts power dynamics and resists the dominant cultural standard of heterosexuality in popular media. And many members of the queer community fully support the waves she's made and how she's made them. Gail Shister, writer for 365Gay.com, asserts, "We've come a long way in three decades, babies. Their numbers may be small, but gays are playing large with mainstream America." And, in reference to Ellen: "it was a woman who broke open the doors."[11] Ellen's very much here, and she's queer.

And yet, when we think about what it means to assert rhetorical power from the margin, we have to ask what being "here" means. When the sex lives of celebrities are such an integral part of celebrity culture—and Ellen often takes it upon herself to ask her guests about their romantic lives—and Ellen less frequently references her own romantic life, then is Ellen still hiding out? In an interview with Bruce Handy for *Time* magazine, Ellen described a conversation with her father about the upcoming coming-out episode: "My father is supportive. My dad said the most hilarious thing when I told him what I was going to do on the show. He said, 'You're not going to go all flamboyant, are ya?' I was like, 'Yeah, Dad, I'm going to completely change. I'm going to start wearing leather vests. I'm going to get one of those haircuts that they all have.' "[12]

When she adamantly (through comedy) resists aligning herself with the butch lesbian stereotype, Hubert's argument is tough to refute. While one could argue that Ellen is challenging dominant discourse by offering what Allen and Faigley call "perspective by incongruity, or setting one assumed truth into an incongruous situation to undermine its truthfulness,"[13] we cannot ignore the fact that Ellen seems to be rhetorically purposeful about separating herself from other "kinds" of lesbians. Thus, we might ask, is she choosing an apolitical, safer, route by asserting her power from the closet? And, moreover, do we laud her for calling out from the closet, or do we criticize her for not calling loudly—politically—enough?

Some would say that Ellen is simply trying to demonstrate that there are lots of kinds of homosexual people, that lines are not so easily drawn. In his article "Queer Eye for Straight TV," James Poniewozik, writing for *Time*, attempts to unveil a secret irony about some of the most successful heterosexually driven shows on TV today: many have been created by gay men. Working against the kind of "monolithic image of camp queers quoting from *What Ever Happened to Baby Jane*" that Hanson also eschews above, Poniewozik asserts the importance of talented gay writers like Marc Cherry (*Desperate Housewives*), Darren Star and Michael Patrick King (*Sex and the City*), and Ryan Murphy (*Nip/Tuck*), who understand that the lines drawn around identity aren't always clear. Poniewozik explains, "Bound up with lies and truth is a sensitivity [in these shows] to ambiguity in a world of black-and-white dualities; boy and girl, straight and gay."[14] In order to challenge these dualities and make the argument "that identity is malleable," these writers have utilized the discourse of "little narratives," which Allen and Faigley (drawing from Lyotard) describe as follows: "If grand narratives offer positions within dominant discourse as common sense, little narratives challenge those positions by providing stories of lived experience that contradict common sense. They challenge the mythic quality of grand narratives by describing the local and particular."[15]

Through little narratives of fiction, these writers have attempted to debunk popular beliefs about how cultural identities, particularly those of sexuality, may be neatly divided.

However, we must further analyze the outcome of such discursive efforts. Let us return to that secret irony that these writers' own sexual preferences are undisclosed to most viewers. Poniewozik asks whether it is "coincidence" that so many of the most successful TV programs today are the creations of gay writers, and responds to his own question: "Gay TV writers will tell you that relationships are universal. (If they talk at all. King, Murphy and Star declined to be interviewed for this article.)" The veiled identities of these writers—which, after all, drives the rhetorical purpose of Poniewozik's article—invites the question of why. Why wouldn't these writers be interviewed? Why avoid a spotlight in *Time* magazine? Poniewozik offers one answer later on in the piece: "There's an old tradition of gay writers (not to mention actors) expressing themselves through straight characters.... Mostly, though, these writers are asserting their right to be gay yet to write straight."[16] His claim echoes that of Freud:

> The artist [says Freud] is originally a man who turns from reality because he cannot come to terms with the demand for the renunciation of instinctual satisfaction as it is first made, and who then in phantasy-life allows full play to his erotic and ambitious wishes. But he finds a way of return from this world of phantasy back to reality; with his special gifts, he moulds his phantasies into a new kind of reality, and men concede them a justification as valuable reflections of actual life. Thus by a certain path he actually becomes the hero, king, creator, favourite he desired to be, without the circuitous path of creating real alterations in the outer world.[17]

Thus, it would seem that rather than utilize the more overtly political rhetoric of speech and self-identification these writers may be sliding their art under the closet door and into the public eye. An important cultural contribution, no doubt, but one that leaves Poniewozik to "out" them, which further points to their closeted identities, to their marginalization.

Poniewozik claims that, because of these gay writers' "special understanding," "these shows question our easy ideas of normality," but in many ways their silence as represented in his article points the rhetorical arrow directly at their homosexuality, highlighting its difference, its ability to see relationships, its need either to "come out" or "stay in."[18] This tendency to "reify" gender identity, claims John M. Sloop, is part of a cultural trend in the last several years: "while cases of gender ambiguity were 'talked about' in ways that encouraged an undermining or questioning of the very notion of 'aberration' as related to sexuality and gender, bi-gender normativity was for the most part underlined and reemphasized."[19] In many ways, it is this assertion and silencing of gender identity that helps and hinders the construction of what Sloop calls the "'messy' changes in the borders between male and female, hetero- and homosexual."[20] It invites the rhetorically interesting, complex, and critical idea of out-but-not-out-enough, and it also continues to normalize the dividing lines between homosexual and heterosexual.

Playing Gay

Further complicating this discussion is the role reversal of gay characters played by "straight" actors, and their public reception. The recent film *Brokeback Mountain*, based on the short story by Annie Proulx (who is believed to be heterosexual), offers American culture an interesting—and, some argue, necessary—twist on the construction of gender roles through performance. Daniel Garrett, in an article for the journal *Film International*, responds to the range of media perceptions of the film, from a story of love that begins with one man inviting another out of the cold and into his tent, to a commentary on the universal nature of love: "Is there nothing between erasure and sexual generalization? Ennis and Jack are two men living what could be described fairly as bisexual lives, though Proulx's text, and [Ang] Lee's interpretation of that text in the film, give focus to the most transgressive or unique aspect of their lives, their ongoing, unlegislated relationship with each other. Must one aspect of their sexuality cancel out another?"[21]

Garrett's dissatisfaction with the public need to type the characters is further aggravated by reviews that complain that the film is not politically discursive enough, that it fails to construct a more blatant pro-gay argument. Garrett quotes Armond White's review of the film in *New York Press* (December 7–13, 2005): "The key to White's complaint is conveyed when he suggests that what the film and men miss and need are 'events that might have given them gay consciousness or put their affair in some workable context that wasn't just imaginary.'"[22] Garrett retorts in his article that neither the writer of the short story nor the filmmakers wanted to make a "gay rights pamphlet in the form of a film."[23] And, in response to Stephanie Zacharek's complaint (on *Salon*, December 9, 2005) that the film is much less than daring and "a closeted movie" (64), Garrett suggests that a few viewers just don't understand the complexities of the film or its characters —they are unable to grasp the "human"[24] element about the film.

While many tout the film as a courageous narrative that takes on a taboo subject (and do it well) and manages to make it universally apply to the subject of love, and while many agree with Garrett's assertion that positive responses to the film are a testament to the "increased health and honesty"[25] of American culture, we must attend to reviews of the film that believe that the film tries too hard or not hard enough, for these views are important in the larger discussion about the rhetoric of sexual identity for characters and the actors who play them. Such responses queer the film's reviews, and thus the films themselves. Certainly, such responses to the film ring like echoes of Hubert's reaction to Ellen's coming out on national television, and they invite challenges to Shister's claim, "we've come a long way, babies." To suggest that *Brokeback* does not sufficiently politicize itself is to ask why it must; and to claim that it is "a closeted movie" is to ask what would make it less so. And for whom? In other words, how better could the argument persuade you?

And yet, claims about the universality of the film don't always hold up. The rhetorical goal of the talk show, that bizarre third space between the screen and the actors' "real lives," is to stage a truth telling of some sort, an opportunity to expose the 'real' behind the imagination of a film or TV program. In an interview with Heath Ledger and Jake Gyllenhaal (the stars of the film), Oprah Winfrey's line of questions reflect a blurry boundary between the perception of *Brokeback* as a-gay-movie, and not-just-a-gay-movie. The segment of her show "Mountain Folk" offers a brief justification that "that label [gay cowboy movie] does not begin to do justice to the heralded film," but quickly shifts its inquiry to the "controversial" nature of the film. Both actors agree on a description of the film as "a beautiful love story" (Gyllenhaal), which seems to discursively include the film among those in the dominantly hetero genre of "romance." However, Oprah pushes them back to the distinction between "gay" and "straight" when she asks them to discuss what she calls the "tent scene." In fact, much of the interview is devoted to the political controversy of the film, asking the actors about the difficulty and risk involved in playing two gay men who do several love scenes together. She also devotes a significant part of the interview to the offscreen, heterosexual relationship between Ledger and Michelle Williams (who plays his wife in the film), and the child they now share. Despite her introduction of the film as "more than a gay cowboy movie," her interview seems to underscore that very identity of the film. Throughout the interview, there seems to be a real effort on the part of the actors to discuss the film in the context of universal love, but Oprah just can't let the show be about that, or about the majestic mountains of Wyoming. She must guide the interview discourse to illustrate a sharp contrast between the character and the actor who plays him, and this rhetorical inquiry, again, reinforces the rhetorical presence of the closet for a heterosexual audience. In constantly reminding her own audience of their heterosexuality, Oprah seems to be trying to help prevent Ledger and Gyllenhaal from being put *in* the closet.

But Where are the Gay Actors?

Not only does Oprah's interview with Ledger and Gyllenhaal seem to purposefully mark both actors as *not*-gay, but the interview also raises other questions: is the public more comfortable with gay portrayal by those actors who identify as heterosexual? Would too much authenticity—be it the discourse of gay talk or gay physical relations—push viewer tolerance over the line? Such inquiry invites this question: where are the gay actors? Allen Ellenzweig's discussion of this dilemma offers critical insight into why we oughtn't to be "dancing in the streets" after *Brokeback* just yet. Though Ellenzweig gives credit to *Brokeback*, and *Capote* (2006), and *Transamerica* (2006), as well as to performances of queer characters in films that have come before (e.g., *Kiss of the Spider Woman* [1985], *Philadelphia* [1993] and *Boys Don't Cry* [1999]) and television shows (*Will & Grace, The L Word*) that help to make queer culture visible,[26] he is still concerned about the invisibility of gay actors. Portraying a homosexual person in TV or film, he argues, seems to be a kind of "rite of passage for non-gay actors, a proving ground to show one's 'chops'"; he likens this trend to those "able-bodied" actors who have garnered prestigious awards for portraying disability on the screen.[27] Ellenzweig suspects that one of the reasons that gay actors are often not recruited to play gay roles comes down to this question: "what's the point of 'playing' gay if you already are?" He seems to suggest a double silencing for gay actors who are not often in gay roles, and who are still not fully permitted to "live openly" in the public eye. He concludes, "The trend I await is the ho-hum appearance of a gay or lesbian actor on the red carpet with his or her current lover, receiving accolades one year for playing a tough Marine and the next for playing a tough 'Mary.' Then I'll break open the champagne."[28]

There's no question that openly heterosexual actors are granted—and encouraged to cultivate—the flexibility to play across the queer spectrum. This kind of talent is often perceived as an act of great theatrical merit. Is it true, perhaps, that the public is more willing to watch a heterosexual actor play a homosexual character because they know that, at the end of the day, that actor is only acting? Does the lack of gay actors playing gay characters raise additional questions about what the public—or even Hollywood—is willing to watch? It would seem that Ellenzweig's discontentment is appropriate, that the progress Hollywood has made in making space for gay actors is still slow, which points back to the continued need for gay constitutive rhetorics in media. Drawing from Foucault, Stockdell-Giesler explains in her introduction to this collection that heterotopia offers "mirrors in which outsiders find themselves reflected in a society which does not really recognize them."[29] The very "absence" of gay representation—even in gay roles—underscores the looming presence of the closet as a kind of barrier. It's a troubling paradox: the existence for gay roles recognizes the existence of homosexuality, which is important, but the lack of gay actors playing gay roles seems to suggest a desire to keep them closeted.

Laura Dern's optimism about gay characters being "completely the norm" on television was further complicated by the concurrent controversy on *Grey's Anatomy*, a show on the very same network as Ellen's talk show. In October 2006, Isaiah Washington (who played one of the main characters on the show) was accused of using the word "faggot" in a homophobic way more than once, a slur that was particularly oppressive to gay actor T. R. Knight (another main character on the show). Washington's response to the media's reaction ranged from denial, to public apology, to his public service announcement (PSA) for the Gay & Lesbian Alliance Against Defamation, where he sent this message in May 2007: "When you use words that demean a person because of their sexual orientation, race or gender, you send a message of hate. A very powerful message. But we all have the power to demand better from one another and for ourselves. We have the power to heal and change the world with the words we use."[30] Neil G. Giuliano, the president of the organization, responded favorably to Washington's announcement, which was due to air on ABC. Likewise, Kevin Jennings, founder and executive director of the Gay, Lesbian and Straight Education Network, was positive: "As an education organization, GLSEN believes in the power of the teachable moment. While there is no excuse for the use of this kind of language, we welcome the opportunity to use this incident to educate millions about the impact of name-calling on young people."[31] It would seem, at least then, that the issue had been resolved.

However, the situation became heightened in the month to follow, and so did its rhetorical complexity. While rumors had spread about whether or not Washington would be fired, the word came in June that Washington had indeed been "written out of the show." CNN released a report that network executives believed that Washington had exhibited a "pattern of behavior" that "represented a potential liability that was too much risk" for Disney.³² While there are myriad aspects of this story that deserve attention—not the least of which is the decision to fire Washington after his public apology and his PSA in which he made an argument *against* hate speech—the situation illustrates major tensions over gay identity that continue to fester in Hollywood, tensions that are not so easily overcome with a PSA. CNN's report paraphrased a comment by Giuliano that very much echoes Ellenzweig's concerns: "Hollywood's image as an unbiased haven for gays is overstated." It's not the gay safe space that some believe it to be. Nevertheless, it would seem that Washington was doing all of the right things to "heal" the situation and to allow himself to be educated during "a teachable moment," including his public statement, "I can neither defend nor explain my behavior. I can also no longer deny to myself that there are issues I obviously need to examine within my own soul, and I've asked for help."³³ One might even argue that he is evidence of the success of constitutive rhetoric.

But there are other messages to be examined, one of which is T. R. Knight's response. In many ways, the media reflected the controversy through talk about Washington, as well as through the words of Katherine Heigl (who plays another main character on the show), who "publicly denounced" Washington in defense of Knight.³⁴ Knight's response for several months was rhetorically confusing. Though he did make a statement reported by the Associated Press about his sexuality, he seemed to do so with much reservation: "'I guess there have been a few questions about my sexuality, and I'd like to quiet any unnecessary rumors that may be out there,' Knight's statement read. 'While I prefer to keep my personal life private, I hope the fact that I'm gay isn't the most interesting part of me'" ("'Anatomy' Star T. R. Knight Says He's Gay"). In his statement, Knight suggests a desire to silence public inquiry, as well as any major connection between his homosexuality and his personal identity, which, rhetorically, suggests that he wants both to come out of and withdraw back into the closet.

Transformations: Cautionary Hope

But there has been a shift.

In MSNBC's January 2007 coverage of the slur, the presence of Knight's perspective on the matter is minimal. The only quote that

MSNBC provides from Knight is, "He referred to me as a faggot. Everyone heard it" ("ABC Rebukes 'Grey's Anatomy' Star"), but should a viewer desire more of Knight's perspective, MSNBC steers its readers toward Knight's upcoming taping of Ellen's talk show. And here we are again—back on the set of Ellen's show, where Knight further expresses his desire for silence in a January 17, 2007, interview. Ellen explains to her audience, and Knight acknowledges once again, that Washington referred to him as a "faggot," in such a way that others also heard it. In the interview Ellen remarks to Knight, "And so then it puts you in a position because you weren't out, and then everyone on the set is hearing this," to which Knight responds that he "was under no delusions that" others (especially his "friends on the set") knew that he was gay. However, he again sends the message of his preference for a low profile when it comes to his sexual identity: "I think, publicly, I mean it's not my, like, thing to, you know, call up *People* magazine and be like, 'Hey, do you wanna know something about me?'" The audience laughs at his wit, but what's so striking about this comment is that Knight, here, is contrasting himself with those who voluntarily and publicly out themselves (remember Ellen's coming-out episode?). As Ellen does with the "butch lesbian" persona, so Knight does with the act of public outing. He seems to be inadvertently putting himself down, reifying his disempowerment as a gay man.

But the issue becomes multivalent. Knight then acknowledges that he's never been called "a faggot" to his "face," and that "when that happened . . . something shifted and it just became something bigger . . . than myself." He then begins to establish a rhetorical alliance with Ellen; he refers to the "bravery" of her coming out "and other people's bravery," and further acknowledges that it has been ten years since Ellen's coming out episode. In many ways, he credits Ellen and others who have publicly come out: "I could have just let it slide and not said anything, but it just, it became important." Ellen—not unexpectedly—praises Knight for his statement about his identity, including the part where he hopes his audience will believe that "there's a lot more interesting things" about him than his sexual identity, and she lets him know that she is glad that "this is out of the way" now and says that she is proud of him. Thus, Knight has identified himself as one who was not inclined to publicly announce his gay identity and who would prefer that people see beyond it, but who also believes that Ellen has helped to inspire him to make his identity known. One wonders, if Washington hadn't slurred at all, would Knight have ever let the public know? The motivation behind the outing is critical—it, too, signals a Hollywood that is still very much alive in its homophobia, and a disturbing need in the queer acting community to both break free from and reconstruct the closet.

And yet, Knight has become "angry" over the months since the event, even sitting down with Michael Glitz of *The Advocate* to do an interview for their Pride 2007 (June 19) issue. Glitz notes Knight's initial trepidation: "At first, his answers are vague and nonspecific (perhaps an unintended result of spending a good chunk of his life in the closet professionally). At times trying to get any specific, personal information out of him feels like dealing with a skittish horse: Move too quickly and he might bolt." But the events have encouraged Knight to develop an edge; he asserts, "I'm not going to keep my mouth closed anymore." And, he admits, though many of his friends urged him not to come out, he was determined to do it anyway. He objects to his previous desire to keep silent, explaining its temptation and aligning himself now with "something that is bigger than [my career]": "Some gay actors cite 'privacy' as a convenient excuse not to come out professionally, even though they love to suck up the spotlight in all other aspects of their lives. Knight isn't like that. 'The reason I act is—' he pauses, starts again. 'You can disappear and not be yourself. You can get out of it for a while. You get away from you. That's what I liked about acting.'"

One of the messages embedded in this article is that Knight will choose a more political route moving forward, which certainly argues against the hopes for silence that he communicated earlier in 2007. And now, he claims, Rosie O'Donnell—one of the outest of the out—has approved; she sent him a toaster.[35] A nod from Rosie means that surely Knight deserves props from his peeps. And, perhaps, he offers Shister another reason to remark on how far we've come.

However, it isn't that Knight and Ellen are out and successful and it's all okay. It isn't that *Brokeback* was an Oscar-nominated film and it's all okay. Though it may pain us to do so, and though some may rejoice in the appellations of gay celebrities who make themselves politically seen and heard, the presence of the closet continues to both dismantle and rebuild anti-gay rhetoric; it continues to queer it. One of Ellen's final statements in her interview with Knight, after he thanks her again for making her homosexuality visible, is, "It was a different time. Things are, things are getting better." There's a lot to be hopeful for when we see the rhetorical journey of transformation that has made queer culture more and more visible in the media, but it's important to notice that the title of *The Advocate's* article on Knight is still couched in the rhetoric of him being "just a regular guy," when we know darn well that the public doesn't see him that way. As Ellenzweig reminds us, we're just not in that regular, pop-open-the-champagne place yet.

Notes

1. Susan Hubert, "What's Wrong with this Picture? The Politics of Ellen's Coming Out Party," *Journal of Popular Culture*, 33, no. 2 (Fall 1999): 31.
2. Ibid., 32.
3. Ibid., 35.
4. Julia A. Allen and Lester Faigley, "Discursive Strategies for Social Change: An Alternative Rhetoric of Argument," *Rhetoric Review* 14, no. 1. (Autumn, 1995): 169.
5. Eve Kosofsky Sedgwick, *Epistemology of the Closet* (Berkeley: University of California Press, 1990), 71–72.
6. Ellis Hanson, "Introduction," in *Out Takes: Essays on Queer Theory and Film*, ed. Ellis Hanson (Durham, NC: Duke University Press, 1999), 4.
7. Ibid., 6–7.
8. Ibid., 10.
9. Ibid., 12.
10. Bruce Handy. "He Called Me Ellen Degenerate?" *Time*, April 14, 1997, http://www.time.com/time/magazine/article/0,9171,986189,00.html.
11. Gail Shister. "Gays on TV," *Gay News* 2006, 365Gay.com, http://www.365gay.com/InTime/History/TVHistory.htm.
12. Handy, "He Called Me Ellen Degenerate?"
13. Allen and Faigley, "Discursive Strategies," 161–62.
14. James Poniewozik. "Queer Eye for Straight TV," *Time* March 12, 2005, http://www.time.com/time/magazine/article/0,9171,1034725,00.html.
15. Allen and Faigley, "Discursive Strategies," 167.
16. Poniewozik, "Queer Eye for Straight TV."
17. Quoted in René Wellek and Austin Warren, *Theory of Literature* (New York: Harcourt, Brace & World, 1956.)
18. Poniewozik, "Queer Eye for Straight TV."
19. John M. Sloop, *Disciplining Gender: Rhetorics of Sex Identity in Contemporary U.S. Culture.* (Boston: University of Massachusetts Press, 2004), 2.
20. Ibid.
21. Daniel Garrett, "*Brokeback Mountain:* You Don't Know What Love Is," *Film International* 4, no. 21 (July 2006): 59.
22. Ibid., 63.
23. Ibid.
24. Ibid., 65.
25. Ibid., 67.
26. Allen Ellenzweig, "Beyond the *Mountain*," *Gay & Lesbian Review* (May–June 2006): 14.
27. Ibid., 15.
28. Ibid.
29. This volume, page 12.
30. "Isaiah Washington PSA—May 24, 2007," Gay & Lesbian Alliance Against Defamation, http://www.glaad.org/stf_app/media_player_lg.php?media_file=http://www.glaad.org/07/207Video/Washington_30_glaad.mov&title=Isaiah%20Washington%20PSA.

31. "ABC to Debut Isaiah Washington PSA Today," Gay & Lesbian Alliance Against Defamation. May 24, 2007, http://www.glaad.org/media/release_detail.php?id=4021.
32. "Why Isaiah Washington Was Let Go From 'Grey's,'" *CNN*, June 14, 2007, http://www.cnn.com/2007/SHOWBIZ/TV/06/14/apontv.greys.anatomy.ap/index.html.
33. "ABC Rebukes 'Grey's Anatomy' Star for Slur," *MSNBC*, Jan. 22, 2007, http://www.msnbc.msn.com/id/16696521/.
34. "'Grey's' Boots Isaiah Washington," *CNN*, June 8, 2007, http://www.cnn.com/2007/SHOWBIZ/TV/06/08/tv.greys.washington.ap/index.html.
35. "T. R. Knight is Just a Regular Guy," *The Advocate*, June 19, 2007, 100.

Bibliography

"ABC Rebukes 'Grey's Anatomy' Star for Slur." *MSNBC*. January 22, 2007. http://www.msnbc.msn.com/id/16696521/.

"ABC to Debut Isaiah Washington PSA Today." *Gay & Lesbian Alliance Against Defamation*. May 24, 2007. http://www.glaad.org/media/release_detail.php?id=4021.

Allen, Julia A., and Lester Faigley. "Discursive Strategies for Social Change: An Alternative Rhetoric of Argument." *Rhetoric Review* 14, no. 1 (Autumn 1995): 142–72.

"'Anatomy' Star T. R. Knight Says He's Gay." *ABC News*. October 19, 2006. June 28, 2007. http://abcnews.go.com/Entertainment/wireStory?id=2588769.

DeGeneres, Ellen, and Laura Dern. "The Puppy Episode, Part I." *Ellen*. By Dava Savell, Mark Driscoll, Tracy Newman, and Jonathan Stark. ABC. April 30, 1997.

———. "The Puppy Episode, Part II." *Ellen*. By Mark Driscoll, Tracy Newman, and Jonathan Stark. ABC. April 30, 2007.

Dern, Laura, interviewee. *Ellen DeGeneres Show*. Host Ellen DeGeneres. ABC. April 23, 2007.

Ellenzweig, Allen. "Beyond the *Mountain*." *Gay & Lesbian Review* (May–June 2006): 14–15.

Garrett, Daniel. "*Brokeback Mountain:* You Don't Know What Love Is." *Film International* 4, no. 21 (July 2006): 48–67.

Glitz, Michael. "T. R. Knight is Just a Regular Guy." *Advocate*. 987 (June 19, 2007): 100.

"'Grey's' Boots Isaiah Washington." *CNN*. June 8, 2007. http://www.cnn.com/2007/SHOWBIZ/TV/06/08/tv.greys.washington.ap/index.html.

Handy, Bruce. "He Called Me Ellen Degenerate?" *Time*, April 14, 1997. http://www.time.com/time/magazine/article/0,9171,986189,00.html.

Hanson, Ellis. "Introduction." In *Out Takes: Essays on Queer Theory and Film*, edited by Ellis Hanson, 1–19. Durham, NC: Duke University Press, 1999.

Hubert, Susan J. "What's Wrong with this Picture? The Politics of Ellen's Coming Out Party." *Journal of Popular Culture* 33, no. 2 (Fall 1999): 31–36.

"Isaiah Washington PSA—May 24, 2007." *Gay & Lesbian Alliance Against Defamation*. http://www.glaad.org/stf_app/media_player_lg.php?media_file=http://www.glaad.org/07/207Video/Washington_30_glaad.mov&title=Isaiah%20Washington%20PSA.

Knight, T. R., interviewee. *Ellen DeGeneres Show*. Host Ellen DeGeneres. ABC. January 17, 2007.

Poniewozik, James. "Queer Eye for Straight TV." *Time*, March 12, 2005. http://www.time.com/time/magazine/article/0,9171,1034725,00.html?promoid=rss_arts.

Sedgwick, Eve Kosofsky. *Epistemology of the Closet*. Berkeley: University of California Press, 1990.

Shister, Gail. "Gays on TV." *Gay News*. 2006. 365Gay.com. http://www.365gay.com/InTime/History/TVHistory.htm.

Sloop, John M. *Disciplining Gender: Rhetorics of Sex Identity in Contemporary U.S. Culture*. Boston: University of Massachusetts Press, 2004.

Wellek, René, and Austin Warren. *Theory of Literature*. New York: Harcourt, Brace & World, 1956.

"Why Isaiah Washington Was Let Go From 'Grey's.'" *CNN*. June 14, 2007. http://www.cnn.com/2007/SHOWBIZ/TV/06/14/apontv.greys.anatomy.ap/index.html.

Winfrey, Oprah, host. "The Stars of *Brokeback Mountain* and Tyler Perry's Next Big Thing." *Oprah Winfrey Show*. CBS. January 27, 2006.

Modernity Baptized in the Spirit: Early Pentecostal Rhetoric in America

JOSEPH W. WILLIAMS

IN A 1907 ISSUE OF THE *APOSTOLIC FAITH*, WILLIAM DURHAM RE-counted a supernatural encounter when he was "baptized with the Holy Spirit."[1] An early Pentecostal leader in Chicago, Durham felt as if his "body had suddenly become porous, and that a current of electricity was being turned on me from all sides." For three days these sensations continued intermittently, energizing his body, until he eventually spoke in tongues. Afterward, Durham knew that a "living Person had come into me, and that He possessed even my physical being, in a literal sense, in so much that He could at His will take hold of my vocal organs and speak any language He chose through me." The intensely physical nature of his encounter proved a crucial component of Durham's absolute assurance of the reality of his experience. Durham confidently proclaimed, the "devil can never tempt me to doubt."[2]

Other early Pentecostals like Durham frequently couched their descriptions of supernatural encounters, whether of baptisms in the Holy Spirit, of healings, or of deliverances from evil spirits, using similar references to liquids, fire, steam engines, electricity, and the like.[3] These physical descriptors drew on scientific and technological advances and reflected Pentecostals' keen awareness of the rapid changes transforming early twentieth-century American society. Though Pentecostal rhetoric lacked the technical sophistication of highly trained engineers or chemists, it nevertheless demonstrated Pentecostals' fascination with modern advances in science and technology. Despite their outsider status in early twentieth-century America, Pentecostals imbibed the intoxicating spirit of the times, transposing themes in the broader American culture into their own plainfolk nomenclature.[4]

On one level, Pentecostal descriptions of their religious experiences using plainfolk references to science and technology can be read as straightforward metaphors meant to convey the physical sensations felt by adherents during their religious experiences. More, however, was at work in these accounts. Like Durham, other Pentecostals frequently juxtaposed these descriptions to claims of assurance regarding the reality of their experiences. The physical language employed by Pentecostals helped concretize otherworldly experiences for the participants themselves. The laboratory-like terminology suggested an empirical basis for their experiential claims. In this manner early Pentecostals tapped an evidentiary rhetorical tradition within American evangelicalism that sought empirical proof to support belief in the supernatural.

In an ironic twist, then, early Pentecostal rhetoric challenged a perceived lack of supernatural power in the mainstream churches and in turn-of-the-century American culture by appealing to the authority of materialistic criteria. Pentecostals creatively harnessed modern assumptions to support otherworldly experiences. On one hand, their discourse regarding supernatural experiences illustrates the powerful hold of technological and scientific advances on the imaginations of average citizens during the early twentieth century. Though often perceived as outsiders and out of touch with modern trends, in many respects Pentecostals imbibed key traits of a rapidly modernizing American culture. Nevertheless, Pentecostals' use of technological imagery to defend the supernatural also reveals how "outsiders" can adopt key components of a dominant culture's rhetorical tools even as they work to subvert that very culture. For many non-Pentecostals, modernizing trends encouraged less of a focus on explicitly supernatural phenomena. Pentecostals, on the other hand, utilized those same trends to bolster their supernatural claims. In short, Pentecostal rhetoric adapted to mainstream American culture in order to authenticate supernatural claims; simultaneously, however, the otherworldly message they substantiated countered modernity's tendency to emphasize material reality. Pentecostal terminology reflected Pentecostals' ambivalent, creative, and even transformational relationship with modernity.[5]

Early Pentecostals as Outsiders in a Rapidly Modernizing American Culture

Rapid industrialization and technical advance characterized the late nineteenth, early twentieth-century world that witnessed the birth of Pentecostalism. Cities grew at exponential rates, big business increasingly dominated the markets, and thousands of inventions—everything from refrigerated railcars to the telephone to the electric motor—flooded the U.S. Patent Office for approval. The "electrification" of the United States during this period exemplified the technological innovations that were dramatically changing everyday life for most citizens. Electrical lines first appeared in cities during the 1880s, quickly transforming the American landscape. Used initially for commercial purposes such as street lights, soon electricity facilitated public transport, provided power to factories, and eventually entered the average home. Telephone, telegraph, lighting, and other power lines crisscrossed downtown areas—so much so that laws were quickly passed requiring underground wires due to concerns over safety and aesthetics.[6] Furthermore, mechanization "took control"—not only of the means of production during this period, but also of the public's imagination. As Alan Trachtenberg suggests, the machine simultaneously functioned as a symbol of supreme optimism and as a symbol of potential devastation for many. Alternately, some Americans were not quite sure how a mechanized vision of the world could be reconciled with their belief in a moral universe where actions and choices were rewarded or punished according to their merits. Regardless of how it was interpreted, however, technological advance permeated the consciousness of Americans.[7]

Significantly, the increased mechanization of society and technological advances bolstered the persuasive power of empirical arguments and appeals to science and were often used to undermine overtly supernatural claims. As the accomplishments of modern science and technology increasingly altered the lives of average citizens, more and more Americans *experienced* the power of empirical science and technology as their day-to-day realities changed in practical ways. These changes increased the potential for conflict between arguments based on empirical data and arguments based on supernatural phenomena. Though the famed Scopes "Monkey Trial" and the ensuing Fundamentalist/Modernist split in the churches did not occur until the 1920s, more and more religious believers even prior to those events encountered modernizing trends that emphasized material reality and posed a challenge to thoroughgoing supernatural accounts of the world.[8]

At first glance, with its clear prioritization of supernatural experiences, Pentecostal spirituality appears ill-adapted to a rapidly modernizing society. The Pentecostal message centered on a distinctive teaching regarding the baptism in the Holy Spirit. According to adherents, the baptism in the Holy Spirit necessarily and inevitably led a believer to speak in tongues. Thoroughly assured of their claims, early Pentecostals called all believers to reclaim the spiritual gifts detailed by the Apostle Paul in the New Testament. Though by no means alone in their belief that God still directly intervened in mundane affairs, relatively few other Christians in the United States followed Pentecostals in placing dramatic otherworldly encounters at the center of their spirituality.[9]

Early Pentecostal periodicals such as *Apostolic Faith* brimmed with accounts of divine healings, speaking in tongues, deliverance from demons, and myriad other accounts of divine activity. These emphases placed Pentecostals increasingly at odds with the growing appeal of modern materialistic assumptions that prioritized this-worldly evidence. In the words of one historian of Pentecostalism, "What distinguished Pentecostals, at least in public perception, was not so much the presence of uninhibited emotion as its centrality.... Any service—indeed any part of any service—that looked like it had been planned seemed a sure sign of nominal Christianity." The Holy Spirit, in other words, was expected to intervene and literally direct each service; far from being anomalous, healings, deliverances from demons, and assorted other spiritual interventions were the norm.[10]

In important respects, then, early Pentecostals stood on the outside of modernizing trends in American society. The fact that few adherents could lay claim to traditional markers of social success in the areas of wealth and education only added to their marginalization.[11] According to one historian, throughout the early decades of the movement, "modernists, fundamentalists, holiness advocates, and ordinary members of traditional churches had many dissimilarities, but they all rejected the Pentecostal message."[12] Though theological disputes, class warfare, and various other trends contributed to the antagonism Pentecostals experienced (and often invited), Pentecostals' tenacious focus on other-worldly phenomena marked them as a people set apart. According to one *Los Angeles Times* reporter, "The night is made hideous ... by the howlings of the worshipers. The devotees of the weird doctrine practice the most fanatical rites, preach the wildest theories and work themselves into a state of mad excitement."[13] To the uninitiated, Pentecostal meetings represented raw, uninhibited fanaticism.

Significantly, Pentecostals themselves actively perpetuated an outsider persona and vigilantly defended their boundaries with non-Pentecostals. Adherents castigated the "dead," "formal" churches who, in their eyes, capitulated to rationalism and squelched the activity of the Holy Spirit. According to Pastor J. N. Hoover, liberal Christians were simply "infidels masquerading as men of God."[14] Those who refused Pentecostal salvation were "starving on theological shavings."[15] Members of other churches, claimed another, were "paying their way to hell." Their offerings supported pastors who taught against the Pentecostal teaching regarding the baptism in the Holy Spirit; these messages poisoned parishioners "against the truth and it is damning their souls."[16] Even seemingly innocent endeavors such as the YMCA and the Student Volunteer Movement were categorized as signs of the coming reign of the Antichrist.[17] This is to say nothing of Pentecostals' vitriolic condemnations of Theosophy, Spiritualism, Christian Science, Roman Catholicism, and hypnotism, to name a few.

Pentecostals' outsider identity, however, was complex. Despite their persistent focus on other-worldly phenomena and their caustic relationship with mainstream society, in other ways, early Pentecostals proved thoroughly in tune with American culture.[18] Grant Wacker, for example, acknowledges the obvious primitivist impulse in Pentecostalism. He notes a persistent and pervasive "longing for direct contact with the divine . . . [an] otherworldliness . . . [and a] heavenly mindedness." Despite the prevalence of these themes, however, Wacker also finds a strong pragmatism that suggests a very this-worldly component to Pentecostal spirituality. This trait displayed a "'realism' . . . [a] 'practicality' . . . [and a] willingness to accommodate themselves to the limits of everyday life." According to Wacker, the primitivist conviction that God actively works on behalf of believers, while world-denying in one respect, also gave early Pentecostals the confidence that "all things are possible for modern-day saints, no less than for the New Testament ones."[19] This ambivalent relationship with the world—at once world-affirming and world-denying—allowed Pentecostals to offer a message at odds with the naturalistic trends in modern societies even as they made numerous practical concessions required for success. To a significant degree, early Pentecostal rhetoric reveals adherents' willingness to make these practical adaptations to modern trends.[20]

Early Pentecostal Rhetoric: Accommodating and Challenging Modernization in American Culture

Early Pentecostals' adherence to literal interpretations of the Bible and their repeated appeals to the divine authority of revelatory experiences usually earn them a position alongside fundamentalists and non-intellectuals. While this portrayal of early Pentecostals captures valid insights, too much focus on these traits obscures the ways in which early Pentecostals attempted to satisfy the empirical criteria demanded by a culture increasingly fascinated with all things scientific. In their own way, Pentecostals sought to harness materialistic evidence of the supernatural in order to prove, both for themselves and others, the reality of their encounters with God. In short, early Pentecostal rhetoric followed Michel Foucault's "rule of tactical polyvalence of discourses." It demonstrated how "discourse can be both an instrument and an effect of power, but also a hindrance, a stumbling-block, a point of resistance and a starting point for an opposing strategy."[21] Rapid industrialization and technological advances associated with modernization tended to promote materialist assumptions and downplay the role of the supernatural. Pentecostals adapted their rhetoric to this empiricism by emphasizing the physical component of their other-worldly encounters; they did so, however, in order to legitimate the supernatural. Though early Pentecostal appeals to modern criteria pointed to the pervasive influence of a dominant culture, they also evidenced the creative potential and agency of "outsiders" as they responded to, negotiated, and reworked the dominant idiom to further their own aims.

Early Pentecostals and the Evidentiary Tradition in American Evangelicalism

Understanding the appeals to empirical proof embedded in Pentecostal rhetoric first requires an examination of the broader evidentiary tradition within nineteenth-century evangelicalism that provided the backdrop for Pentecostal claims. Highly influenced by the Common Sense philosophy of Scottish Realists of the late eighteenth century, American evangelicals believed their immediate perceptions of the world around them confirmed their deepest religious convictions. In what historian Mark Noll has termed "methodological Common Sense," evangelicals heartily embraced Baconian scientific assumptions, asserting that "truths about consciousness, the world, or religion must be built by a strict induction from irreducible facts of experience."[22] In the words of one nineteenth-century theologian, "Protestant christianity and the Baconian philosophy originate in the same foundation."[23] God had not left believers unarmed in their confrontations with critics. Powerful, this-worldly proof justified their positions. Any reasonable observer could ascertain the order in the universe, an order which pointed to the necessity of a creator. As William Paley argued in his *Natural Theology* (1802), if an intricate watch implies a watchmaker, so an intricate universe implies a universe-maker. Though the marriage of religion and science began to deteriorate in the late nineteenth and early twentieth century due to the influence of scientific theories such as Darwin's evolutionary theory, evangelical theologians nevertheless continued to press the argument from design throughout the twentieth century.[24]

Alongside nature, the Bible also stood as a wellspring of evidence in defense of the faith. Put simply, the numerous miraculous references in scripture, it was believed, offered irrefutable evidence of the veracity of the Christian message. "The Bible is to the theologian what nature is to the man of science," wrote the Presbyterian theologian Charles Hodge. "It is his store-house of facts; and his method of ascertaining what the Bible teaches, is the same as that which the natural philosopher adopts to ascertain what nature teaches."[25] Though theologians increasingly felt a need to defend their assumptions regarding the accuracy of the biblical record due to the steady rise of biblical criticism, on a popular level, the Bible continued to be accepted as authoritative by the majority of evangelicals and other Protestants throughout the nineteenth century. These tendencies were so pervasive, in fact, that not until the 1920s and 1930s—the same period that witnessed the famed Scopes trial—would historians find enough evidence to claim the demise of "biblical civilization" and widespread disavowal of biblical authority in the United States.[26]

Whether they realized it or not, early Pentecostals, like other evangelicals, inherited evangelicals' Common Sense approach to scripture and spirituality. "This Bible becomes a new book to those baptized with the Holy Ghost," asserted an *Apostolic Faith* commenter. "You eat it down without trimming or cutting, right from the mouth of God."[27] Importantly, for this Pentecostal, a supernatural encounter with God did not provide access to an esoteric reading of the text. Rather, it cut away any artificial impediment to reading the text "as is." When taken at face value, without any addition or emendation, the Bible represented a book of irrefutable facts. Though early Pentecostals went farther than most of their fellow believers in their openness to divine intervention in their personal lives, and though they never received plaudits for theological sophistication, they nevertheless embraced other evangelicals' desire to read scripture in a "scientific," straightforward manner.

Early Pentecostals also shared other evangelicals' Common Sense confidence that their beliefs would withstand demands for evidence and the scrutiny of scientific observation. Whereas most evangelical theologians tended to locate scientific proof of Christianity in the miracles described in scripture or in observation of nature, participants within the Pentecostal movement discovered this same assurance in daily events and in their own physical experiences of the supernatural. One of the clearest examples of the influence of these evidentiary trends on Pentecostal practices involved their rhetoric surrounding the Pentecostal distinctive of the baptism in the Holy Spirit with the evidence of speaking in tongues. For Pentecostals, speaking in tongues did not simply set them apart from other communities. Rather, speaking in tongues provided a ground of assurance regarding the reality of their special relationship with God. "Praise God for a salvation that brings a witness," exclaimed one *Apostolic Faith* commenter. Upon receiving the Holy Spirit, present-day believers relived the disciples' original experience of the Holy Spirit's presence as recorded in Acts 2:4: they spoke in tongues. For this participant, speaking in tongues lacked the mysterious, otherworldly quality perceived by outsiders. "Why not have the Bible witness," the account continued, "a supernatural witness that people will not have to take your word for?"[28] One adherent emphasized the distinct difference between sanctification, which occurred internally, and the baptism in the Holy Spirit, which was accompanied by external signs. "When you are sanctified," this individual wrote, "people have to take your testimony and watch your life." But when baptized with the Holy Spirit, "you know it and everybody else knows it. That is one thing you cannot hide."[29] Brother G. W. Batman's testimony, also captured in the *Apostolic Faith*, brimmed with confidence regarding the physical, objective nature of his Christian experiences. Batman testified to his "know-so salvation—no guess work about it." The changes in his life offered "real evidence that I was sanctified and the Blood applied." In the same evidentiary vein, the distinctly corporeal nature of his baptism in the Holy Ghost provided a similar "know-so" confidence. Far from a mystical, detached experience, Pentecostals saw the baptism in the Holy Spirit, accompanied by speaking in tongues, as an undeniable physical proof of the Holy Spirit's presence—a proof that not only the participant but outsiders should also recognize.

Language of evidence also saturated early Pentecostals' testimonies of divine healing. Officially, many early Pentecostals denounced the use of medicine. In a "Questions Answered" section of a 1908 issue of *Apostolic Faith*, the editor responded to the direct question: "Do you teach that it is wrong to take medicine?" "Yes," the editor wrote. "Medicine is for unbelievers, but the remedy for the saints of God we will find in Jas. 5:14," which detailed the need for prayer and anointing the sick with oil.[30] A. J. Tomlinson, eventual founder of the Church of God, a Pentecostal denomination, would later be more direct. "Haven't you sworn to obey the commands of your Lord?" he asked his readers. "Doesn't He tell you what to do in case of sickness? And does He say if that fails to call for a physician?" Tomlinson continued, "Die rather than go contrary to the plain teaching in God's Word!"[31]

For a community where many found medicine anathema, however, early Pentecostals revealed a remarkable willingness to draw on the authority of doctors to corroborate their healings. One man who suffered from paralysis for over eighteen years, for example, had the foresight to hold off prayer for his illness until he "called a physician to be a witness." Healing of his distress then occurred "in the presence of the physician," lest anyone doubt the authenticity of the man's claims. In a similar vein, physicians proved a major prize if they could only be lured into the fold. After one healing of a deaf man, the editor was careful to point out that the man was a "practicing physician in Oakland."[32] The *Apostolic Faith* editors also included an analogous story that they borrowed from Charles Parham's Pentecostal periodical. When Pentecostal revival broke out in Melrose, Kansas, a physician in the town who knew several languages visited the meetings in order to denounce the speaking in tongues and other practices as fraud. To the delight of those present, the physician reportedly heard a women revealing his life secrets in Italian, and then experienced a profound transformation. As a result, he "now says he would rather pray for the sick than give drugs, and is seriously thinking of leaving his profession and going into the Lord's work."[33] While these statements may be read simply as Pentecostals celebrating the spiritual power of the Holy Spirit over even the most hardened unbeliever, the attention paid to evidence and to the verification of miracles by doctors suggests an awareness of the power of empirical evidence and a willingness to draw on doctors' authority to gain credibility.[34] In sum, the language of evidence, imported from the Common Sense tradition in American evangelicalism, permeated Pentecostal rhetoric.

Technology and the Body in Pentecostal Rhetoric

Other aspects of Pentecostal rhetoric also revealed evidentiary concerns. Though more subtle than the explicit appeals to evidence addressed above, Pentecostals' descriptions of their supernatural encounters and their depictions of the Holy Spirit also reflected an attunement to the growing focus on the material world in American culture. Pentecostals stressed the bodily component of their encounters with the Holy Spirit, often describing him using physical terminology. One common theological theme recalled the image of the "Shekina glory." Though the term does not occur in the Bible, it was generally used to refer to physical manifestations of God in scripture, as when a cloud filled the Jewish temple at its dedication. Significantly, in the biblical account, priests were physically unable to stand when God's presence enveloped the temple.[35] Pentecostals built on these examples. "The great Shekina glory is still resting upon us," wrote one believer. Another recounted, "The great Shekina glory rests upon us day and night, and we are filled and thrilled with the power of the Holy Spirit."[36]

In the context of turn-of-the-century America, a reference to the Shekina glory of God would have functioned in part as an apologetic tool; it highlighted the tangible nature of Pentecostals' experiences and pointed to the very this-worldly, verifiable nature of their interactions with God.

Other aspects of Pentecostal rhetoric functioned in an analogous manner. In addition to theologically informed images, Pentecostals frequently likened the Holy Spirit to electricity, liquids, fire, and modern forms of energy production. Each identifier suggested a malleable, transient entity even as it connected Pentecostal experiences to physically verifiable phenomena. These word choices allowed early Pentecostals to employ laboratory-like terminology and subtly invoke the objectivity of physical observation and experience without ceding thoroughgoing materialist assumptions. The majority of their descriptions contained no reference to the person of Christ. Instead, they focused on the Holy Spirit as a substance-like force. Significantly, participants frequently juxtaposed these descriptions to claims of certainty regarding the factuality of their encounters.

Electricity served as one of the more prominent themes. Celia Freeman, for example, recounted that on "March 13th, 1907, the electrical shock of the Holy Ghost from heaven fell on me. I died seemingly and I became helpless as a babe."[37] William Durham's description, recounted earlier, described how his "body had suddenly become porous, and that a current of electricity was being turned on me from all sides."[38] A Brother Hezmalhalch told how the Holy Spirit manifested through a young girl. "As I went toward her," he reported, "*I shall never forget* the power I felt when about two feet from the child, I felt as if batteries of mighty power had seized my body and the whole was one great reservoir of electric forces."[39]

Similarly, references to fire frequently appeared. Howard Goss noted that when he received the baptism in the Holy Spirit the "fire of God flamed hotter and hotter, until I thought that I must be *actually* on fire." Similarly, T. B. Barratt felt himself "filled with light and such a power that I began to shout as loud as I could in a foreign language."[40] A. A. Boddy described how a "strange flame" spread in meetings "liable at any moment to be swept by a wave of spiritual power." In a curious reference to sound, Boddy continued, "At times the noise is strangely awesome, almost appalling to an 'outsider.' "[41] In the fourth issue of the *Apostolic Faith*, Brother George E. Berg claimed that the Holy Spirit felt like "balls of fire . . . [that] went through me from the crown of my head to the soles of my feet." He literally felt his heart enlarged. Far from a mere metaphor, Berg recounted real fear that that the "vessel might not hold the glory and power that seemed to rush into me like water."[42]

Liquids also figured prominently in early Pentecostal testimonies. A Brother Burke "asked the Lord to put the Holy Ghost on me." The Lord answered his prayer, "It came like the outpouring of water on the crown of my head . . . and my heart seemed to expand ten time [*sic*] larger. Then something rushed through me like I was under a fawcet." Glenn Cook felt as if a "large pipe was fitted over my neck." The Holy Ghost poured into his body like oil being pumped "under terrific pressure. . . . This was *undoubtedly* the baptism into the death of Christ."[43]

As these examples suggest, early Pentecostals found in the Holy Spirit a malleable symbol of the divine and attributed numerous physical characteristics to him. Theologically, the doctrine of Christ's incarnation served as the paradigmatic example within Christianity of God taking on a physical form. The vague, impersonal nature of the Holy Spirit, however, allowed Pentecostals to treat God as a substance-like force that facilitated very physical, this-worldly encounters. To some degree, the easy transition from theological language to physical terminology regarding the Holy Spirit built on biblical precedents. For example, early Pentecostals would have been very familiar with passages in scripture that likened the Spirit to forces of nature such as wind and fire. Jesus himself, in a conversation with a Pharisee named Nicodemus, compared the activity of the Holy Spirit to the movement of wind. Just as the "wind bloweth where it listeth, and thou hearest the sound therof, but canst not tell whence it cometh, and whither it goeth: so is every one that is born of the Spirit."[44] Similarly, in the book of Acts, the arrival of the Holy Spirit coincided with "a sound from heaven as of a rushing mighty wind, and it filled all the house where they were sitting. And there appeared unto them cloven tongues like as of fire, and it sat upon each of them."[45] Read in context, and viewed through the lens of American culture during the early twentieth century, however, Pentecostals' physical representations of the Holy Spirit also pointed to the very this-worldly, verifiable nature of Pentecostals' interaction with God.

Of course, the laboratory-like images used by Pentecostals can also be read merely as symbolic references that communicated to others the powerful impact of their experiences. Electricity in particular proved a rather fluid concept for many and took on a variety of meanings during this time period. In various contexts it was claimed that electricity "promoted growth, quickened intelligence, enlivened the personality, and was a mysterious fluid connected to the life processes."[46] As Amanda Porterfield notes in her discussion of Pentecostal healing, viewed from this type of perspective, "The association of religious experience with electrification can be understood as a metaphor for conveying the transformational impact of conversion and sanctification." On another level, though, the use of "clinical, scientific language imputed a kind of objective reality to the metaphysical power and subjective experience. . . . Electrification was more than a metaphor for describing conversion and sanctification; it was also a way of making those experiences real."[47]

Pentecostal rhetoric contributed to the objectification of experience in part based on a simple appeal to the concrete nature of bodily sensations. Electricity, liquid, fire—each represented an elusive yet verifiable phenomenon that could stimulate a physical response. Physical sensation, in turn, connected individuals to the visible, external world—the world of *certain* experience. By linking supernatural encounters directly to their bodies, early Pentecostals grounded their testimonies in individuals' shared certainty in their own bodily existence. As Elaine Scarry has argued in her discussion of the body and pain, an immaterial object such as an idea, a theory, or belief in God may "not take a materialized and hence physically experienceable form . . . ; still that it is 'real' or 'true' will be certified by materialized or experienceable instances of it, supporting facts (the theory of gravity cannot itself be seen but the falling apple can)." A "disembodied idea that has no basis in the material world," can nevertheless gain credibility and substantiation by being juxtaposed to "the realm that from the very start has compelling reality to the human mind, the physical body itself."[48] In short, Pentecostals' repeated association of the Holy Spirit with the physical world and their descriptions of his direct interaction with their bodies served as key bridges between their very otherworldly beliefs and very this-worldly evidence. In a plain-folk, unsophisticated manner, they attempted to satisfy the increasing demand in American culture that material evidence substantiate immaterial claims and ideas.

To be sure, it is important to note that most outsiders did not find Pentecostals' appeal to evidence convincing. In this sense, early Pentecostals resembled what Grant Wacker terms an "intellectually coherent subculture." According to Wacker, for such closed groups, "what counts for good evidence, reliable warrants, and sound conclusions in their fixed social universe remains stubbornly distinct from what counts for good evidence, reliable warrants, and sound conclusions outside their subculture."[49] From the outside looking in, many observers saw a smug community content to snub its nose at the doubts of unbelievers. When Nazarene evangelist A. M. Hills assessed Pentecostals, for example, he described them as "dogmatic, unteachable, schismatic and anathema-breathing souls."⁵⁰ Hills echoed earlier criticisms of the holiness movement that helped shape the early Pentecostal ethos. As a writer for the *Journal of the Methodist Episcopal Church, South* insisted, "We deplore their methods in so far as they claim a monopoly on the experience, practice and advocacy of holiness."⁵¹ While these types of claims undoubtedly reflected a variety of motivations and by no means offered an unbiased portrait of Pentecostals, the consistent appearance of such accusations suggested that early Pentecostals to some degree did see themselves as a breed set apart. Though Pentecostals' attunement to evidentiary demands in their rhetoric demonstrated key continuities with modern trends in the broader American culture, in the end, the absolute certitude in this same rhetoric regarding their beliefs and experiences enabled them to rebuff any outside criticisms and served to reinforce their social isolation.

Conclusions

Pentecostals' commitment to this-worldly proofs of their claims reflected the shaping influence of scientific and technological advances on their subculture. Though out of step with mainstream American culture in many respects, they (wittingly and unwittingly) sought in their own way to meet the growing demand in society for empirical evidence. In this manner, Pentecostal rhetoric reflected continuity with broader cultural trends. Despite their persistent and strident denunciations of the lack of supernatural power and holiness in other churches and spiritual communities, Pentecostals did not escape the materialism in the United States at the beginning of the twentieth century.

Ironically, however, Pentecostal appeals to empirical evidence helped justify a belief in the supernatural that challenged the materialistic assumptions often associated with modernization. For Pentecostals, their intense physical experiences of the supernatural confirmed the ancient words of a biblical prophecy regarding a massive end-times revival of the supernatural. According to the book of Joel, God promised, "And it shall come to pass afterward, *that* I will pour out my spirit upon all flesh; and your sons and your daughters shall prophesy, your old men shall dream dreams, your young men shall see visions: And also upon the servant and upon the handmaids in those days will I pour out my spirit."⁵² Pentecostals posited themselves at this crucial apex of history described by the prophet Joel. In their eyes, the rise of Pentecostalism represented the restoration of authentic religious experience and intense supernatural visitation that prepared the way for Christ's Second Coming. Pentecostals' focus on the body and on physical experience gave them confidence in the reality of their claims and helped them envision a massive spread of revivalistic fervor around the world. In sum, Pentecostals imbibed the empiricism of the modern world to a large extent, but they also reworked it, tailoring it to their own agenda. They accepted the modern world—that is, as long as it was baptized in the Holy Spirit.

Interestingly, despite major demographic changes that have lessened the social isolation of Pentecostals, many of these same evidentiary themes continue to appear and can also be found within the burgeoning Charismatic Movement that shares many traditional Pentecostal emphases.[53] In a recent article of *Charisma*, a widely popular magazine for Pentecostals and Charismatics, a prominent leader related her encounter with the Holy Spirit. "I felt a great sense of the sovereign presence of God," she wrote. "I felt empowered, as if someone had plugged me into an electrical socket. . . . This was definitely an *experience* I could not deny."[54] Another Charismatic, Carolyn Parker, recounted her experience when a leader prayed for healing for her kidney problems. "I could feel [something] like an electric current go all through that kidney." She added, "I knew that God had done something."[55] In these examples the same rhetorical themes utilized by early Pentecostals appear: an intensely physical encounter coupled with a very this-worldly characterization of the Holy Spirit, all of which contributes to an absolute assurance regarding the reality of the supernatural.

In conclusion, early Pentecostal rhetoric offers valuable insights regarding the way in which modernizing forces have helped shape the development of outsider rhetoric among specific religious communities in contemporary societies. Pentecostal rhetoric exemplifies just how difficult it is for religious groups to escape the cultural authority of science and technology in a context such as the United States during the twentieth and twenty-first centuries. Here, even amid a group frequently dismissed by others due to its overt supernaturalism, assurance of the reality of the supernatural is bolstered by references to technology and scientific advances. Early Pentecostals also demonstrate that the adaptation of religious rhetoric to fit with modern sensibilities moves well beyond the walls of obviously modern groups such as Protestant Modernists in mainline denominations; religious outsiders seemingly out-of-step with modernity have also adapted their rhetoric to meet demands for empirical proofs rooted in this-worldly evidence. The key difference, of course, is that Pentecostals and others like them have co-opted the dominant culture's rhetorical tools in a creative effort to subvert aspects of that same culture, in particular its prioritization of the material world and its tendency to downplay the authority of supernatural claims. As such, early Pentecostal rhetoric provides one model of the evolution of religious outsider rhetoric within modern societies. Undoubtedly, many more trajectories are yet to be explored.

Notes

1. Much of the material for this essay derives from the *Apostolic Faith* [Calif.] periodical published out of the Azusa Mission in Los Angeles. Printed from 1906 through 1908, it has been dubbed "the Pentecostal revival's flagship periodical." For further discussion of the *Apostolic Faith*, see Edith Blumhofer and Grant Wacker, "Who Edited the Azusa *Apostolic Faith* Papers?," *Assemblies of God Heritage* 21 (2001): 15–21.

2. *Apostolic Faith* 1, no. 6 (Feb.–Mar. 1907): 4. The "baptism in the Spirit," accompanied by speaking in tongues, served as *the* distinguishing practice of early Pentecostals. According to Allan Anderson, most early Pentecostal testimonies "spoke of a longing for the experience, followed by extreme physical sensations and feelings of elation, and culminating in a release usually involving speaking in tongues." See Allan Anderson, *An Introduction to Pentecostalism: Global Charismatic Christianity* (Cambridge, UK: Cambridge University Press, 2004), 197–98.

3. Throughout the essay, I intentionally bypass questions regarding the physical, social, and/or supernatural causes that shaped Pentecostal experiences. Rather, I am specifically interested in the rhetoric that developed around these experiences and the role this language played in defining the Pentecostal subculture.

4. Here I follow R. G. Robins's application of the term "plainfolk" to describe early Pentecostals. For Robins, "Plainfolk were not necessarily poor folk: the status was largely self-ascribed. . . . Nevertheless, most came from ranks of society low enough to have grounds for discontent with the status quo but high enough to aspire to reshape it and to have enough resources to form institutions capable of bearing those aspirations. More important to plainfolk status than one's economic level, then, was one's appropriation of the lore of the honest, hardworking ordinary American. . . . Plainfolk culture in the late nineteenth century . . . nourished its own religious forms, which responded to modernization in ways that were compatible with its fundamental habits and instincts. . . . Its message, of course, was theoretically universal, but it targeted a specialized market and proved most effective at converting those who shared its pre-understandings." R. G. Robins, *A. J. Tomlinson: Plainfolk Modernist* (New York: Oxford University Press, 2004), 31.

5. Stuart Hall provides a useful summary of key characteristics of modern societies. According to Hall, modern societies are characterized by: "1) The dominance of secular forms of political power and authority and conceptions of sovereignty and legitimacy, operating within defined territorial boundaries, which are characteristic of the large, complex structures of the modern nation-state. 2) A monetarized exchange economy, based on the large-scale production and consumption of commodities for the market, extensive ownership of private property and the accumulation of capital on a systematic, long-term basis. . . . 3) The decline of traditional social order, with its fixed social hierarchies and overlapping allegiances, and the appearance of a dynamical social and sexual division of labor. . . . 4) The decline of the religious world-

view typical of traditional societies and the rise of a secular and materialist culture, exhibiting those individualistic, rationalist, and instrumental impulses now so familiar to us." Stuart Hall, "Introduction," in *Modernity: An Introduction to Modern Societies*, ed. Stuart Hall et al. (Cambridge, MA: Blackwell, 1996), 8. In this essay, I focus on the fourth characteristic of modern societies mentioned above. Whereas some scholars see modernization as value-neutral in its impact on religion, I emphasize the tendency of modern trends—in particular the impact of technology—to distract from other-worldly concerns. That said, I do not claim that this process is somehow inevitable, or that it cannot be reversed (also see note 8).

6. David E. Nye, *Electrifying America: Social Meanings of a New Technology, 1880–1940* (Cambridge: MIT Press, 1990), 48, 156.

7. Alan Trachtenberg, *The Incorporation of America: Culture and Society in the Gilded Age* (New York: Hill and Wang, 1982), 38–69.

8. Any simple correlation between modernization and the secularization of society requires important qualifications. To begin, the conflict between overtly religious claims and appeals to empiricism initially proved most intense in intellectual circles and among the highly educated. Nevertheless, as Paul Carter emphasizes, this should not obscure the way in which practically everyone during the late nineteenth century, "no matter how little might be their own scientific expertise, had to live in the same culture with a burgeoning science and technology that made the most extraordinary claims" regarding what could be known and accomplished. Paul Allen Carter, *The Spiritual Crisis of the Gilded Age* (DeKalb: Northern Illinois University Press, 1971), x. Also, some historians have begun to refute common assumptions regarding the challenge modernization posed for religion. In his work on early Pentecostalism, R. G. Robins sees the forces of modernization as value-neutral in their impact on religion, emphasizing the way in which Pentecostals embraced overt supernaturalism even as they celebrated innovation, change, and technological advances, see *A. J. Tomlinson: Plainfolk Modernist*, 18–25. At a minimum, the work of scholars such as Robins indicates that the secularization usually associated with modernity is not inevitable and the relationship can be reversed. That said, it is no accident that numerous scholars have linked modernization with the "decline of the religious world-view typical of traditional societies and the rise of a secular and materialist culture, exhibiting those individualistic, rationalist, and instrumental impulses now so familiar to us." Hall, "Introduction," 8. For the purpose of this essay, then, on the one hand I emphasize the tendency of modern trends—in particular the impact of technology—to distract from other-worldly concerns, and to downplay the need for overtly supernatural forms of religious belief and practice. On the other hand, I also stress Pentecostals' creative engagement with modernizing trends that counteracted what was for most the seemingly natural connection between modernization and a focus on the material world.

9. George Marsden notes the irony of Pentecostalism's appeal at the turn of the twentieth century. "Perhaps the most interesting cultural question suggested by the rise of holiness and Pentecostal movements in the late nineteenth and early twentieth centuries," he writes, "is why such teaching began to spread widely just at the period when industrialization and new technology were revolutionizing the world." George M. Marsden, *Religion and American Culture*, 2nd ed. (Fort Worth, TX: Harcourt College Publishers, 2000), 167.

10. Grant Wacker, *Heaven Below: Early Pentecostals and American Culture* (Cambridge: Harvard University Press, 2001), 100.

11. Many historians of the movement have depicted early Pentecostals as social outcasts on the losing side of the changes rapidly transforming American society at

the turn of the twentieth. For a classic study of Pentecostalism that emphasizes the economic deprivation experienced by believers see Robert Mapes Anderson, *Vision of the Disinherited: The Making of American Pentecostalism* (New York: Oxford University Press, 1979). Recent historians in the field suggest that in actuality "plainfolk" best captures the average Pentecostal's status, despite the fact that the movement had its fair share of poor adherents. (See note 4 for further discussion of the term "plainfolk.") That said, Pentecostals were often perceived as social outcasts, and were very much religiously marginalized for their beliefs. For more recent analyses of Pentecostals' socioeconomic status, see Wacker, *Heaven Below*, 197–216; and Robins, *A. J. Tomlinson: Plainfolk Modernist*, especially 31–32.

12. Edith Waldvogel Blumhofer, *Restoring the Faith: The Assemblies of God, Pentecostalism, and American Culture* (Urbana: University of Illinois Press, 1993), 158.

13. Quoted in Wacker, *Heaven Below*, 100.

14. Ibid., 181.

15. *Apostolic Faith* 1, no. 2 (Oct. 1906): 3.

16. *Apostolic Faith* 1, no. 3 (Nov. 1906): 2.

17. See Anderson, *Vision of the Disinherited*, 200.

18. In fact, as Protestants, Pentecostals stood squarely within the most dominant religious tradition in the United States. Many early Pentecostals displayed nativist tendencies, for example, which implied a strong identification with the mainstream. Nevertheless, observers often associated Pentecostals with a lower socioeconomic status and treated them as outsiders.

19. Wacker, *Heaven Below*, 12–13, 268. A growing body of research on Pentecostalism has emphasized a more positive portrayal of Pentecostalism's relationship with modernity and modernization. In his recent biography of the early Pentecostal leader A. J. Tomlinson, R. G. Robins contends that Pentecostals represented a form of plainfolk modernism. Robins, *A. J. Tomlinson: Plainfolk Modernist*. Similarly, Edward Gitre argues that the 1904–5 Welsh Revival (a precursor to Pentecostal revivals in the United States) was the first "modern revival." He notes the way in which Pentecostal spirituality sacralized the technologies of modernity, in particular those associated with mass transit, such as the railway. Instead of "receding into oblivion in the face of 'modernity,'" he claims, "believers reinscribed the sacred onto physical bodies and physical space—and technologies of modernization." Edward J. Gitre, "The 1904–05 Welsh Revival: Modernization, Technologies, and Techniques of the Self," *Church History* 73, no. 4 (2004): 827.

20. My argument explicitly builds on Wacker's description of Pentecostal pragmatism, focusing on pragmatic aspects of their rhetoric. While Wacker discusses the practical aspects of Pentecostal rhetoric, he focuses on issues of style more than content. For example, he details their platform charisma, verbal agility, plainness of speech, dramatic tension, and humor. This essay, on the other hand, stresses the way which the content of Pentecostal rhetoric adapted to the growing appeal of this-worldly criteria. See Wacker, *Heaven Below*, 112–20.

21. Michel Foucault, *The History of Sexuality*, 1st ed. (New York: Vintage Books, 1988), 101.

22. Far from being relegated to a few intellectual elites, Common Sense assumptions filtered down to the average evangelical parishioner during the nineteenth century. See Mark A. Noll, "Common Sense Traditions and American Evangelical Thought," *American Quarterly* 37 (1985): 222–23; and George M. Marsden, "Everyone One's Own Interpreter: The Bible, Science, and Authority in Mid-Nineteenth-Century America," in *The Bible in America: Essays in Cultural History*, ed. Nathan O. Hatch and Mark A. Noll (New York: Oxford University Press, 1982), 81–84.

23. Samuel Tyler, quoted in Marsden, "Everyone One's Own Interpreter," 82.

24. See E. Brooks Holifield, *Theology in America: Christian Thought from the Age of the Puritans to the Civil War* (New Haven: Yale University Press, 2003), especially 173–96.

25. Charles Hodge, *Systematic Theology* (Grand Rapids, MI: Eerdmans, 1979), I, 10.

26. See Grant Wacker, "The Demise of Biblical Civilization," in Hatch and Noll, *The Bible in America*. For discussion of Pentecostals' response to Darwin's theory of evolution, see Ronald L. Numbers, "Creation, Evolution, and Holy Ghost Religion: Holiness and Pentecostal Responses to Darwinism," *Religion and American Culture* 2 (1992): 134. Numbers indicates that Pentecostals would pay less attention to the creation-evolution controversies than fundamentalists, though they both shared similar responses to these trends.

27. *Apostolic Faith* 1, no. 5 (January 1907): 3.

28. *Apostolic Faith* 1, no. 2 (Oct. 1906): 4.

29. *Apostolic Faith* 1, no. 2 (Oct. 1906): 2.

30. *Apostolic Faith* 1, no. 11 (Oct.–Jan. 1908): 2.

31. A. J. Tomlinson, *The Last Great Conflict* (Cleveland, TN: Press of Walter E. Rodgers, 1913), 15–16.

32. *Apostolic Faith* 1, no. 1 (Sept. 1906): 4.

33. Ibid.

34. Of course, the question remains as to *who* the Pentecostals were trying to convince, those already within the community or skeptics on the outside. Given the animosity directed toward early Pentecostals by outsiders, it seems likely that these accounts largely reassured the faithful against the accusations leveled against the group.

35. 1 Kings 8:10–11, King James Version (KJV). For a more detailed discussion of early Pentecostals' conceptions of "Shekina glory," see Ann Taves, *Fits, Trances, & Visions: Experiencing Religion and Explaining Experience from Wesley to James* (Princeton: Princeton University Press, 1999), 337–41.

36. *Apostolic Faith* 1, no. 4 (Dec. 1906): 1, 2.

37. *Apostolic Faith* 1, no. 8 (May 1907): 4.

38. *Apostolic Faith* 1, no. 6 (Feb.–Mar. 1907): 4.

39. *Apostolic Faith* 1, no. 5 (Jan. 1907): 4 (emphasis mine).

40. Goss and Barrat quoted in Wacker, *Heaven Below*, 38–39.

41. *Apostolic Faith* 1, no. 6 (Feb.–Mar. 1907): 1.

42. *Apostolic Faith* 1, no. 4 (Dec. 1906): 3.

43. *Apostolic Faith* 1, no. 3 (Nov. 1906): 3, 2 (emphasis mine).

44. John 4:8 (KJV).

45. Acts 2:2–3 (KJV).

46. Nye, *Electrifying America*, 48, 156.

47. Amanda Porterfield, *Healing in the History of Christianity* (New York: Oxford University Press, 2005), 170. In her chapter on Pentecostalism, Porterfield also finds historical precedent for Pentecostal rhetoric regarding electricity in the writings of John Wesley during the eighteenth century.

48. Elaine Scarry, *The Body in Pain: The Making and Unmaking of the World* (New York: Oxford University Press, 1985), 125.

49. See Grant Wacker, "Understanding the Past, Using the Past: Reflections on Two Approaches to History," in *Religious Advocacy and American History*, ed. Bruce Kuklick and D. G. Hart (Grand Rapids, MI: Eerdmans, 1997), 172.

50. Torrey and Hills quoted in Grant Wacker, "Travail of a Broken Family: Radical Evangelical Responses to the Emergence of Pentecostalism in America, 1906–16,"

in *Pentecostal Currents in American Protestantism*, ed. Edith Waldvogel Blumhofer, Russell P. Spittler, and Grant Wacker (Urbana: University of Illinois Press, 1999), 31, 32.

51. Quoted in Edith Blumhofer, *Restoring the Faith: The Assemblies of God, Pentecostalism, and American Culture* (Urbana: University of Illinois Press, 1993), 28.

52. Joel 2:28–29 (KJV).

53. I use the term "Charismatic" to refer to individuals and religious communities who, like Pentecostals, emphasize the work of the Holy Spirit and the spiritual gifts identified in I Corinthians 12:8–10, yet remain outside of traditional Pentecostal denominations. For useful overviews of the movement, see Peter Hocken, "Charismatic Movement," in *The New International Dictionary of Pentecostal and Charismatic Movements*, ed. Stanley M. Burgess and Ed M. Van der Maas (Grand Rapids, MI: Zondervan, 2002); Richard Quebedeaux, *The New Charismatics II*, rev. ed. (San Francisco: Harper & Row, 1983); Stanley M. Burgess, "Charismatic Revival and Renewal," in *Encyclopedia of Religious Revivals in America*, ed. Michael James McClymond (Westport, CT: Greenwood Press, 2007); and Margaret M. Poloma, *The Charismatic Movement: Is There a New Pentecost?* (Boston: Twayne Publishers, 1982).

54. Darlene Zschech, "Darlene Zschech," *Charisma & Christian Life* 31, no. 1 (2005): 50.

55. "Focus on Healing," *Word of Faith* 37, no. 9 (2004): 12.

Bibliography

Anderson, Allan. *An Introduction to Pentecostalism: Global Charismatic Christianity*. Cambridge, UK: Cambridge University Press, 2004.

Anderson, Robert Mapes. *Vision of the Disinherited: The Making of American Pentecostalism*. New York: Oxford University Press, 1979.

Apostolic Faith (Los Angeles, CA), 1906–8.

Blumhofer, Edith Waldvogel. *Restoring the Faith: The Assemblies of God, Pentecostalism, and American Culture*. Urbana: University of Illinois Press, 1993.

Blumhofer, Edith Waldvogel, and Grant Wacker. "Who Edited the Azusa *Apostolic Faith* Papers?" *Assemblies of God Heritage* 21 (2001): 15–21.

Burgess, Stanley M. "Charismatic Revival and Renewal." In *Encyclopedia of Religious Revivals in America*, edited by Michael James McClymond, 99–102. Westport, CT: Greenwood Press, 2007.

Carter, Paul Allen. *The Spiritual Crisis of the Gilded Age*. DeKalb: Northern Illinois University Press, 1971.

"Focus on Healing." *Word of Faith* 37, no. 9 (2004): 12.

Foucault, Michel. *The History of Sexuality*. 1st Vintage Books ed. New York: Vintage Books, 1988.

Gitre, Edward J. "The 1904–05 Welsh Revival: Modernization, Technologies, and Techniques of the Self." *Church History* 73, no. 4 (2004): 792–827.

Hall, Stuart, David Held, Don Hubert, and Kenneth Thompson, eds. *Modernity: An Introduction to Modern Societies*. Cambridge, MA: Blackwell, 1996.

Hocken, Peter. "Charismatic Movement." In *The New International Dictionary of Pentecostal and Charismatic Movements*, edited by Stanley M. Burgess and Ed M. Van der Maas, 477–519. Grand Rapids, MI: Zondervan, 2002.

Hodge, Charles. *Systematic Theology*. 3 vols. Grand Rapids, MI: Eerdmans, 1979.

Holifield, E. Brooks. *Theology in America: Christian Thought from the Age of the Puritans to the Civil War.* New Haven: Yale University Press, 2003.

Kern, Stephen. *The Culture of Time and Space 1880–1918.* Cambridge: Harvard University Press, 1983.

Marsden, George M. "Everyone One's Own Interpreter: The Bible, Science, and Authority in Mid-Nineteenth-Century America." In *The Bible in America: Essays in Cultural History,* edited by Nathan O. Hatch and Mark A. Noll, 79–100. New York: Oxford University Press, 1982.

———. *Religion and American Culture.* 2nd ed. Fort Worth, TX: Harcourt College Publishers, 2000.

Noll, Mark A. "Common Sense Traditions and American Evangelical Thought." *American Quarterly* 37 (1985): 216–38.

Numbers, Ronald L. "Creation, Evolution, and Holy Ghost Religion: Holiness and Pentecostal Responses to Darwinism." *Religion and American Culture* 2 (1992): 127–58.

Nye, David E. *Electrifying America: Social Meanings of a New Technology, 1880–1940.* Cambridge: MIT Press, 1990.

Poloma, Margaret M. *The Charismatic Movement: Is There a New Pentecost?* Boston: Twayne Publishers, 1982.

Porterfield, Amanda. *Healing in the History of Christianity.* New York: Oxford University Press, 2005.

Quebedeaux, Richard. *The New Charismatics II.* Rev. ed. San Francisco: Harper & Row, 1983.

Robins, R. G. *A. J. Tomlinson: Plainfolk Modernist.* New York: Oxford University Press, 2004.

Scarry, Elaine. *The Body in Pain: The Making and Unmaking of the World.* New York: Oxford University Press, 1985.

Taves, Ann. *Fits, Trances, & Visions: Experiencing Religion and Explaining Experience from Wesley to James.* Princeton: Princeton University Press, 1999.

Tomlinson, A. J. *The Last Great Conflict.* Cleveland, TN: Press of Walter E. Rodgers, 1913.

Trachtenberg, Alan. *The Incorporation of America: Culture and Society in the Gilded Age.* New York: Hill and Wang, 1982.

Wacker, Grant. "The Demise of Biblical Civilization." In *The Bible in America: Essays in Cultural History,* edited by Nathan O. Hatch and Mark A. Noll, 121–38. New York: Oxford University Press, 1982.

———. *Heaven Below: Early Pentecostals and American Culture.* Cambridge: Harvard University Press, 2001.

———. "Travail of a Broken Family: Radical Evangelical Responses to the Emergence of Pentecostalism in America, 1906–16." In *Pentecostal Currents in American Protestantism,* edited by Edith Waldvogel Blumhofer, Russell P. Spittler, and Grant Wacker, 23–49. Urbana: University of Illinois Press, 1999.

———. "Understanding the Past, Using the Past: Reflections on Two Approaches to History." *Religious Advocacy and American History,* edited by Bruce Kuklick and D. G. Hart, 159–78. Grand Rapids, MI: Eerdmans, 1997.

Zschech, Darlene. "Darelene Zschech." *Charisma & Christian Life* 31, no. 1 (2005): 50.

Techno-Mob Movements: Public Performances and the Collective Voices of Outsiders
Jessica Ketcham Weber

San Francisco, 2007: It's five-thirty in the afternoon, rush hour on the last Friday of the month; close to eight hundred people pedal, skate, and walk down some of the busiest streets in the city. People on mountain bikes, cruisers, and skateboards converge once a month to reclaim the streets, to bike in safety, and to profess an alternative to driving. "We aren't blocking traffic, we *are* traffic!" is a commonly heard retort to the honks of angry motorists.

Washington D.C., 2005: Fed up with the War on Terror, thousands of people march in front of the White House. Clowns wearing Blood for Oil T-shirts, Black Bloc affinity groups dressed head to toe in black, Code Pink women waving cleverly designed banners, and 50-foot Bush and Cheney puppet theater dotted the city on the anniversary of the occupation of Iraq. The events lasted for two days straight.

New York City, 2003: Close to four hundred people descend upon the Toys R Us in Times Square at the same time to meet in front of an enormous, animatronic Jurassic Park dinosaur display. They are men and women, hipsters, tourists, and businesspeople, in running clothes, backpacks, and service industry uniforms. As the dinosaur roars, the people fall to their knees and moan, arms extended, as if praying to a god. Within ten minutes, they disperse.

Manila, Philippines, 2001: The impeachment trial of President Joseph Estrada is aborted and immediately denounced corrupt. Within an hour over fifteen thousand people amass at Edsa, the city center, to protest. His regime ends after four days of demonstrations by more than one million citizens clothed in black, fists in the air.

THERE WAS A MOMENT IN U.S. HISTORY WHEN POLITICAL ACTION. was equated with large protests, banners, and street theater. A time when the sheer volume of people at a political protest meant that it would be covered by the media, that it would be talked about, and that it could affect change. Mainstream as well as outsider activists alike were *taking it to the streets* and demanding *power to the people*. Today however, many activists and academics claim that "60s-style" protest is outdated, that political action is dead, and that we are in a culture of apathy. Another camp claims that twenty-first century protest is just different—that it is digitized, that it includes people mobilizing through text messages, Web sites, and e-mails (oftentimes for a 60s-style protest), "writing" petitions through the push of an online button, or adding political campaigns or political action committees as their "friends" on MySpace and Facebook. Yet another group argues that protest is an outmoded form of political resistance and that the only way to affect change is through policy. I mention these three views in order to provide a taste of the increasingly varied ideas about what constitutes political action in the twenty-first century and how technological tools are helping shape these ideas.

The four aforementioned performances, while seemingly unrelated, are all popular examples of a new force in transnational society: what I call the techno-mob sociopolitical movement. While the prefix "techno" summons stereotypical images of information technology professionals in a lab or highly knowledgeable experts of the latest technological gadget, the least revolutionary aspect of this movement is the technology itself. The main feature that unites all four of these examples is that they were made possible by the creative use of **techno**logy to **mob**ilize citizens in public performances. These actions are referred to by such names as flash mobs, smart mobs, and Critical Mass but they are united in that they are dynamic, fluid collectives of citizens whose voices are being heard despite their lack of traditional political power.

It has been fifty-five years since movement studies theorist Leland Griffin asked us to "turn our attention from the individual 'great orator' and undertake research into such selected acts and atmospheres of public address as would permit the study of a multiplicity of speakers, speeches, audiences, and occasions."[1] These acts and atmospheres, social and political movements, have much to contribute to the story of outsider rhetoric. The rhetorical strategies and characteristics of any movement necessarily include a wide media of symbols—bodies, words, images, sit-ins, chants, signs, and petitions—and the techno-mob movement is no exception. The major rhetorical differences from other movements are the mode and medium through which the voices of the outsiders unite and the kinds of performances occurring in reclaimed public spaces. In the techno-mob movement, the most important rhetorical features are not the words of the chants or letters on the signs, it is the mode of mobilization, what that mode allows in terms of collective action, and how the organization of power structures echo that mode. It is a rhetoric based on action—and interruption.

The individual citizen's voice is an outsider to social or political power. Corporate globalism and media conglomerates increasingly regulate which voices are heard. CEOs and media moguls have joined national leaders in their role of policy makers—a woeful situation for democracy in North America, for example. Citizens are left wondering exactly whose voices, or what groups, are being privileged. The dissatisfaction among citizens who feel unrepresented has prompted an explosion in the past five years of independent media sources (i.e., indymedia.org), personal publishing tools (i.e., Weblogs), and personal radio stations (i.e., podcasting). Everyday citizens have begun to embrace their outsider position by creating alternative news and media sources, and through technology they are building upon the fact that collective social action is the only way for resistance to turn into political change.

Global society has undoubtedly been "transformed radically by media and technology, which have introduced new forms of communication and representation into contemporary life."[2] Critical of a techno-utopia, many critics have written on "the digital divide"[3] or "cyberbalkanization"[4] as if technology is to blame for a culture of isolation and divisiveness. Some scholars blame identity politics and assert that because people separate themselves "into categories based on race, gender, ethnicity, sexual orientation, environmental awareness, or religion, special interest groups in the U.S. competitively grab for power, undermine a sense of an American collectivity, and threaten the opportunities of others."[5] In truth this is the result of a system that does not provide for all, rather than the result of people networking based on special interests. Furthermore, Weblogs and media-based social networks like Friendster, Blogger, LiveJournal, MySpace, and Facebook seem to fall in line with the necessity of "the social multiplicity [managing] to communicate and act in common while remaining internally different."[6] Like cultural critics such as Checker, Fishman, and Rheingold, I contend that this kind of networking, identity based or not, offers "a multitude of possibilities and promises for coalition building, and for harnessing collective power."[7]

Howard Rheingold uses the term "Smart Mob" to detail "the new social form made possible by the combination of computation, communication, reputation, and location awareness."[8] This form, combined with the nonhierarchical organization of the groups, and the public and political performances it inspires, is the focus of this chapter. After situating the tensions and dialogues between performance and political protest, I'll share a bit of historical background that contributes to each major rhetorical feature of the techno-mob sociopolitical movement, in-depth descriptions of slices of the movement, and analyses of the common rhetorical characteristics. I will also locate the immediacy of technologically organized performance of techno-mobs as a politically aware rhetorical method, which citizens are participating in across the world to gain agency, transform the meaning of outsider, and to unsettle normalizing practices of society.

I'm certainly not the first person to look at political acts of resistance and protest through a performance lens, especially since many activists themselves have moved toward explicitly using performance as an activist tool. In fact, it may be that the iconic protest marches of the '60s was the height of political action and that now performance is the height of political action. Like "the political" though, performance doesn't come without its own existential problems. Many young twenty-first century activists fear that performative protests may simply reinforce the depiction of the left and center-left as nonrational and too radical to be trusted with political control. On the other side of the spectrum, there is the danger that performances, even the most radical in content, will evaporate into the society of the spectacle[9] unnoticed or become co-opted by hip marketing and business people. Confident that this danger can be overcome, in *The Radical in Performance: Between Brecht and Baudrillard*, Baz Kershaw asserts "the performativity of protest is a key index of its ability both to subvert the commodifying hyper-realism of the globalised media industry and to contribute effectively to the construction of future realities for a more democratic world."[10]

In this era of globalization, at the end of the twentieth and beginning of the twenty-first century, when the social and cultural landscape claims messy, fluid, decentered, and liminal boundaries, artists and activists are simultaneously asking themselves how to even stage oppositional resistance. Practitioners of performance and protest are asking the same questions about these boundaries (or lack thereof). Are we to consider all political acts of resistance equally as forms of protest? Likewise, are we to consider all performative acts as performance? When do the terms become useless? And for whom? Baz Kershaw asks, "How might we judge one aesthetic approach to be more politically promising than another?" and offers the answer that we can't because everything is situated—"it all depends on where you're standing when."[11] As members of subcultures and margins (at least, the ones that can be marketed to) become swallowed by the mainstream, it becomes harder to articulate opposition. One theory, as Jill Lane points out in "Reverend Billy," referring to the philosophy of the activist arts group Critical Art Ensemble, is "rather than to stage opposition, our only viable option is to create calculated disturbance in these networks of power."[12] Performance can function as a subversive, playful, and political do-it-yourself tactic for injecting disturbance into the cultural sphere. It can also offer political activism both creative potential for subverting dominant ideologies and strategies for allowing the spectator to transform into a participant.

Performance taps into and offers political protest what it needs—a way into the media circus. One argument for the continued development of performative protest is that it helps get media coverage, however small the clip. Following this line of reasoning, we enter into a different kind of thinking about political efficacy where it's not about the end goal (e.g. policy change), but the means. Calling for a closer look at performance and protest in the field of anthropology, Angelique Haurgerud recently described some of these means: "Today both trans-border and national activist networks are animated by new protest styles—some with roots in medieval festivals of resistance or carnival, and others apparent information-age novelties. Media-savvy activists now offer street theatre processions with colorful giant puppets, skits, music, ritual performances, newspaper wraps and inserts, leafleting, and parodies and subversions of advertisements (culture jamming)."[13] In this realm, raising awareness and disrupting dominant ideologies is the game. It's nonviolent direct action meets spectacle. And because it seems that the mainstream media is less concerned with the content of a story than the level of hyper-real pizzazz surrounding it, activist-artists and artist-activists are borrowing from performance. Following McLuhan's tenet, "the media is the message," offers more of an understanding into twenty-first century protests and collective political acts of resistance. Leftist resistance is fragmented—it's anti-war, pro-civil rights, antidiscrimination, and pro-environment—but it seems to be unified against rampant consumerism, capitalist globalization, and corporate ownership of the world.

The appropriate media for this message is collective, radical, oppositional performance. Jan Cohen-Cruz writes that "political art relies on an energized context,"[14] and collective public performance, frequently mobilized through technological means, is one way to energize communities, to find solidarity, and subvert hyperindividualism, even if just for a moment.

Tensions in Radical Performance and Performance Art

Analyzing protest as performance illuminates the radical possibilities of performance in everyday contexts. Without a doubt many disciplines have an increasing interest in performance studies which, while risking the promiscuity of performance, is in part because of the performativity of a heavily branded, capitalist society. Kershaw speculates that "performance has gained a new kind of potency because multiparty democracy weaves ideological conflict visibly into the very fabric of society" and as such "the performative becomes a major element in the continuous negotiations of power and authority."[15] Arguing for a look at performance beyond the theater house, Kershaw writes that it "has a much better chance of turning the trick of cultural production back against the commodifying depredations of late-capitalism."[16] Political theater, or theater which features explicitly political plots or themes, certainly has its place, but it may be that radical performances in everyday life have more potential to expose oppression and move participants to action, in large part because the performances are often not mediated through frames and stages.

There are, of course, numerous tensions within performance studies about the political efficacy of any performance. Kershaw bluntly states one of the root issues for radical performance: "In capitalist democracies, confidence in the legitimacy of established political processes is in a state of continual crises, and that, paradoxically, undermines any performance that aims to be politically oppositional: if few people believe in the state then it is hardly worth attacking."[17] Additionally, he states, "the representational styles of a performative world" are mass distributed through global media channels, which contributes to our voyeuristic love/hate relationship with humanity-becoming-spectacle. Put succinctly and playfully, Kershaw writes:

> So long as we accept the full force of the post-modern paradigm and allow that Barthes has finally done for the intentional fallacy by murdering the author, Foucault has incontrovertibly shown that power is everywhere, Derrida has uncoupled the signifier from the signified forever, Lyotard has raised incredulity about master narratives to a new order of intensity, Butler has demonstrated that even gender is a cultural construct, and Baudrillard has possibly capped it all by banishing the real, we will be plagued by an acute indecision about the politics of theatre and performance in the contemporary world.[18]

Performance artists raise questions about the threat of ideological subsumption and appropriation of performances and performative acts. Artists such as Guillermo Gómez-Peña worry that audiences will "misinterpret our 'radical' actions and our complex performative identities as merely spectacles of radicalism or stylized hybridity,"[19] while many mainstream political activists ask the same question. While many scholars will continue to debate the question of performance's efficacy on the political (and/or entertainment) sphere, I think it is more useful to not look for an answer but to continue to look for a way to reveal, restructure, and play with power configurations. We are in the midst of what Gómez-Peña terms "the culture of the mainstream bizarre . . . (which) has effectively blurred the borders between pop culture, performance, and 'reality,'"[20] and it makes sense to engage in play as a way to navigate the bizarre.

Borrowing from Others

As artistic genres have blurred, and as access to digital graphic tools becomes greater, there seems to be an explosion in the crossover lives of activists and artists. Collective acts of resistance, from large protests and marches to the staged ten-minute performances of flash mobs borrow from performance movements and evolutions. Like performance art and community-based theater, protest is situated—created in response to a particular situation; Marvin Carlson writes of performance artists that "its practitioners, almost by definition, do not base their work upon characters previously created by other artists, but upon their own bodies, their own autobiographies, their own specific experiences in a culture or in the world."[21] In these next few pages, I'll illustrate how a few specific forms of performance, are used in protests as tactics to (1) create a spectacle that is more likely to be picked up by mainstream media and thus injected into the infotainment sphere, and (2) encourage spectators to become participants.

Street theater, or guerilla theater refers to a type of performance staged in the street, a park, or other public places, generally for an unintentional audience. Probably one of the most recognized strands of street theater is agit prop, or: "the use of satire as a weapon against the powers that be, in an effort to agitate the body politic by injecting unwelcome and disruptive propaganda into its main ideological arteries."[22] Agit prop is far from the carnivalesque, anarchic style that is commonly thought of in association with street theater. On the contrary, agit prop uses satire and irony to clearly articulate a particular message. Popular manifestations of agit prop include blogs like Liberal Agit-Prop: Fighting Fascism with Photoshop which creates downloadable and printable critiques of the current administration, or the myriad of satirical T-shirts available on the Internet and bookstores.

Comprised of pieces of agit prop and performance art, electoral guerilla theater is an example of a particular kind of performative protest against the democratic electoral system. Disillusioned activists use drag, camp, and personification of inanimate objects to provide satirical insight into issues like the lack of real choice in the voting booth. Examples from the last thirty years include the citizens of Amsterdam voting for a gnome and a houseplant and a clown running for office in the United States. Through electoral guerilla theater, activists have actually successfully won some elections, though it is not the goal and can sometimes backfire. In his book *Electoral Guerrilla Theatre: Radial Ridicule and Social Movements*, L. M. Bogad writes, "Oppositional, collective identity and resistance are encouraged and enacted as the guerilla electioneers' absurdist participation exposes the theatricality and symbolic ritualism of an electoral system which defines itself as natural, optimal, and democratically inclusive of all of its citizenry."[23] Street/guerilla theater is rooted in the Brechtian tactic of making the familiar strange, which is also part of the tactic in flash mob activism. Unlike flash mobs and other hyperreal forms of performed spectacle, electoral guerilla theater specifically confronts the process of our democratic elections: "Electoral guerillas are political actors and performance artists, guided by aesthetic concerns and theories as well as sociopolitical agendas and grievances. To be politically effective, their work must entertain and engage their chosen audiences. Brechtian distantiation, Boalian spect-actorship, and the Bakhtinian carnivalesque intermingle in this complex exercise."[24] In general, street theater's mission is to incite and provoke, to make spectators question and wonder, and to create a moment of playful critique. The purposefully bizarre performances and delightfully celebratory rebellion frequently catch the media's attention, which even if only mentioned briefly, receives more coverage than traditional marches. As long as the mainstream media continues to function as the primary hegemonic tool, capturing its attention will be an important activist strategy, if only to provide mediated solidarity with those who question dominant ideologies.

The second main tactic that activists borrow from performance artists is creative ways to engage or involve spectators. Augusto Boal's Theatre of the Oppressed encourages the audience to take an active role as SpectActor, which allows people to engage in action from the margins, and from various outsider positions. For Boal, "all human beings are Actors (they act!) and Spectators (they observe!) . . . they are SpectActors."[25] The dissolution of the traditionally separated roles of actor and spectator that Boal's notion of SpectActor offers is particularly resonant with the nonhierarchical decision making of many activist collectives. Political organizing with the SpectActor in mind challenges everyone involved to act collectively and in response to specific problems. Broadly conceived, Theatre of the Oppressed is made up of a myriad of games and techniques in response to the monologue of traditional theater, with the goal of creating dialogue and critical thinking about particular problems in our communities. As Augusto Boal notes, "I hope no one can be satisfied with the world as it is; it must be transformed."[26] Two techniques that seem to be the most frequently adapted from Theatre of the Oppressed in the activist communities are Image Theatre and Forum Theatre. In Image Theatre, people create image-based, body-based sculptures, while in Forum Theatre they stage improvisational scenarios depicting specific scenes of oppression. Participants of these techniques are "concerned with whatever problems were of greatest urgency and importance for the communities at the time"[27] and for that reason, the workshops might be best understood in situations where there is a shared context. As Theatre of the Oppressed techniques continue to resurge in popularity and as derivatives continue to be developed, it will be helpful to look at the activist communities adopting the techniques through a performance lens.

Another closely related theater movement is community-based theater, which brings people into dialogue to try to examine community issues. Community-based theater, focused more on process than product (or content), is intent on "democratizing access to art making."[28] Similar in goal to Theatre of the Oppressed workshops, community-based theater is immediately focused on the local. In fact, the grassroots sticker "Think Globally, Act Locally" might be an appropriate motto for community-based theater companies as well. Jan Cohen-Cruz writes "in bringing people together to address a local problem, community-based theater has contributed to new, perhaps more modest ways of understanding political efficacy."[29] Like a more embodied town hall meeting, community-based theater has yet to infiltrate mainstream protests—perhaps because of the hyperlocal focus—but as more mainstream activists become frustrated and disillusioned with the attempts of high-profile, media-laden performative protests, it may be a form of increasing interest.

The trend to act locally, think locally, and affect change locally, while a useful starting place, does risk the danger of hyperindividualistic thought, which can lead to political action only when it affects the individual's life. An example of this can be seen right now in the U.S. Green movement. Simply put, the environmental movement suffered a major splintering in the past ten years. On the one side, eco-activist performance was at its high point—from EarthFirst!'s yearlong tree-sits and machinery sabotage to massive Greenpeace actions, the media's attention was captured. On the other side, mainstream activists were fed up with the lack of policy action by these performative eco-activists and started friendly Green organizations. A little bit of market research and the movement has become co-opted by consumerist ventures and all of a sudden "acting locally" is equated with buying energy-efficient lightbulbs. But at least the eco-activist performances spurred the mainstream activists enough to create some kind of change, because that's what our definition of radical performance is here: performance which invokes, calls for, or demands political and social change.

To look at Protest as Performance is to recognize the performativity of everyday life while discerning the specific performance practices of particular activist communities. While much scholarship is dedicated to the politics of performance, and there are certainly many tense questions about the political efficacy of performance as protest, the sites of possible interdisciplinary research are abundant. As Gómez-Peña puts it, "the illusion of interactivity and citizen participation has definitely changed the relationship between live art and its audience,"[30] and the way artists and activists design dialogic spaces is a direct result of this. Reclaiming pseudopublic spaces (coffee shops, bookstores, shopping malls, etc.) as public ones seems to be one tactic. Rather than marching in front of state capitols or the White House, activists and artists are going where they can be heard: Starbucks, Macy's, Best Buy, or Wal-Mart.

While this speaks volumes about civic discourse in contemporary America, it deserves a closer look—especially in light of the question of efficacy, which is quite problematic to measure. If the goal is primarily to disrupt and raise awareness then the efficacy of the performance could be measured simply through spectator response, but if the goal were to change public policy or affect direct political or electoral change, the measurements would be quite different. Ultimately, performance is "a means by which discourses of ideology and politics are communicated and promoted,"[31] and viewing performances as means rather than an end makes any measurement difficult. Transcending any measure of worth quantitatively, Alan Read simply states that performance and theater is worthy "because it is antagonistic to official views of reality."[32]

Movement Studies: A History of Conflict

To study literary, historical, political, social, or cultural movements is to study their forms. Movement studies were quite dense in the 1960s, 1980s, and true to the twenty-year pattern, are recently making another comeback. In Leland Griffin's "The Rhetoric of Historical

Movements," he distinguishes between two broad types of rhetorical movements: (1) Pro movements, in which the rhetorical attempt is to arouse public opinion to the creation or acceptance of an institution or an idea; and (2) Anti movements, in which the rhetorical attempt is to arouse public opinion to the destruction or rejection of an existing institution or idea.[33]

Many of Griffin's predecessors claim that Anti movements are the only real movements, citing that the Pro movements, by his definition, are no different than any other rhetorical attempt. Some, such as the controversial movement studies theorist Robert Cathcart agree that confrontation, or at least conflict, are requisite parts of a movement. In fact, Cathcart believed that "confrontation is not anti-communication but rather is an extension of communication in situations where confronters have exhausted the normal means of communication with those in power."[34] Contrary to a mere adjustment to an existing order, movements require rejection of the current system by outsiders of that system.

As if anticipating the political climate that Hardt and Negri would write about in *Multitude: War and Democracy in the Age of Empire*, Robert Scott and Donald Smith advised in 1969 that: "A rhetorical theory suitable to our age must take into account the charge that civility and decorum serve as masks for the preservation of injustice, that they condemn the dispossessed to non-being, and that as transmitted in a technological society they become the instrumentalities of power for those who 'have.'"[35] While this is still true, citizens have always used technology subversively, as far back as the printing press, to counter the message of the ruling ideology. However, the accessibility and ease of use of technology have increased individual citizens' ability to create rather than consume. A group's access to resources was the major approach to studying movements in the 1980s because it was thought to be the only variable to that movement's organization and success. Current movement theory rejects this notion, arguing that there must be more of a cultural component, one that reflects current identities and societies. The main concern of the new social movement approach (NSM) is "the connection of contemporary social movements to broad structural changes in society as a whole," and it is thought that the main difference between NSMs (movements after 1960s) and earlier movements is that they are "a complex social base decoupled from the class structure, [and] have an ideological outlook centered on autonomy and identity."[36]

The techno-mob movement is one of very few movements whose cultural critiques are verbalized via satirical action. The Cynics, of the Hellenistic period, are perhaps the most similar movement in terms of action, rhetoric, and purpose. According to Kristen Kennedy, they "advocated a public exercise of resistance to social conventions."[37] Techno mobs, and specifically the flash mobbers within the movement, also draw from the Cynic tradition of "physicality," "disruption," and the "pairing of their verbal and visual tactics." Just as the Cynic "used his position on the margins of culture to intervene,"[38] the techno mobs force their outsider positions into mainstream arenas through public performances of resistance.

Anarchism and the Internet

Most movement studies concern themselves with the leaders of the movements—Malcolm X, Betty Freidan, Martin Luther King, Jr., Mother Jones, Gandhi, Kennedy—and their speeches. Techno mobs, however, do not follow a hierarchical structure and have no leader in the traditional sense. This type of organization structure is not unique, and finds many of its roots in anarchist theory. Though many types of anarchism exist, the fundamental desire of anarchists is to eliminate all forms of hierarchy and to maximize individual freedom and equality. The Internet has often been compared to anarchy due to its structure, as cyberpunk author Bruce Sterling notes: "The Internet is a rare example of a true, modern, functional, anarchy."[39] The Internet is also referred to as a space in which geographical boundaries are moot and hierarchy is not applicable—which many anarchists see as a favorable model for society. Quick to dismiss the widespread notion of "techno-utopianism," social theorists such as Armin Medosch state: "Wireless broadcasting technology, radio, television, and mostrecently, computers and the Internet have served over the past hundred years as sources of inspiration and bearers of hope for social revolution. It is not the idea that these technologies cause social change that needs criticising here, but the way in which the link between technology and social change is imagined."[40] Without romanticizing the Internet too much, there are three features which are particularly relevant to the techno mob movement: (1) the opportunity for high levels of networking, (2) the lack of a forced control system, and (3) the retainment of autonomy.

Perhaps indisputable is the idea that networks are the newest form of social organization (see John Arquilla, David Ronfeldt, and Howard Rheingold). Networks "use many possible paths to distribute information from any link to any other, and are self-regulated through flat governance hierarchies and distributed power."[41] Deleuze and Guattari wrote about network theory in *A Thousand Plateaus* though they conceptualized it as rhizomal: "unlike trees or their roots, the rhizome connects any point to any other point, and its traits are not necessarily linked to traits of the same nature; it brings into play very different regimes of signs, and even nonsign states."[42] The social networks of citizens emulate the very technology which organizes them, but will this phenomenon, be it rhizome or network, help to "overcome the paradigms of consumerism and broadcast media,"[43] or will the networks exponentially grow until chaos breaks out? In former protest movements, after all, it is the popularity of the movement that brings about the destruction or dissolution of it. In the techno-mob movement, it is precisely the popularity that encourages spin-offs to be created; like anarchist "affinity groups," autonomy is not compromised as the numbers grow. Affinity groups, which hark back to the nineteenth-century Spanish anarchists, are small nonhierarchical groups of activists who collaborate to perform direct action. For larger direct action, members from each affinity group from an area (local, state-wide, across the nation, etc.) gather together to make collective decisions. One of the reasons that these affinity groups have been so successful is because they are made up of friends or people who trust each other. On the contrary, techno mobs are rarely made up of trusted friends; rather, they come together with anyone "in the network."

Performance and Activism in Everyday Life

Some of the basic characteristics of new social movement theory in the late 1980s—such as a lack of distinction between the participants and the leaders, as well as independence from specific institutions—seem to echo anarchism. Yet, this could also be a result of postmodernism. For instance, NSMs "tend to structure themselves in a fluid, decentralized style, to emphasize the reflexive construction of collective identities and the moral meaning of everyday life, and to rely on cultural and symbolic forms of resistance at least as often as more conventional political activism."[44] Most postmodern and poststructuralist theorists dismiss the notion that people have "core identities" and instead concentrate on the fluid, fragmented, isolated, performative aspects of identities. Yet, fundamental features of the techno-mob movement counteract these concepts head-on. For instance, the fragmentation or fluidity of individuals, which shares many concepts with what cultural theorists refer to as *the performance of everyday life*, seems to permeate Internet culture already. Also, because many of the people in a particular techno-mob occurrence don't know each other, performative identities are often assumed and even welcomed through anonymity or pseudonyms. While critics of the Internet will often cite it as the cause for social isolation and virtual (and therefore inferior) relationships, the kind of networking and collective social action that results from the creative use of technology can actually be community building.

Citizens are paying closer attention to the role of activism in everyday life. In a consumerist society, people are making conscious, daily-life decisions about where to shop, what products to buy, and what to eat. The definition of activism is expanding. On a message board discussing activism, it is defined in multiple ways, including "educating family and friends" (Sarah Chee) to "when someone acts on something that moves them" (Ayako Hagihara) or "when someone makes the choice between moving forward and perpetuating status quo" (Kim San). The extension of the meaning of "activism" has begun to diminish the stigma of "the activist."

Resistance and activism are not just words associated with wild-eyed liberals anymore; citizens are beginning to see activism in every conscious action. As I describe examples of techno mobs in the next pages, I will demonstrate how they are forms of political activism which empower citizens' voices using a pastiche of rhetorical acts, from postmodern performance to digital social networking, and how these acts engage citizens in performance and activism in everyday life.

An Exploration of Specific Techno Mobs

The *most threatening* aspects of the 1960s' rhetoric of the streets are arguably the *most successful* rhetorical features of contemporary techno mobs; they create a sense of anarchy in times, places, and manners that are not traditionally viewed appropriate for protest. Techno mobs differ from other movements in their membership, organizational structure, resources, and tactics. It is important to make it clear that the entire movement, which often claims to be "organized coincidences" or "coincidental performances," shares a rhizomal structure. One of the defining features of the movement is the fact that there are no leaders, organizer meetings, or memberships. The other distinguishing feature of the movement is that technological tactics such as Listservs, text messages, Web sites, blogs, digital social network programs, and virtual community boards as well as traditional word of mouth and flyers alert participants. Various examples of techno mobs will exemplify their differences among each other, for instance, in goals and kinds of performances.

The outsider status of participants of techno mobs does not only refer to people who previously had no voice in public policy, but also citizens who are acting outside of their traditional political identity markers: conservatives, liberals, and independents are joining together. One reason for this might be because techno mobs can fit any kind of schedule. Flash mobs usually last less than ten minutes, and Critical Mass only requires one afternoon a month. Another reason that citizens from all walks of life are gathering to participate might be because many of the messages conveyed or questions raised are not political party specific. For example, Critical Mass, which began in 1992 in San Francisco, aims simply to "raise awareness of the bicycle as an alternative means of transportation, and have a fun monthly ride ... by riding en masse on downtown streets during the Friday evening rush hour."[45] The activist nature of this monthly performance becomes tangible as officials begin to incorporate cyclists' needs in city planning, but it was not a politically affiliated request.

According to its unofficial Web site, critical-mass.org, since 1992 Critical Mass has spread to more than 350 cities across the world with major cities such as Tokyo, New York, Dublin, and Moscow boasting an average of a thousand participants at their rides. One of the reasons for the widespread success of the movement is that it harbors no racial,

Fig. 3.

gender, political, or class boundaries. An open letter on San Francisco's Indymedia Web site "states, 'being in the streets, disrupting the continuation of ordinary life, is what made Critical Mass what it is today—a global, decentralized mass movement, a powerful voice for change that is difficult to ignore.'" Ordinary people interrupting ordinary life is the common rhetorical strategy that Critical Mass's participants use to illustrate the importance of alternate transportation in an oil-dependent nation.

Turning the ordinary into the extraordinary is also a tactic used by Guerilla gardeners. Since the creation of the New York-based "Green Guerillas" in 1973, small groups have formed, armed with the equipment to plant flowering or vegetable gardens in community spaces. In Europe, "some of the group behind the [United Kingdom-based] Reclaim the Streets demonstrations have adopted 'guerilla gardening' as the latest tactic in their campaign to take back public spaces for the

Fig. 4.

community."[46] Like Guerilla Gardening, Reclaim the Streets in the United Kingdom, which blocks off major streets and highways for community parties, flirts with the ideas that public space is dwindling, and that there should be community ownership of public spaces.[47] These two performances of activism, along with Critical Mass, are all nonviolent expressions of resistance to ideas such as consumerism and gentrification in a global society. These performances are sustained, in part, because of the regularity in the cities which they occur in. Critical Mass always meets at the same day, time, and place and Guerilla Gardening always meets at the same day and time. Consistency was certainly key to pre-Internet success, but as technology evolved, so did the potential for these groups.

A strong rhetorical message that is made through techno mobs is in the number of people engaged in collaborative, and seemingly preconceived, collective actions. Howard Rheingold refers to the phenomena as the "mobile power of many," which echoes, in many ways, the media theory of Marshall McLuhan. The number of people involved can tell more than the message itself, as Franklyn Haiman points out: "Is it reasonable to limit marches to no more than 500 persons? From the police department's viewpoint, yes; for the same message can be communicated by 500 as by 5000 and at much less strain to community resources. From the viewpoint of the marches, as well as the theory of Marshall McLuhan, the medium of 5000 marchers does not communicate the same message as 500. Furthermore, what of the constitutional rights to free speech of the potential 501st marcher?"[48] The number of participants in the Filipino takedown of President Estrada had everything to do with its effectiveness. As Rheingold describes it:

> The "People Power II" demonstrations of 2001 broke out when the impeachment trial of President Estrada was suddenly ended by senators linked to Estrada. Opposition leaders broadcast text messages, and within seventy-five minutes of the abrupt halt of the impeachment proceedings, 20,000 people converged on Edsa. Over four days, more than a million people showed up. The military withdrew support from the regime; the Estrada government fell . . . largely as a result of massive nonviolent demonstrations.[49]

The extraordinary part of this story is that it occurred because of SMS—short message service, also known as text messaging. Texting is significantly cheaper than using landlines, computers, and even talking on the mobile phone. In rural areas, and in places like the Philippines, where at least a third of the population lives on less than a dollar a day, this is significant.

The messages relayed through SMS were urgent. In fact, mere minutes after the Senate vote, text messages were rampant: "Hundreds of thousands converged on the capital, following directions to, as one message put it, WEAR BLACK TO MOURN THE DEATH OF DEMOCRACY. Said another text message: EXPECT THERE TO BE RUMBLES."[50] The action was unified even if the reasons for coming together differed. A thirty-two-year-old Filipino woman admitted on an online message board that, "[she] felt safer protesting the government when [she] knew that other women and children would be involved and not just the usual rebels." Many participants of techno mobs, especially those from nondemocratic nations, seem to feel more comfortable making their voices heard alongside everyday citizens. Gloria continued to say, "I know that I do not share all of the radical views of the Estrada Regime opponents, but I also know that I want my children to grow up without corruption."

When the WTO decided to host their 1999 meeting in Seattle, dissenters immediately sent out an alert not only to anti-WTO groups across the country, but also to all anti-globalization groups as well. Rheingold explains that, "a broad coalition of demonstrators who represented different interests but were united in opposition to the views of the World Trade Organization planned to disrupt the WTO's 1999 meeting in Seattle. The demonstrators included a wide range of 'affinity groups' who loosely coordinated their actions around their shared objectivity."[51] Hundreds of thousands of citizens met in Seattle over the course of a week, coordinating actions such as street theater, mock forums, and puppet shows, among more traditional protest tactics. Campsites and "temporary towns" were set up outside of Seattle proper to accommodate such a large number of visitors. Web sites were created with the sole purpose of facilitating carpool rides to Seattle. For about nine months prior to the events, I received Call for Action e-mails from Students Against Sweatshops, Amnesty USA, Democratic Citizens, and even local Listservs. The "Battle of Seattle," as it was called by the media, was collectively organized by official groups, individual protesters, and also local businesses. Many participants such as Reverend Joe, an infamous U.S. protester, saw the real success in the kinds of people organizing, "It was truly beautiful to see business owners and gutter punks unite in voices and cry out together, 'we don't condone the WTO's worker-policies!'"[52]

The Seattle, Washington, and Manila, Philippines, mass protests were undoubtedly political, but there are many other actions which don't seem to be. Flash mobs are described as "an 'inexplicable crowd' . . . summoned to a particular location via e-mail or SMS to engage in a loosely choreographed activity."[53] They are described as wacky stunts, art, social revolution, and silly fun (Ray). The first flash mob

Fig. 5.

occurred in New York City in 2003 when "a hundred people grouped at Macy's to inquire about buying a giant 'love rug' for their 'suburban commune.' "⁵⁴

The organizer of this occurrence, known simply as Bill, claimed to have been experimenting in the power of mobilizing citizens to reclaim public space. Most often, word is spread when anonymous organizers send out e-mails and text messages and post on blogs specifying a date and time to meet. Within the next few months, flash mobs were occurring all over the world, mainly at large companies or corporate stores such as Starbucks, Toys R Us, or McDonald's, but also at high-end stores and pseudopublic places like street crosswalks. Bill and other participants seemed to initially be drawn to the transgressive nature of the events; a flash mob in Singapore for instance, simply self-identified as "urban misadventurers bent on breaking up the blah . . . in a city that is used to a routine of shopping and consuming."⁵⁵ These urban misadventurers who place themselves outside of the dominant corporate or commercial sphere are drawn to parody—to cultural pastiche. They are citizens who are used to the familiar jingle of adver-

Fig. 6.

tisements and who know marketing psychology; consequently, they use the master's tools to begin to dismantle the master's house.

Citizens ran with the idea all over the country in the next few months. Gay and lesbian students would organize to "flash mob" military recruiters on campus claiming "we really want to join the military, but we're gay!" and a variety of ethnic groups would target restaurants with known racial biases. By August of 2003, the concept had spread to Asia, the United Kingdom, Australia, Latin America, and Europe, with spaces on the Internet dedicated to the movement. As a social commentary on the lack of freedom of speech for journalists in Romania, over one hundred people gathered in Bucharest in front of national television with duct tape over their mouths. Brazilian citizens gathered on San Paulo's busiest street in front of a giant screen. The one hundred or so people all pointed remote controls at the screen, symbolically trying to turn the TV off.[56] The duration of flash mobs, contrary to the more traditional protests in Seattle or Manila, is usually less than ten minutes. While the venue and participants are always different, and according to the flash mob creation Web site, flashmobwiki, the situations are always chosen by "whoever comes up with an idea and spreads it"—the messages are clear. Citizens are mobilizing to nonviolently protest cultural concepts in society, and attempt to reclaim public space.

Not everyone sees flash mob and other ephemeral performances in a positive light. On Howard Rheingold's Smart Mob Web site he says, "One of the side-effects of this rather silly phenomenon has been the opportunity to tell journalists that whether or not today's fun and meaningless flash mob events evolve into anything more meaningful, people around the world have been awakened to the way online media afford collective action in the face to face world." On another Web discussion board, OnLisaReinsRadar, Rheingold says, "I think we need to see collective action in a broader and longer-term context than flash-crowds and mobs." In fact, entire discussion threads on Rheingold's Web site have been devoted to belittling flash mob occurrences as meaningless or silly acts. While Rheingold himself seems to try to see the benefits of flash mobs as spreading the word about the phenomena of smart mobs, I believe that they are both forms of techno mobs. Just as Critical Mass and Reclaim the Streets were earlier forms of techno mobs, so are smart mobs and flash mobs different pieces of the same techno mob movement.

The Relevance of Techno Mobs to Outsider Rhetoric

The performative and social actions of techno mobs are part of a larger call for mainstream culture jammers.[57] They can be traced back to the Situationists, Surrealism, and even further back to the protests of Cynics in ancient Greece. The concepts are not new; instead, the way they are being used is the revolutionary aspect of techno mobs. Participants in flash mobs and other performative events choose spaces that are driven by and drowning in consumerism. Members are cultural critics engaging in dialogues about the lack of true public spaces and the epidemic of consumerism, and they are catching the eye of the media through their subversive and ironic tactics. The members of technology-facilitated protests are also critics, but their aim is to directly change policies rather than raise awareness, which is the primary goal of technology-facilitated performances. George Packer proclaims that, "Internet democracy allows citizens to find one another directly, without phone trees or meetings of chapter organizations, and it amplifies their voices in the electronic storms or 'smart mobs' (masses summoned electronically) that it seems able to generate in a few hours."[58] Everyday citizens are using the technology of the twenty-first century in innovative ways to connect with each other and to gain insider-agency. By mobilizing in large numbers, with strangers, in attention-grabbing, often satirical, ways they are unsettling traditional power structures. At times, they affect public policy, and other times they ask audiences to reconsider the normalizing aspects of society.

There is much to be researched about the techno mob movement, as it is necessarily interdisciplinary. My current research has drawn me to look at how technology is changing literacy formation as well as how powerful voices are conceived in a technologically enhanced society. Clearly, as demonstrated by two new Internet bans in China[59] and the extension of the U.S. Patriot Act, 2005 has marked a year when governments are increasingly worried about the effectiveness of technologically organized protest and citizen dissent. This chapter serves as an introduction to performance as an outsider form of political protest as specifically illustrated through the techno-mob movement, but also calls for a closer look at independent media as a crucial, albeit untraditional site for rhetorical participation by citizens. There is currently an insurgence of independent media around the world, led by a focus on creation rather than consumption. The techno-mob movement is sustaining this effort, and encouraging citizens to assert their autonomy. The area of protest and performance certainly offers many possible sites for research, and precisely because political protest is a constantly fluid and changing phenomena, pinning it down long enough to write about it, and potentially stripping it of its ephemeral nature, may indeed be the most difficult task.

Notes

1. Leland M. Griffin, "The Rhetoric of Historical Movements," in *Readings on the Rhetoric of Social Protest*, ed. Stephen H. Browne and Charles E. Morris III (State College, PA.: Strata, 2001), 5.
2. Sonja K. Foss, *Rhetorical Criticism* (Prospect Heights, IL.: Waveland Press, 2004), 241.
3. Pippa Norris, *Digital Divide: Civic Engagement, Information Poverty and the Internet Worldwide* (Cambridge: Cambridge University Press, 2001). Benjamin M. Compaine, *The Digital Divide: Facing a Crisis or Creating a Myth* (Cambridge: MIT Press, 2001).
4. Robert Putnam, *Bowling Alone: The Collapse and Revival of American Community* (New York: Simon & Schuster, 2001).
5. Melissa Checker and Maggie Fishman, eds., *Local Actions. Cultural Activism, Power, and Public Life in America* (New York: Columbia University Press, 2004), 2.
6. Michael Hardt and Antonio Negri, *Multitude: War And Democracy In The Age Of Empire* (Cambridge: Harvard University Press, 2005), xiii–xiv.
7. Checker and Fishman, *Local Actions*, 2.
8. Howard Rheingold, *Smart Mobs: The Next Social Revolution* (Cambridge, MA: Perseus, 2002), 169.
9. Throughout this paper, I will draw upon Debord's conception of Spectacle as hypermediated reality, or reality which privileges appearances and image-based realities.
10. Baz Kershaw, *The Radical in Performance: Between Brecht and Baudrillard* (London: Routledge, 1999), 124.
11. Kershaw, *Radical in Performance*, 17.
12. Jill Lane, "Reverend Billy: Preaching, Protest, and Post-industrial Flânerie," in *The Performance Studies Reader*, ed. Henry Bial (London: Routledge, 2004), 300.
13. Angelique Haurgerud, "The Art of Protest," *Anthropology News* (November 2004): 4–5.
14. Jan Cohen-Cruz, "Motion of the Ocean," *Theater* 31, no. 3 (2001): 96.
15. Kershaw, *Radical in Performance*, 13.
16. Ibid., 84–85.
17. Ibid., 6.
18. Ibid., 16–17.
19. Guillermo Gómez-Peña, "Culturas-in-Extremis: Performing Against the Cultural Backdrop of the Mainstream Bizarre," in *The Performance Studies Reader*, ed. Henry Bial (London: Routledge, 2004), 288–89.
20. Ibid., 287–88.
21. Marvin Carlson, "What is Performance?" in Bial, *The Performance Studies Reader*, 71.
22. Kershaw, *Politics of Performance*, 68.
23. L. M. Bogad, *Electoral Guerilla Theatre: Radical Ridicule and Social Movements* (New York: Routledge, 2005), 5.
24. Ibid., 8.
25. Augusto Boal, *Games for Actors and Nonactors*, trans. Adrian Jackson (London: Routledge, 1992), xxx.
26. Ibid., 47.
27. Augusto Boal, *Legislative Theatre: Using Performance to Make Politics*, trans. Adrian Jackson (London: Routledge, 1998), 213.
28. Jan Cohen-Cruz, "Motion of the Ocean," *Theater* 31, no. 3 (2001): 101.

29. Ibid., 104.
30. Gómez-Peña, "Culturas-in-Extremis," 290.
31. Lizbeth Goodman, introduction to *The Routledge Reader in Politics and Performance*, ed. Lizbeth Goodman and Jane de Gay (London: Routledge, 2000), 2.
32. Alan Read, "Theatre and Everyday Life," in Goodman and de Gay, *Routledge Reader in Politics and Performance*, 189.
33. Griffin, "Rhetoric of Historical Movements," 7.
34. Robert Cathcart, "Movements: Confrontation as Rhetorical Form," in Browne and Morris, *Readings on the Rhetoric of Social Protest*, 103.
35. Robert L. Scott and Donald K. Smith, "The Rhetoric of Confrontation," in Browne and Morris, *Readings on the Rhetoric of Social Protest*, 32.
36. Joseph E. Davis, ed., *Stories of Change: Narrative and Social Movements* (New York: State University of New York Press, 2002), 6.
37. Kristen Kennedy, Cynic Rhetoric: The Ethics and Tactics of Resistance, *Rhetoric Review* 18 (1999): 30.
38. Ibid., 42.
39. Bruce Sterling, "Short History of the Internet," *Fantasy and Science Fiction* (February 1993): 5.
40. Armin Medosch, "Society in Ad-hoc Mode: Decentralised, Self Organising, Mobile," *European Journal of Higher Arts Education* 2 (2004): 2.
41. Howard Rheingold, *Smart Mobs: The Next Social Revolution* (Cambridge, MA: Perseus, 2002), 163.
42. Gilles Deleuze and Felix Guattari, *A Thousand Plateaus: Capitalism and Schizophrenia* (Minneapolis: University of Minnesota Press, 1987), 21.
43. Medosch, "Society in Ad-hoc Mode," 2.
44. Davis, *Stories of Change*, 7.
45. Todd Underwood, "Critical Mass Movement Has Colorful Past and an Enjoyable Future," *Chicago Daily Herald*, October 6, 2004.
46. Scott Millar, "Irish Anarchists Sow Seeds of Flower Power," *Sunday Times*, May 8, 2005, Home News Edition, Section 11.
47. Blending the philosophies of Guerilla Gardening and Reclaim the Street, an annual Park(ing) Day has popped up all over the United States since 2005. See http://www.parkingday.org.
48. Franklyn S. Haiman, "The Rhetoric of the Streets: Some Legal and Ethical Considerations," in Browne and Morris, *Readings on the Rhetoric of Social Protest*, 18.
49. Rheingold, *Smart Mobs*, 160.
50. Sandra Burton, "People Power Redux," *Time Asia*, (Jan. 29, 2001). Available from: http://www.time.com/time/asia/magazine/2001/0129/cover1.html.
51. Rheingold, *Smart Mobs*, 161.
52. "Just Say No To The WTO" (2005). Available from: Infoshop, www.infoshop.org.
53. Tom Vanderbilt, "Follow the Crowd: Tom Vanderbilt on New-Model Flash Mobs," *Artforum International* 42 (2004): 71.
54. Ibid.
55. Ibid.
56. "Flash Mobs: A New Protest Strategy?" (2003). Available from: Independent Media Center, www.indymedia.org.
57. See Adbusters magazine or go to www.adbusters.org for examples of and writings about culture jammers.
58. George Packer, "Smart-Mobbing the War," in *Media and Messages: Strategies and Readings in Public Rhetoric*, ed. Greg Barnhisel (New York: Pearson, 2005), 281.

59. Anick Jesdanun, "New Bans Show China's Concerns About Tech," *Washington Post*, October 1, 2005. Available from http://www.*washingtonpost.com*.

Bibliography

Battle of Seattle Photo (image). *Infoshop.* Available from http://www.infoshop.org.org/octo/wto-pix3.html.

Boal, Augusto. *Games for Actors and Nonactors.* Translated by Adrian Jackson. London: Routledge, 1992.

———. *Legislative Theatre: Using Performance to Make Politics.* Translated by Adrian Jackson. London: Routledge, 1998.

Bogad, L. M. *Electoral Guerilla Theatre: Radical Ridicule and Social Movements.* New York: Routledge, 2005.

Burton, Sandra. "People Power Redux." *Time Asia*, January 29, 2001. Available from http://www.time.com/time/asia/magazine/2001/0129/cover1.html.

Carlson, Marvin. "What is Performance?" In *The Performance Studies Reader*, edited by Henry Bial. London: Routledge, 2004.

Cathcart, Robert. "Movements: Confrontation as Rhetorical Form," in *Readings on the Rhetoric of Social Protest*, edited by Stephen H. Browne and Charles E. Morris III. State College, PA: Strata, 2001.

Checker, Melissa, and Maggie Fishman, eds. *Local Actions: Cultural Activism, Power, and Public Life in America.* New York: Columbia University Press, 2004.

Cohen-Cruz, Jan. "Motion of the Ocean." *Theater* 31, no. 3 (2001).

Critical Mass (image). *Wikipedia.* Available from http://en.wikipedia.org/wiki/Critical_Mass.

Davis, Joseph E., ed. *Stories of Change: Narrative and Social Movements.* New York: State University of New York Press, 2002.

Deleuze, Gilles, and Felix Guattari. *A Thousand Plateaus: Capitalism and Schizophrenia.* Minneapolis: University of Minnesota Press, 1987.

"Flash Mobs: A New Protest Strategy?" *Independent Media Center* (2003). Available from www.indymedia.org.

Foss, Sonja K. *Rhetorical Criticism.* Prospect Heights, IL: Waveland Press, 2004.

Gómez-Peña, Guillermo. "Culturas-in-Extremis: Performing Against the Cultural Backdrop of the Mainstream Bizarre." In *The Performance Studies Reader*, edited by Henry Bial. London: Routledge, 2004.

Goodman, Lizbeth. Introduction to *The Routledge Reader in Politics and Performance*, edited by Lizbeth Goodman and Jane de Gay. London: Routledge, 2000.

Griffin, Leland M. "The Rhetoric of Historical Movements." In *Readings on the Rhetoric of Social Protest*, edited by Stephen H. Browne and Charles E. Morris III. State College, PA.: Pennsylvania: Strata, 2001.

Guerilla Gardening (image). *Times-Up.* Available from http://www.times-up.org/gardengrow.php.

Haiman, Franklyn S. "The Rhetoric of the Streets: Some Legal and Ethical Considerations." In *Readings on the Rhetoric of Social Protest*, edited by Stephen H. Browne and Charles E. Morris III. State College, Pennsylvania: Strata, 2001.

Hardt, Michael, and Antonio Negri. *Multitude: War And Democracy In The Age Of Empire*. Cambridge: Harvard University Press, 2005.
Haurgerud, Angelique. "The Art of Protest." *Anthropology News* (November 2004).
"Just Say No To The WTO." *Infoshop* (2005). Available from: www.infoshop.org.
Kennedy, Kristen. "Cynic Rhetoric: The Ethics and Tactics of Resistance." *Rhetoric Review* 18 (1999).
Kershaw, Baz. *The Politics of Performance: Radical Theatre as Cultural Intervention*. London: Routledge, 1992.
———. *The Radical in Performance: Between Brecht and Baudrillard*. London: Routledge, 1999.
Lane, Jill. "Reverend Billy: Preaching, Protest, and Post-industrial Flânerie." In *The Performance Studies Reader*, edited by Henry Bial. London: Routledge, 2004.
Millar, Scott. "Irish Anarchists Sow Seeds of Flower Power." *Sunday Times*, May 8, 2005, home news edition, sec. 11.
Medosch, Armin. "Society in Ad-hoc Mode: Decentralised, Self Organising, Mobile." *European Journal of Higher Arts Education* 2 (2004).
NY Flash Mob (image). *Wikipedia*. Available from http://en.wikipedia.org/wiki/Flash_mob.
Packer, George. "Smart-Mobbing the War." In *Media and Messages: Strategies and Readings in Public Rhetoric*, edited by Greg Barnhisel. New York: Pearson, 2005.
Read, Alan. "Theatre and Everyday Life." In *The Routledge Reader in Politics and Performance*, edited by Lizbeth Goodman and Jane de Gay. London: Routledge, 2000.
Rheingold, Howard. *Smart Mobs: The Next Social Revolution*. Cambridge: Perseus, 2002.
Scott, Robert L. and Donald K. Smith. "The Rhetoric of Confrontation." In *Readings on the Rhetoric of Social Protest*, edited by Stephen H. Browne and Charles E. Morris III. State College, PA: Pennsylvania: Strata, 2001.
Sterling, Bruce. "Short History of the Internet." *Fantasy and Science Fiction* (February 1993).
Underwood, Todd. "Critical Mass Movement Has Colorful Past and an Enjoyable Future." *Chicago Daily Herald*, October 6, 2004.
Vanderbilt, Tom. "Follow the Crowd: Tom Vanderbilt on New-Model Flash Mobs." *Artforum International* 42 (2004).

Strategic Essentialism and the Representation of the Natural: The Case of Ecofeminist/Scientist Wangari Maathai

RAYMOND OENBRING

Introduction

WITH ONLY SLIGHTLY GREATER FANFARE IN THE INTERNATIONAL press than that she caused by presenting controversial views on the provenance of AIDS at a press conference a day later, Wangari Maathai, Kenyan environmentalist, political activist, leader of the influential pan-African Non-Governmental Organization NGO the Green Belt Movement, and the first East African woman to receive a PhD, was proclaimed the first female African Nobel Peace Prize laureate on October 8, 2004. Speaking to the press in Nairobi on the ninth, Maathai claimed, echoing a common belief in sub-Saharan Africa, that HIV was created by a scientist in the West in order to kill off Africans. Journalists quoted Maathai as stating that: "some say that AIDS came from the monkeys, and I doubt that because we have been living with monkeys [since] time immemorial; others say it was a curse from God, but I say it cannot be that.... Us black people are dying more than any other people in this planet.... It's true that there are some people who create agents to wipe out other people.... In fact it [the HIV virus] is created by a scientist for biological warfare."[1]

As could be expected, several conservative international publications quickly derided Maathai's view on the provenance of AIDS as inconsistent with science. Op-ed writers in the *Spectator* and the *Sunday Telegraph* decried Maathai's "globophobia"[2] and suggested that she "looks set to join the Crackpot Club."[3] The *Economist*, alluding to her PhD in veterinary anatomy, excoriated Maathai for disavowing the findings of science, suggesting that "coming from one of the first women in east Africa to earn a doctorate, Ms. Maathai's views might be seen as surprising. Coming from a freshly crowned Nobel laureate, they might be considered inexcusable."[4] The *Economist* article, furthermore, connected Maathai's controversial views on AIDS with those of well-known AIDS skeptic South African president Thabo Mbeki.[5]

While Maathai and Mbeki[6] share the laudable common goal of drawing the world's attention to the pandemic of poverty—in addition to the pandemic of AIDS—ravaging sub-Saharan Africa, Maathai's utterance in the October 9, 2004, press conference has garnered interest on an international scale arguably on par (in current visibility, not total media attention over time) with that of Mbeki's statements on the origin of HIV/AIDS even after years being South Africa's president. This interest is, undoubtedly, due to Maathai's utterance's tight rhetorical packaging. Mbeki routinely expresses his complaints against the West's cultural and institutional subjugation of Africa in the highly-coded and verbose language of postcolonial criticisms. Maathai, however, created in her utterance a strategic and highly emotive fabrication (read: lie[7]), thereby garnering the attention of the international media.[8]

As this chapter will suggest, however, the October 9 press conference has not been the only time in Maathai's activist career in which she has promoted nonstandard representations of scientific concepts and natural objects (i.e., differing from those of the Western research establishment) for the purpose of building international awareness of her project. Indeed, Maathai routinely represents natural objects in ways that facilitate communication with Western activists and progressives. Maathai, I would like to suggest, frequently represents nature in a manner that demonstrates greater interest in building communicative bridges with the West than offering the most scientifically accurate representation of natural processes and objects. That is to say, one can defuse possible critiques of Maathai's seeming unscientific statements by locating her representations within a broader strategic project. Maathai, this chapter will suggest, like the promoters of science and technology, desires to put nature in the service of humankind rather than, as some postmodern Western environmentalists wish to do, extricate all human cultivation from the natural world.

In order to further these claims, I shall, after taking some time building up a theoretical framework, analyze a handful of selected texts from Maathai's activist work. As a rhetorician of science, I am primarily interested in how scientists in various situations use language to represent nature in the achievement of particular ends. As such, I will largely limit the scope of my analysis to Maathai's representation of *the natural*. Of course, rhetoricians, particularly those interested in notions of "strategic essentialism," should have much more to say about Maathai's use of language in order to navigate the discursive divide between the developing world and the West; this chapter has no pretensions of being the final word on Maathai's rhetorical formations—or even the strategies she uses to raise awareness of her work in the West. As suggested, in my textual rhetorical analysis I shall specifically focus on how Maathai frames and represents certain scientific concepts and issues, from the status of nature and biological organisms to the use of biotechnology, in her utterances specifically addressed to the West. The texts that this chapter will analyze, ranging from an op-ed in the *New York Times*,[9] to an official Green Belt Movement communiqué,[10] to her book *The Green Belt Movement*,[11] describing activities of her NGO, and to her recent memoir *Unbowed*,[12] demonstrate Maathai at work selling her movement to the West, speaking to the postmodern left in ways that enact—potentially strategically—some of its prominent essentialist and unscientific myths.[13]

This chapter's most important contribution to rhetorical theory and, furthermore, studies of outsider rhetorical agency, I would like to suggest, is its move to extend the domain of rhetorical analyses of outsider appropriations of the language of power beyond traditional hegemonic discourses[14] and to include institutionalized Western progressive discourses. Unlike the traditional critical school of marginal rhetor discourse appropriation that argues for the political efficacy of momentary carnivalesque subversions of the formulations of the hegemon (e.g., "culture jamming")—a somewhat dubious claim, the theory of outsider rhetor discourse appropriation promoted by this chapter instead looks for moments of obviously efficacious rhetorical navigation across the discursive divide between the developing world and the West.

Wangari Maathai and The Green Belt Movement

After completing the remarkable dual feats of obtaining her BS. and MS. from American universities (Mount St. Scholastica College [1964] and University of Pittsburgh [1966]) despite being raised in a rural Kenyan farming family, Maathai returned to Kenya, finishing a PhD in anatomy at the University of Nairobi in 1971, thereby becoming the first East or Central African woman to receive a doctoral degree.[15] In 1976, she was elected chair of the University of Nairobi's Department of Veterinary Anatomy. The early and mid seventies were also a formative time in Maathai's activist career. At that time, Maathai worked as the chairman of the board for Nairobi's Environment Liaison Center (ELC) and became intimately involved at a high level with coordinating action between NGOs (both Western and local) and

United Nations (UN) system. Maathai first promoted large-scale tree planting operations, the hallmark of her current NGO, in 1974 while working on a political campaign for her then husband. Maathai's original reasons for promoting tree planting were, however, very practically focused and deeply intertwined with the immediate goals of her husband's election campaign; as Maathai acknowledges in *The Green Belt Movement*, her main reason for organizing tree planting in the early days of her then NGO Envirocare was to create jobs for rural people.[16]

Indeed, it took several years of interaction with Western activists before Maathai began to present tree planting as a panacea. By early 1977, when Maathai moved to the upper echelons of another, more influential Kenyan NGO, the National Council of Women of Kenya (NCWK), she had developed two other central reasons to promote tree planting (both, however, still largely focused on concrete issues of human health and nourishment): trees prevent soil erosion and desertification; and, in regions where people rely heavily on wood for cooking (as was the case with Kenya in those days), increased tree density reduces malnutrition and hunger by allowing (and speeding up) the preparation of food. As Maathai acknowledges, her increasing concern with environmentally focused, rather than human-focused, critiques in this time period was largely the product of her participation in the United Nation's first conference on Human Settlement in Vancouver, Canada, in June 1976. Maathai's account in *The Green Belt Movement* of her intellectual and activist development during the conference makes it clear; she came to the conference concerned with "improved societal living conditions" and left "calling for . . . more trees and green vegetation."[17] Maathai's increased focus on explicitly environmental critiques while working at NCWK led her to organize the first "Save the Land Harambee,"[18] a single day massive tree plant that later developed into a standing organization: the Green Belt Movement.

The scope of the Green Belt Movement's achievements in the past three decades is truly impressive; the organization has planted over thirty million trees in Kenya and across sub-Saharan Africa, developing six thousand working tree nurseries.[19] Another truly remarkable aspect of the Green Belt Movement is the uniquely progressive organizational structure that Maathai has developed. Unlike many NGOs, the GBM does not promote development or environmental conservation exclusively; GBM believes in sustainable development and is committed to the idea that development and conservation can go hand in hand. Maathai's ability to fuse environmental critiques, a notion of unique interest to Western audiences, with the goal of social development has, I would like to suggest, been central in helping Maathai develop and maintain her profile in the West. Indeed, it is interesting to note that Maathai's Nobel citation puts great emphasis on her work to integrate environmental protection with social development.[20]

Central to the implementation of GBM's sustainable development goals has been the organization's grassroots structure. Unlike most NGOs operating in Africa, GBM is not a branch of a foreign organization; its headquarters are located in Nairobi.[21] Moreover, the vast majority of the members of the organization are rural women.[22] While GBM's primary raison d'être remains the planting of trees in order to combat soil erosion, the organization has in recent years expanded its goals to include critiques of gender, class, and power relations, transforming GBM into a de facto social movement.[23]

As a sub-Saharan African woman, Maathai's success in garnering the attention of international institutions suggests that she must not only be a skilled activist but must also be a rhetorically adept communicator. Indeed, in her memoir *Unbowed*, Maathai at several points demonstrates a remarkable degree of rhetorical awareness. Maathai, for example, critically and carefully analyzes Kenyan media discourse surrounding a specific flare-up of strife between GBM and the Kenyan government, trenchantly scrutinizing how both she and actors in the government were represented and how their various statements played out in the pages of local Kenyan newspapers during the controversy.[24] At several points in *Unbowed*, Maathai, furthermore, directly comments on how working with local and international media was integral to GBM's achievements.[25] Maathai credits her work with the media with increasing her profile both locally and in the West, suggesting, for example, that "I always made sure the press was with us, so they could record what was happening and take the news to Kenyans and the world."[26] Maathai also at several points in *Unbowed* connects her increasing profile abroad with greater success as an activist at home, stating, for example, that "[international] awards brought attention to our efforts, as well as making news at home. Both helped protect me from increasing criticism and threats I faced in subsequent years from the Kenyan government."[27]

Strategic Essentialism and Rhetorical Practice

I would like to suggest that Gayatri Spivak's familiar notion of 'strategic essentialism" may be of particular value when analyzing Maathai's representations of natural objects. Spivak, in her 1985 essay "Subaltern Studies: Deconstructing Historiography," praises the Indian subaltern studies group for crafting coherent and one-sided narratives to describe subaltern history and consciousness. Spivak suggests that the subaltern studies group's work demonstrates "a *strategic* use of positivist essentialism in a scrupulously visible political interest."[28] As Spivak's quote intimates, the writers of strategic essentialisms self-consciously acknowledge that what they are providing are oversimplified narratives and/or cultural myths that make affectations of direct access to truth. Consciously avoiding the complete moral relativism of some versions of poststructuralism, these writers seek to contest the supposed superiority of the hegemonic formulations such as masculinity and the West by privileging and mythologizing the cultural practices of marginalized peoples.[29]

In many ways, the strategic deployment of essentialist rhetorics ask marginalized peoples to affect, for the audience of the hegemon, the pretensions of access to absolute Truth, destabilizing the West's and masculinity's claims to naturalness. In the academic literature, notions of strategic essentialism have been deployed by numerous authors describing approaches used by marginalized groups seeking to contest the privileged status of the West, the patriarchy, and/or whiteness. McPhail's "From Complicity to Coherence: Rereading the Rhetoric of Afrocentricity,"[30] for example, describes how the strategic essentialism of Afrocentrism serves to challenge the perceived normativity of Eurocentric ideologies.[31]

In recent decades, notions of ecofeminism, a field of thought fusing the critiques of a myriad of critical frameworks including environmentalism, feminism, postcolonialism, and (oftentimes) Marxism, have received a great deal of attention in the Western academic left. As a discourse, one of ecofeminism's main projects is to valorize the work of females (especially those working in developing countries) who, like Maathai,[32] challenge everything from government corruption, to female subjugation, to environmental degradation. While emerging from a deconstructive critical framework, ecofeminist ideas, by their symbolic elevation of marginalized peoples, and, moreover, their frequently hagiographic descriptions of developing world feminists, naturally promote essentialist notions of the purity of nonhegemonic, feminine, indigenous, and nontechnical knowledges. Jackson's "Radical Environmental Myths,"[33] for example, criticizes Western academics promoting notions of ecofeminism for providing oversimplified portraits of "indigenous" femininity, arguing that "ecofeminism seems ... to be beached on a combination of essentialized female loving and caring qualities, the invention of feminized spirituality and the 'true for me' approach to myths and knowledge."[34]

Sturgeon's "Ecofeminist Appropriations and Transnational Environmentalisms"[35] argues that Western academic ecofeminists' essentialized depictions of non-Western women and their supposed greater intimacy with nature can, in fact, be a valuable political tool to facilitate communication between marginalized peoples and Western progressives. By describing the language of ecofeminism as a possible political tool for the empowerment of developing world activists, allowing them to "speak" to the West, Sturgeon posits ecofeminism as rhetoric to be deployed for strategic purposes rather than just as an alternative critical epistemology.

As a scientist, Maathai recognizes that there is nothing correct, pure, or transcendent about any particular way of being for biological organisms; she understands them as technologies—the collective products of their DNA sequences—sequences that have constantly been changing through the action of natural selection since the beginnings of life on earth. This scientific understanding of nature is, of course, markedly different from the holistic and essentialist view of organisms that permeates much postmodern environmental discourse.[36] One of the great villains in contemporary holistic environmental discourse is, of course, genetically modified (GM) food. As a whole, anti-GM activism relies largely on appeals to the notion that exists a *natural* or *true* prototypical form to species—a form from which GM organisms, as they have been *tampered with* by humans, deviate. Such an understanding necessarily construes organisms not as a complex set of technologies, charges, and rates of flow as scientists do, but rather as beings either *true* or *false*. Scientists, however, acknowledge that the altering of crops' genomes, a genetic engineering of sorts, has been going on in agriculture since time immemorial (see, for example, Pinstrup-Andersen and Schiøler);[37] every year farmers have retained seeds from the heartiest plants to sow the following year.[38]

I would like to suggest that in her descriptions of nature Maathai frequently engages in rhetorical moves similar to those that have been described under the label of strategic essentialism. That is to say, there exists a more than circumstantial degree of evidence to suggest that Maathai may, in her descriptions of nature, overlook her other, self-consciously recognized "more correct" understandings, for, as Spivak puts it, "a scrupulously visible political interest." Maathai, I would like to suggest, recognizes Western progressive discourses' nonmaterially driven respect for living beings and nature—a respect that seems to imbue organisms and landscape with a nonscientific, transcendent essence.[39] Maathai echoes these sentiments quite clearly in her memoir, noticing distinct differences between the romanticized "holstic" understanding of scientific concepts espoused by Western activists and the understanding of scientific concepts she had developed both through her training as a biologist and through her work as a developing world activist concerned with day-to-day basic human needs. Describing her early encounters with the ideas of Western activists, Maathai suggests that

> for me, a biologist who had grown up in a rural area where our daily lives depended on the health of the environment, the issues raised at the Liason Centre were not completely strange. For example, when we discussed biological diversity, my study of genetics was relevant. But a great deal of the information I was exposed to through the meetings at UNEP, books and articles, and discussions with people working in environmental NGOs in different countries was new to me. Much of it dealt with natural science from a holistic perspective.[40]

As one can see from this quote, Maathai, in the early days of her activist career, recognized a clear distinction between the holistic and romanticized view of nature promoted by Western activists and the scientific understanding of nature she was familiar with as a biologist. Although she was, even at that time, sympathetic to the holistic view of nature promoted by Western activists, suggesting it to be "not completely strange," she still makes a sharp distinction between the view of nature promoted by Western activists and that of natural science. It is, however, interesting to note that this quote come from a text aimed at a Western audience that, as a whole, wholeheartedly embraces the rhetoric of holism. For example, several of the chapter titles in *Unbowed* (e.g., "Cultivation"; "Seeds of Change"; and "Epilogue: Canopy of Hope") suggest Maathai's development as an activist to have followed a narrative of organic growth.

Textual Rhetorical Analysis

Nielsen et al., in their "Traditional blue and modern green resistance,"[41] recognize two separate strands of thought in Western anti-biotechnology discourse: the preindustrial, Mephistopheles critique, suggesting that tampering with nature is a Faustian bargain; and the Frankenstein critique, evoking the possibilities of biotechnology one day manufacturing a potentially dangerous monster which could cause great havoc for its progenitors. Maathai's 1998 Green Belt Movement press release "The Linkage between Patenting of Life Forms, Genetic Engineering, and Food Insecurity," now available through several Western activist Web sites including the United Kingdom-based Agricultural Biodiversity Coalition, is an excellent example of Maathai framing a representation of nature in order to appeal to the interests of a Western audience. That is to say, Maathai promotes, through the agency of the press release, a multifaceted critique of the workings of Western power agents in Africa that, by virtue of its topic, is of specific interest to a certain common type of Western activist, but that, underneath, the text has little to do with the specific interests of the groups to which the utterance appeals to on the surface (i.e., the text has little to do with Western Mephistopheles or Frankenstein critiques).

Although framing her text as an argument against the expanded use of biotechnology and GM crops, Maathai uses the utterance as an opportunity to promote a far-reaching critique of Western neo-colonialist activities in the developing world. Maathai argues specifically that "traders have appropriated other people's resources, including human 'resources' and territories, as free goods for centuries, usually by buying-off misinformed, unsuspecting or corrupted nationals. Biotechnology and patenting of life forms is now the new frontier for conquest, and Africa ought to be wary because a history of colonialism and exploitation is repeating itself."[42]

In this quote, Maathai frames the operation of contemporary Western interests using notions taken directly from the colonial era, describing biotechnology as a "new frontier for conquest." By invoking notions such as "traders," Maathai develops an extended metaphor, representing Africa as space on the verge of being thrown back into the power relations of the colonial era. Furthermore, by locating the use of biotechnology within what she sees as the West's centuries-old project of expansion and dominance in Africa, Maathai equates contemporary battles against GM crops in Africa with the battles for independence from their colonial masters that Africans fought decades before.

As suggested before, in the piece it is clear that Maathai's concerns with GM crops have nothing to do with the purity-nostalgic Frankenstein and Mephistopheles critiques that dominate the anti-GM discourse of the West.[43] Instead, Maathai's concerns with GM crops have to deal with African farmers' loss of sovereignty over their land and its products by planting GM seeds bought from Western multinationals. Maathai suggests that "the idea that African farmers should have to buy seeds, developed from their own biological materials, from transnational corporations, because such companies have given themselves the exclusive rights to those seeds, is outrageous. The rights and the capacity of communities to feed themselves would be completely undermined, if industry managed to assert its self-given rights."[44]

As one can see in the quote, Maathai makes a strong claim to the sovereignty of African farmers over the products of their land, describing the seeds of their farms as "their own biological materials." Maathai, furthermore, opposes the "right and capacity of communities to feed themselves" with Western multinationals' illegitimate "self-given rights."

While framing the text as merely an argument against expanding the use of biotechnology, it is clear that Maathai's main goal in the text is to promote the cause of sub-Saharan Africans left marginalized in the global economy; Maathai acts as an advocate, telling the story of those that cannot "speak" to a Western audience that could not otherwise hear them. To do this effectively, Maathai hides her explicitly political and structural critique in the Trojan horse of anti-GM discourse. While Maathai could have expressed similar concerns by deploying any one of a host of critical perspectives regarding Western involvement in Africa (e.g., multinationals' profit-driven motivations for working in developing countries, and the West's frequent support of nondemocratic regimes friendly toward business interests), Maathai's framing of her text as a statement against biotech and GM foods makes her utterance accord with the goals of a widespread form of activism within the postmodern left. One could, furthermore, argue that this reframing has increased the overall circulation of her critique.

Maathai's rhetorical strategy in the press release allows her to build communicative bridges to the West because it both arouses and involves a widely held holistic essentialism within the contemporary West: anti-GM discourse. While her goals are to draw attention to the material, structural plight of sub-Saharan Africans, Maathai's framing of her utterance as against GM foods allows her to access the institutions of the West. Maathai's seeming antiscientism (that is to say, her denigration of a technology nearly universally accepted by the West's scientific research establishment) is now a twice moot point; she merely expresses her concerns within an antiscientific discourse now dominant in the postmodern left in order to converse with Western progressives, and, moreover, speaks out, justifiably, against a technology which would serve only to make money for Western multinationals and further African material and cultural subjugation.

On multiple occasions in *The Green Belt Movement*, Maathai exalts the nontechnical, "indigenous" knowledge of rural peoples employed by GBM to plant trees, seemingly demonstrating disdain for the findings and products of science. Maathai, for example, discusses several examples in which the local women employed to plant trees eschewed the technical knowledge that they received in their training from GBM. Although GBM's foresters had taught the women a handful of technical skills, the woman were not able to deploy these skills effectively when performing the planting and cultivating. Subsequently, many of the trees that the women planted died. The women were, however, much more successful when they started to deploy their local, nonscientific knowledge when planting and cultivating the seedlings. Using inspiring language, Maathai describes this change as a "revolution."[45] To account for the women's greater success once they disregarded the scientific approach, Maathai, however, invokes the somewhat problematical notions of "common—and perhaps women—sense,"[46] seemingly describing the women as having been imbued with a unique form of technical knowledge as part of their essential nature as women.

Maathai's exalting of nonhegemonic knowledges does not mean, however, that she disavows the advancements of Western science. Rather, she is describing a unique situation in which logistical, practical, and time constraints all led to a realization that reliance upon and promotion of local knowledge seemed the best planting strategy for the NGO to deploy. Indeed, as the women largely lacked formal educations, and as the organization lacked the resources to give the women extensive training in the technical knowledge of forestry science, encouraging the women to rely on the knowledge of agricultural practices they had learned from their immediate, farming-based culture proved to be the best practice; that is, it was the strategy that seemed most likely, given the organization's financial and logistical constraints, to eventually produce the most and the healthiest trees.

Although introducing the notion of "women sense," Maathai does not suggest that the women's essential nature itself magically promoted the seedlings' growth. Maathai, moreover, does not suggest that the women's essential nature as females immediately gave them access to transcendent truths regarding the best practices to use when tree planting. Instead, Maathai praises the women for their ingenuity in developing practices for cultivating the seedlings, stating that "women substituted broken pots for seedbeds, used granaries or any raised ground to keep seeds and seedlings away from domestic animals and learned to observe the flowering cycle of plants so they could harvest seeds, and also how to differentiate weeds from seedlings."[47] This respect for the invention of new knowledge and technical practices, I would like to suggest, demonstrates Maathai's esteem for both instrumentalism and the cumulative accumulation of knowledge by a culture over time, both hallmarks of a scientific perspective. Therefore, by praising the knowledge of the women, Maathai is not showing disrespect for the products of science; she is instead lauding a technological system that was most effective in allowing her NGO to perform its goals given the logistical constraints of governing her organization's work.

Maathai, furthermore, has yet another reason for emphasizing the valuable work done by the rural African women, construing their abilities using an essentialist concept like "women sense": it allows her to further the hegemon-challenging mythology she crafts, potentially strategically, throughout her activist work. As a sub-Saharan African female with a truly inspiring story leading an NGO that employs developing world women to plant trees, Maathai (and the GBM as a whole) naturally excite a whole host of romanticized essentialisms in play in the discourse of the postmodern left. Taking advantage of these romanticized essentialisms by privileging all things female and all things local in her rhetorical formations, Maathai, in her overarching rhetorical project, constructs a hegemon-challenging mythology inspiring to both local members of the GBM and the elements in the West.

In addition to exalting indigenous knowledges, Maathai also demonstrates obvious preference for "native" organisms. Speaking of GBM's promotion of the planting of indigenous African trees rather than the "exotic" species that were encouraged for short-term economic gain (for the powerful) under the project of colonialism, Maathai states in *The Green Belt Movement* that

> both the colonial and current education system promoted exotic biological diversity of trees and crops at the expense of indigenous species. . . . This is because the exotic species of trees such as eucalyptus (from the southern hemisphere) and the pines (from the temperate zones of the northern hemisphere) were (and are still) promoted for rapid economic returns. . . . Even in forestry schools and research institutions, exotic species continue to receive preference over local ones. Convincing farmers to plant indigenous trees has been challenging. However, with persuasion and constant education, farmers have begun to appreciate the short and long-term economic value of the indigenous trees.[48]

As this quote suggests, Maathai argues for the economic value of indigenous trees without satisfactory explanation as to why indigenous trees are superior to the exotic trees introduced by colonial agriculture. While biologists recognize that introduced exotic species can sometimes have deleterious effects on local biodiversity and the health of human populations (see, for example, Mack et al.'s "Biotic Invasions"[49]), the introduction and cultivation of nonnative species for the purposes of agriculture is a ubiquitous practice nearly universally accepted by scientists and agronomists.[50] Most scientists, moreover, recognize that, despite the existence of both complex webs of interdependence between species in biological communities and highly refined and specified organismal niches, nothing ontologically makes a "native" species a more "natural" or "correct" member of a biological community than a nonnative one.[51]

As such, Maathai's preference for indigenous species would, at first, seem to suggest that she is imbuing native species with a spiritual essence. This privileging of the indigenous seems to pit Maathai against all large-scale agriculture and forestry, suggesting that she is against the instrumental use of nature for human purposes. While Maathai's stated preference for indigenous and local species seems to endorse uncritically postmodernist progressive purity-nostalgia, I would like to suggest that this may be yet another example of Maathai crafting a strategic-essentialist rhetoric for the purposes of facilitating communication between herself and the West. While one could certainly charge Maathai in the above passage of adopting an unscientific perspective critical of all large scale human cultivation of the natural world, I would like to suggest that her reasons for expressing preference for native species are consistent with both the findings of science and scientific instrumentalist logic and stem from a genuine desire to increase the economic standing of rural Africans.

Sturgeon's "Ecofeminist Appropriations and Transnational Environmentalisms" argues that the left's recent coronation of grand notions of "the Environment" has served as a valuable organizing framework from which to advance a myriad of progressive critiques of the current state of the globe. Sturgeon states that "in [the contemporary] political context, 'the environment" has served . . . as a medium for the connection of critiques of militarism, sexism, capitalism, and neo-colonialism, similar to the way militarism functioned in the 1970s and 1980s."[52] As the quote suggests, invoking grand notions of "the environment" can serve to coordinate various disparate social and political problems into an intelligible—and thereby potentially politically malleable—whole. Drawing upon this rhetorical strategy, Maathai similarly connects environmental degradation with a host of undesirable results of global scope, stating in a 2004 *New York Times* op-ed that "unless we properly manage resources like forests, water, land, minerals and oil, we will not win the fight against poverty. And there will not be peace. Old conflicts will rage on and new resource wars will erupt unless we change the path we are on."[53] As this quote suggests, Maathai directly connects environmental degradation with a host of problems including poverty, social decline, and war.

Maathai's connection of environmental management directly with many of the most vexing social problems plaguing sub-Saharan Africa, and the globe as a whole, may seem a bit tenuous, and, moreover, her prescriptions for the world may seem rather romanticized, unscientific, and even naive. However, as suggested by the GBM's formal mission statement, Maathai's more lofty goals like the advancement of females and other marginalized peoples—those goals that can participate in arousing Western progressive mythologies—remain secondary effects of the primary objective of tree planting; GBM wishes "to mobilize consciousness for self-determination, equity, improved livelihood securities and environmental conservation *using trees as the entry point*" (my emphasis).[54] Desertification is a real phenomenon, a phenomenon that prevents sub-Saharan farmers from engaging in their livelihood. Although probably not the panacea that Maathai sometimes romanticizes it to be, tree planting, is, certainly, a task that actually serves directly to advance the material situation of sub-Saharan African peasants. If, indeed, it is true that increasing forest density in the developing world leads those living there to more secure and prosperous livelihoods, then Maathai's suggestion that environmental conservation can, in the long run, function as a tool to advance a myriad of progressive transformative changes seems much more plausible.

Although tree planting in sub-Saharan Africa is an act with material benefits, it is also a symbolic act. Maathai highlights both the powerful symbolism of the act of tree planting and the feelings of autonomy and efficacy that tree planting brings in a 1999 interview in the *UNESCO Courier*, stating: "*The act of planting trees conveys a simple message*. It suggests that at the very least you can plant a tree and improve your habitat. It increases people's awareness that they *can take control of their environment*, which is the first step toward greater participation in society"[55] (emphasis added).

Maathai's statement, seemingly equally applicable in both Western and developing countries, emphasizes that the simple act of tree planting can function to affirm the planter's control over their environment, inspiring them to engage in broader progressive action. GBM's tree planting, moreover, functions as a metonymy, standing in symbolically for Maathai's NGO's entire project. (After all, the organization's name is the Green Belt Movement.) This metonymy, seemingly imbuing trees with a spiritual, unscientific essence, is a prominent element of the hegemon-challenging mythology that Maathai engenders, potentially strategically, through the rhetorical formulations of her activist work. What's more, the tree metonymy serves as yet another simplifying and organizing symbol—a symbol that facilitates communication between Maathai and the West.

Conclusion: Appropriation and the Language of Power

Scholars broadly acknowledge that marginalized peoples must learn to converse in the language of power if they wish to gain agency within the West's institutional apparatuses; as there exists no institutionally promoted subject position in the discourse of the West from which an outsider can articulate their concerns, marginalized peoples must affect a Western voice in order to promote institutional and structural change. Numerous feminist and cultural theorists[56] have, of course, proposed a possible way out of the quagmire of powerlessness: the appropriation of the genres and forms of the language of power. These theorists suggest that outsiders must, in order to be heard, articulate their concerns within the available discursive forms of the West.

As a sub-Saharan African woman, Maathai's reception of the Nobel Peace Prize demonstrates that she is not only a marvelous activist working for truly beneficial change, but also reveals that she is an extraordinary rhetor. As this chapter has argued, there is a more than circumstantial amount of evidence to suggest that Maathai frames her representation of natural and scientific objects in a strategic manner; while her representations of nature directed to Western progressive audiences may not always be scientifically "correct," she effectively harnesses the mythological apparatus of her Western audience. That is to say, she has exploited "the reality effect" of her nonstandard representations of nature in order to increase the interest of her Western audience.

Notes

1. "Kenyan Nobel peace laureate claims AIDS virus deliberately created," *Agence France Presse*, October 9, 2004.
2. Ross Clark, "Globophobia; A weekly survey of world restrictions on freedom and free trade," *Spectator*, October 30, 2004.
3. Robert Matthews, "And this year's backstabbing prize goes to," *Sunday Telegraph* (London), October 17, 2004.
4. "The woman who planted trees; Kenya's Nobel laureate," *Economist*, October 16, 2004.
5. President Mbeki widely promotes his suspicion that HIV is not the cause of AIDS, instead suggesting that rampant poverty is the primary cause of the pandemic ravishing his country (see, for example, Mbeki's 2002 African National Congress press release "Health, human dignity and partners for global poverty reduction"). What's more, Mbeki believes that hysteria over AIDS is a racist tool used by the West and whites in his country in order to stigmatize black Africans as a whole; according to Mbeki, AIDS is a neocolonialist strategy deployed by the West in order to maintain black Otherness. For example, as recently as October 2004, when asked explicitly in South Africa's parliament by an opposition Member of Parliament whether he believes that HIV causes AIDS, Mbeki avoided directly answering the question, stating instead: "I for my part will not keep quiet while others whose minds have been corrupted by the disease of racism accuse us, the black people of South Africa, of Africa and the world, as being, by virtue of our Africanness and skin colour, lazy, liars, foul-smelling, diseased, corrupt, violent, amoral, sexual depraved, animalistic, savage and rapist" (cited in "Mbeki, DA racism row continues")

6. While it is not my intention to defend AIDS skepticism, it is interesting to note that Western attention regarding AIDS skepticism by certain African leaders has largely disregarded those leaders' central points of contention: that the challenge of AIDS in Africa cannot be answered by science and medical attention alone, but requires economic and social development.

7. See Maathai's cautious, eloquent, and "scientifically-accurate" (i.e., consistent with the findings of the Western research establishment) retraction of her comments about the origin of AIDS ("The Challenge of AIDS in Africa").

8. At several points in her memoir *Unbowed*, Maathai directly acknowledges the importance of garnering the attention of media for documenting events and promoting ideas (e.g., 204, 242).

9. Wangari Maathai, "Trees for Democracy," *New York Times*, December 10, 2004.

10. Wangari Maathai, "The Linkage between Patenting of Life Forms, Genetic Engineering and Food Insecurity," *Green Belt Movement*, May 28, 1998, http://www.ukabc.org/gaiam4_1.htm.

11. Wangari Maathai, *The Green Belt Movement* (New York: Lantern, 2004).

12. Wangari Maathai, *Unbowed: A Memoir* (New York: Knopf, 2006).

13. As many who read this chapter will indubitably question my political/theoretical motivations, I believe I should clear them up now. I make the claims I present in this article with full respect for the myriad progressive movements whose rhetorics I analyze. To label a rhetoric as "essentialist" or a "myth" does not necessarily mean disrespect for that rhetoric's underlying political motivations and goals. The ongoing debates among feminists regarding the value of essentialist rhetorics prove this. To say that the postmodern left harbors essentialist myths regarding the purity of marginalized groups is merely to state a fact—and is not designed to denigrate these critical projects and their overarching goals.

14. See, for example, Helene Shugart "Counterhegemonic acts: Appropriation as a feminist rhetorical strategy," Quarterly Journal of Speech 83 (1997): 210–30.

15. For more biographical information, see either Maathai's *The Green Belt Movement* or her personal Web site http://wangarimaathai.or.ke/.

16. Maathai, *Green Belt Movement*, 9.

17. Ibid., 15.

18. Maathai's translation of *Harambee* is "let us all pull together!" (Ibid., 20.)

19. Ibid., 30.

20. "The Nobel Peace Prize for 2004," Norwegian Nobel Committee, October 8, 2004, http://nobelpeaceprize.org/eng_lau_announce2004.html.

21. Maathai, *Green Belt Movement*, 6.

22. Ibid.

23. That is to say, the ideologies and mythologies developed within the GBM have expanded beyond the domain of the institution.

24. Maathai, *Unbowed*, 186–93.

25. E.g., ibid., 242 and 193.

26. Ibid., 240.

27. Ibid., 178.

28. Gayatri Spivak, "Subaltern Studies: Deconstructing Historiography," in *Subaltern Studies: Writings on South Asian History and Society* volume 4, (Delhi: Oxford University Press, 1985), 342.

29. Debates among Western academics, furthermore, are making it increasingly clear that all critical values and critical rhetorics rely, to some extent, on a priori and essentialized theories of the marginalized groups and/or objects being championed.

Indeed, academic feminists widely acknowledge this split between theory and praxis regarding essentialist and constructivist discourses; while constructivism rules the discourse of (most) contemporary academic feminist discussion, (oftentimes strategic) essentialism governs the rhetorical formations of most popularly focused feminisms. A similar split between theory and praxis seems to exist in queer activism as well; many Gay, Lesbian, Bisexual, and/or Transexual (GLBT) activists whose work engages real-world, nonacademic audiences prefer rhetorics of biological naturalness in order to challenge those who claim the divine "naturalness" of heterosexuality (see, for example, Smith and Windes's "The progay and antigay issue culture"). These GLBT activists favor essentialist rhetorics to the opaque and convoluted rhetoric of constructivism offered by poststructuralism, the language of the academy, because of their powerful simplicity and seemingly greater potential to effect persuasion.

30. Mark McPhail, "From Complicity to Coherence: Rereading the Rhetoric of Afrocentricity," *Western Journal of Communication* 62 (1998): 114–40.

31. Perry, in her article "Muslim Child Disciples," recognizes, furthermore, that international development NGOs, the very type of organization which Maathai leads, frequently provide oversimplified and moralized depictions of developing world cultural practices for the purposes of increasing Western interest in (and thereby funding for) their projects. Examining how activists and NGOs have represented Senegalese talibés, Perry suggests that Western NGOs working in Senegal have overlooked how the local culture views the practice; Western NGOs fan moral outrage over the practice for their Western audience in order to keep the funds flowing, despite the talibé institution being viewed by most Senegalese as "a conscientious child-rearing strategy that is in decline" (72). Perry labels this practice of selective ethnography "strategic structuralism," recognizing that NGOs, even when their goals in the country are entirely benevolent, are not immune to calculated representation of cultures in order to promote their broader project.

32. Indeed, Maathai, for several years, has been one of the most important and prominent faces on the pantheon of developing world ecofeminist activists.

33. Cecile Jackson, "Radical Environmental Myths: a Gender Perspective," *New Left Review* 217 (1995): 124–41.

34. Ibid., 140.

35. Noël Sturgeon, "Ecofeminist Appropriations and Transnational Environmentalisms," *Identities* 6 (1999): 255–79.

36. Drawing on the model of the Green Revolution of the twentieth century and its subsequent massive increases in crop yields, scientists and agronomists widely acknowledge biotechnology's tremendous potential in the battle against world hunger. These scientists unapologetically promote the advancement of the use of genetically modified (GM) foods, citing what they see as unlimited potential and an impeccable safety record (see, for example, Guerinot's article in *Science* [2000] and Macilwain's report in *Nature* [2000]). The discussion in the scientific and peripheral literature has, however, articulated a handful of concerns regarding the increased use of GM foods, including the following: the safety of the food for both the consumer and for the ecological community in which the GM crops are grown, whether the patenting of genes is an ethical practice, and whether GM foods will lead to deleterious effects upon the livelihoods of Western and developing world farmers.

37. Per Pinstrup-Andersen and Ebbe Schiøler, *Seeds of Contention: World Hunger and the Global Controversy over GM Crops* (Baltimore: Johns Hopkins University Press, 2001).

38. It is, furthermore, interesting to note that an understanding of organisms that does not look for an essential, romanticized nature—namely, a scientific view of or-

ganisms—is, in many ways, compatible with contemporary ideas regarding social construction.

39. As several developing world scholars have suggested, the Western postmodern concepts of the "Environment" and "Environmentalism" are notions largely at home solely in wealthy, industrialized nations in which large sections of the population have the time and resources in which to engage in recreational activities (see, for example, Guha's "Radical American Environmentalism and Wilderness Preservation: A Third World Critique"). In these Western countries, spending time enjoying nature is seen as a means for spiritual and aesthetic fulfillment. Developing world critiques of attempts to preserve ecological habitat in their countries call Western attempts to spread their environmentalist agenda at the expense of economic and social development "eco-imperialism." Suggesting that the romanticization of nature is a luxury that countries in which large segments of the population remain perpetually very close to starvation simply cannot afford, these critics encourage underdeveloped countries to retain an instrumentalist (i.e., functional) rather than aesthetic view of nature. To put this another way, these critics charge that Western environmentalists are attempting to promote the material relations of postmodernism in regions where the project of modernism never took place.

40. Maathai, *Unbowed*, 120.

41. T. Nielsen et al., "Traditional blue and modern green resistance," in *Biotechnology: the Making of a Global Controversy*, edited by Martin Bauer and George Gaskell (New York: Cambridge University Press, 2002).

42. Maathai, "Linkage."

43. Maathai's discussion of organic food in *The Green Belt Movement* (43) works in a similar manner; the passage says nothing regarding nutrition and is largely focused around the undesirable economic position the use of fertilizers induces developing world farmers into.

44. Maathai, "Linkage."

45. Maathai, *Green Belt Movement*, 27.

46. Ibid., 28.

47. Ibid.

48. Maathai, *Green Belt Movement*, 71

49. Richard, Mack, Daniel Simberloff, W. Mark Lonsdale, Harry Evans, Michael Clout, and Fakhri Bazzaz, "Biotic Invasions: Causes, Epidemiology, Global Consequences and Control,"*Ecological Applications* 10 (2000): 689–710.

50. Indeed, advanced agriculture is impossible without human introduction, promotion, and cultivation of plants different from the wild flora. Even when the process involves species native to an area, the development of advanced agriculture necessarily involves some form of domestication (and thereby alteration) of the native organism.

51. Philosophers, historians, and numerous other academics have noted, furthermore, that overzealous concern with the eradication of nonnative species has a long history of attachment with xenophobic beliefs (see, for example, Simberloff's "Confronting introduced species: a form of xenophobia").

52. Sturgeon, "Ecofeminist Appropriations," 272.

53. Maathai, "Trees for Democracy."

54. Maathai, *Green Belt Movement*,112.

55. Wangari Maathai, "Wangari Muta Maathai: Kenya's Green Militant," Interview by Ethiragan Anbarasan, *UNESCO Courier*, December 1999, http://www.unesco.org/courier/1999_12/uk/dires/txt1.htm.

56. See, for example, Shugart's "Counterhegemonic acts: Appropriation as a feminist rhetorical strategy" and Christine Harold's "Pranking rhetoric: 'culture jamming' as media activism," *Critical Studies in Media Communication* 21 (2004): 189–212.

Bibliography

Beverley, John. "The Margin at the Center." In *The Real Thing: Testimonial Discourse and Latin America*, edited by Georg Gugelberger, 23–41. Durham, NC: Duke University Press, 1996.

Clark, Ross. "Globophobia: A weekly survey of world restrictions on freedom and free trade." *Spectator*, October 30, 2004.

Galinat, Walton. "The origin of maize." *Science* 225 (1984): 1094.

Guerinot, Mary Lou. "The Green Revolution Strikes Gold." *Science* 287 (2000): 241–43.

Guha, Ramachandra. "Radical American Environmentalism and Wilderness Preservation: A Third World Critique." *Environmental Ethics* 11 (1989): 71–83.

Harold, Christine. "Pranking rhetoric: 'culture jamming' as media activism." *Critical Studies in Media Communication* 21 (2004): 189–212.

Jackson, Cecile. "Radical Environmental Myths: a Gender Perspective." *New Left Review* 217 (1995): 124–41.

"Kenyan Nobel peace laureate claims AIDS virus deliberately created." *Agence France Presse*, October 9, 2004.

Leakey, R. R., and A. J. Simons. "The domestication and commercialization of indigenous treesin agroforestry for the alleviation of poverty." *Agroforestry Systems* 38 (1998): 165–76.

Little, Adrian. "Feminism and the politics of difference in Northern Ireland." *Journal of Political Ideologies* 7 (2002): 163–78.

Maathai, Wangari. "The Challenge of AIDS in Africa." December 12, 2004. http://greenbeltmovement.org/a.php?id=30.

———. *The Green Belt Movement*. New York: Lantern, 2004.

———. "The Linkage between Patenting of Life Forms, Genetic Engineering and Food Insecurity." *The Green Belt Movement*, May 28, 2004. http://www.ukabc.org/gaiam4_1.htm.

———. "Trees for Democracy." *New York Times*, December 10, 2004.

———. *Unbowed: A Memoir*. New York: Knopf, 2006.

———. "Wangari Muta Maathai: Kenya's Green Militant." Interview by Ethiragan Anbarasan, *UNESCO Courier*, December 1999. http://www.unesco.org/courier/1999_12/uk/dires/txt1.htm.

Macilwain, Colin. "US academy study finds GM foods are safe." *Nature* 404 (2000): 693.

Mack, Richard, Daniel Simberloff, W. Mark Lonsdale, Harry Evans, Michael Clout, and Fakhrii Bazzaz. "Biotic Invasions: Causes, Epidemiology, Global Consequences and Control." *Ecological Applications* 10 (2000): 689–710.

Matthews, Robert. "And this year's backstabbing prize goes to." *Sunday Telegraph* (London), October 17, 2004.

Mbeki, Thabo. "Health, human dignity and partners for global poverty reduction." *ANC Today*, April 11, 2002. http://www.anc.org.za/ancdocs/anctoday/2002/at14.htm.

McPhail, Mark. "From Complicity to Coherence: Rereading the Rhetoric of Afrocentricity." *Western Journal of Communication* 62 (1998): 114–40.

Mies, Maria, and Vandana Shiva. *Ecofeminism*. Highlands, NJ: Zed, 1993.

Mustapha, Abdul Raufu. "Colonialism and Environmental Perception in Northern Nigeria." *Oxford Development Studies* 31 (2003): 404–25.

Nielson, T. V., E. Jelsøe and S. Öhman. "Traditional blue and modern green resistance." In *Biotechnology: the Making of a Global Controversy*, edited by Martin Bauer and George Gaskell. New York: Cambridge University Press, 2002.

Norwegian Nobel Committee. "The Nobel Peace Prize for 2004." October 8, 2004. http://nobelpeaceprize.org/eng_lau_announce200 4.html.

Perry, Donna. "Muslim Child Disciples, Global Civil Society, and Children's Rights in Senegal: The Discourses of Strategic Structuralism." *Anthropological Quarterly* 77 (2004): 47–86.

Pinstrup-Andersen, Per, and Ebbe Schiøler. *Seeds of Contention: World Hunger and the Global Controversy over GM Crops*. Baltimore: Johns Hopkins University Press, 2001.

Sanchez, Pedro. "Delivering on the promise of agroforestry." *Environment, Development, and Sustainability* 1 (1999): 275–84.

Shugart, Helene. "Counterhegemonic acts: Appropriation as a feminist rhetorical strategy." *Quarterly Journal of Speech* 83 (1997): 210–30.

Simberloff, Daniel. "Confronting introduced species: a form of xenophobia." *Ecological Applications* 10 (2000): 689–710.

Smith, Ralph, and Russel Windes. "The progay and antigay issue culture: interpretation, influence and dissent." *Quarterly Journal of Speech 83 (1997): 28–49*.

South African Press Association. "Mbeki, DA, racism row continues." October 22, 2004. http://iafrica.com/news/sa/15889.htm.

Spivak, Gayatri. "Subaltern Studies: Deconstructing Historiography." In *Subaltern Studies: Writings on South Asian History and Society* volume 4, 330–63. Delhi: Oxford University Press, 1985.

Sturgeon, Noël. "Ecofeminist Appropriations and Transnational Environmentalisms." *Identities* 6 (1999): 255–79.

Williams, Gareth. "The Fantasies of Cultural Exchange in Latin American Subaltern Studies." In *The Real Thing: Testimonial Discourse and Latin America*, edited by Georg Gugelberger, 225–53. Durham, NC: Duke University Press, 1996.

"The woman who planted trees; Kenya's Nobel laureate." *Economist*, October 16, 2004.

Conclusion

Anne Stockdell-Giesler and Rebecca Ingalls

Genius Child

This is a song for the genius child.
Sing it softly, for the song is wild.
Sing it softly as ever you can—
Lest the song get out of hand.

Nobody loves a genius child.

Can you love an eagle,
Tame or wild?
Can you love an eagle,
Wild or tame?
Can you love a monster
Of frightening name?

Nobody loves a genius child.

Kill him—and let his soul run wild.

Langston Hughes's poem "Genius Child"[1] offers up an effective, if unintended, example of the outsider ethos that is described within the chapters of this book. Hughes (1902–67), an African American writer, lived as an outsider during the United States' mid-twentieth-century civil rights struggles. As an African American and as a man of letters, Hughes recognized the particular difficulties facing outsiders who desire to make themselves heard. The "monster" and "genius" Hughes references can be read as those who stand out/apart from the mainstream of rhetorical agency; the genius, who struggles with his or her ethos, is cursed by self-awareness in that he or she becomes monstrous, incapable of fitting into the mainstream or of living quietly on the margins. The purpose of this book is to explore how these "monsters," these outsiders, have managed to access and wield rhetorical agency from those marginal spaces where they felt themselves to be confined. Hughes's use of jazz rhythms in his poetry; his exploration of the African American experience in drama and fiction; and his lifelong struggle with his own outsider identity while seeking a literary, social, and political audience represents the kind of rhetorical struggles that inspired this collection.

Though the rhetorical tradition is filled with the examples of individual, masculine-influenced oratory both by dominant-class males and minorities who sought to emulate them, what the authors of this collection seek to expose and to fill are the gaps in the tradition that fail to show how people who are neither dominant nor have access to dominant sites and modes of communication manage to make themselves heard anyway, from the margins. While a potential outsider like Barack Obama became a presidential front-runner in the 2008 elections by echoing past rhetors like Abraham Lincoln, outsiders have stayed outside, seeking to make change through alternate sites and modes of rhetoric. What links each of these chapters together are the concepts of constitutive rhetoric and of Foucault's heterotopia; that is, each of these chapters provides examples of outsiders constituting themselves as outsiders, and then inhabiting a space, a heterotopia, in which they are able to function rhetorically. Sometimes, outsider status is self-defined—Jessica Ketcham's techno mobs, for example, could theoretically be populated by individuals who might at first glance seem to easily fit into dominant rhetorical groups. But those who participate in such events are establishing rhetorical agency through an outsider ethos with deliberate rhetorical purpose and end in mind. A heterotopia has been constructed in which the rhetors are able to see themselves mirrored as agents of a particular kind; they harness a particular kind of rhetoric—outsider rhetoric—because it is the available means of persuasion in a particular rhetorical situation.

As mentioned in the introduction, the question which serves as both the catalyst and the foundation for this book is: do people who perceive themselves to be without rhetorical agency, without access to language-as-power, simply give up and lead lives absent of any rhetorical expression? Or do they find available means of persuasion outside the tradition—do they constitute themselves, creating a rhetorical ethos outside the utopia? The chapters in this book show how groups and individuals have in fact garnered and wielded rhetorical power by using the very ethos that would seem to marginalize them from rhetorical power. These are not rhetors who look like outsiders who manage to take on traditional means of persuasion and frame themselves as outsiders while speaking like—and in the spaces belonging to—those in power. Langston Hughes, for example, lived his life identifying himself as an outsider—writing about African American struggles and identity not as an overt social activist or politician—his rhetoric came through literature. Florida turpentine workers used a subtle, subversive rhetoric to gain some control in their lives, because outright protest simply was not available to them.

Certainly, one dreams of a world where the inside-outside dichotomy does not exist, a world where there is rhetorical access for all—a rhetorical utopia where heterotopias are unnecessary. In a sermon delivered at St. Andrew's Presbyterian Church on August 5, 2007, journalism professor Robert Jensen from the University of Texas at Austin proclaimed to his audience, "We are all prophets now," asserting that leadership may not be our guiding light into social change. Rather, he suggested, "We need to go deeper than leadership can take us." He explains, "Perhaps there are no inspiring figures on the scene because authentic leaders know that we are heading into new territory for which old models of movements and politics are insufficient, and rather than trying to claim a place at the front of the parade they are struggling to understand the direction we should be moving, just like the rest of us."[2]

Jensen's message argues for a unified resistance to the hegemonic structures that keep the marginalized down, and he imagines a shared human experience of self-examination and rising above domination, a "collective struggle to understand the truth."

Jensen's call from the pulpit is praiseworthy; his challenge to the "privileged" is critical because it asks us to see the delineations of inside-outside. But as we take his message to heart, we must also consider his mode. We know that rhetoric cannot be limited by individual public oratory if we are to consider the most ancient concepts of rhetoric itself, including Aristotle's own idea of available means. Before we can dissolve the margins, as Jensen seems to suggest, we must honor the ways in which outsiders have steadfastly recognized and defied barriers to equality and acceptance, have cultivated and utilized the resources indigenous to the societal spaces they have inhabited for decades and centuries. In these chapters, we have seen "otherness" spun into empowerment; and some of us have seen ourselves. Without the rhetorical work behind the seemingly invisible walls of dominance, would we even know enough about the subjugation of outsiders to preach against it? It is the voicing of these voices that propels Jensen's message of solidarity forward.

These margin-dwelling rhetors are no twenty-first century creations; the chapters in this book show that there is a history of outsider rhetoric to be explored and theorized about. Certainly technology can affect agency—Jessica Ketcham Weber's essay in this collection shows how digital technology has been used in twenty-first-century culture to create agency for impromptu social expression. Furthermore, cultural restraints define the margins in which the outsider lives—Coretta Pittman demonstrates nuances of outsider identity and rhetorical expression across decades in her chapter on how socially conscious rapper Common communicates using a medium accessible to him, though he does not fall neatly into the genre he employs. The margins, in this book, are revealed to be heavily populated and successfully negotiated domains, rather than spaces of isolation and silence.

To return briefly to Hughes's poem, we can read the last line, "kill him—and let his soul run wild," through the lenses of outsider rhetoric. For the outsider, what must be "killed" is the desire to fit into the mainstream. Once an outsider finds a space to be heard from the margins, he or she can "run wild" to find agency and audience. This book will, hopefully, provide examples to begin many discussions about how rhetoric works from nontraditional sites, modes, and agents. Certainly people can be silenced, especially in mainstream academic/political rhetorical sites. But the state of being silenced in one space does not necessitate total silence or, by extension, utter powerlessness. There is a richly textured and diverse space to be explored in the margins. It is the hope that this text will inspire further exploration beyond the studies in these chapters.

And here, at the conclusion of this text, we might ask, "Where do we go from here?" and further, "Where is *here?*" Our discussion of marginalization gives rise to questions of location—as we share in this collective recognition of outsider rhetorics, we might consider ways to move forward socially and intellectually "as one," ways to eradicate marginalization by maintaining an enlightened understanding of subjectivity that helps us to be witnesses to our own domination, to rescue the marginalized in our/their struggle. Some may argue that the margin is an inevitable space, a necessary social divider that *must* be occupied in order for cultural shifts to take place. Stuart Hall, in his "Notes on Deconstructing the 'Popular,'" argues, "In the study of popular culture, we should always start here: with the double stake in popular culture, the double movement of containment and resistance, which is always inevitably inside it."[3] There is an inherent tension, he claims—"the people versus the power bloc"[4]—in culture that maintains dominant and subordinate groups; the former continues to try to restrict the latter, while the latter continues to push against the former. Hall's theory comes to life in the delicate balance of taming and wildness that Hughes discusses in his poem. Simply put, dichotomies of inside-outside—of controller and controlled—will continue as this organism we call culture continues to form, break down, and reform.

And yet, perhaps there is hope in the constant cultural struggle. In many ways, we can find promise embedded in the rhetoric of the individuals illustrated in this text; their struggles may be emblematic of an endless human desire to "right" itself even amid its most despicable errors, another facet of the inherent cultural contradiction Hall describes. In our exploration, we may see the reconstruction of identity, the empowerment of previously marginalized groups through visibility, and the gradual—often painstakingly slow—realization that the dominant cultural standard is in dire need of revision. In his theorizing of "reverse discourse,"[5] a phrase he used to described the ways in which homosexuals used the very language used against them to call attention to their work in the margins and empower the civil rights efforts of future queer communities, Foucault helped to shed light on the courage that comes from standing up to one's own subjugation. Richard Meyer argues further that such rhetorical moves have attempted to "restage one's own outlaw status within a different register of representation and thereby to reopen the question of homosexuality for further inquiry."[6] Our exploration is not, then, simply to "rescue" the outsider; if this text proves anything, it is that outsiderness has so often been an ever freer space for many who have inhabited it. Our study is, more critically, to perpetuate the continued identity work involved in how we determine belonging, how we view ourselves in relation to Others, and how we intend to rebuild the cultural demolition that has resulted from historical suppression and make ourselves wary of the unavoidable collective moves that will undoubtedly push entire groups to the periphery of society.

Notes

1. Langston Hughes, *Selected Poems of Langston Hughes* (New York: Vintage, 1990).
2. Robert Jensen, "We Are All Prophets Now: Responsibilities and Risks in the Prophetic Voice," http://uts.cc.utexas.edu/~rjensen/freelance/propheticvoice.html.
3. Stuart Hall, "Notes on Deconstructing 'The Popular,'" *People's History and Socialist Theory*, ed. R. Samuel (London: Routledge and Kegan Paul, 1981), 238.
4. Ibid, 228.
5. Michel Foucault, *History of Sexuality, Volume 1* (New York: Pantheon Books, 1978), 101.
6. Richard Meyer, *Outlaw Representation: Censorship and Homosexuality in Twentieth-Century American Art* (New York: Oxford University Press, 2002), 8

Bibliography

Foucault, Michel. *History of Sexuality, Volume 1.* New York: Pantheon Books, 1978.

Hall, Stuart. "Notes on Deconstructing 'The Popular.'" *People's History and Socialist Theory.* Edited by R. Samuel. London: Routledge and Kegan Paul, 1981.

Hughes, Langston. *Selected Poems of Langston Hughes.* New York: Vintage, 1990.

Jensen, Robert. "We Are All Prophets Now: Responsibilities and Risks in the Prophetic Voice." http://uts.cc.utexas.edu/~rjensen/freelance/propheticvoice.html.

Meyer, Richard. *Outlaw Representation: Censorship and Homosexuality in Twentieth-Century American Art.* New York: Oxford University Press, 2002.

Contributers

ANNE MEADE STOCKDELL-GIESLER, PhD, is Assistant Professor of English at the University of Tampa. Her research is in the areas of the rhetorics of ethics, politics, and social identity. Her most recent publications include articles in *Academe, Inventio,* and a chapter in *Compositions in the New Liberal Arts* (eds. Joanna Castner Post and James Inman 2008).

LINDA BANNISTER is the Daum Professor of the Bellarmine College of Liberal Arts at Loyola Marymount University and Professor of English specializing in Rhetoric, contemporary literature by underrepresented groups, and playwriting.

MICHAEL DONNELLY is Assistant Professor of English and Director of the Writing Program at Ball State University. His primary area of interest is in cultural rhetoric and composition, with special emphases on civic literacy and public discourse in composition studies. He is currently at work on a book project focusing on freedom of speech.

DR. IAN EDWARDS teaches and lectures at the University of Birmingham. His research interests include twentieth-century U.S war fiction, psychoanalysis, and cultural criticism, and forms of marginalized discourse within U.S. culture.

JAMES E. HURD, JR. is a writer, actor, and director in Los Angeles, co-authoring civil rights-themed dramas with his partner, Linda Bannister. Their latest full-length drama, *Turpentine Jake,* which concerns Black laborers enslaved under debt peonage in 1930s Florida, was selected for a reading at the National Black Theatre Festival 2007 and premiered at the Del Rey Theater in Los Angeles in August 2008. Hurd and Bannister's short film, *Poet of the Swingin' Blade,* won Best Message Film, San Diego Black Film Festival 2007. Hurd and Bannister are the founders of The Kohl Players, a Los Angeles-based theater company *www.kohlplayers.com.*

REBECCA INGALLS is Assistant Professor in the Department of English and Philosophy at Drexel University. Her current research interests include the study of spoken-word performance, plagiarism, queer theory, and the religious rhetoric of *Harry Potter*.

RAYMOND OENBRING is a PhD Candidate at the University of Washington, Seattle in the Department of English. His research interests include the fields of rhetorical theory, rhetoric of science, linguistics, and discourse analysis. His dissertation is a critical rhetorical reading of Chomskyan generative grammar.

CORETTA M. PITTMAN is an Assistant Professor of English at Baylor University. Her area of specialization is in Composition and Rhetoric. Her research interests include: composition and rhetorical theory, literacy studies, and cultural studies.

ILARIA SERRA is in the Program of Italian Studies at Florida Atlantic University. Her research spans Italian cinema and literature to the history of Italian immigration to the United States. She has recently published "The Value of Worthless Lives: Writing Italian American Autobiographies" (2007). *The Imagined Immigrant* is forthcoming with Farleigh Dickinson University Press (1909).

ZOE TRODD teaches in the History and Literature department at Harvard University. Her books include *Meteor of War: The John Brown Story* (2004), *American Protest Literature* (2006), *To Plead Our Own Cause: Personal Stories by Today's Slaves* (2008), *The Long Civil Rights Movement* (2008), and *Modern Slavery* (2009). She has also published numerous articles on American literature, history, and visual culture.

JESSICA KETCHAM WEBER is a PhD Candidate in Writing, Media, and Cultural Studies in the Department of English at Louisiana State University. She has written articles about feminist spaces and discourses in academia, multiliteracies and activist pedagogy, Julia Kristeva, identity, and performativity. Her current research explores the cultural production and digital literacy practices of contemporary anti-oppressive social movements in the U.S., alongside how these practices are imaged in popular media.

SCOTT WHIDDON is an Assistant Professor of Writing, Rhetoric, and Communication at Transylvania University in Lexington, KY. He earned his doctorate from Louisiana State University in 2006. His scholarly interests include writing center theory and practice, first-year writing pedagogy, and the literature of confinement. He also plays guitar and collects rare rock and soul records.

JOSEPH WILLIAMS earned his MA in the History of Christianity from Wheaton College (IL) in 2002. In 2008 he completed his doctorate in American Religious History in the Department of Religion at Florida State University.

Index

Aesop, 15
Agency, feminine, 198, 206, 219
Agit prop, 267–68
American Indian Movement (A.I.M), 28
Angolite, The, 165–96
Aristotle, 22, 95, 119, 138 n. 1, 157, 309
Attucks, Crispus, 73
Austin, J. L., 144, 145
Autobiography as rhetoric, 144
Auto-ethnography, 43, 58

Baldwin, James, 95, 103, 112
Benjamin, Walter, 69
Bildungsroman, 109
Black Panther Party, the, 128–31, 136
Booth, Wayne, 116 n. 19
Bricolage, 74
Brokeback Mountain, 231–33
Brown, Henry "Box," 71
Brown, John, 69, 73, 74
Brown, William Wells, 69, 73
Burke, Kenneth, 97, 99, 144, 146
Butler, Judith, 92–95, 198–99, 208, 211, 217, 221 nn. 1, 2, and 6

Charland, Maurice, 9, 10, 11, 12
Churchill, Ward, 14, 23–34
Common Sense, 16, 119–21, 131–38, 310
Constitutive Rhetoric, 10, 12, 167–68, 171, 226
Coulter, Ann, 28, 31
Critical Mass, 275–76

DeGeneres, Ellen, 228–29
De Man, Paul, 96–97
Douglass, Frederick, 16, 69, 74–87, 99–101, 119
DuBois, W.E.B., 102–3

Ecofeminism, 292–93, 299
Ellen, 225–26, 228, 236–37

Ellison, Ralph, 16, 91–115; *Invisible Man*, 91–118
Ethos of the survivor, 151–52

Fanon, Franz, 103–4, 111, 221–22 n. 11
Farm, The: Life Inside Angola Prison, 165–66
Fish, Stanley, 24–26
Florida turpentine industry, 39–60
Folktales, 40, 57–58
Foucault, Michel, 10, 11–12, 15, 21, 166, 168, 171, 245–46, 308, 311
Free Speech, 14, 23–34
Freud, Sigmund, 230

Gashé, Rudolph, 91–92, 97
Gates, Henry Louis, Jr., 105
Gee, James Paul, 167
Generative rhetoric, 17, 144–47
Geschichstraum, 69
Gilyard, Keith, 43–44, 65 n. 12
Girl Fight, 220
Green Belt Movement, 289–91, 296–300

Horowitz, David, 28–30
Howe, Irving, 95
Hughes, Langston, 307–10
Hurston, Zora Neale, 41–43, 46–47, 58

Immigration to United States, Italian, 143–64
Individualism, 215–17
Invisible Man. See Ellison, Ralph

Jacobs, Harriet, 11, 16, 68–87

Kennedy, Stetson, 41
King, Martin Luther, Jr., 17, 21, 185

Licona, Angela, 169. *See also* third space
Lionnet, Francoise, 43

INDEX

Literacy studies, 167, 183–84, 187–89

Maathai, Wangari, 287–301
Malcolm X, 16, 17, 119–42, 189
Million Dollar Baby, 200, 202, 205–20
Modern society: definition of, 255–56 n. 5
Mosley, Walter, 112–15
Movement studies, 262–63, 271–72

Nation of Islam, 123, 126
Nat Turner Rebellion, 70
Newton, Huey P., 16, 17, 119–42

Oates, Joyce Carol, 203–5
Obama, Barack, 308
Ong, Walter, 144, 149
O'Reilly, Bill, 14, 28–30

Pentecostalism, 241–60; and the Charismatic Movement, 254; and materialism, 249–53; and medicine, 248–49; and science, 246–49
Peonage, 39, 42, 51, 64 n. 1
Performative rhetoric, 144–45; and protest, 264–82

Quiet individualism, 154–56

Rheingold, Howard, 263, 272, 277–78, 281

Rich, Adrienne, 199
Rideau, Wilbert, 17, 165–90

Scientific rhetoric, 246–49, 288–89, 293–94
Seale, Bobby, 128
Selective democracy, 159 n. 9
Signifyin(g), 105, 114
Social Movement Rhetorics, 10, 11, 273–74
Socially conscious rhetoric, 119–42
Speech Act Theory, 145. *See also* Austin, J. L.
Spivak, Gayatri, 291–92. *See also* Strategic Essentialism
Stowe, Harriet Beecher, 72
Strategic Essentialism, 287–301
Subversion, 40, 47, 49, 52, 56, 271, 309

Technology, 261–86; and religion, 242–46. *See also under* Pentecostalism
Techno-mobs, 308
Third space, 169–70

Uncle Tom's Cabin, 72–73

Wacquant, Loïc, 203, 221 n. 8
Wright, Richard, 16; *Native Son*, 89–118, 125–26